D0876215

Visual
Thinking

ALSO BY TEMPLE GRANDIN

Emergence: Labeled Autistic (with Margaret M. Scariano)

Thinking in Pictures: And Other Reports from My Life with Autism

Genetics and the Behavior of Domestic Animals (editor)

Livestock Handling and Transport (editor)

Animals in Translation (with Catherine Johnson)

Unwritten Rules of Social Relationships (with Sean Barron)

Developing Talents (with Kate Duffy)

Humane Livestock Handling (with Mark Deesing)

The Way I See It

Animals Make Us Human (with Catherine Johnson)

The Autistic Brain (with Richard Panek)

Temple Grandin's Guide to Working with Farm Animals

Calling All Minds (with Betsy Lerner)

Navigating Autism (with Debra Moore)

The Outdoor Scientist (with Betsy Lerner)

Visual
Thinking

The Hidden Gifts of People Who
Think in Pictures, Patterns, and Abstractions

TEMPLE GRANDIN

with Betsy Lerner

RIVERHEAD BOOKS NEW YORK 2022

RIVERHEAD BOOKS
An imprint of Penguin Random House LLC
penguinrandomhouse.com

LIBRARY OF CONGRESS CATALOGING-IN-PUBLICATION DATA
Names: Grandin, Temple, author. | Lerner, Betsy, author.
Title: Visual thinking : the hidden gifts of people who think in pictures,
patterns, and abstractions / Temple Grandin ; with Betsy Lerner.
Description: Hardcover edition. | New York : Riverhead Books, 2022. |
Includes bibliographical references and index.
Identifiers: LCCN 2022006436 (print) | LCCN 2022006437 (ebook) |
ISBN 9780593418369 (hardcover) | ISBN 9780593418383 (ebook)
Subjects: LCSH: Visual perception. |
Art—Psychological aspects. | Thought and thinking.
Classification: LCC BF241 .G683 2022 (print) | LCC BF241 (ebook) |
DDC 152.14—dc23/eng/20220210
LC record available at https://lccn.loc.gov/2022006436
LC ebook record available at https://lccn.loc.gov/2022006437

International edition ISBN: 9780593543115

Printed in the United States of America
1st Printing

Book design by Alexis Farabaugh

To all the people who think differently

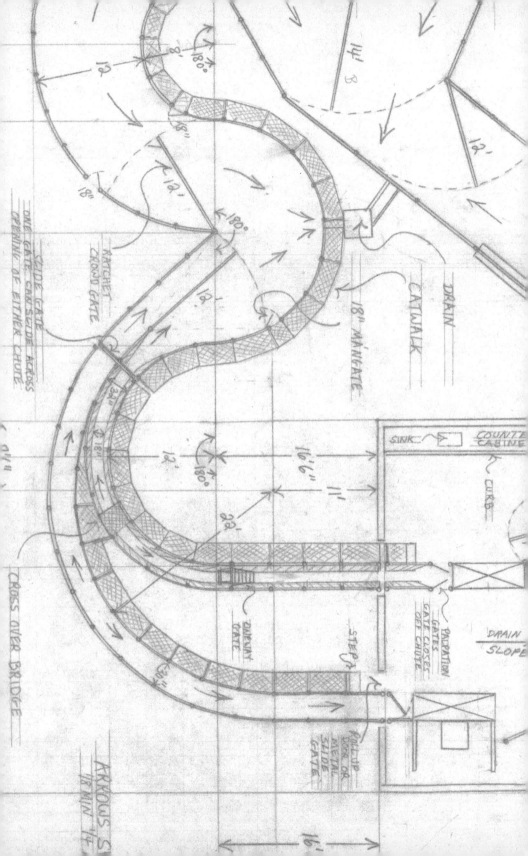

Contents

Drawings by Temple Grandin

Visual
Thinking

Introduction

We come into the world without words. We see light, recognize faces, differentiate colors and patterns. We can smell and start recognizing tastes. We have a sense of touch and start grasping things and sucking our thumbs. Soon we start to recognize songs, which explains the universal existence of lullabies and nursery rhymes. Babies make lots of sounds. "Mama" and "Dada" are more random than anxious new parents want to believe. Gradually, language gains ascendancy: By one and a half, most toddlers will have a bunch of nouns and verbs under their belts. By two, they start to make sentences. By the time most children go to kindergarten, they can speak in complex sentences and understand the basic rules of language. When it comes to communication, language is the water we drink, the air we breathe.

We assume that the dominance of language forms not only the foundation of how we communicate, but also the foundation of how we think—and in fact for centuries, we have been taught to believe just that. The seventeenth-century philosopher René Descartes cast a long shadow when he wrote, "I think, therefore I am." Specifically, Descartes claimed that it is language that separates us from "beasts": our very humanity was predicated on language. Flash forward a few hundred years, and we are still describing theories of mind based primarily on language. In 1957, linguist Noam Chomsky published his groundbreaking book *Syntactic Structures*, which claims that language, specifically grammar, is innate. His ideas have influenced thinkers for more than half a century.

The first step toward understanding that people think in different ways is understanding that different ways of thinking *exist*. The universally accepted belief that we are all hardwired for language may be why it took me until I was nearly thirty to understand that I am a visual thinker. I am also autistic, and I didn't have language until I was four. I didn't read until I was eight, and that was only with considerable tutoring in phonics. The world didn't come to me through syntax and grammar. It came through images. But unlike what Descartes or Chomsky might have expected, even without language my thoughts are rich and vivid. The world comes to me in a series of associated visual images, like scrolling through Google Images or watching the short videos on Instagram or TikTok. It's true that I now have language, but I still think primarily in pictures. People often confuse visual thinking with vision. We will see throughout this book that visual thinking is not about how we see but about how the brain processes information; how we think and we perceive.

Because the world I was born into did not yet distinguish between different ways of thinking, it was disconcerting to discover that other people didn't think the same way I did. It was like being invited to a costume party and discovering I was the only one wearing a costume. It was difficult to fathom the differences between most people's thought processes and my own. When I figured out that not all people think in pictures, it became my personal mission to discover how people *do* think, and to find out if there were other people like me. I first wrote about this in my memoir, *Thinking in Pictures*, twenty-five years ago. Since then, I've continued to investigate the prevalence of visual thinking in the general population through research of the literature; close observation; conducting informal surveys at the hundreds of autism and education conferences I've addressed; and talking to thousands of parents, educators, disability advocates, and people in industry.

It wasn't exactly a eureka moment, because it dawned on me gradually rather than all at once, but I came to see that there were two different kinds of visual thinkers. Though I couldn't prove it at the time, I recognized a kind of visual thinker who was distinct from me. This is the spatial visualizer who sees in patterns and abstractions. I first became aware of this distinction while working with various kinds of engineers, machinery designers, and welders. Later, I was ecstatic to see my observations confirmed in the scientific literature. The work of the researcher Maria Kozhevnikov showed that there are object visualizers like me, who think in pictures, and, as I suspected, a second group of mathematically inclined visual-spatial thinkers, an overlooked but essential subset of visual thinkers, who think in patterns.

The impact was powerful. I knew I had to scale up my personal experience as a visual thinker to meet the larger story of visual thinking in our culture, from schools to safety to work and beyond. This book explores these two kinds of thinking, how they impact people personally and impact our world. Along the way, I'll introduce you to what I call the "clever engineering department"— stories drawn from my professional experience over nearly fifty years, working with both kinds of visualizers: the people who are object visualizers like me, who see in pictures, and the spatial visualizers, who see the patterns. Think of it this way: the object thinkers build the trains, and the spatial visualizers make them run.

This book also grows out of two major revelations—true eureka moments— I had over the past few years that were game changers for me. In 2019, I set out to tour three state-of-the-art US poultry- and pork-processing plants. This is a regular component of my job as a consultant in the food-supply business. I am brought in basically to make sure plants are operating according to code and not violating any protocols. I look for signs of mistreatment of animals, equipment failure, and employee misbehavior. I'm in demand in my field because of the way I see things. Details, no matter how small, jump out at me. I'm known for spotting something as insignificant as a piece of string that may halt the progress of cattle in a chute, causing expensive delays. At one plant I visited, something else entirely caught my eye. Until then, nearly every plant I'd ever worked on or consulted with used equipment made in America. The parts were manufactured here, and there were workers at the ready who could put together new components and repair any malfunction. At this plant, the equipment was brand-new. It was beautiful, meticulously crafted and made of gleaming stainless steel, with many intricate moving parts. Looking at it, I imagined the highly skilled, high-wage workers who had designed and installed the equipment. Then I discovered that it had been transported from the Netherlands on a container ship, in more than one hundred shipping containers.

I stood on an overhead catwalk and looked at all the complicated conveyors and exclaimed to no one, "We don't make it anymore!" This is the price we have paid for removing most hands-on classes from our schools, such as shop, welding, drafting, and auto mechanics. The kids who should have grown up to invent this equipment are often considered poor performers, academically or behaviorally, and are shunted into special education. But many of them are simply visual thinkers who are being screened out because the current curriculum favors verbal, linear thinkers who are good at taking tests. The hands-on classes where some of these "poor students" might have shown great ability are now gone.

My second eureka moment arrived later that year when I visited the Steve Jobs Theater at Apple headquarters in Cupertino, California. It looks like a pristine glass disk from another galaxy. The twenty-two-foot walls are sheer glass. There are no support columns. The electrical wiring, the sprinkler, audio, and security systems are invisible, concealed inside the seams between the glass panels. It is magnificent. As I often do when something interests me, I drilled down, researching how it was constructed. I discovered that the entire roof is supported by those structural glass walls, and that the glass is manufactured by the German company Sedak, which has become a state-of-the-art industry leader in producing large glass sheets. The fantastic lightweight carbon-fiber roof was imported from Dubai. And the glass cladding and roof of the theater were designed, engineered, fabricated, and installed by the Italian company Frener & Reifer. The theater was empty when I visited. I stood in the middle of the lobby and again cried out, "We don't make it anymore!"

What I quickly came to realize was that those two instances were not the exception. Instead, they were evidence of a seismic shift in American industry. By the spring of 2021, I was discovering brand-new meat-cutting and packaging equipment from the Netherlands, Denmark, and Italy at another pork-processing plant. Some weeks later, the latest issue of a meat trade magazine featured a gigantic foldout spread of equipment made by a huge Dutch company. I was witnessing a tipping point in the crisis in American ingenuity.

We are losing essential technical skills, for three main reasons. First, the people who had manufacturing expertise are not being replaced at the same rate at which they're leaving the job market. Second, we've ceded the manufacture of not only volume goods such as clothes and toys and appliances to foreign companies but high-tech goods as well (about 30 percent of iPhones are made in China). Last, and this is my main area of focus: we've screened out visual thinkers. When we fail to encourage and develop the talents and skills of people who think in different ways, we fail to integrate ways of learning and thinking that benefit and enrich society. Imagine a world with no artists, industrial designers, or inventors. No electricians, mechanics, architects, plumbers, or builders. These are our visual thinkers, many hiding in plain sight, and we have failed to understand, encourage, or appreciate their specific contributions. One reason I was driven to write this book is that the loss of skills in this country terrifies me. And it is entirely preventable, if only we stop screening out the very people who could save us.

Most people don't fully comprehend the way their mind works. Most scientists don't know, either. I'll begin by describing what we know about visual thinking and how visual thinking works, in a way that both visual and non-visual thinkers can recognize. From there I'll identify what we're doing wrong in education, from imposing uniform curricula to relying on a biased and outdated testing system, and in the process screening out talented kids in both the short and the long term, to our collective detriment. It turns out that algebra is a barrier that keeps some students from completing high school or a community college technical degree. These are the visual thinkers who can invent machinery but can't solve for x, and we are screening them out. Next, we'll look at how the crisis in education leads to an unemployment or underemployment crisis, abetted by prejudices about the trades and community colleges. We mostly agree that maintaining and improving infrastructure is critical, but are we identifying, encouraging, and training the builders, welders, machinists, and engineers to manifest it? In other words, where are today's clever engineers?

From there we'll look at the brilliant collaborations between verbal and visual thinkers, including the work of Richard Rodgers and Oscar Hammerstein, Steve Jobs and Steve Wozniak, and architect Rem Koolhaas and engineer Cecil Balmond. We'll look at studies that show how diverse thinkers advantage teams. Then we'll explore the intersection of genius, neurodiversity, and visual thinking. Here we'll describe artists and inventors, among them many visual thinkers and some on the autism spectrum as well. Their towering contributions to art, science, and invention have changed the course of history.

Then we'll turn to the sometimes life-and-death, real-world consequences of not having visual thinkers on your team. We'll see how disasters such as the devastating failure of the Fukushima power plant in Japan and the twin Boeing 737 MAX crashes that took the lives of hundreds of people might have been averted by someone with a visual skill set. While visual thinkers are not seers, enlisting our perspective can help avert not only small mishaps but larger catastrophes. We'll look at studies that show how teams consisting of one kind of thinker underperform compared with mixed groups of visual and non-visual thinkers. Having a visual thinker on your team could make all the difference.

Last, I'll return to a subject I've written about extensively. As an animal scientist, I've spent a lifetime teaching, studying, and consulting on the behavior of animals. Here I want to focus on animals precisely because they are nonverbal; what can they teach us about the ways we think?

How can you tell if you're a visual thinker? You probably know if you are musical, good at art, or good at putting mechanical things together, or if you'd rather draw than write. These are clues. It's important to remember that visual thinking, like most traits, exists on a spectrum. Most people use a combination of verbal and visual thinking to navigate their world. Through the stories, research, and ideas I present in this book, you should be able to find your place on the spectrum. I also aim to help parents guide their kids according to their strengths. It's super important to set up kids for success, and that starts with understanding how they think, and therefore how they learn. I also want to encourage employers to assess their workforce and to look beyond résumés to see what visual thinkers and neurodiverse people can offer. I hope visual thinkers will see themselves in these pages and non-visuals will recognize the possibilities and opportunities that come from different ways of thinking. And, finally, I want us collectively, as citizens of the world, to reclaim our ability to create and innovate in a rapidly changing world, recognizing what we gain by harnessing the power of every kind of mind.

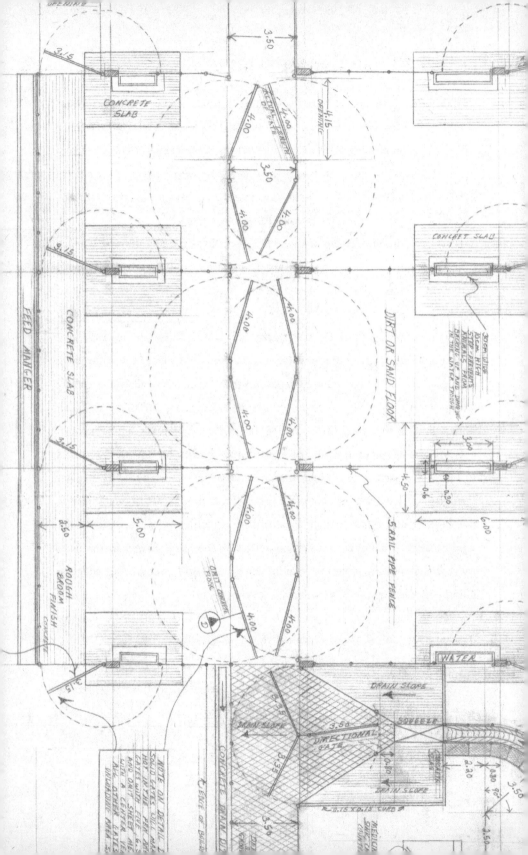

ONE

What Is Visual Thinking?

When I was born in 1947, the medical profession had not started applying an autism diagnosis to children like me. I was exhibiting most of the behaviors now fully associated with autism, including lack of eye contact, temper tantrums, lack of social contact, sensitivity to touch, and the appearance of deafness. Chief among my symptoms was late speech, which led the neurologist who examined me when I was two and a half years old to conclude that I was "brain damaged." I've since learned that a good deal of my behavior at the time (tantrums, stuttering sounds, screaming, and biting) was connected to the frustration I experienced due to my inability to talk. I was fortunate that a lot of early speech therapy eventually helped me gain speech, but I still had no idea that not everyone thought like me, or that the world could be roughly divided into two kinds of thinkers: people who think in pictures and patterns (more on the difference later), and people who think in words.

Word-based thinking is sequential and linear. People who are primarily verbal thinkers tend to comprehend things in order, which is why they often do well in school, where learning is mostly structured sequentially. They are good at understanding general concepts and have a good sense of time, though not necessarily a good sense of direction. Verbal thinkers are the kids with perfectly organized binders and the adults whose computer desktops have neat rows of folders for every project. Verbal thinkers are good at explaining the steps they take to arrive at an answer or to make a decision. Verbal thinkers talk to themselves silently, also known as self-talk, to organize their world. Verbal thinkers easily dash off emails, make presentations. They talk early and often.

By default, verbal people tend to be the ones who dominate conversations, and are hyper-organized and social. It makes sense that they are drawn to and tend to succeed in the kind of high-visibility careers that depend on facility with language: teachers, lawyers, writers, politicians, administrators. You probably know some of these people. The editors I've worked with over the years have all been verbal thinkers. I've noticed that they strongly prefer to work sequentially, meaning they are linear thinkers and need to connect thoughts in a beginning-middle-end sequence. When I gave my editor a few chapters of this book out of sequence, she had a hard time working with them. They didn't line up in her mind. Pictures are associational, sentences go in order. Logic for her was lost without verbal order, and she needed me to present my ideas in an unbroken sequence she could follow.

Visual thinkers, on the other hand, see images in their mind's eye that allow them to make rapid-fire associations. Generally, visual thinkers like maps, art, and mazes, and often don't need directions at all. Some visual thinkers can easily locate a place they've been to only once, their internal GPS having logged the visual landmarks. Visual thinkers tend to be late talkers who struggle with school and traditional teaching methods. Algebra is often their undoing, because the concepts are too abstract, with little or nothing concrete to visualize. Visual thinkers tend to be good at arithmetic that is directly related to practical tasks, such as building and putting things together. Visual thinkers like me easily grasp how mechanical devices work or enjoy figuring them out. We tend to be problem solvers, and sometimes appear to be socially awkward.

When I began to study cattle behavior, as a graduate student in animal science at Arizona State University, I still did not know that other people did not think in pictures. It was the early 1970s, I was in my twenties, and word-based thinking remained a second language to me. My first major breakthrough in understanding that people have different ways of thinking came when I was trying to figure out why cattle sometimes balked when they walked through chutes. I've written and talked about this experience many times: it was the eureka moment that defined my approach to working with animals and launched my career.

The cattle handlers at the time resorted to yelling, hitting, or pushing the animals through with electric prods to keep the line moving. To experience a cow's-eye view, I jumped down into the chute. Once inside, I saw what kinds of things were halting the cattle in their tracks: shadows, a slant of sunlight, a distracting object such as a dangling chain, or even something as simple as a rope draped over the top of the chute caused them to stop. To me, getting inside the chute was the obvious thing to do, but none of the cattle handlers had thought to do it, and some of them thought I was nuts. Looking at the world from the cattle's point of view was a radical idea when I first started out in the field, yet it became the hallmark of my approach to working with all animals.

I have worked with the cattle industry for many years to improve the way cattle are handled, and I've consulted with zoos and other animal-handling facilities to help unlock other questions of animal behavior. When I wrote about this in *Thinking in Pictures*, I believed that my connection with animals, especially prey species like cattle, was on account of my autism. I believed we shared a flight response when threatened. I understood their fear. In some ways, I related more to animals than to people.

I came to realize that my visual thinking has a component that contributes to my ability to see things that other people miss. I notice details that are amiss or faulty, sometimes dangerously so, an awareness I'll elaborate on in the chapter on disaster. I didn't just see that slant of sunlight or chain in the chute; these things jumped out at me. When I walk into a room, I immediately see anything that is off-kilter, the way a verbal thinker will pick out a misplaced comma or a typo in a sentence. The stuff that shouldn't be there or is slightly off jumps out.

It turns out that this ability has roots in both autism and visual thinking. Laurent Mottron, a psychiatrist and researcher in cognitive neuroscience and autism at the University of Montreal, and his colleague Sylvie Belleville have worked with many people on the spectrum. Their research encompasses studying perceptual processing abilities. In one study, they administered a series of tests to a patient known as E.C., who was a savant (more on savants in a later chapter). E.C. could draw from memory in perfect proportion, with great spatial detail. Mottron observed, "Autistic subjects are known to detect minor modifications in their surroundings more rapidly than normals, and to fixate on small morphological details." Mottron later conducted another study looking at visual and verbal thinkers using more complex visual tasks to locate perceptual functioning. Here, too, visual perception played "a superior role in autistic cognition."

Uta Frith is the pioneering developmental psychologist who helped pave the way for autism to be viewed as a cognitive condition and not the result of frigid mothers (referred to at the time as "refrigerator mothers"). In an early study, she and Amitta Shah compared how autistic people, "normal" people, and those with intellectual disabilities would complete a task where colored blocks were assembled into different patterns. They found that autistic subjects, "regardless of age and ability, performed better than controls."

I don't think it would have occurred to me to jump in that chute if I weren't a visual thinker. I had to see things from the cows' point of view. To me, it was the most natural response in the world. Then again, I still believed everybody thought the same way I did, in a series of associated photorealistic pictures or in short, trailer-like films playing in my mind. Just as verbal thinkers had a hard time understanding visual thinkers like me, I had difficulty understanding that verbal thinkers existed. I didn't know about the work of researchers like Mottron and Frith back then. It would never have occurred to me that you could study and quantify visual thinking or that there was a name for it. Since then, I've given a lot of thought as to why this is the case.

Visual Thinking in a Verbal World

The fact is, we live in a talky culture. Verbal thinkers dominate the national conversation in religion, media, publishing, and education. Words fill the airwaves and the internet, with preachers, pundits, and politicians taking up most of the real estate. We even call commentators "talking heads." The dominant culture favors verbal people; theirs is a language-filled world.

Psychologist Charles Fernyhough is director of the Hearing the Voice project at Durham University. His book *The Voices Within* describes the pervasive and multiple ways and reasons that people talk to themselves: to motivate, self-focus, regulate mood, direct attention, change behavior. In essence, to become conscious. As we'll see, even highly verbal thinkers do visualize, but information comes to them mostly in the form of language. Yet Fernyhough, like many, falls prey to a certain bias in reporting on his research. He contends that thinking is primarily linguistic, more closely "tied up with language than it initially appears to be." He acknowledges that imaging is involved, along with sensory and emotional elements, but "they are only parts of the picture." While it's true that I talk to myself, sometimes even out loud when I'm concentrating really hard on a livestock-design project, my mind is not a raft on a sea of words. It's an ocean of images.

———

Most children connect language to the things in their lives at a remarkable rate. Speech comes naturally to verbal people. A toddler picks up, in addition to words and syntax, the intonations and expressiveness in a parent's language. Many visual thinkers on the spectrum, however, must learn to adapt to the dominant culture. They don't understand that the rest of the world communicates thoughts and feelings through words. Language does not come naturally to us. We struggle to master it, as well as how to modulate our voices with the right intonation, pitch, and tone. I learned to modulate my voice through close observation of the way verbal thinkers speak. It did not come naturally. It is not innate. I still struggle with remembering long sequences of verbal information. Sometimes jokes go over my head, especially if they are delivered rapidly or involve wordplay. To understand the joke, I have to convert the words to images. If the joke includes a verbal leap or strange syntax, I probably won't get it.

For a long time, I mistakenly believed that all people with autism were visual thinkers. As it turns out, some people on the spectrum are highly verbal. But according to psychologist Graham J. Hitch and his colleagues at the University of Manchester, all children exhibit an early propensity toward visual thinking. He studied how children process information to see if they rely on visual rather than phonological cues in their memory. The results showed that in older children, visual memory is "masked by the more pervasive phonological component of recall," meaning that words soon paper over images, like one layer of wallpaper covering another. Gabriela Koppenol-Gonzalez, a psychologist and data analyst who has also tracked the ascendancy of language as children's primary means of communication, found that until five years of age, children rely heavily on visual short-term memory (STM). From six to ten, they start using more verbal processing, and from age ten onward they resemble adults with respect to verbal STM. As their verbal and visual systems develop, children become more inclined to verbal thought. But the researchers also reported on previous studies of STM in adults and concluded that, contrary to what one might assume, not all adults process information verbally first and foremost.

Psychologist Linda Silverman of the Institute for the Study of Advanced Development and the Gifted Development Center in Denver has been working with gifted individuals, including many on the spectrum, for more than forty years. Their cluster of traits includes difficulty with reading, spelling, organization, and sequencing. Yet many of these kids could readily take things apart and put them together and solve complicated equations, though they would not be able to tell you how they did it. They tended to like calculus and physics and were good at map reading. Silverman's work has been in service of teaching different kinds of learners, acknowledging their very different brains not as a disability but as an asset. In a presentation about the differences in learning styles, Silverman flashes a slide showing a person with a tidy file cabinet and a person surrounded by messy piles of paper. The "filer" and the "piler," to use her terms. You probably know which one you are. What does it say about the way you think?

Silverman rightly points out that you can't make any definitive inferences about the messy versus the neat person in terms of intelligence, abilities, and so on, yet it's the messy people who tend to get stereotyped as lacking. When we compare a student with a perfectly organized binder and one with a backpack stuffed with papers, we generally assume that the organized kid is the better student and is smarter. It's possible that they are just better at school. The geniuses, as we'll see, are usually "pilers." Silverman also correctly notes that if you made the person with the messy pile organize those papers, he or she would never find anything again. Such people know where everything is. For them, the "mess" is organized. They see it in their mind's eye.

That is absolutely true for me. My office has messy piles of journal and magazine articles and stacks of drafts that look like a random mess. Yet the piles are not random. Each contains the source material for a different project. I could easily locate the right pile and find any paper I needed. Finding a specific paper in a messy pile might not be an indicator of genius, but it's definitely a clue to how the mind works.

Yet the benefit of the doubt always seems to go to the verbal thinkers. Simon Baron-Cohen, professor of psychology and psychiatry and director of the Autism Research Centre at Cambridge, puts forth a fascinating theory in his book *The Pattern Seekers: How Autism Drives Human Invention,* in which he posits that people with autism are responsible for much of the world's innovation. "These hyper-systemizers struggle with even the simplest of everyday social tasks, like making and keeping relationships, yet they can easily spot patterns in nature or via experimenting that others simply miss." This is an accurate description of how I think. But Baron-Cohen goes on to acclaim the importance of verbal thinking, asserting that the cognitive revolution gave rise to "our remarkable human capacity for language." This idea dominates the history of human understanding: through some alchemical process, language is presumed to transform thought into consciousness, while visual thinking gets erased somewhere along the way.

The Visual-Verbal Continuum

I am asked all the time how you can determine if a child is a visual thinker. The signs may show up in a child as young as three, but they more often become apparent when the child is six to eight years old. The propensity for visual and spatial thinking will turn up in the activities they gravitate toward. Often, they create beautiful drawings that are highly detailed and realistic. They also like building with toys like blocks, Legos, and Erector sets, or putting things together with materials they find around the house, such as cardboard or wood. They may light up at the sight of a thousand-piece jigsaw puzzle or spend hours in the basement or garage tinkering with tools or electronics, taking things apart and putting them back together. Theoretical physicist Stephen Hawking took apart model trains and airplanes before making a simple computer out of recycled clock and telephone parts. Pioneering computer scientist and mathematician Grace Murray Hopper took apart all seven of the clocks in her family home. You probably wouldn't be happy if your teen took apart your laptop, though you might be happier if he or she turned out to be the next Steve Wozniak.

With adults, I suggest taking what I call the IKEA Test to help identify where you fall on the visual-verbal spectrum. It's not strictly scientific, but it's a fairly reliable shortcut to separating the more verbally inclined from the more visually inclined. Here's the test: You buy a piece of furniture and are ready to put it together: Do you read the instructions or follow the pictures? If I attempt to read verbal instructions, I become totally lost, because I cannot follow the sequential steps. But if I look at the drawings, my mind will start associating all the things I have put together in the past, and I'll know how this piece of furniture is supposed to look. You may have noticed that IKEA instructions come as a series of illustrations—no written instructions at all. I wasn't surprised to learn that the man who created the company was dyslexic, privileging pictures over words. I've heard of some verbal thinkers who completely fall apart in the face of IKEA furniture instructions, becoming highly frustrated as they try to follow them. What is a perfect road map for me is a confusing mess for them. That must be why IKEA partnered with TaskRabbit, employing visual thinkers to help English majors assemble their bookshelves.

Bookcases aside, there is no definitive test or scan for visual thinking (yet), but Linda Silverman's "Visual-Spatial Identifier," which she and her team in Denver developed over many years, does a very good job of distinguishing between what Silverman calls "auditory sequential" thinkers (language based) and "visual spatial" (picture based). If you're interested in where you fall on the spectrum, take a moment to answer the eighteen questions on the Visual-Spatial Identifier opposite.

If you answer yes to ten or more of the questions, you are very likely to be a visual-spatial learner.

Remember, it's a verbal-visual continuum, not a binary. Very few people will reply yes to all the questions. I replied yes to sixteen out of eighteen, which puts me at the far end of the visual-thinking spectrum. Writers, editors, and lawyers will typically have far fewer yes answers. My cowriter, a highly verbal person, answered yes to only four of the questions. Most people will likely fall somewhere in the middle, showing a blend of both kinds of thinking. Highly creative or mathematical people will likely answer yes to many of the questions.

People often ask me what percentage of people are visual thinkers. There isn't a whole lot of data on that yet. But Silverman's team, conducting a study that included 750 fourth-, fifth-, and sixth-graders with a wide range of socioeconomic backgrounds and IQ scores, found that roughly one third were strongly visual-spatial, about one quarter were strongly auditory-sequential, and about 45 percent were a mix.

When I first realized that I was a visual thinker, I went into scientist mode and created my own survey. I believed that if I surveyed enough people, asking the same questions designed to reveal how they accessed visual memory, I could build a database of people out there who thought like me. Neurologist and author Oliver Sacks picked up on this propensity of mine to gather information and wrote about it in a *New Yorker* article that then became the title of his book *An Anthropologist on Mars*. It was an accurate description of how I

VISUAL-SPATIAL IDENTIFIER

		YES	NO
1.	Do you think mainly in pictures instead of in words?	☐	☐
2.	Do you know things without being able to explain how or why?	☐	☐
3.	Do you solve problems in unusual ways?	☐	☐
4.	Do you have a vivid imagination?	☐	☐
5.	Do you remember what you see and forget what you hear?	☐	☐
6.	Are you terrible at spelling?	☐	☐
7.	Can you visualize objects from different perspectives?	☐	☐
8.	Are you organizationally impaired?	☐	☐
9.	Do you often lose track of time?	☐	☐
10.	Would you rather read a map than follow verbal directions?	☐	☐
11.	Do you remember how to get to places you visited only once?	☐	☐
12.	Is your handwriting slow and difficult for others to read?	☐	☐
13.	Can you feel what others are feeling?	☐	☐
14.	Are you musically, artistically, or mechanically inclined?	☐	☐
15.	Do you know more than others think you know?	☐	☐
16.	Do you hate speaking in front of a group?	☐	☐
17.	Did you feel smarter as you got older?	☐	☐
18.	Are you addicted to your computer?	☐	☐

make sense of the world. I'm like Margaret Mead among so-called normal, or "neurotypical," people. In lieu of certain kinds of social connection, I'm more comfortable studying the ways and habits of people. "Fitting in" is a complicated business. I didn't realize it then, but in searching for fellow visual thinkers through my survey, I was also searching for my tribe.

I started my survey by asking people to describe their home or their pet. Almost everyone, it turned out, described their homes or pets with specific visual detail. When I asked people to describe ordinary things such as toasters and ice cream cones, I got similar results. People had no trouble visualizing and describing them. Were they all visual thinkers? As a scientist, I did what I always do: I analyzed my results and hypothesized. I suspected that familiarity with these objects might be responsible for the detailed recall.

I decided to focus on something that people were aware of but didn't encounter in their everyday lives. Driving by the church in my town, I lit on steeples. Everyone knows what a steeple is and probably sees one from time to time, but they're not hugely present in our lives. Even if you attend church, the steeple may not be something you take notice of. I've spoken to ministers who barely noticed the steeples on their own churches. Asking people to access their memories about church steeples completely changed the results.

Without fail, I get one of three distinct responses. The visual thinkers like me describe specific steeples, often naming several actual churches. There is nothing vague or abstract about the picture in their mind. They might as well be staring at a photograph or photorealistic drawing; they see it that clearly. Then there are the people like my cowriter, on the far end of the verbal spectrum, who see two vague lines in an inverted V, as if roughly sketched in charcoal, not at all specific. Generally, these folks are verbal thinkers. But there are also many people who have a response somewhere in between the two extremes. They see a generic New England–style steeple, an image they piece together from churches they've seen and from steeples they may have read about or seen in movies. This person falls in the middle of the spectrum, a mix of verbal and visual. So almost from the beginning I recognized that there were not two distinct categories of thinker but rather a continuum.

Another informal experiment I've conducted over the years to screen for visual thinkers involves two disparate groups I regularly give talks to: elementary school kids and school administrators. I show each group a picture of a steer exiting a chute, staring at a bright spot of sunlight on the floor. The caption says: NON-SLIP FLOORING IS ESSENTIAL. I ask for a show of hands: How many see that the animal is looking at the sunbeam? The results remain consistent: With the kids, half the hands go up. When I present the same slide at a conference of school administrators, almost no hands go up. The administrators focus on the caption.

The Visual Brain and the Verbal Brain

In a brief history of the discovery of the visual cortex, Professor Mitchell Glickstein highlights a series of doctors who homed in on different aspects of how vision works in the brain. Francesco Gennari, a medical student in eighteenth-century Parma, Italy, who put brains on ice and dissected them, "initiated the field of cerebral architectonics: the study of regional differences in cortical structure." Scottish neurologist David Ferrier, looking for the part of the brain that controls vision, accidentally discovered visually guided movement or motor functions. With the advent of Russian rifles with bullets that didn't shatter the soldiers' skulls, Japanese physician Tatsuji Inouye was able to record the entry and exit point of the bullets and calculate the location of vision damage in the brains of twenty-nine soldiers wounded in the Russo-Japanese War of 1904–1905. British neurologists came up with an even more accessible diagram from working with wounded English soldiers at around the same time.

The two parts of the brain most closely associated with speech are named for two nineteenth-century neurologists who figured out that different parts of the brain play unique roles. French surgeon Paul Broca identified the language center in the brain after working with a patient who had lost his speech (aphasia). An autopsy showed the presence of a lesion in the left frontal portion of the brain. This finding was corroborated in subsequent autopsies. A person with an injury to Broca's area will often be fully able to understand language but cannot speak. Influenced by Broca's work, Polish neurosurgeon Carl Wernicke discovered a similar pattern of lesions, only this time in the posterior portion of the temporal lobe. Broca's area became associated with speech production, the ability to form words. It's also responsible for our understanding of nonverbal cues such as gestures, facial expressions, and body language. This part of the brain is close to the motor cortex, which enables your brain to run your mouth. Wernicke's area is the locus of language comprehension and is close to the auditory cortex. A person whose Wernicke's area is damaged will often have scrambled thoughts, but will be able to speak, though without making much sense. These areas are connected by a big associative bundle that doesn't contain information but merges both speech and comprehension into thought. Our bundle is larger than any other animal's, which helps explain our complex speech and sophisticated communication.

At the same time, experiments using highly invasive procedures, including electrodes connected to different parts of a person's or animal's brain, aimed to show exactly what the brain did. In one experiment, stimulating one side of the brain caused the opposite side of the body to move. Two German physiologists, Gustav Fritsch and Eduard Hitzig, were treating soldiers with head injuries and figured out what part of the brain produces voluntary movement by prodding the back of their heads with electrical stimulation. They repeated the experiment with a dog. David Ferrier, the same neurologist who discovered motor function, removed the prefrontal lobes of monkeys and found their motor skills intact but their personalities profoundly changed. (He would also become the first scientist to be tried under the Cruelty to Animals Act of 1876.)

Oliver Sacks pointed out that most studies of the brain emanate from lack of capacity. A patient with a specific deficit gives us a chance to look for the cause, and by locating it, to learn about brain function. In perhaps the most famous early case, a railway worker named Phineas Gage was pierced by a metal rod that entered below his cheekbone and penetrated through the top of his skull. He miraculously survived and was able to see, walk, and talk, but he had significant personality changes, constantly spewing expletives and dispensing with social decorum. This was perhaps the first window into the function of the prefrontal cortex. In 2012, more than 170 years later, researchers at UCLA's Laboratory of Neuro Imaging, using a combination of high-tech tools and 110 images of Gage's virtual skull, were still trying to explain the loss of executive and emotional functions and how it might shed light on the effects of brain trauma and degenerative conditions such as dementia.

Over time, tools have been developed that allow researchers to peer inside the brain without such invasive procedures. PET scans gave way to EEGs, CAT scans, and MRIs, which produce highly accurate images of the brain that can be used to diagnose brain injuries, tumors, dementia, strokes, and more. The fMRI (functional magnetic resonance imaging) takes the technology one step further and shows brain activity.

Still, fMRI has its limitations. I think of the technology as an airplane cruising at night over a complex of houses that all get their electricity from a single generator. If the house that contains the generator is struck by lightning, all the houses will go dark. If a house that does not have the generator is hit, the others will continue to keep their lights on. With fMRI technology, we have no idea where the "generator" is unless we hit it, as with an electrode. It doesn't allow us to determine which node in a neural network turns on the entire system.

It's important to remember that we rely on sight more than any of our other senses. Research studies have shown that both seeing something and imagining it activates a wide area of the occipital (visual) cortex and the temporal lobe. These two areas make up approximately a third of the brain. That's a lot of real estate. The primary visual cortex is located at the back of the head in all mammals, the farthest point from the eyes. We don't know why it's lodged back there, but the location may have assisted in the evolutionary development of depth perception.

Data is stored in basically three places in your brain. I think of them as your phone, your desktop, and your cloud for archiving detailed visual memories. Visual information enters the brain through your eyes and is stored at the back of the brain in your visual cortex along with some associated structures, including a hot zone for dreaming. Imagine you are taking pictures or video with your phone. Do you want to store your photos on your desktop (mid-brain), where you can file and categorize them (dogs, family, trees, videos, etc.), or do you need to put them away for safekeeping in the cloud? The frontal cortex sorts through all this data, just as you do when you decide how to organize your photos, dragging them for storage to your desktop or the cloud. Nothing is stored in the frontal cortex, but it's where you arrange your life, a process known as executive functioning. How does all the information travel through the brain? To extend the analogy: through high-speed internet, Wi-Fi, or dial-up.

Over the years, I have participated in many brain-scan studies, each time using the newest technology. As a scientist, I had a tremendous urge to explore the unknown aspects of my own brain, to see if I could unlock some of the mysteries of autism or better understand how I think. My first brain scan was done on a then-state-of-the-art MRI scanner in 1987 by Eric Courchesne at the University of California San Diego School of Medicine. Cutting-edge at the time, the technology measured brain structure in beautiful, sharp detail.

When I saw the images, I exclaimed, "Journey to the center of my brain!" From this scan, I learned why I had balance problems. My cerebellum was 20 percent smaller than in the average brain. Another MRI explained why I had high levels of anxiety before I started taking antidepressants. My amygdala (emotion center) was three times larger than average.

The scans that really blew my mind were done at the University of Pittsburgh by Walter Schneider, the inventor of a new technology called Diffusion Tensor Imaging (DTI). This technology images the nerve fiber bundles that carry information between different parts of the brain. His research was funded by the Defense Department to develop high-definition fiber tracking (HDFT) to diagnose head injuries in soldiers. This technology provided clearer images than other devices at the time and was able to distinguish where nerve fibers connected to each other and where they only crossed each other. My speech circuits were much smaller than those in the control, which may explain why my speech was delayed as a child. But my visual results were off the charts—400 percent larger than those in the controls. It was as if I had a huge internet trunk line from my rear visual cortex to my frontal cortex. Proof positive that I was a visual thinker.

It's deep inside these circuits where things run smoothly or where developmental problems can occur. One example: Your eyes are always moving but the words on the page don't jump around when you read. That's thanks to the stabilization circuitry in your brain that keeps words from jiggling. Poor circuitry can be responsible for visual distortion or bandwidth problems, as well as stuttering, dyslexia, and learning disabilities.

Once again, it's important to remember that visual thinking is not about seeing, per se. Everyone sees unless they are blind. Visual thinking refers to the way the mind works, to *the way we perceive*. For all our poking and prodding into the brain, we still don't have a whole lot of information on how visual files are created, stored, or accessed. We know that while visual perception and mental imagery use many of the same brain structures, they are distinct neural phenomena. Put plainly, we understand how the physiological hardware works, but not the software.

Neuroscientist Sue-Hyun Lee and her colleagues at the National Institute of Mental Health in Bethesda, Maryland, moved the ball up the field when they were able to differentiate the way the brain processes objects as a person is looking at them versus when the same object is imagined in the mind's eye. When a subject was asked to look at pictures of common objects, fMRI scans revealed that information from the eyes streamed into the input point in the primary visual cortex, then the information moved forward into mid-brain areas for processing and storage. When the same subjects were asked to imagine the same objects, the mid-brain areas were activated; the information moved through the circuits differently.

In an older study, a man in his early thirties had a head injury that destroyed his ability to recognize common objects, though he could visualize them in his imagination. When he was given a cup of coffee, he did not drink it because he could not recognize it among all the other objects on a desk. When he visited a buffet, he was not able to recognize the array of different foods. They appeared as colored blobs. When shown common objects, he thought a pair of pliers was a clothespin. His brain scans revealed possible damage in the occipital temporal area, the area of the brain that processes visual information. Studies like these began to articulate how our mind's eye relies on a processor different from the visual cortex.

In even earlier neurological research about how we think, pathbreaking studies began to focus on visual thinkers. In an influential 1983 paper, neuropsychologist Mortimer Mishkin described two separate cortical processes in the brains of monkeys, one for identifying objects and a separate pathway for locating them. A 2015 study from Japan looked at brain activity associated with verbal and visual thinking. Kazuo Nishimura and his colleagues tasked their subjects to recall in turn a famous Japanese temple, the twelve signs of the zodiac, and a personal conversation, all while the researchers measured the attendant neurological activity. They found a "significant correlation between an individual's subjective 'vividness' of visual imagery and activity in the visual area." Magnetoencephalography (MEG) showed that visual thinkers created images during these tasks, while the verbal thinkers relied more on self-talk. This method makes it possible to measure rapid changes in the areas of the brain that are activated.

Additional research seemed to correlate the two different types of thinking, visual and verbal, with the right and left hemispheres of the brain. In 2019, Qunlin Chen of Southwest University in Chongqing, China, who studies the underlying cognitive mechanisms of creativity, together with a colleague administered four tasks to 502 subjects. They were asked to improve a toy elephant to make it more fun, to draw ten figures, to come up with alternative uses for a can, and to look at ambiguous figures and list ideas they got from them. Under an MRI scan, brain imaging showed that those who performed these tasks easily—the visual thinkers—had a higher concentration of activity on the right side of the brain, while verbal thinkers, who had a harder time with the assignments, had greater activity on the left side of the brain. These ideas have been popularized as right-brain/left-brain thinking. The right-brain hemisphere is associated with creativity, while language and organization are associated with activity in the left brain. Roger Sperry, the American neuropsychologist and neurobiologist whose split-brain experiments earned him a Nobel Prize in physiology, recognized the bias toward left-brain thinking, acknowledging that we tend to "neglect the non-verbal form of intellect. What it comes down to is that modern society discriminates against the right hemisphere."

As research was beginning to validate the existence of visual thinking, I was coming to see that the verbal/visual construct was too simplistic. Visual and verbal thinking isn't a binary, either/or prospect but rather describes the endpoints of a spectrum along which all of us fall, with some of us much closer to one end than the other. Chen's study, in fact, highlighted that a "hemispheric balance" among the regions of the brain was essential to verbal thinking. The lines between kinds of thinking are not so easily drawn, in the brain itself or in the skills where different kinds of brains excel. You might be a verbal thinker who is also good at math. Or a rocket scientist who likes to write poetry.

The genetics of brain science are even more complex. Some researchers have hypothesized that the genes that make the brain large are related to the genes that contribute to autism, suggesting a genomic trade-off: higher intelligence at the cost of some social and emotional skills. Recent research on genetic sequencing shows that many genes are related to autism. Dr. Camillo Thomas Gualtieri, a child psychiatrist in North Carolina, calls them "multiple genes of small effect." This would explain why autism occurs on a spectrum ranging from a few traits to disabling. The complexity of our genetic makeup provides the ability for humans to adapt to a wide range of environments. The price is that a few individuals will be severely disabled.

Other such trade-offs have been observed in people who are blind from birth; all that valuable brain real estate can get repurposed for other functions. In a study by Rashi Pant and her colleagues at Johns Hopkins University, the researchers were able to show that people who were born blind used portions of their visual cortex to respond to math equations, simple yes-or-no questions, and a semantic judgment task, while people who became blind later did not. This shows that there are channels of communication between visual and language systems.

One of the best analogies I've found to describe how visual thinking works is the way some blind people learn to navigate via echolocation, most commonly used by bats. The bat emits high-frequency clicking noises and uses the echoes to detect prey and any obstacles in its flight path. Echolocation allows bats to "see" with sound. About 25 percent of blind people learn to echolocate using mouth clicks, finger snaps, or cane tapping to "see" with both the auditory cortex and some repurposed visual cortex. A skilled echolocator can detect the shape, motion, and location of large objects. It appears that the brain can adapt to use sound—nonvisual information—to perform tasks of visual perception. In a very young person, the brain has more flexibility for repurposing. Another interesting study showed that when people blind from birth did algebra, their brains used early visual cortices that received no input from the eyes. This was not true for sighted people. The brain starts with a sizable portion dedicated to visual thinking. If it is not used, another function will take it over. The brain will not allow valuable real estate to sit vacant. This research also suggests that the brain is designed to create images. When the eyes stop providing information, the brain learns how to create images by using the other senses.

An extreme example is Matthew Whitaker, whom I first saw featured on *60 Minutes*. Born prematurely, at twenty-four weeks, Matthew was not expected to survive. He defied the odds. But he became blind as a result of a condition known as attendant retinopathy. When he was three, his grandfather gave him a small electronic keyboard. Matthew immediately started playing it, easily sounding out songs he had heard, such as "Twinkle, Twinkle, Little Star." At the age of five, Matthew became the youngest student to be admitted to the Filomen M. D'Agostino Greenberg Music School for the blind and visually impaired in New York City. His teacher reported that the morning after he attended a concert of her performing a Dvořák piano quintet, she heard him playing not only the piano part but all four parts for strings. Matthew now travels the world playing jazz professionally.

Dr. Charles Limb, who studies neural networks in artists and musicians, scanned Matthew's brain while he was playing a keyboard, listening to some of his favorite music, then listening to a dull lecture. When he listened to the lecture, his visual cortex was unengaged. When he listened to some of his favorite music, the entire visual cortex activated. Limb observed, "It seems like his brain is taking that part of the tissue that's not being stimulated by sight and using it or maybe helping him to perceive music with it."

At least twelve new brain-scan studies conducted in the past few years have focused on visual thinking and how it is activated in different parts of the brain. The new generation of scanners can detect activated brain areas more quickly and accurately. That said, the next generation of MRI testing can still produce skewed results due to inaccurate or incomplete methods sections that make it difficult to replicate the studies accurately. In my own field, I've seen important details left out of the methods section, such as how subjects were chosen, the breed of pig, or the ingredients in the feed. Like the slant of sunlight in the chute, these are troubling details that jump out at me. The conflicting results in MRI studies may be due to such seemingly minor inconsistencies as the timing of prompts given to subjects, or their duration. But they may also be the product of the same confirmation bias we've already seen at work: most visual tests are designed and conducted by psychologists, who mostly happen to be verbal thinkers. Depending on who is analyzing the experiment, results may conflict or be skewed. Spatial and object visualizers see the world differently, as we'll explore.

Object Visualizers and Spatial Visualizers

Discovering the difference between visual and verbal thinking was, as I've said, mind-blowing. The realization that visual and verbal thinking exist along a continuum was another breakthrough. Encountering the groundbreaking work of Maria Kozhevnikov further transformed how I thought about modes of visual thinking.

Kozhevnikov, a lecturer at Harvard Medical School and a researcher at the visual-spatial cognition lab at Massachusetts General Hospital, is one of the first scientists to differentiate between two kinds of visual thinkers: spatial visualizers and object visualizers. In her 2002 landmark research, she developed a battery of questionnaires and skill tests that have become the gold standard in studies about spatial and object visualization. Using her Visualizer-Verbalizer Cognitive Style Questionnaire (VVCSQ), she identified seventeen undergraduates at the University of California at Santa Barbara as high visualizers. The subjects were then given a series of visual tests, including a paper-folding test that was originally developed in 1976 as part of a cognitive test kit to determine aptitude in naval recruits. In the test, researchers show subjects a drawing of a folded piece of paper perforated by a hole. The subjects are then asked to use spatial reasoning to choose which of five drawings accurately depicts what the paper will look like—where the holes will appear—when the paper is unfolded. In another test, the participants were shown a schematic drawing that represented motion of an object. When I looked at the drawing, I saw photorealistic pictures of a real situation, such as riding my sled down a hill. The more mathematically visual-spatial thinkers interpreted the drawing as an abstract schematic representation of motion. They did not see pictures in their mind's eye. Depending on a subject's performance on this and other tests, Kozhevnikov would measure spatial visualization abilities in processing, apprehending, coding, and mentally manipulating spatial forms.

Overwhelmingly, the fine artists and interior designers tested as object visualizers and the scientists tested as spatial visualizers. More specifically, the low-spatial visualizers interpreted graphs as pictures, whereas the high-spatial visualizers correctly interpreted the graphs as abstract representations of spatial relations. The verbalizers didn't show a clear preference for either visual or spatial imagery.

Kozhevnikov articulated what I had started to suspect: visual thinkers couldn't all be lumped together. In the most basic terms, there are two kinds of visualizers. "Object visualizers" like me see the world in photorealistic images. We are graphic designers, artists, skilled tradespeople, architects, inventors, mechanical engineers, and designers. Many of us are terrible in areas such as algebra, which rely entirely on abstraction and provide nothing to visualize. "Spatial visualizers" see the world in patterns and abstractions. They are the music and math minds—the statisticians, scientists, electrical engineers, and physicists. You'll find a lot of these thinkers excel at computer programming because they can see patterns in the computer code. Here's a way to think of it: The object thinker builds the computer. The spatial thinker writes the code.

A team of scientists led by María José Pérez-Fabello from the University of Vigo in Spain tested 125 fine arts, engineering, and psychology students for verbal, spatial, and object thinking and independently corroborated Kozhevnikov's results. Kozhevnikov then tested the same subjects again to assess their abilities in different types of visualization. Some had high object-visualization skills, while the others had high visual-spatial skills, but none excelled in both types of visual skills. A person who has both superior visual-spatial and object-visualization skills would be a supergenius. Imagine Mozart doing rocket science.

In a recent study, Tim Höffler and colleagues at the University of Duisburg in Germany studied eye-gaze patterns of object visualizers, spatial visualizers, and verbal thinkers, using a questionnaire to determine their cognitive processes, followed by the paper-folding test. Information was then presented in both detailed pictures and writing on topics ranging from tying a knot to how a toilet tank works. The object visualizers spent more time looking at the pictures, and the verbal thinkers spent more time reading the instructions.

As soon as I encountered Kozhevnikov's new distinction between kinds of visual thinkers, I knew immediately that I was an object visualizer. For starters, I was terrible at the paper-folding test. My talents are mechanical, and I think in concrete, highly detailed images. The mechanical engineers I've worked with, the welders, machinists, and equipment designers, the people who just do stuff and build stuff, they also fit this description. The pattern thinkers known as "spatial visualizers" have the ability to extract principles and patterns from the relationships between sets of objects or numbers. Yet the difference between object-visual thinkers and visual-spatial thinkers, important as it is, is almost always overlooked in brain studies of verbal and visual thinking. Searching the scientific literature on object thinking and mechanical ability, with the exception of Kozhevnikov's work, yields very little.

Then Kozhevnikov developed another test to measure detailed visual thinking and perception, or how a person acquires and processes information. It is called the Grain Resolution Test. The subject hears the names of two different substances—for example, a pile of salt versus a heap of poppy seeds, or a grape versus the strings on the head of a tennis racquet—and is asked to determine which has the finer grain, which is denser. In assessing how a person uses imagery to solve problems, Kozhevnikov showed that object thinkers were faster and more accurate, creating "high quality images of the shapes of individual objects." The visual-spatial thinkers excel at a more abstract imagining of the relationships between objects. I aced the Grain Resolution Test. For the tennis racquet string example, I saw in my mind's eye the grapes being squashed because they were too big to fit through the spaces between the racquet strings. My score on the Grain Resolution Test was much better than that of Richard Panek, my coauthor for *The Autistic Brain*, but his score on the paper-folding test was much better than mine. These results indicated that he is a visual-spatial thinker, while I am an object visualizer.

Just for fun, I took an online mechanical aptitude test that measures the ability to understand common mechanical things, using timed questions. As a visual thinker, I expected to ace it. The test initially asks you to choose between pairs of images, identifying the one with the superior construction—for example, a bolt cutter with long or short handles. I could immediately see the performance of the two bolt cutters as short video clips in my imagination. From experience, I also know that longer handles provide more leverage and will cut through a bolt more easily. Another test features two cars located on a bridge, one closer to the bridge support and the other in the middle of the bridge. Which car would do more damage to the structure if the bridge construction were defective? I could easily picture where the weight-bearing load would be distributed on the structure, which quickly revealed to me that the car in the middle would be more dangerous. Next were multiple-choice questions about the mechanics of different objects. Here, however, I got only seven out of ten questions right.

My score reflected one of the aspects of object-visual thinking: some object visualizers like me need more time to process information, because we first need to access the photorealistic picture bank to process information. In other words, I need to do the equivalent of a Google search in my mind to access the images to solve a given problem. Different types of thinking provide strengths in one area and deficits in another. My thinking is slower but it may be more accurate. Faster thinking would be helpful in social situations, but slower, careful thought would enhance production of art or building mechanical devices.

Rapidly delivered verbal information is even more challenging for object-visual thinkers like me. Standup comedians often move too quickly through their routines for me to process. By the time I have visualized the first joke, the comedian has already launched two more. I get lost when verbal information is presented too fast. Imagine how a student who is a visual thinker feels in a classroom where a teacher is talking fast to get through a lesson.

The New Normal

These days, "neurotypical" has replaced the term "normal." Neurotypicals are generally described as people whose development happens in predictable ways at predictable times. It's a term that I shy away from, because defining what is neurotypical is as unhelpful as asking the average size of a dog. What's typical: a Chihuahua or a Great Dane? When does a little geeky or nerdy become autistic? When does distractable become ADHD, or when does a little moody become bipolar? These are all continuous traits.

Most recently, the stereotype of the monotone scientist was portrayed in the character of the physicist Sheldon Cooper on the TV sitcom *The Big Bang Theory*. Sheldon speaks in a stream of unmodulated sentences and has the emotional range of a spatula. Among his geeky roommates, though, he's probably the one whose intelligence could save the planet. They are smart; he is off the charts. In the show, Sheldon's spectrumlike qualities are played for laughs, but that's not usually how it goes. Math geeks are often bullied or shunned. It's only when the geeks become brilliant coders, mathematicians, entrepreneurs, and rocket scientists that we appreciate the way they see the world.

Elon Musk was so badly bullied in school, he needed to have surgery after a group of bullies threw him down a flight of stairs. He also taught himself coding, and at age twelve sold his first video game for $500. According to his biographer Ashlee Vance, Musk ran out of books to read at school and the local library. He then churned through two sets of encyclopedias. His photographic memory of facts and his proclivity for sharing them did not win friends and influence people. Instead, he was thought of as a "fact factory" and came off as a classic know-it-all. I think it's fair to wager that Musk is off the charts. Not long ago, when he hosted *Saturday Night Live*, he revealed that he has Asperger's syndrome.

I was pretty geeky myself, badly bullied in middle school. I didn't really find my tribe until I started working on construction projects. The engineers and welders I worked with were generally visual thinkers like me. It explained why we collaborated so well and got along. We spoke the same language. It was an arena where all that mattered was our skills, not how we looked, our background, our college education, and so on. My weirdness didn't matter once they saw my work.

Early on in my career, I gained respect for my ability to draw accurate blueprints. People marveled at my work. I had never taken a single drafting class. Some people thought I had savant skills. But savants are people who can re-create a piece of music or memorize mind-bogglingly long pieces of writing or mathematical sequences with a single exposure. (More on this in the chapter on neurodiversity and genius.) Figuring out how to draft took me several weeks. I observed how a colleague drafted blueprints, and copied everything he did, down to the kind of pencil and bond paper he used. Then I took a set of blueprints out to the plant and walked every inch of the place, relating every line on the paper to the physical equivalent in the plant. In retrospect, this was pure visual thinking. I wasn't going to understand a blueprint unless I connected the drawing to its physical manifestation.

Once again, the cattle handlers thought I was nuts, traipsing through the muddy facility with blueprints flapping in the breeze. But eventually I was able to connect the abstract shapes on the floor plan of the plant to the elements of the structure itself, such as connecting squares to the supporting columns. In all likelihood, a spatial visualizer would have been able to make the mental leap simply by reading the blueprint. But by physically surveying the plant, I was able to run a visual simulation in my head that enabled me to draw my renderings with a great deal of accuracy. It was as if I were tracing a picture from a diagram in my mind onto the drafting paper.

I've spent a lifetime working with the Sheldons of the world, brilliant people who are marginalized for their weirdness. I worked with a guy who was extremely socially awkward and had no college degree. If he were a child today, I'm convinced he'd be diagnosed with autism. As an adult he has developed about twenty patents, owned a metal shop, and invented custom-designed equipment for his customers. He does this *in his head*. I worked with another guy who is dyslexic and stutters. He sells his patented equipment all over the world. I wonder what would happen to him in today's educational system. His successful career was started with a school welding class that enabled him to showcase his skills. I've worked with people whose minds can automatically morph two-dimensional renderings into three-dimensional structures like Tony Stark in the *Iron Man* movies, when he touches the screen in his garage workshop and a 3D interface of his imagination blossoms.

These visual thinking skills were studied by Ji Young Cho of Kyung Hee University in South Korea and and Joori Suh of the University of Cincinnati. They assessed the impact of mathematical visual-spatial skills by measuring their effect on an interior-design project. Interior-design students were first given tests to assess their visual-spatial skills. Then they were instructed to design a 3D sunscreen from discarded materials. The designs were judged by an independent panel. The object visualizers, who had scored poorly on the more abstract mathematical visual-spatial skills, easily won the design competition. The lack of those skills had absolutely no effect on their ability to create the best design. This finding confirms exactly what I had been witnessing at every welding and construction company I'd ever worked with. Cho and Suh's study, conducted independently of Kozhevnikov's work, confirms her results.

Let's look at the verbal thinkers with respect to visual thinking. The scientific literature agrees that some verbal thinkers at the far end of the spectrum have no idea what to do with pictures or diagrams. In one of Kozhevnikov's original papers, students were shown a graphlike image that looked like a hill. For object and spatial thinkers, the hill overwhelmingly suggested downward motion. But in responding to the image, the verbal thinkers failed to mention downward motion and instead offered seemingly random interpretations. For instance, one respondent described a little girl pushing a cart along a street and leaving it there. Another recalled a stopped car. A more recent study in *Computers in Human Behavior* tested visualizers and verbalizers who were shown both text and pictures to learn something new. Not surprisingly, eye tracking showed that visualizers focused on pictures and verbalizers focused on words. But when the verbalizers looked at the pictures, they often looked at areas such as the border of the picture that were not helpful to learning the new information.

Another piece of the puzzle came together when I found a gem of a paper by Kozhevnikov and her colleague Olesya Blazhenkova that was published in 2016, about a study that didn't require a brain scanner, control groups, surveys, or questionnaires. Teams of six to eight middle school and high school students gifted in the arts, sciences, and humanities, respectively, were instructed to draw an unknown planet. That's all the information they received. The researchers wanted to see if their work reflected different types of creativity. The drawings were then evaluated by professionals who were blind to the purpose of the study.

The art students (object visualizers) created vivid, fantastical planets. One was a square shape with pictures that spanned the globe, from pyramids to penguins. Another drawing was of a unique crystal planet, and a third had a fantastic building sticking out of it. The scientists (visual-spatials) had clearer concepts about the nature of their planets, which they rendered as spherical and lacking color, more like conventional depictions of planets. The drawings from the humanities students (verbals) lacked imagery and looked like splotchy abstract paintings. They had put words on their drawings but then had painted over the words because they thought they should not use them. (Word-based thinkers are often rule followers.)

Kozhevnikov and Blazhenkova took their work a step further. They wanted to determine *how* the different types of thinkers developed their ideas for creating their planets. Both art and science students developed their "key creative ideas" at the beginning of the project, as did mixed teams of different kinds of thinkers. The object-visualizing art students discussed their planet's appearance. The more visual-spatial science students discussed functions such as gravity, chemistry, and types of life. The verbal humanities types named the objects they had drawn but were unable to describe much planning that had gone into drawing them. The ways the three types of students approached their work and then described it align with the three styles of thinking we have been talking about.

The Strange Worlds of Aphantasia

At the ends of the visual spectrum are people described as having aphantasia and hyperphantasia. The person with aphantasia has no or almost no visual imagery. The term was first coined by neurologist Adam Zeman at the University of Exeter in England when a man came to his office claiming that he had lost all capacity for visual memory: he could no longer see images of friends, family, places. When asked which green was lighter, the color of a leaf or a pine needle, he could answer from memory but couldn't see the difference in his mind's eye. He became known as patient MX, and his mind-blindness had probably resulted from a stroke. Until that point, he had been able to vividly picture the people and things in his world. An fMRI showed that when he was asked to visualize something, the parts of his brain associated with visualization no longer "lit up."

Using the Vividness of Visual Imagery Questionnaire (VVIQ) developed by D. F. Marks in 1973 (and updated in 1995), Adam Zeman and his colleagues continued to study aphantasia, administering the test to nearly seven hundred subjects. The VVIQ consists of sixteen questions that examine mental imagery, including memory, spatial reasoning, and the ability to visualize objects not in one's direct line of vision, and is scored on a five-point scale, from 1 (no image) to 5 (vivid as normal vision). In all, 2 percent of the students qualified as having aphantasia. (If you're curious about where you fall on the spectrum, you can take the VVIQ online.)

Zeman's research group has also studied differences between people who have aphantasia and those who fall at the opposite extreme, with hyperphantasia, an overabundance of visual imagery. Cognitive neurosurgeon Joel Pearson described the condition in *The New York Times* as "like having a very vivid dream and not being sure if it was real or not." Participants were asked to describe in their mind's eye three imaginary places: a beautiful tropical beach, a museum, and a busy street market. People with hyperphantasia produced excessively detailed memories.

Further research with functional MRI brain scanning showed that hyperphantasic visual thinkers had greater brain activity between the prefrontal cortex and the network in the occipital visual cortex. A *New York Times* article by Carl Zimmer headlined "Many People Have a Vivid 'Mind's Eye,' While Others Have None at All," describes how researchers are looking into the brain circuitry responsible for these two extreme conditions. "So far, that work suggests that mental imagery emerges from a network of brain regions that talk to each other," he wrote. These brain characteristics may be linked to creativity and novel ways of solving problems.

Not surprisingly, people with aphantasia tend to go into science and math fields, while people with hyperphantasia gravitate to more visually creative jobs. Paradoxically, however, according to Zeman, it's not unusual for people with aphantasia to dream in images. He distinguishes between how the sleeping mind works and how the awake mind works. He explains that dreaming is a "bottom up" process that comes from the brain stem, whereas seeing images when you're awake is "top down" from the cortex. In other words, "What the brain is doing in wakefulness and dreaming are different." According to Zeman, 63 percent of people with aphantasia dream in pictures and 21 percent dream without images.

My dreams come to me much like the way I think, in vivid movies in color, with few words. They mostly involve some sort of fear or anxiety with balance, like being on a steep roof, driving down a steep hill, or riding a bike. I also have a recurring dream of trying to get to the airport and something makes me late, like a huge crater on I-25 (I have almost never been late to the airport). And like most people, I've had the occasional dream where I show up naked or partially naked in a public place.

Two studies being done on hyperphantasia look at the correlation between hyper-vividness and PTSD. In some cases, people such as soldiers or trauma victims who can't stop replaying the terrifying images in their mind report images so vivid that they believe their thoughts or flashbacks are real. According to psychologist Chris Brewin, flashbacks are an adaptive mechanism that stores information until it can be processed, after the danger is past. In a study of visual imagery and PTSD, researchers Richard Bryant and Allison Harvey looked at eighty-one motorcycle accident survivors and determined that visual imagery, including flashbacks and nightmares, plays a central role in PTSD. Even something far less traumatic can trigger repetitive visual remembering.

In the paper "The Blind Mind," researchers Rebecca Keogh and Joel Pearson at the University of New South Wales show that people who do not think in pictures often rely on verbal strategies to recall pictures. Other studies go so far as to say that people with aphantasia have a poorer ability to remember their past because they are less likely to visualize it. When asked to recall their living room or office, people with aphantasia will describe the location using directional words such as right, left, up, and down instead of using imagery.

Visual people might say that their office is across the hall from the Matisse poster. People with aphantasia will say it's three doors down on the right. They remind me of a speech therapist who heard the bell but couldn't visualize the steeple. Her husband put it this way: The camera in her brain is turned off.

When I look back on my own childhood, I have clear pictorial memories of coasting down snow-covered hills on toboggans or flying saucers. I see three-dimensional pictures and videos in my imagination, complete with sensory memories. I can start to feel the flying saucer bumping up and down on the snow. In kindergarten and first grade, I had a favorite swing that both swung and slid along an overhead trolley. During recess, I would swing and slide on it multiple times. While writing this, I can see, hear, and feel it. In elementary school, I loved embroidery class. Embroidery uses a special thread called embroidery silk, made of three strands. When I recall these kinds of details, many people ask me, "How can you remember that?" To check myself, I did a Google search and saw that I had remembered correctly: embroidery thread is made of three strands. If I had not been able to "see" the threads in my imagination, I would not have been able to recall the correct number of threads. I can even feel and see the needle poking the underside of the fabric, making a tiny tent before it pierces the fabric to complete the stitch.

I really appreciate something Zeman said in Zimmer's article: "This is not a disorder as far as I can see. It's an intriguing variation in human experience."

The Visual Thinking Advantage

I always end my talks at both animal behavior and educational conferences with a Q&A session. I generally get two kinds of questions: general and specific. The specific questions, such as what age I started speaking, are easy to field. The generalized questions are impossible to answer without more information. Verbal thinkers tend to use top-down thinking, which is like doing an internet search using one keyword. A zillion things come up. The more you refine the search, the more likely you are to find what you're looking for. Laurent Mottron has found that autistic people rely less on the verbal parts of the brain. His colleague researcher Michelle Dawson is autistic. He describes her as a bottom-up heuristic, meaning she comes up with ideas only from available facts. "As a result, her models never over-reach, and are almost infallibly accurate." By contrast, he describes his top-down approach: "I grasp and manipulate general ideas from fewer sources, and after expressing them in a model, go back to facts supporting or falsifying this model. Combining the two types of brains in the same research group is amazingly productive."

My bottom-up thinking works a little like the elimination game twenty questions that I played as a child. I'll use it, for instance, when I'm asked about the prognosis for an autistic child without speech—the kind of general question I am often asked by parents at conferences. In order to help them, I need specific information; using the process of elimination enables me to determine the best options for them. I respond by asking a series of questions to narrow down the possibilities—in this case, the possible causes for the child's lack of speech. First, I ask the age of the child. Teaching a hitherto nonverbal three-year-old to talk is totally different from attempting the same with an older child. I attempt to discern whether the parents might be on the spectrum by asking what they do. Are they programmers, scientists, math professors? Is there a history of family members on the spectrum? This is when some people start to remember an "odd" uncle or a cousin with cognitive issues. I want to know what kind of schooling the child has had and what kind of testing has been done. I want to know if the child has table manners, if he or she can take turns playing, and answers to other questions to get at some of the behaviors. I'm not a doctor, but in asking a series of questions I get a picture of the silent child. It is essential for the child to be given a way to communicate. There are many options, such as typing, picture boards, sign language, and electronic talking devices. Sometimes, I can suggest an intervention to help. Being a bottom-up thinker keeps me grounded in the facts; autism prevents emotions from clouding my judgment.

Most recently, Dr. Kasia Chawarska and her colleagues at the Yale Child Study Center have shown the efficacy of using puppets to communicate with kids on the spectrum. Their findings are beautifully illustrated in the 2016 documentary *Life, Animated*. In it, Owen Suskind, a young boy, loses his speech at age three and is diagnosed with autism. We see a breakthrough when his father realizes that his son's obsession with Disney movies provides a key to reaching him. He uses the puppet of Iago from *Aladdin* to communicate with his son, and for the first time Owen responds verbally. They begin to unlock the prison of silence.

I am aware that I may be missing certain experiences that are emotion-based, but for me, thinking that is less impacted by emotion is likely focused more on concrete problem-solving. Most autistic people, regardless of their thinking style, rely more on logic than emotion. It may be another genomic trade-off, but I don't bring a whole lot of emotional baggage to any situation. I don't get caught up in the emotion; instead, my mind starts to problem-solve. That's one advantage.

In some ways, I could say that visual thinking saved my life. I first wrote about my aunt's ranch twenty-five years ago, in *Thinking in Pictures*. Even then I didn't fully understand how my teenage fixation on cows, certainly a by-product of my autism, led to my work as a designer and animal behavior professor. When I turned forty, I realized I was able to think about things more clearly, compared with when I was twenty. When I looked back at my old diaries from the 1970s, I was astonished at how jumbled my thought patterns were. I was making a lot of associations that did not make much sense. This was owing to huge gaps in my visual database. The larger my database grew, the more connections I could make. It's like an open-ended accordion file. As I've grown older and had more experiences, I can solve problems much more easily, because my memory contains more visual data. My world has gotten bigger and bigger.

Navigating visually often means finding visual metaphors to explain novel situations, and I still use them. Most recently, I was particularly concerned about COVID-19 because I am in the at-risk older population. To get a grip on it when the pandemic first started, I did what I always do, by applying bottom-up thinking. I gathered numerous research papers about medications to treat the virus. Then I categorized the treatments: the antivirals and the anti-inflammatories. Then a visual analogy came to me. I imagined the body as a military base. If the soldiers in the immune system successfully attack the virus, it will be repelled. If the military base gets overrun, a "cytokine storm" can occur. This is where I see the soldiers in my immune system going berserk. They become confused and start attacking the base and lighting it on fire. The cytokine storm can destroy the lungs and other body systems. At that point, anti-inflammatory drugs would be needed before the entire military base is in flames.

I often struggle with verbal metaphors, but my mind is like a visual metaphor-making machine. Sometimes people ask me if visual thinking is like having X-ray vision. It's not. Visual thinking is the ability to see associated images from your "visual memory files" and access them in different ways to problem-solve, navigate, and interpret the world. That's why object thinkers are often designers, builders, architects, mechanics, and artists. And visual-spatial thinkers are often mathematicians, coders, composers, musicians, scientists, and engineers. Many visual thinkers are hiding in plain sight. (We'll meet many more over the course of the book.) We don't necessarily attribute their skills to their being visual thinkers. We say they're good with their hands, they're great at computers, can do math in their head, and so on. Both kinds of visualizers may have aptitudes for types of problem solving we don't necessarily associate with visual thinking.

In a program called Innovation Boot Camp, the Marine Corps demonstrated their superior ability for improvising. Brad Halsey, the originator of the program, created a hell week to weed out the scientists and engineers who wouldn't be able to contribute under high-pressure conditions. He found that truck mechanics and radio repairmen from the Marines were better than engineers with degrees from Stanford or MIT at improvising rapid-fire solutions to problems such as making a rudimentary vehicle out of a pile of junk, creating a device to track cars, and devising grenade sensors. Halsey explained that "engineers tend to overthink" and do poorly when an innovative solution needs to be determined quickly. "They don't like to operate outside their comfort zones. . . . They're very good at their particular specialties but not so good at executions— at translating ideas into things." My interpretation is that the truck mechanics were more likely to be object visualizers whose abilities to see it, build it, and repair it were fused. When we say people are good with their hands, it's this exact melding of skills: it's as if they see with their hands. The engineers are abstract spatial thinkers, essential for developing certain systems, but maybe not the best folks to share your foxhole.

Sometimes a visual analogy will unlock a mystery. There is the famous case of chemist August Kekulé dreaming about a snake forming a ring by holding its tail in its mouth. This provided insight into the structure known as the benzene ring in organic chemistry. Science writer Mike Sutton explained that the ability of Kekulé to hold complicated visual images in his mind was extremely helpful to his understanding of molecular structures. A more recent visual analogy was made by Kim Nasmyth at the University of Oxford. Geneticists have known for a long time that genomes form a loop, but they had been trying to figure out how DNA stays organized when it is folded up inside a cell. Nasmyth's hobby was mountain climbing. One day, while he was tinkering with the ropes and carabiners, he had a visual epiphany. Threading the ropes in loops through the carabiners reminded him of the long strands of DNA connecting the chromosomes. Pure visual connection. It was like the string on a bolo tie or the multiple loops that I embroidered to make daisies in third grade.

According to Raffi Khatchadourian, in a *New Yorker* article titled "The Elusive Peril of Space Junk," astronauts on a spacewalk were horrified to find that the Hubble Space Telescope's cylindrical surface had been pockmarked by tiny pieces of debris, the way sand on a highway will pit your truck. Astronaut Drew Feustel said, "A fleck could come from anywhere, any time." A satellite research project known as RemoveDEBRIS was launched to develop technologies to combat interstellar debris. Engineers built a satellite loaded with ballistic instruments, including a titanium harpoon and Kevlar net. These proposed approaches to capturing the floating junk reminded me of early whaling methods. When the engineers viewed the video of their satellite, one said, "As engineers, we had visualized this as charts, as graphs, as timetables. I don't think we thought about what it would *look* like." As engineers, their brilliant spatial minds could develop complicated abstract simulations, but it would have helped to have object thinkers on the team. I could immediately see the futility in trying to sweep the cosmos of debris. It would be like trying to rid the earth of rocks. One small step for mankind. One giant leap for object visualizers.

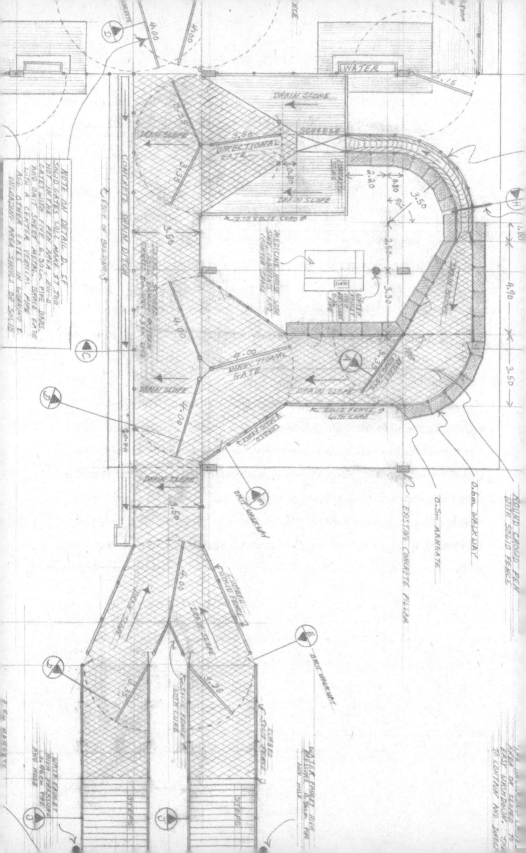

TWO

Screened Out

Back when I went to school in the 1960s, shop class was nearly ubiquitous. I can vividly recall our fifth-grade shop. It was an industrial-style room with a roll-up garage door. There were wooden workbenches and a huge bin for plyboard and wood scraps. Coping saws, hammers, pliers, screwdrivers, and eggbeater drills hung from a pegboard in a neat row, in descending order from largest to smallest. It was there that I started learning to use tools and make things. (One of my first projects was a wooden boat, which, sadly, failed to float.)

What I remember even more was respect for the shop. It was always meticulous. Before we were dismissed at the end of every class, we put the tools back in their proper place and swept up wood shavings like curls of hair on a barbershop floor. At home, my room was always a disaster area, and my mother would constantly admonish me to clean it, threatening to dock TV watching and allowance. But I had complete regard for shop and always followed the dictum of Mr. Patriarca, our teacher: Leave this place cleaner than you found it. I liked Mr. Patriarca, not least because he allowed me and one other girl who had expressed interest to take the class. It was the highlight of my day.

On the other side of the gender aisle, schools used to offer home economics to girls. Starting in the nineteenth century, these courses were designed to teach the domestic arts, such as cooking, sewing, gardening, raising children, and balancing a checkbook. Most people might assume that I'd hate home economics, since I was something of a tomboy and loved shop. But I loved working with my hands in all kinds of ways.

In third grade, we started with embroidery, which taught me how to use a needle and thread. Some kids today have no idea how to thread a needle or sew on a button. When I was in fourth grade, my mother gave me a toy sewing machine that actually sewed. It was one of my favorite things, and I used it to sew costumes for the school play. In seventh grade, we got to use real, full-sized sewing machines, which really fired up my technical mind. Class was held in a special room with a sewing machine on every desk. I couldn't wait to get there. One of my favorite inventors was Elias Howe, who received the first patent for the lockstitch sewing machine, which joined the thread from the needle to one from the bobbin below. Pure "clever engineering department," my term for brilliant inventors and visualizers, wherever they are found. I loved tracing patterns, measuring fabric, cutting it accurately, and sewing it together. Later, I would apply these skills toward putting together livestock-handling systems, connecting some of the skills I still use today back to those sewing classes. Same for the cooking classes. They were process-oriented, teaching us how to measure and add ingredients in order. Measuring liquids is the same, whether it's a cup of milk or a 3,800-gallon dip vat.

I also participated in the drama program, opting for the behind-the-scenes jobs I excelled in. I worked on the set crew in every grade of high school, culminating in a senior-year production of Gilbert and Sullivan's *Trial by Jury*, for which I built the jury's box and judge's bench using cardboard and plywood. I watered down paint to give it the appearance of wood and inked in black lines to approximate the panels. Programs like these give kids with technical skills the opportunity to show off. They also provide a community for geeky kids like me who gravitate toward things such as lighting and scenery design.

If you went to public school in the 1990s or after, you may not remember such programs. They were largely scrubbed from the public school curricula around that point, along with art, theater, welding, and auto mechanics, with some regional variation. The culmination of these policies arrived in 2001, when the education reform bill known as No Child Left Behind "hit American education like a tsunami," according to Nikhil Goyal's critique of the legislation in his book *Schools on Trial*. Now, not only was the stripping away of hands-on learning a reality, but a new philosophy had supplanted it: teach to the test. The policy, otherwise known as "drill, kill, bubble fill," became the norm. The legacy of the previous twenty years of federal education policy, from No Child Left Behind to the Every Student Succeeds Act, has created a culture that has simultaneously overemphasized testing and stripped our schools of multifaceted curricula.

The goal of raising national academic standards through comprehensive testing decimated the classes that didn't lend themselves to standardized testing. "Beginning in third grade, the amount of instructional time in the arts, music, science, and history was reduced, because basically what was tested got taught, and these subjects were not equally tested," writes Goyal. In 2015, the president of the National Education Association, Lily Eskelsen García, and the president of the National Parent Teacher Association, Otha Thornton, wrote in *The Washington Post*: "Schools with the most limited resources have been most likely to cut back on history, art, music and physical education, simply because they aren't covered on standardized tests."

For the first twenty years of my career, all engineering and architectural drawings were done by hand. When the industry switched to computerized drafting in the mid-1990s, I started seeing strange discrepancies in drawings. The center of a circle was not always in the center, or reinforcing rods for strengthening concrete were left out. Drawings often lacked detail, becoming more like schematics. Many of the people who were learning to design on computers had never picked up a pencil or touched a piece of drafting paper or built anything.

I had a disturbing discussion with a doctor who was training interns. Some of them had great difficulty learning how to sew up cuts because they had never used scissors. Dr. Maria Siemionow, a transplant surgeon at the University of Illinois, has trained many surgeons. She credits their dexterity to hands-on activities in their early years. But lots of kids no longer have experience working with their hands. Dr. Siemionow crocheted as a child. She also used scissors to create elaborate collages from pictures cut out of magazines. *New York Times* reporter Kate Murphy profiled a brain surgeon whose piano playing may have helped develop his superior manual dexterity. Grades may not be the best way to choose doctors who will specialize in complex surgery.

Discussions with parents indicate that many of those children who are missing in action are in their basements playing video games. There is no doubt in my mind that I would have become a video game addict had I been born thirty years later. The rapid visual stimulation would have been intoxicating. Research has shown that autistic individuals are more prone to excessive video game playing. To wean a young adult who is addicted requires replacing the games with something equally compelling. I know of two cases where replacing them with auto mechanics proved successful. Fixing real cars and learning about engines became more interesting than racing simulated cars. I've heard many parents complain that they can't get their kids off their screens. That might be in part because the parents themselves are glued to their screens. And they may be afraid to exert their authority. My mother restricted our television time to one hour per day, as a reward for doing homework and chores. Some of today's parents will do anything to avoid a meltdown. Meltdowns are scary, but kids need the chance to discover what they're good at in order to find meaningful work. You'll never find out if you don't get off the screens and expose them to different environments. For me it was my aunt's ranch.

I travel a lot, and wherever I go, I see almost no one reading books or magazines. Parents and teens are on their phones. Kids are playing video games. I'm hardly the first person to take note of this, but from my vantage point, the addiction is directly connected to a larger failure: the loss of trained workers in this country, the loss of people who are good at working with their hands and who are likely visual thinkers. Every minute a child is on a video game is a lost opportunity to learn about cars, planes, working with tools, getting out in nature. Most students never have the chance to learn what they might be good at. Restoring shop, art, music, and home economics to schooling would help.

Another great way to expose kids to different ideas and potential careers is through field trips. When I was growing up, field trips were a big deal. I was in elementary school when I first visited a car factory. I can still vividly recall watching an air wrench screw in all five bolts on a wheel at once. I'd seen my dad laboriously change a tire by removing and replacing it one lug at a time. I remember being fascinated by the lug wrench, jack, and lever—intimations that my mechanical mind was already at work. I could have stared at it for hours—the machine that achieved at warp speed what had taken my father ages. The budding clever engineer in me was on fire.

School field trips have been another casualty of the "teach to the test" approach. A report called "Why Field Trips Matter" cites a survey by the American Association of School Administrators that found that more than half of planned field trips were eliminated as early as 2010. The report also mentions that museum visits promoted critical thinking, historical empathy, and interest in art. The benefits were two to three times greater in students from less advantaged backgrounds. Lack of funding is often blamed for the diminishing number of field trips. *New York Times* reporter Michael Winerip profiled a

New York City teacher who took her kindergarten class on "field trips to the sidewalk." There, she taught them everything from math to vocabulary as they encountered and studied Muni-Meters and new words like *parking* and *violations*. The students visited an auto repair shop, a municipal garage, the subway, a market, several bridges, and a hospital emergency room. This is ingenious. You don't have to go to a famous museum or monument. Curiosity is all you need, and administrators who are willing to let teachers find the learning opportunities in everyday things.

The head of the school's network lamented that more teachers didn't adopt the sidewalk field trip. "There is so much pressure systematically to do well on the tests, and this may not boost scores right away. . . . To do this you'd have to be willing to take the long view." Imagine the possibilities field trips might offer to students in a variety of settings: factory, farm, mill, distribution center, professional kitchen. These experiences supply direct exposure to careers students may have never imagined, along with a window into the way everyday things work and are made.

One of the most useless questions you can ask a kid is: "What do you want to be when you grow up?" It's one of those vague verbal-thinker questions. The more useful question is concrete: "What are you good at?" That's a real starting place to develop interests. Kids need broad exposure to discover their talents. There is no subject I am more passionate about, and the reason is two-fold. First, by depriving students of that exposure, we are failing them. And in the process, we are also dismantling the healthy and diverse workforce our country needs.

Removing hands-on learning from schools is the worst thing to happen to education in recent memory, in my opinion. Wittingly or unwittingly, its disappearance screened out an entire generation of visual thinkers, whose abilities might have flourished in such so-called extracurriculars. There is no way for kids, especially kids who are object-visual thinkers, to find out what they're good at by sitting behind a desk all day. Plus, it's torture for kids like I was, with excess energy that could be better channeled into *doing* things, *making* things. These abilities need to be developed starting when kids are young. Without exposure to such classes, we can't nurture the budding builder, engineer, or chef. We screen out designers, inventors, and artists. We need future generations who can build and repair infrastructure, overhaul energy and agriculture, create tools to combat climate change and pandemics, develop robotics and AI. We need people with the imagination to invent our next-generation solutions.

———

This chapter is about the high cost of screening out kids in school and, as a result, denying them a satisfying future. Screening out kids virtually extinguishes their chances at success, whether they're shunted off to special ed or denied the opportunity to advance because of learning orthodoxies that are based on a one-size-fits-all model. Look at any group of kids in a classroom, or talk to any teacher, and it's obvious that one size does not fit all.

There is another reason that I highlight the danger of screening out kids, and it's personal. As a person with autism, I've had to persevere through educational challenges on every level: developmental, behavioral, and academic. Eventually, I fulfilled my dream of working with animals, both in industry and as a professor with graduate students in animal science, with whom I work to keep improving our understanding of animal behavior. The irony has never been lost on me: Now I teach veterinarians, but I couldn't get into veterinary school. The reason? I got screened out.

Do the Math

It may sound simple, but it's true: I was screened out in school because I couldn't do math. Actually, that's not quite true. The traditional arithmetic I learned in the early grades made sense to me because I could relate it back to real-world things. Fractions could be related to cutting up a pizza, for example. I did fine in old-fashioned arithmetic the way it was taught in the 1950s. Working with protractors and angles in fourth grade was fun. In sixth grade, I learned how to find the area of a complex space by dividing it up into squares, circles, and triangles. This practical math would prove necessary in my work designing livestock facilities.

Later, when I was learning how to design, I was good at finding the area of a circle, which proved essential to practical tasks such as sizing hydraulic and pneumatic cylinders. What I couldn't do was algebra. That is where I hit a wall. Like a lot of object visualizers, I couldn't grasp abstract concepts, and algebra is all about abstract concepts. In high school, my teachers tried to pound the subject into me, but without images to visualize, it was hopeless. I should have been jumped to geometry and trigonometry. I learn best if a problem can be visualized, and I could learn the concepts involved in trigonometry by visualizing, for example, the cables on a suspension bridge. I needed real-world examples for each equation.

As a result, I was screened out. I had to drop a physics and a biomedical engineering course because I could not do the math. This screened me out of veterinary school and engineering. I had to choose majors with lower math requirements, such as psychology and animal science. Today I would probably be screened out of those majors as well, because they now have even higher math requirements. I recently received an email from a student who informed me that calculus was required for his undergraduate biology major. I would never have gotten past that barrier. Calculus was not a requirement for biology when I was in college. Biology was the one class that I loved in high school and did well in.

Fortunately, in college I was able to avoid algebra by taking other required courses in probability, matrices, and statistics. Even so, I got tutoring immediately after I failed my first math quiz. In my job as a professor, I've noticed that the biggest mistake my students make is waiting too long before they ask for help. In college, I got about two hours a week of tutoring during the math professor's office hours. And in graduate school, I paid another student to tutor me. Without all that tutoring, I doubt I would have gotten through. To save myself from failing the statistics course I needed for my PhD, I created specific examples of real research projects for each type of statistical test. The examples had to be things I could visualize, such as a trial comparing two types of feed on the weight gain of cattle or the effect of environmental enrichment on the behavior of pigs. I'm convinced that eliminating the algebra barrier and substituting other forms of math, such as geometry, trigonometry, and statistics, would solve the problem for many students who are getting screened out.

A 2012 op-ed by political scientist Andrew Hacker, "Is Algebra Necessary?" landed like a bombshell in the education world. Hacker assailed the insistence on algebra in schools, pointing out that the math taught there was nothing like the math people use at their jobs. He questioned why we subject students to an "ordeal" so many are likely to fail, reporting that most of the educators he talked with "cite algebra as the major academic reason" children fail to finish high school.

"Making mathematics mandatory," writes Hacker, "prevents us from discovering and developing young talent. In the interest of maintaining rigor, we're actually depleting our pool of brainpower." He didn't advocate dropping things like basic or quantitative skills, and I don't, either. As a visual thinker who has worked with a wide range of engineers, software developers, welders, CEOs, and other professionals, I understand that math is important. But there are different kinds of math and different kinds of learners and different kinds of real-world applications. The issue is what will help students down the road in their careers.

In a 2017 *New York Times* article, "Trying to Solve a Bigger Math Problem," Emily Hanford contributes some staggering statistics: Nearly 60 percent of community college students need remedial math—more than twice as many as those who need remedial English. Four-year public colleges are close to that, with 40 percent of their students needing to take at least one remedial class, 33 percent in math. But again, maybe the decline in performance points to a deficiency not so much in how well students are mastering material but in what we are asking them to master. Two-year colleges have traditionally required students to take algebra. According to Hanford, some policy makers are finally beginning to question the logic.

Andrew Hacker says, "Yes, young people should learn to read and write and do long division, whether they want to or not." It is essential for students to learn basic skills such as being able to write clearly. Some of my recent graduate students have terrible writing skills. When I questioned a few of them, I discovered that they'd seldom been required to write a term paper, and that their teachers had never corrected their grammar or given detailed comments on their writing. This is clearly not acceptable. In any profession, a person must be able to explain things clearly in writing. To improve their writing skills, I have corrected the grammar in students' journal articles and then had them rewrite them. But as Hacker puts it, there is no reason to force students to "grasp vectorial angles and discontinuous functions. Think of math as a huge boulder we make everyone pull, without assessing what all this pain achieves."

Christopher Edley Jr., a former dean of the UC Berkeley School of Law, is on a mission to move the boulder. Edley wants to close the equity gap and increase graduation rates by eliminating algebra requirements for students who are not on a STEM track. "The culprit is Intermediate Algebra, a high school–level course of technical procedures that most college students will never use, either in college or in life," Edley notes. He reports that of the 170,000 California community college students who are placed into remedial math based on a standardized test, more than 110,000 will not complete the requirements for getting an associate degree or transferring to the University of California. But a pilot program at California State University that allows students to substitute a series of statistics courses for algebra has shown that completion rates for math classes increase when algebra isn't required. Edley is eager for greater implementation. "The inequity, and the legal problem, remain, grounded in a dirty secret about math requirements: the requirements are largely arbitrary."

Mathematician Paul Lockhart rails against the modern approach to teaching math in his paper "A Mathematician's Lament." He's speaking, of course, to people who wince when they hear the word *math*, resolutely claim they are no good at math, hate math, or people like me who thrived at one kind of math and not another. Most of us were required to take three or four years of coursework in high school, starting with algebra and working up the chain: geometry, algebra 2, trigonometry, precalculus, calculus. Lockhart writes, "If I had to design a mechanism for the express purpose of *destroying* a child's natural curiosity and love of pattern-making, I couldn't possibly do as good a job as is currently being done—I simply wouldn't have the imagination to come up with the kind of senseless, soul-crushing ideas that constitute contemporary mathematics education." A New York principal quoted in a 2014 *New York Times* article echoed the sentiment. "I fear that they are creating a generation of young students who are learning to hate mathematics."

Margaret Donaldson, professor of developmental psychology at the University of Edinburgh, studies the disconnect between teaching and learning in her paper "The Mismatch between School and Children's Minds." In it, she ponders why kindergartners and first-graders are happy and excited to learn, but by high school so many students are bored and unresponsive. "This desire [to learn] is still strong in most children when they enter school. How is it that something that starts off so well regularly ends up so badly? Why do many children learn to hate school?"

Donaldson's work represents a departure from that of the influential thinker and childhood psychologist Jean Piaget. Piaget believed that until age seven, children were limited in their cognitive understanding of the world. He based this belief in part on a famous study known as "The Conservation Tasks," in which children's ability to understand concepts such as "same" and "not same" was measured by showing them two pictures. The first presents two lines of objects of equal size and equal number. In the second picture, the objects on the second line are rearranged so that they are closer together, though they are the same in number as the first line. Most children are not able to grasp that both rows have the same number of objects until they are around age six or seven.

But Donaldson and her colleague James McGarrigle questioned whether Piaget's approach to the study, rather than a deficiency in the children's reasoning, had produced this result. They devised a similar test, in which children four and six years of age were shown that a naughty teddy bear had rearranged the objects in the second row. Presented with a "real world" explanation or narrative, a much higher percentage of children arrived at the right answer, fifty out of eighty versus thirteen out of eighty. The difference, theorized Donaldson, is that the naughty teddy bear gave the children context. The objects weren't just clinically presented. Donaldson believes that "humanly meaningful context" informs our thinking. We need ideas to be connected to real-world examples in order to grasp and implement them.

Angeline Lillard at the University of Virginia has studied play in preschool children. She says, "Kids like to do real things because they want a role in the real world." Her study showed that even four- to six-year-old children prefer real activities over pretend activities. When teachers apply math to real-world work or personal interests such as sports, shopping, and even video games, kids see the sense in learning.

For spatial visualizers, a teaching tool can be made out of nearly any sport or game in which calculating, scoring, and evaluating the odds is fundamental to play. One great example is chess, which, in and of itself, is a dynamic math problem. Imagine a class of elementary school students playing chess for almost a year (with instruction), and then getting tested in math. That's exactly what Danish researcher Michael Rosholm and his colleagues did when they replaced one out of four weekly math classes with chess instruction for 482 students in first through third grade. On average, the students who studied chess improved their math scores. For some children, chess can evidently be a gateway to grasping math. Pepe Cuenca, a professional chess player with a PhD in applied mathematics, credits chess for teaching calculation, visual memory, spatial reasoning, capacity to predict and anticipate consequences, and geometry. For another kind of child, chess wouldn't help at all. I would have been one of the students who was not good at chess. For an object visualizer like me, the patterns were too abstract to remember, but it is easy for me to visualize what a remodeled building will look like. As I've said, if I can't find a visual correlative, I'm not going to get it. A variety of approaches is needed to provide an on-ramp for developing skills.

For any type of learner, a key question is brain development: When are a child's cognitive skills able to handle abstract reasoning? Piaget believed children become capable of logic by age eleven or twelve. Ana Sušac and her colleagues at the University of Zagreb suggest that the development from concrete to more abstract thinking may occur in late adolescence, when the prefrontal cortex, associated with abstract mathematical reasoning, more fully matures. Their research suggests that, at the very least, we're teaching algebra too early and too fast, that the road from concrete to abstract reasoning takes more time. It's not a switch you can turn on in the summer between seventh and eighth grade. A researcher at the University of Kansas raises the possibility that abstract reasoning is developed through experience, which is a good argument for keeping all those extracurriculars.

Tracy Goodson-Espy, a professor and researcher at Appalachian State University, posed the question this way: "Why can one solver formulate an arithmetical solution to the problem and yet be unable to think of the problem in algebraic terms?" Her study entailed nine learning tasks, all "real world" problems. Like Margaret Donaldson's naughty teddy bear, the problems were intended to provide context and meaning using examples drawn from familiar situations, such as car rentals and employee benefits. Goodson-Espy evaluated the students to assess each one's internal problem-solving process. Then the students were extensively interviewed and videotaped to track their mental processes as they worked through the problems. The subjects fell into three categories. First, students who used arithmetical methods that were not based on imagery to find solutions. Second, students who relied on charting methods. And third, students who used algebraic methods. Her research clearly shows how each group problem-solved, but it doesn't say why.

Here's how I interpret Goodson-Espy's findings: The student who didn't use any visual tools is the verbal thinker. The student who transfers the problem to a chart to visualize (but still can't make the algebraic leap) is the object thinker like me. And the student who used algebraic methods is the spatial visualizer. Goodson-Espy concludes that, to make a successful transition from math to algebra, students need to be capable of reflective abstraction. "Imagery," she writes, "is an inherent part of the development from one level of reflective abstraction to the next." This is visual thinking.

And yet we persist in an abstract approach to math education. Donaldson uses the term "disembedded" to describe things without a context or direct experience to ground them. These skills, she writes, "underlie our mathematics, all our science, all our philosophy. It may be that we value them too highly in comparison with other human skills and qualities, but we are not likely to renounce them. We have come to depend on them too much." Donaldson sees how the education system rewards those who "get it" and leaves the rest with a sense of profound failure. That failure, it turns out, is more pervasive than I had imagined.

The 2019 National Assessment of Educational Progress (NAEP)—known as the "Nation's Report Card"—showed that only "37 percent of 12th-graders have the math skills needed for entry-level college course work." In presenting these dismal numbers, David Driscoll, chair of the National Assessment Governing Board, said, "Clearly this [is] not acceptable. . . . We see our kids losing their place. . . . We should be holding them to higher standards." Of course, higher standards translates to more bubble filling, when what kids need is engagement with real-life projects.

Even in the wake of President Obama's Race to the Top fund, aimed at promoting innovation and achievement in grades K through 12, through $4.35 billion in grants, the future for STEM education remains grim. In a *New York Times* article, "Why Science Majors Change Their Minds," Christopher Drew writes, "Freshmen in college wade through a blizzard of calculus, physics and chemistry in lecture halls with hundreds of other students. And then many wash out." Forty percent of engineering and science students change majors or drop out. When premedical students are added to the equation, that figure jumps to 60 percent, "twice the attrition rate of all other majors." David E. Goldberg, professor emeritus of engineering at the University of Illinois at Urbana-Champaign, is quoted as calling the system a "math-science death march."

And then, every three years, like a comet, a report called PISA (Program for International Student Assessment) comes hurtling into the American consciousness. While the test is considered extremely flawed by some educators and policy makers, the headlines with which it is greeted never fail to shock:

We suck at math. Big-time. In 2018, six hundred thousand students from seventy-nine countries took a two-hour test that is designed to assess problem solving over rote memorization. It's like the Olympics of secondary education, and America has yet to take the gold or silver or bronze. In fact, if this were the Olympics, we wouldn't even qualify. In math, American students don't measure up to peers in other wealthy countries, and even struggle against peers from less wealthy countries. In the most recent PISA, the top-performing country in math and science, by a wide margin, was China.

In a 2016 *New York Times* article, "What America Can Learn from Smart Schools in Other Countries," Amanda Ripley writes, "For now, the PISA reveals brutal truths about America's education system: Math, a subject that reliably predicts children's future earning, continues to be the United States' weakest area at every income level." She sums up by saying nearly a third of fifteen-year-old students are unable to meet the "baseline level of ability."

When these reports land, there is a tendency to throw more of the same at the problem. The more students fail math, the more math we throw at them, and the more we test them. That has been the illogic of the past two decades.

In 1983, developmental psychologist Howard Gardner published his influential book *Frames of Mind: The Theory of Multiple Intelligences*. His theory emerged from his work with children and adults who had suffered from brain damage; their injury-based abilities and deficits provided a compelling landscape for study. Gardner also observed that no two people have the same intelligence, even twins. And yet, we test people in the same way, with IQ and standardized tests. The odds are stacked against anyone whose strengths don't correspond with the testing methodology, which favors mathematical and linguistic intelligence.

Gardner looked at research on the brain, human development, evolution, and cross-cultural comparisons to arrive at his eight categories of intelligence: musical, logical-mathematical, linguistic, spatial, interpersonal, intrapersonal, naturalistic, and kinesthetic. He urges us to stretch our definition of intelligence. "It is of the utmost importance that we recognize and nurture all of the varied human intelligences, and all of the combinations of intelligences. We are all so different largely because we all have different combinations of intelligences." He wants us to stop assessing all children in the same way and find new entry points to help them. Even if you insist on teaching algebra, he points out, "algebra can be taught three or even thirty ways." Though Gardner doesn't recognize visual thinkers (let alone the different kinds of visual thinkers) as a separate category of intelligence, we are in agreement that our educational system fails to recognize different types of intelligence. "How to educate individuals so that each develops his or her potential to the fullest is still largely a mystery," he wrote. But, he was certain, "we cannot afford to waste any more minds."

Learning Fast and Slow

At age eight, I was not yet able to read. It's hard to say how long I would have struggled with reading had I continued with Dick and Jane and the sight-word learning taught at my school. Instead, my third-grade teacher and my mother developed a plan for my mother to teach me reading at home. I was highly motivated to learn to read, because my mother read to my sister and me almost every day. Sometimes she would read interesting passages from *Oliver Twist* by Charles Dickens. Oliver lived in a poorhouse, and I will never forget the passage where he asked to be served more food.

Every afternoon after school, Mother spent an hour teaching me phonics, which correlates sounds and letters, having me "sound out" syllables. Instead of Dick and Jane, she turned to *The Wonderful Wizard of Oz*. She would read a page of the book and then stop in the middle of an exciting part, fueling my desire to find out what happened next. But before we continued, I was required to sound out every letter of the alphabet that Mother had taped to the wall. I was always asked to say them out loud. Then she had me sound out a word, then two words, then three, and so on before we could continue with the story. Gradually, she read less and less, and eventually I was reading full sentences. Phonics, one-on-one tutoring, and my mother's instinct to choose stories that kept my attention were all key. Within a few months, I jumped to a sixth-grade reading level. Without this intervention, I would have totally failed in school.

The work my mother did teaching me to read is the equivalent of an IEP, or Individualized Education Program, which provides children with disabilities special help in public school. These weren't around when I was in school. The special help and intensive tutoring came from my mother. By the time I reached high school, conventional schooling was a disaster for me, filled with constant bullying and teasing. My parents were able to afford to send me to a special boarding school for kids with learning disabilities. I wasn't happy to go, but it turned out to be one of the most formative experiences of my life. Two things in particular happened there: I was mentored by a science teacher, and I learned working skills taking care of the school's horses. As a result, I found the subject I would pursue for the rest of my life, and I was instilled with a really strong work ethic.

In a paper titled "Autistic Children at Risk of Being Underestimated," Valérie Courchesne and colleagues focused on the cognitive abilities of autistic children with minimal verbal skills. Using what is known as the Children's Embedded Figures Test, the researchers administered four separate cognition and intelligence evaluations to thirty autistic children with low verbal skills and an age-matched control group. While none of the autistic kids were able to complete the standard intelligence test (Wechsler Intelligence Scale), twenty-six completed the Embedded Figures Test, and they finished it faster than matched neurotypicals. Laurent Mottron, in a *Nature* article, reports that autistic people display more activity in the visual-processing network than the speech-processing network of the brain. He writes, "This redistribution of brain function may nonetheless be associated with superior performance."

The challenge is in how to offer a more effective assessment and education to visual-object thinkers. The bottom line is that kids who can't do the math are potentially being underestimated, and we are losing the skills they do have, ones we need. For some, homeschooling is an option. It's something I'm frequently asked about for kids with autism.

According to the National Center for Education Statistics (NCES), approximately 1,770,000 kids are homeschooled. Of that number, 16 percent are identified as having special needs. The most frequent reasons parents cite for choosing to homeschool kids on the spectrum are bullying, managing behavioral problems, a child's happiness or well-being, and dissatisfaction with the level of school support. But it's not a decision anyone should go into lightly, as it often puts tremendous stress on the family. In the chapter on genius and neurodiversity, I talk about Thomas Edison, who was homeschooled. It's a romantic story about how his mother, a former teacher, plied him with all the right books to ignite his brilliant mechanical mind. That story is rare (and in Edison's case, possibly apocryphal). Parents ask me about homeschooling all the time. I can't advise if I don't know more about the child, but I always say that if you choose to homeschool, make sure the child has opportunities to do activities with other children. Many parents who homeschool belong to homeschool groups that provide these opportunities. I think the groups are good for the parents, too. It takes a village to raise a child. It takes a village and a whole lot of support to raise a child with autism.

Finding the right entry point for a particular brain and learning style can be a game changer. Learning to write clearly was a struggle for me, and many teaching methods of my day were similarly meaningless and incomprehensible to me—diagramming sentences, for example. Yet by the ninth grade, my writing ability was better than that of many of my recent graduate students. When I write, the words provide a description of the images I see in my imagination. There were three ways I learned how to write well: Reading my writing out loud to determine if it sounded right. Paying close attention to the way teachers marked up my papers and corrected my grammar. And writing book reports, which taught me how to pick out the main points in the material I read. My writing skills are what got my first articles published, and those articles are what got me jobs. All the writing I do now is for either technical or practical transfer of information, and I apply all of the skills I learned back in school. Over the course of my career, I've written over one hundred scientific journal articles and eight books, two on my own and the others with cowriters.

So how is it that so many of my students are unable to explain the methods and results of their research in clear language? Today, as I am forced to go back to basics with masters and PhD students, I'm convinced that with less emphasis on testing and more on basic math and grammar, students would be far better off when they set out in their careers.

There's another way we screen out kids via schooling. Standardized curricula assume that all students develop at the same rate. Even when a child is seriously underchallenged, many parents discover that educators insist on restricting them to so-called age-appropriate materials. And many parents hesitate to allow or ask that their kids be accelerated, out of social and developmental concerns, or fears of pushing them too hard and too fast. This dilemma is captured in the wildly exaggerated 1989 sitcom *Doogie Howser, M.D.*, about a boy who graduates from Princeton and then medical school by the age of fourteen. The teenage physician and prodigy balances treating patients and treating pimples.

For all these reasons—institutional resistance and parental concern—only 1 percent of students skip grades or subjects, even though research shows the benefits of acceleration where appropriate. According to Gregory Park and his colleagues in the study "When Less Is More," published in the *Journal of*

Educational Psychology, accelerated students outperform nonaccelerated peers in the long term. They are more likely to obtain advanced degrees, publish, receive patents in STEM, and have successful careers.

Just as we are screening out kids who can't do math, I worry that we're hindering the kids who *can* do the math (and other subjects), because we're not advancing their potential. One solution is to let the kids with clear passions and abilities follow their strengths. Take the incredible case of Katherine Johnson, first brought to public awareness in the book and film *Hidden Figures*. As a little girl, Johnson loved counting, and then calculating, and then computing. Johnson's teachers recognized her ability when she was in elementary school and accelerated her education by allowing her to skip grades. At ten, she started high school. When she was fifteen years old, she attended West Virginia State College, from which she graduated summa cum laude at age eighteen, having taken every math class the college offered. After graduation, Johnson worked as a teacher, one of the few jobs available to Black women at the time.

Johnson's genius was put to the test when NASA needed more "manpower" and turned to the female workforce. She started working at NASA in the 1950s, when overt racism and sexism were pervasive. The women were referred to as "computers who wore skirts," and Black employees were segregated in every area, from where they worked and ate to what bathrooms they used. Yet Johnson's mathematical calculations made manned spaceflight possible before computers were advanced enough to handle the complicated computations required. She calculated the orbital and reentry paths of the Mercury and Apollo space capsules. Her calculations enabled the safe return of the astronauts. When Katherine Johnson calculated orbital paths, I imagine she saw multidimensional patterns in her brilliant mind.

What is the profit in holding back any student with clear aptitude beyond their grade level? What if we routinely let students who love math double down by increasing their math courses or taking classes at local colleges? Bill Gates, Steve Jobs, Mark Zuckerberg and Elon Musk all dropped out of college or graduate programs. They were eager to test and apply their advanced skills in the marketplace, heading straight for Silicon Valley. But in Jobs's case, at least, there was also a desire to skirt required courses in which he had no interest. I would wager that the curriculum on offer just wasn't challenging enough for any of them.

The Testing Trap

"Is it going to be on the test?" That's the feeble cry of students everywhere. As a professor, that question bothers me more than any other. You can almost hear the mental doors closing, as if anything outside the test were superfluous and not worth consideration. How have we raised a generation of people for whom learning has come down to passing a test? Learning should prepare a student for both life and a career.

In my livestock handling class, one of the assignments is creating a scale drawing. Compared with ten years ago, many students are having a harder time with it. Some of them have never learned to use a ruler to measure things. Sometimes they question the value of the assignment. I tell them that if they go to buy a couch, they will need to measure it to determine if it will fit in their living room.

The obsession with testing has landed us in very unfortunate places, namely cutting corners, cheating, and failure. According to Daniel Koretz, a professor at the Harvard Graduate School of Education, the tests reveal inequities among the student population more than they do achievement. Koretz has spent three decades issuing damning critiques of the testing system. In his book *The*

Testing Charade: Pretending to Make Schools Better, he reports how educators' jobs are on the line if results are not achieved. And as discussed, the pressure to raise scores influences which subjects are taught. The collateral damage is huge: teachers waste precious time teaching to the test, and an overall corruption of teaching ideals begins to permeate the classroom as the pressure to raise scores mounts. Bob Schaeffer, public education director of the nonprofit FairTest, has witnessed every kind of cheating as a result of our fixation on test scores, including the use of impersonators to take exams, faking disability to be allotted extra time, paying someone to fix or fill in the answers, and bribing proctors to look the other way.

All of that seems tepid in comparison with the cheating scandal that rocked the nation when two high-profile actresses were charged and served prison time for bribing coaches with large sums of money to manipulate their daughters' college applications. Over fifty additional indictments were served to CEOs, real estate developers, and standardized test administrators. Cheating is ubiquitous, according to Koretz, and to explain why, he points to something known as Campbell's Law, which says that any metric used to determine social decision-making will become corrupted by people who want to affect those decisions.

Today, nearly 70 percent of American kids go on to college, a percentage that has greatly increased since 1975. It sounds like good news, but on average, only 41 percent of those kids will graduate in four years. According to Ellen Ruppel Shell, in a bracing *New York Times* article, "College May Not Be Worth It Anymore," the staggering cost of higher education has reached $1.3 trillion in student loans, more than doubling over the course of a decade. She also notes that the 40 percent of people who drop out of college earn just slightly more than high school graduates, barely enough to cover their college debt. She writes, "We appear to be approaching a time when, even for middle-class students, the economic benefit of a college degree will begin to seem dim." Shell tops it off with an eye-opening statistic: "25 percent of college graduates now earn no more than does the average high school graduate."

The Scholastic Aptitude Test, originally an extension of the IQ test, was developed in the 1920s. It was first showcased in 1926 and was intended to test for learning aptitude and standardize the way we evaluate college applicants. Over the decades, the test gained popularity despite charges that it is culturally biased. Today, the test has become a big business. With millions of students taking the exam, it generates a large portion of the College Board's $1 billion in annual revenue. It has now been well documented that the test discriminates against people of color and lower-income students, not only because of its cultural biases but because those populations are generally less able to afford tutoring. Alongside the exam, a test prep industry has mushroomed, beginning in 1938 when Stanley Kaplan started tutoring students on the SAT in his Brooklyn basement. The college prep business has ballooned into a $1.1 billion industry, serving, of course, those who can afford it.

In 1959, an alternative and competitor to the SAT was developed. The ACT (American College Test) is extremely similar to the SAT but purports to test what is learned in school as opposed to the SAT, which primarily tests cognitive reasoning. The ACT includes a science section and a forty-minute optional essay component. Though it's impossible to know which test a student will do better on without taking practice tests on both, the ACT, like the SAT, displays the same achievement gaps for minority and low-income students. In any case, the luxury of taking both tests, let alone having the money for tutoring or adequate guidance counseling, is not an option for many students.

In our public schools, on average, there are 478 students to each guidance counselor. According to Elizabeth A. Harris's reporting in *The New York Times*, this is almost double what the American School Counselor Association recommends. According to the US Department of Education's Office for Civil

Rights, one in five schools doesn't have a single counselor. That's eight million children without any access to a counselor. The American School Counselor Association says, "Thirty-eight states are shortchanging either their students of color, students from low-income families, or both." According to the Princeton Review, another indicator that the system is broken is poor level of retention. Many counselors quit the field after the first couple of years.

The internet provides services and resources that were unimaginable when I was in high school, but it is no substitute for the experience and judgment required to harness those services and resources effectively. If a family has the means, it can fill in the gap with expensive college consultants who will guide a student through the application process, prepare them for the admissions tests, handhold them through writing essays, and consult on extracurriculars and impressive summer internships. The Cadillac of these services is IvyWise, which will work with students for their entire high school careers and can cost over $100,000. The way I see it, the whole process has been hijacked by big business and it screens out most kids, not just the visual thinkers.

As with any institution, practice is slow to change, but with respect to access to higher education, it is coming. With the University of California leading the charge, some colleges have announced that they will no longer use SAT or ACT test scores in considering applicants. According to a *Forbes* investigation by Susan Adams, more than five hundred colleges, including all the Ivy League schools, have adopted a "test optional" position. This is progress.

With test requirements removed, student applications have skyrocketed, especially at Ivy League schools, says a February 2021 *New York Times* article. "First generation, lower income, as well as Black, Hispanic, and Native American students were much less likely to submit their test scores on college applications," Anemona Hartocollis reported in the *Times* in April 2021. During the COVID-19 pandemic, 650 more schools dropped the test requirement. Students who would have screened themselves out based on test scores now have an opportunity to showcase their public service, hobbies, recommendations, work experience, and personal essays. This is progress, especially for visual thinkers.

Conventional aptitude testing, among its many limitations, fails to recognize object visualizers. Two studies done by Erhan Haciomeroglu at the University of Central Florida show that high school students' ability in calculus is related to what kind of thinker they are, with those who are high object visualizers performing poorly compared with visual-spatial thinkers. Haciomeroglu also looked at verbal skills. Students with high verbal skills were also better at calculus compared with students who had high ability in object visualization. This research clearly supports the existence of two types of visualizers. No difference was observed between the groups with respect to performance on verbal skills assessments. The results of these studies really concern me. They support my fear that schools and aptitude tests are screening out talented object-visual thinkers.

Why do students who score well on traditional standardized tests often perform so poorly in more complex "real life" situations where mathematical thinking is needed? Why do students who have poor records of performance in school often perform exceptionally well in relevant "real life" situations? Steffen M. Iversen at the University of Southern Denmark and Christine J. Larson at Indiana University set out to answer those questions in their study "Simple Thinking Using Complex Math vs. Complex Thinking Using Simple Math." The study was conducted with two hundred first-year students in the University of Southern Denmark's science and engineering departments. The students had all completed the highest level of math in secondary school and were taking a calculus course for the first time. They worked individually and then in small groups to solve what is known as the "Penalty Throw Problem," in which subjects are challenged with figuring out a procedure to select the best handball players to throw penalty shots on the basis of sets of data about the players. Coming up with the right solutions requires skills that include aggregating both qualitative and quantitative information, using multiple formulas, creating graphs, recognizing patterns in the data, and understanding the rules of the game.

One goal of the test was to see whether standardized testing, with its narrow focus on certain kinds of problem-solving, overlooked certain students. It showed that students with low pretest scores used a multiphase ranking system for the handball players, while those with high pretest scores focused on a narrower area of investigation, trying to fit the data into preexisting mathematical constructions. That is, the students who scored low on the initial test fared better in solving a real-world problem because their thinking was more flexible, while students who tested well found themselves stuck in ruts because of their rigid approach. The research affirms the difference between the kind of computations students can ace in a classroom and what they accomplish in the real world.

In a piece titled "Do Grades and Tests Predict Adult Accomplishment?" Leonard L. Baird, professor of educational policy and leadership at Ohio State, reviews the literature measuring the relationship between academic ability and high-level accomplishment. He looks at studies on a range of professionals, from scientists to middle managers, along with research on both high school and college students, including gifted students. It's clear that academic ability will get you into good colleges and open doors to high-paying jobs. It's also assumed that high-achieving students will be high achievers in life. But Laird concludes, "It should be noted that high academic ability is no guarantee of high-level attainment."

The Illinois Valedictorian Project followed eighty-one valedictorians for fourteen years after high school. Karen Arnold, assistant professor at Boston College, set out to see if high school success was a predictor of life success. High school success did correlate with college success, but after that, things got dicey. "Scholastic performance is at best an indirect predictor of eminent career achievement," Arnold observed. One quarter of the valedictorians worked in top professional careers. Three quarters were "solid but not outstanding career prospects." Most worked in traditional fields (engineering, medicine, science), but few pursued creative careers. Arnold writes, "They're not mold breakers. They're just the best of the mainstream people."

Success in jobs may be correlated with many qualities not captured on tests, including resilience, creativity, working well with others, good communication skills, and work ethic. Success also happens when a person marshals their resources and creates something people need or want. The owner of an amazing specialty food-processing plant was a kid who would have received every diagnostic label in the book in today's educational system, as he and I have discussed at length. He would certainly have been labeled oppositional and defiant, and he would probably have received an autism diagnosis. Now in his seventies, he is a self-made man. He started out washing food-processing equipment and quickly moved into fixing and maintaining it. His next step was building and creating new devices. He is a mechanical genius, and he built his own factory using a combination of off-the-shelf equipment and totally original patented devices. The factory looks like Willy Wonka's candy factory in stainless steel. Today, he has a multimillion-dollar business. Recently, I boarded his corporate jet to visit his plant. I had to sign a nondisclosure agreement, so I cannot tell you what Willy Wonka makes, but it's enough to say he is a brilliant, eccentric visual thinker.

I still credit the time I spent taking care of the horses at my boarding school with helping me develop my strong work ethic. As I did in Mr. Patriarca's shop, I meticulously cleaned the stables, which was not a pretty job. I fed and groomed the horses, and my reward was getting to ride them. It was a big job for a teenager to do every day. I didn't have the option of skipping a day if I was tired or needed more time for homework. It developed character and responsibility, and it earned the trust of my teachers and headmaster.

There are people in my industry who run successful businesses with only a high school diploma, and whose "real world" skills outstrip those of many people with multiple degrees. People who hire veterinarians and field staff to solve problems out on ranches and feedlots have told me that a solid B+ student often performs better than a straight-A student, and I have observed the same.

The Disabilities Trap

My primary identities are professor, scientist, livestock industry designer, and animal behavior specialist. To this day, autism is secondary. I credit my mother again. It's possible that the most important thing my mother did for me was to not see herself primarily as the mom of a disabled child. It may also explain why she took me to a neurologist instead of a psychologist when it became clear that I was struggling with speech and motor control. That doctor referred us to a speech therapist, and that intervention was critical in my development. Today, I meet loads of parents at disability conferences who call themselves disability moms. They can't think outside the disability box. I've met eight-year-old kids on the autism spectrum who tell me they want to be autism advocates. I tell them to get outside and play. My mother always encouraged me to put work over autism. Autism was always secondary in our household, and that mentality set the course for my life.

You can't learn the value of something, and you certainly can't gain any independence if other people do everything for you. Julie Lythcott-Haims, a former dean and associate vice provost at Stanford University, described the "helicopter parent" in her 2015 book *How to Raise an Adult,* sounding an alarm about parents who overprotect and do too much for their children. Helicopter parenting produces smart adults who do not have the skills to live independently.

When I was in college in the 1970s, my mother didn't call my professors to find out how I was doing in a particular class. It's not that she wasn't concerned. College was a huge step for me. But she knew that learning independence was more important. Today it's not uncommon for parents to contact professors to express concerns about a student's workload or to dispute a grade (it's happened to me). Some parents I've spoken with have shared that they've even called their child's workplace to solve a problem, or just to check in with the boss. There is a new breed of parents who are even more overprotective than the helicopter parents. They are the snowplows and bulldozers. They can't bear for their child to experience any adversity at all, so they clear a path for them.

Snowplow parents are not doing their child a favor, either, because a child raised with this kind of constant intervention will never learn to solve problems. Kelly Lambert at the University of Richmond in Virginia has done research with rats that clearly shows how rats that had to explore and dig to find sugar-cereal treats (Froot Loops) were more persistent when confronted with a new problem. The rats that got their treats dumped on the floor gave up more quickly. Similarly, parents who get their kid out doing things in the world have reported to me that they "blossom" and "flourish."

Hovering is bad for neurotypicals, but it is even worse for kids with disabilities. I have observed many children held back by the label. Some parents embrace the disability mindset so fully that they fail to teach their child useful skills that they could easily learn. I'll never forget meeting a couple, both computer programmers, who wanted advice for their autistic son. They described him as brilliant at math but content to spend all his time in the basement playing video games. I asked if they ever thought of teaching him coding. It had never occurred to them.

I've met parents of fully verbal children with an autism label who are so overprotective that the children never learn basic skills such as shopping and having a bank account. In a book I cowrote with Debra Moore, *Navigating Autism*, we call this "label locking," which is a failure to see the whole child.

This may also keep parents from exposing their kids to things that could develop their abilities, such as tools, math books, or art materials. I recently met a young autistic adult who had figured out how to make accurate working replicas of vehicles from Legos. Neither his teachers nor his parents thought to expose him to tools or a machine shop class. They were locked into the label. I see it all the time: the child is pathologized and never given the opportunity to explore the world or potential gifts. So many object visualizers (neurotypical and neurodiverse) can build the most complex Lego structures. These are the people who should be building our infrastructure, inventing twenty-first-century solutions, and making art to inspire us. But for too many people with disabilities, too much of the world is off-limits.

When parents seek my advice about their spectrum kids, I can often tell by the way they ask their questions that they are much too overprotective. Often, they will make excuses for their child's failure to thrive before getting to the question. There are many definitions of independence, whether it is tying your shoe, making a sandwich, or getting on a bus to go to school on your own. Maybe even going to college and living on your own. I believe that all children need to be encouraged to grow. I wasn't happy when my mother sent me to boarding school. But it was the most formative experience of my life. Becoming independent is one of life's great rewards.

Autism diagnosis covers such a wide range that one person might be an engineer at Apple, and another can't dress himself. In 1980, when autism first appeared in the *Diagnostic and Statistical Manual of Mental Disorders* (*DSM*) as a separate diagnosis from schizophrenia, children had to have both obvious delayed speech and a lack of responsiveness to their surroundings and other people to be labeled autistic. In 1994, Asperger's syndrome was added. It could apply to a child who is socially awkward with no obvious speech delay. This greatly increased the number of kids who would get an autism label, which, according to *The New York Times*, "ballooned to one child in 100." Dr. Laurent

Mottron contends that the definition of autism may "get too blurry to be meaningful." I have observed that, more and more, even just slightly geeky kids are getting labeled. To make the criteria even murkier, in 2013 Asperger's was merged with autism into one big spectrum.

Diagnosis of many of the milder versions of these disorders is creating a blurry mess. When does a little "geeky" become autistic? The diagnostic method is not precise; it is a behavioral profile. This is especially true when a child has just a few traits. There is a point at which mild forms of various disorders are just part of neurotypical behavior and skill variation. It's also a problem that people with disabilities get lumped together. In the autism community, there are big disagreements between parents of kids with severe autism and individuals on the spectrum who say autism is part of neurodiversity.

To me, it is ridiculous that adults who cannot dress themselves have the same label as people with undiagnosed mild autism who work in Silicon Valley. I know families who cannot go to church or eat dinner in a restaurant because of a child who is nonverbal and has other problems such as epilepsy and outbursts. One mother shared that her adult son who is nonverbal breaks everything in her house. How did autism get into such a diagnostic mess?

One diagnostic challenge is that it is difficult to determine which children will become fully verbal and which will remain nonverbal. Even at age three or four, both cases may look severe. Intensive early speech therapy and lots of turn-taking games enabled me to become fully verbal at age four. Other children with the same therapy might remain nonverbal, but still might be able to learn basic skills such as eating with utensils, getting dressed, and brushing their teeth. The same goes for manners, taking turns, and presentation, all of which my mother insisted on. These are not just vestiges of the fifties. They teach the necessary skills and provide the essential tools to learn cooperation, communication, and compromise, all of which are life skills and essential for forging a career path.

In high school, my psychology teacher could see that I wasn't particularly interested in his class, so he challenged me to build a miniature Ames optical-illusion room. The Ames room creates the illusion that two objects of the same size appear as two different sizes. No one knew that I was a visual thinker at that point, but my teacher intuited how to keep me challenged when most schoolwork didn't interest me that much. The project held my attention for over a month as I used trial and error to arrive at the solution: the key to constructing the Ames room and achieving the illusion is that the box is a trapezoid. I still visually reference it when I'm constructing new equipment or problem solving on projects. These things can stay with you for life. These things are not found on standardized tests.

Today, I see too many students give up on projects when they meet any resistance. I was driven to do my work. A big motivation for me was proving to people that I wasn't stupid. I didn't feel entirely respected, even when I was getting great grades in college, including an A in physiology, considered one of the most difficult biology classes. The professor was a reproductive physiologist, and his specialty was studying how heat stress affects dairy cows. His examples were more visual than abstract, in a field known for abstraction. It's possible that his approach enabled me to better grasp the concepts. I've seen throughout my life, first as a student and then as a professor, that when a student fails to grasp something, the student is usually blamed. But not everyone learns the same way.

———

People with disabilities have a long history of being screened out in schooling—in life in general, for that matter. In ancient times, the treatment of people born with disabilities was shockingly atrocious. If you want to get really depressed, you can read about the cruel acts that humans have committed against disabled people, including infanticide, starvation, abandonment, and chaining them up. For economic reasons, Plato and Aristotle recommended infanticide—weeding out the weaker or less perfect. The ancient Greek physician Hippocrates had a more enlightened view. He believed that mental illness was caused by either something wrong with the brain or factors in the environment. People in the early American colonies thought that mental illness was a punishment from God, and the mentally ill were often burned or hanged. For over a century, up until the 1950s, eugenics dictated that individuals with intellectual disabilities be sterilized so they could not pass on their "defective" genes. The worst treatment of the developmentally disabled in more modern times was in Nazi Germany. Hitler's extermination campaigns included forced sterilizations and "euthanasia" centers where thousands of disabled people were killed. Later, more painful methods of death became more common, including lethal injection, experimentation, poisoning, gas chambers, and starvation. If I had been a three-year-old child in Nazi Germany, I would have been designated a "useless eater"—a drain on society—and killed.

The road toward civil rights for people with disabilities has been long and difficult. Within my own lifetime, there has been tremendous change in this arena, centering on three important laws. Each incrementally increased the rights of individuals with physical and intellectual disabilities to receive education. The 1975 Individuals with Disabilities Education Act (IDEA) and Section 504 of the Rehabilitation Act had the greatest impact on education, ensuring the right to fair access to a free public education. This law specified that an individual with a disability had a right to be educated in the "least restrictive environment" and be mainstreamed into classrooms with nondisabled children to the extent possible. This law also required that each eligible child with a disability would have an Individualized Education Program (IEP). These plans are created for each student by a team of teachers, education specialists (often a school psychologist), and parents. The law opened the doors of the public school system to students with autism, ADHD, dyslexia, physical disabilities, and many other diagnostic categories.

One of my favorite anecdotes about a person with disabilities involves Stevie Wonder. In an interview, he describes climbing trees and running around with the neighborhood kids as a small child. It's a fact that's always stayed with me. Stevie Wonder's mother didn't let his blindness hold him back and keep him inside. He didn't get stuck in a disability mindset. He also had access to many musical instruments from a very young age, and by age ten he had taught himself to play piano, drums, and harmonica. At church he sang in the choir. Stevie was told by some of the people at his school that all a blind person could do was make pot-holders. He more than proved them wrong.

Thomas West, an author who is dyslexic himself and was "not reading until way too late," has written powerfully about the need to appreciate and recognize different ways of thinking. His mission is much like my own: to help people appreciate different kinds of minds and ensure that they are not screened out by a one-size-fits-all educational system. "What is being suggested here," he writes in his book *In the Mind's Eye*, "is that for a certain group of people the handicap itself may be fundamentally and essentially associated with a gift . . . too often the gift is not recognized and is regarded only as a problem."

In retrospect, failing algebra may have been one of the best things that ever happened to me.

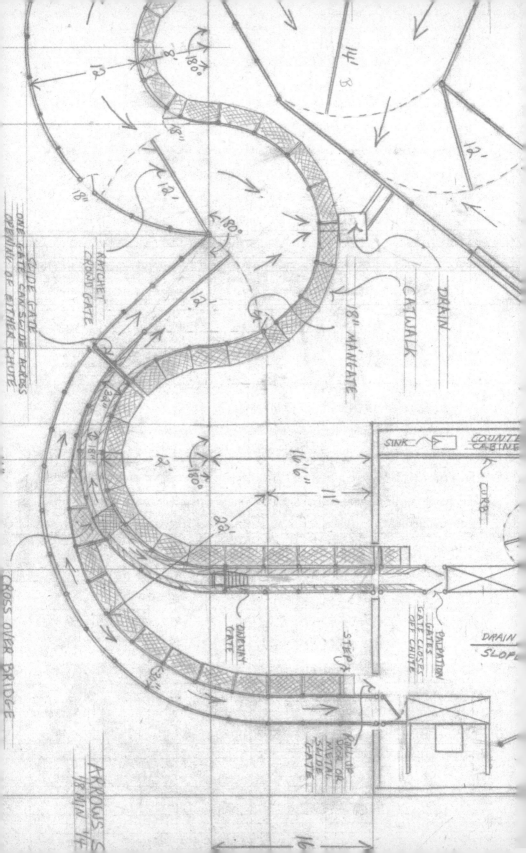

THREE

Where Are All
the Clever Engineers?

I magine a dollhouse for geniuses. A museum of the mind. A place where history pops up in three dimensions and tells the story of human ingenuity. That's what it felt like when I entered the United States Patent and Trademark Office two years ago. I had been invited there to give a talk on different kinds of minds, and my own mind was blown when I encountered the models for inventions that I had read about my entire life.

As a kid, I was given a book on inventors. Sadly, it's long gone, but I still have visual recall of the pages that interested me most, such as those on Elias Howe, who invented the sewing machine, the Wright brothers, who ignited my lifelong interest in aerodynamics, and my hero, Thomas Edison, who held the record for the most patents. My grandfather, who had a huge influence on my life, was a co–patent holder for the autopilot that guides planes.

The US Patent Office came into being in 1790. Until the 1870s, inventors seeking a patent had to include a model or prototype with their application. In its first hundred years, the Patent Office housed inventions for agriculture (the first patent was for a new method to make potash), chemistry, hydraulics, electricity, printing, and paper manufacture. By 1823, patents had been filed for plows, threshing machines, watermills, windmills, locks, guns, bridges, and pumps. Steam power was harnessed in myriad ways to fuel trains, mills, boats, and factories. Unfortunately, the Patent Office burned down twice, and with it the models of early inventions. At the centennial celebration of the Patent Office, Connecticut senator Orville Platt remarked, "All history confirms us in the conclusions that it is the development by the mechanical arts of the industries of a country which brings it greatness, power, and glory." Platt traced this mechanical knowledge back to the unacknowledged clever inventors, "the blacksmith, the carpenter, the millwright and the village tinker." I would add that these are all unquestionably visual thinkers.

At the same celebration, the venerable commissioner of patents, Charles E. Mitchell, recalled that he had seen the tallow candle become electric light, the messenger boy become the telephone and telegraph, and the saddle become the car. The age of invention was inextricably tied to the men and women who were able to see in their mind's eye how to solve a problem, enhance a system, enact a solution. The first thing that caught my eye when I entered the atrium of the Patent Office was the model of a cannon with an elaborate mechanism to absorb the recoil. Clever engineering department, one hundred percent.

Where have all those tinkerers gone? Why has the United States fallen behind other countries in manufacturing? If we zoom out, the bigger global picture shows a conflagration of complex political and economic forces. My focus is on something more tangible—the loss of essential technical skills, for the reasons I've mentioned: our failure to replace people with manufacturing expertise as they leave the job market, our ceding the manufacture of not only cheap volume goods but high-tech products to foreign companies, and an education system that screens out the very people most suited to perform the skilled work we've lost.

———

Here are some things you probably don't think about: your garage door opener, the conveyor belt at the supermarket, the drum inside your printer, your building's elevator, even the phone you keep on your person at all times. We take these gadgets for granted, as part of the fabric of our lives. Who invented the ice maker, the touch screen, the ballistic missile? The origin story behind each gizmo is likely longer than *War and Peace*, except it's told through thousands of pages of patent applications and drawings that reveal how inventors seek to create and improve upon those creations. But long before patents, clever people were figuring out how to make and fix things, not necessarily for profit but just because it would make life easier or make something possible. Civilization would not have progressed without the mechanical inventions—starting with the humble lever and the simple pulley—that enabled people to dig wells, erect dams, or build the roads that gave access to clean water, allowed agriculture to flourish, and made possible the transport of goods. The mechanical inventors are generally object visualizers. The picture-thinking mind can see how a not-yet-created mechanical device will work.

In the earliest renderings on view at the Patent Office, you can see the mechanical mind of the object thinker at work. The same ingenuity was captured in that book about inventors that I loved as a child. Four examples come to mind that show the impact their inventions had on society. The cotton gin invented by Eli Whitney separated the seeds from the cotton fiber, revolutionizing the textile industry. The reaper invented by Cyrus McCormick used a vibrating blade to harvest grain; a version of this device would be used in all subsequent mechanical reapers, revolutionizing our food supply. Elias Howe didn't invent the sewing machine, per se, but he put together all the existing elements: the overhanging arm, the lockstitch, an automatic feed for the fabric, and his own ingenious design of a needle with an eye placed at the point of insertion into the fabric. It seems like a small thing, but, combined with the cotton gin, it ushered in the age of cheaper, faster clothing production. The six-shooter pistol invented by Samuel Colt had a revolving cylinder, whittled out of wood, that automatically rotated the next bullet into position and allowed the gun to be fired multiple times without reloading, something that changed the face of warfare. All four of these inventors were mechanically clever; none of them would have needed higher math for their creations.

Visual problem-solving is the stock in trade of the clever engineer. It's how mechanical information has been transmitted through the centuries. In a seminal paper on visual thinking published in *Science*, Eugene S. Ferguson, an engineer and historian of technology, presented the visual record of technical knowledge that mushroomed with the advent of the printing press. In compiling artists' and engineers' notebooks, technical workbooks and manuals from the fifteenth to the twentieth century (including Leonardo da Vinci's thousands of pages of technical drawings), Ferguson traces the record of human ingenuity in the detailed drawings of every known device and mechanism. These notebooks are filled with exquisite photorealistic drawings of complex gear assemblies, water pumps, sawmills, cranes, and military machinery. Ferguson writes, "As the designer draws lines on paper, he translates a picture held in his mind that will produce a similar picture in another mind and will eventually become a three-dimensional engine in metal. . . . It rests largely on the nonverbal thought and nonverbal reasoning of the designer, who thinks with pictures."

Every century brought with it an incredible record of mechanical innovation and refinement. Ferguson credits the craftsmen, designers, inventors, and engineers—those who see with their mind's eye "by a visual non-verbal process"—for advancing technology. He concludes, "Much of the creative thought of the designers of our technological world is nonverbal, not easily reducible to words. . . . Technologists, converting their nonverbal knowledge into objects . . . or into drawings that have enabled others to build what was in their minds have chosen the shape and many of the qualities of our man-made surroundings. This intellectual component of technology, which is nonliterary and nonscientific, has been generally unnoticed because its origins lie in art and not in science."

Fifteen years after the publication of his 1977 paper on visual thinking, Ferguson wrote a book titled *Engineering and the Mind's Eye*. He confirms what I've been observing in the field, that engineering has moved away from "knowledge that cannot be expressed in mathematical relationships." He warns that an engineering education that ignores visual, nonverbal thinking will produce engineers who are ignorant of how the "real world differs from the mathematical world their professors teach them."

———

I recently toured the shop of a twenty-first-century visual thinker whose canvas is the cosmos. He designs planetary equipment, in this case the mechanism that launches satellites out of the nose cones of rockets. I was taken with the array of gleaming machinery in his workshop, but what really caught my eye was something I can only describe as a golden milk crate, a gleaming, latticed box used to store the satellites. I'm pretty sure he got the idea from an actual milk crate. His client list is a who's who of space exploration. Most of them probably don't know that he was a C student and barely got through engineering school. Or that he got the idea for the sophisticated mechanism that launches satellites from the gadget that unlatches your car trunk. This mechanism ensures that the satellite is always released and never gets stuck in the nose cone. For inspiration, this inventor will go to Home Depot and buy a drill or other tools just to take them apart and get ideas for new mechanisms. We didn't have Home Depot when I was a kid, but I remember trips to the hardware store. I'd fiddle with every lock and latch. I could watch the paint mixer rotate a can for hours. Not all Home Depot nerds are rocket scientists, but a lot of us are visual thinkers.

Some mechanical inventors may be strong visual-spatial thinkers as well; the research to date has not yet separated them from object visualizers. But it's clear that most of the mechanical inventions over the centuries did not come about through abstract thinking. They were conceived of and executed by object visualizers who could see in their mind's eye how physical things work, people who used a hands-on approach. People with exceptional visual skills— members of the clever engineering department—have transformed society. Gutenberg's movable type revolutionized the printing press and advanced literacy. Henry Ford didn't invent the car, but he figured out how to build a transmission mechanism that made driving easier, and he introduced improvements along the assembly line that would change the face of transportation.

Object thinkers have mechanical minds; they tend to be specific and practical. Spatial thinkers understand abstraction; they not only grasp but discover the scientific principles that organize the world. I recently came across a quote by the Swiss chemist Richard R. Ernst, who was awarded a Nobel Prize for paving the way for the MRI. It goes to the heart of this critical difference between the two kinds of visual thinkers: "I'm not really what one would imagine to be a scientist who wants to understand the world. I'm a toolmaker and not really a scientist in this sense, and I wanted to provide other people these capabilities of solving problems."

I got to witness the sheer beauty of mechanical invention up close throughout the 1970s, 1980s, and early 1990s, when I worked in the field supervising the construction of stockyards, chutes, and handling systems that I had designed for cattle and pigs. It's not an exaggeration to say that these operations would have failed to thrive if not for the many talented and ingenious machinery designers. Generally, in the food-processing industry, the spatial visualizers are the engineers with advanced degrees who build the infrastructure that requires advanced mathematics, such as boilers and refrigeration, power, and water systems. The object visualizers from the clever engineering department almost never have an engineering degree, but they can build anything mechanical. In a food-processing plant, it's these "quirky" people who design and build all the mechanically intricate specialized equipment. In today's digital age, the equipment may be controlled by computers, but it is still mostly mechanical.

"Quirky," of course, is a euphemism for people who don't exactly "fit in." Many I've worked with have been socially awkward and intensely focused, with a preference for working on their own and often a disregard for hygiene. One of these designers, a colleague, was a terrible student, struggled with dyslexia, and had many autism traits; he still stutters. A welding class in high school saved him. He started building equipment and selling it in the exhibit halls at county and state fairs, and eventually started his own business. He now owns a large metal fabrication company and sells his products all over the world. He can build just about anything, and he doesn't even need to sketch it out. He holds multiple patents. Pure object-visual thinker.

Another colleague, who is also an object visualizer and holds many patents, was poor at algebra. His career was successfully launched with a high school FFA program and welding class. FFA stands for Future Farmers of America. This is a national high school program for educating high school students in agriculture, leadership, and public speaking. Learning skilled trades, such as welding and engine repair, is an important part of FFA programs. He now owns a large construction company and builds large turnkey beef-processing plants. A turnkey project is one in which the contractor constructs the building and also provides and installs all the specialized machinery. It's worth underscoring that while one of these businesses has remained local and the other gradually grew into a huge company with many employees, both started out as tiny shops. That's where innovation happens.

When I was starting out in my career, I believed that the bigwigs at the corporations had all the answers. Experience has taught me that this is not always the case. My motto now is: Little guys innovate. I geeked out over the camera on the Mars rover *Perseverance*. Michael Malin, who invented it, is a geology professor at my alma mater, Arizona State University. He also works at the Jet Propulsion Lab and at NASA, where he first pitched the idea for the camera. NASA initially rejected it, stating that it had all the photos it needed. Malin disregarded the rejection and started a small company with other geologists to study other planets. Eventually, NASA helped fund their efforts. The Mars rover looks like a cross between a desert jeep without the shell and a Transformer. It has nine engineering cameras, seven science cameras, and seven entry, descent, and landing cameras mounted on it—twenty-three cameras in all. Each has a different purpose. The one that blows my mind is the Super-Cam, which fires a laser at mineral targets that are farther out than the robotic arm can reach, then analyzes the vaporized rock to determine its element compound. Malin's cameras are responsible for the photographs that show evidence of water on Mars. Very clever.

Another company that was critical to the success of the latest rover was Forest City Gear in Illinois. They worked with NASA to create the tiny gears that turned the camera. This was a big challenge, because very precise tolerances were required to enable them to survive the harsh Martian environment. To execute, extraordinary attention to detail is required. It turns out the perfect candidate for such a job is a person with autism. Dr. Ivan Rosenberg started a unique program with College of the Canyons in Santa Clarita, California, to train autistic students to run computerized metal machinery equipment for Forest City. The twelve-week program combines classroom and hands-on learning, matching the vocational skills taught with those needed in the workplace.

Both the camera company and the gear company are excellent examples of small, privately owned US businesses that excel at highly specialized work. It is also worth noting, however, that the machinery they use to make the highly machined parts of their products come from Europe. We don't make precision computerized metal-milling machinery anymore.

The high-tech fabric in the parachutes that landed *Perseverance* softly on Mars was made by the British company Heathcoat Fabrics, although the parachute itself was sewn and assembled in the United States. Peter Hill, the head of the woven fabric department, watched the landing on Mars "on his knees in front of the TV."

The rover has some cool hot wheels, machined from a single block of aircraft-quality aluminum. Most people don't know that there's a kind of "Batcave" signal embedded in the aluminum treads of one of the earlier rovers. When the wheels turn, the initials JPL (for Jet Propulsion Lab) are imprinted in the surface it travels over. NASA calls this a visual odometer, making it possible to measure how far the rover has moved. Insiders believe that the techies who engineered this didn't have permission to use the laboratory's initials. But techies, as we'll see in future chapters, love to show off.

At trade shows, I always ask companies about the origins of their latest machines. Often, it's the guy working in the shop who comes up with the idea and builds the prototype. Then the more mathematically inclined engineers perfect it. When I first started working with meat companies, they had their own in-house engineering departments and equipment-manufacturing facilities. These engineering departments invented lots of new equipment. To save money, the engineering offices and their extensive metal fabrication facilities were phased out in the late 1990s. As people retired, they were not replaced. Instead of being passed down, their skills and institutional knowledge were irretrievably lost.

Most people may not know that the modern industrial conveyor belt was invented in the United States. Nor do they know that conveyance is an area in which we no longer excel. The first patent was awarded in 1896, but the inventor largely credited for it was Thomas Robins, who started out by transporting coal and ore for Thomas Edison's Ore-Milling Company. Robins quit Princeton after two years. He received a patent in 1905 for his improvements to the conveyor belt and started his own company. But the part of the conveyor industry where the United States stopped excelling is in highly automated systems. The company Robins founded to produce conveyor belts is now owned by an Indian multinational conglomerate.

In general, automated conveyor systems are an area where Europe now excels. The German-based Kion Group is a leader in manufacturing automated warehouse systems. The company is developing a workforce trained in the skilled trades to improve supply-chain conveyor systems for maximum efficiency. In the most highly automated systems, there will always be a need for highly skilled people to install and repair the machines, the service that makes rapid delivery to your doorstep possible. American companies such as Amazon, Walmart, and Frito-Lay are customers. The most advanced robotic warehouse comes from the UK, and Japan reigns supreme for automated machine tools. According to Market Research Reports, the top five manufacturers of industrial robots are located in Switzerland, Japan, and Germany. In addition to making most of the world's iPhones, China builds the clever machines that put the popular chocolate swirls in soft-serve ice cream cones. As of 2014, Europe had 37 percent of the elevator-modernization market and the United States only 17 percent. Huge cranes for loading and unloading massive container ships come from Europe and China. Vast amounts of the merchandise you buy online travel to the United States on container ships built in other countries.

Also in the blow-my-mind department is a huge computer chip—making machine that I first read about in 2020 in *The Economist*. This incredible machine could have come from a long time ago in a galaxy far, far away. It was a huge rectangular box the height of a bus, and the outside, with white panels all around, gave no hint whatsoever what it would be like inside. Inside, a maze of silver pipes both big and small were connected to boxes, valves, and electronic devices. This is the part where you could hear the *Star Wars* theme song: ultraviolet light beams bounced back and forth between multiple mirrors to create the thinnest of lines, thinner than a strand of hair. These gossamerlike light beams etch the circuit patterns onto the computer chips. If you're a tech geek, you would find it incredibly beautiful, especially when compared with earlier generations of chip-making machines, which made patterns that looked as if they had been crudely scrawled on the circuit boards with a thick piece of chalk. Creating this futuristic device requires both the object-visualizing clever engineer and the mathematically inclined visual-spatial engineer. I was astonished to learn that the most advanced equipment for making electronic chips now comes from a Dutch company named ASML. How did this happen, when America invented the computer chip?

According to a global manufacturing scorecard compiled by the Brookings Institution, American workers are falling far behind other countries in a range of areas. With respect to manufacturing output, China leads the world, and the United States is second. But with respect to the percentage of people employed in manufacturing, the United States ranked sixteenth out of eighteen countries surveyed. The study notes that one significant problem is the lack of skilled workers to fill the positions that still exist, concluding, "Vocational training programs and education focused on incentivizing individuals to study STEM fields is imperative."

Countries such as Germany and the Netherlands have kept their skilled-trades classes. In the United States, the exodus of manufacturing to other countries has left a vacuum of skilled tradespeople to supply hands-on labor. According to a 2021 report by the Associated General Contractors of America, 61 percent of contractors struggled to find qualified workers. When

COVID restrictions eased up, I was allowed to go back into the beef plants. At one, there was equipment that needed to be rebuilt. It was simple steel work that required standard off-the-shelf hydraulic components. I was shocked to learn that the only metal shop capable of building it was booked for the next eight months. On top of that, there were no skilled metalworkers available to construct it. A conversation with the plant's maintenance department further revealed that they did not know if they would be able to replace their skilled maintenance workers once they retired. According to every report I've read, we are facing an unprecedented skills gap at a time when the need for skills is ever more pressing.

The employment landscape is going to be in deep trouble if we don't address the lack of all kinds of skilled workers. The COVID-19 pandemic highlighted the urgency for specific needs: medical technicians, EMTs, caregivers, Zoom and video-platform specialists, and nurses' aides, among others. But COVID didn't create the crisis: a 2008 report from the Association of Schools of Public Health had already forecast a workforce crisis that would result in a shortfall of 250,000 public health workers by 2020. Here we are.

It all adds up to what I call the failure to launch. By that I mean the failure to identify visual thinkers early on and to encourage their talents and skills toward meaningful work they would naturally be good at. And the failure to integrate different ways of thinking to benefit society. There are real-world consequences of this failure, collectively and individually. There are real-world solutions to this failure, individually and collectively.

While some European countries have trained and promoted their clever engineers, we have screened them out.

Cultivating Clever Engineers

I've always collected stories of people who prevail against the odds. They affirm my deep belief that hard work and independent thinking pave the way for true discovery. Lynn Margulis, a biologist at Boston University, persisted after her research was rejected from fifteen scientific journals. When her paper was finally published, it proved that the mitochondria that provide energy to animal cells and the chloroplasts that enable plants to use sunlight for photosynthesis were once independent organisms. This is now accepted fact. Another scientist I admire is Bob Williams, the astronomer responsible for the Hubble Deep Field image. When Dr. Williams suggested pointing the telescope at sections of space where there was nothing to observe, his peers thought it was a waste of valuable telescope observation time. He chose a dark area of space near the Big Dipper constellation. When the Hubble Space Telescope was pointed at what appeared to be nothing, it revealed thousands of galaxies and the vastness of the universe, all wonders that lay beyond the visible stars.

Cultivating clever engineers begins at home and in early childhood education. In addition to affording kids the opportunity to build things and experience the tactile world (through sewing, cooking, gardening, assembling, tinkering, and experimenting), we need to encourage them to develop patience, resilience, and curiosity. My mother valued perseverance, and she imparted that to my siblings and me. Quitting, or not trying in the first place, was one of the most disappointing things you could do, in her book. Once, when the neighborhood kids got together on their bikes to ride to the local Coca-Cola bottling plant, I begged my mother to drive me there. She refused. I'd have to learn to ride my own bike if I wanted to go. I learned! It may seem like tough love, but my mother had an innate sense of how to stretch me without breaking me.

Coming of age in the 1950s with autism was difficult because there was so little research or available knowledge about the condition. The nascent disability movement had not yet galvanized in any significant way. The wealth of books, conferences, videos, support groups, and therapeutic protocols that we have now did not exist. Doctors were clueless and often recommended institutionalization for people like me, with delayed speech and other autistic traits. On the other hand, I wasn't weighed down with labels and protocols. My mother, always a bit of a rebel, was happy to do things her way.

People are right to talk about the 1950s as a conservative and restrictive time, but for me it was also a godsend, helping me move beyond my autistic traits. If I had a temper tantrum, Mother would take away my hour of television. Not getting to watch my favorite show was more than enough incentive. By the time I was in elementary school, I could participate in most social situations, such as going to Granny's for Sunday dinner, or sitting at a table without making a scene or having a tantrum. My mother's insistence on manners and polite behavior prepared me to go to a restaurant, to church, and to the movies, because I knew how to behave. I also learned about the value of money from a very early age. My parents gave me an allowance of fifty cents. I knew exactly what I could get for my money at the local five-and-dime and saved up for my favorite toy airplane.

I was a terrible student but getting to work at the horse stables at my boarding school taught me work skills. My reward was getting to ride those beautiful animals. I get asked all the time about how I got into the cattle industry when I came from an East Coast, nonagricultural background. Age fifteen was a pivotal time for me. I visited my aunt's ranch in Arizona and experienced the West and ranching. I loved everything about it: the horses and cattle, leatherworking, the handling chutes, the barn, and the big open sky. It all fascinated me, and it launched me on my career path.

On the entrepreneurial side, I started painting signs while I was in high school and sold a few. (Remember, I got the chance to develop my skills by painting sets for our school shows. Without that experience, I doubt I would have attempted my signs.) In college, I went on to paint signs for feedlots, a thrift store, and the Arizona State Fair. To get jobs, I showed people photos of completed signs. This experience, too, would pave the way to future work, and future work skills. I realized that examples of my work were more persuasive than a résumé. When I started my business designing livestock-handling facilities, I showed prospective clients my portfolio. I would lay my drawings on their desks and show them photos of completed projects. I called this the "thirty-second wow." To further promote my work, I wrote about it in the livestock-industry trade press.

All these experiences encouraged me to figure out how to do things for myself and made me stronger, more resilient. That's a trait that many kids today are no longer developing. In her bestseller *Grit*, Angela Duckworth defines grit as a quality that combines both passion and persistence to achieve a long-term goal. Anyone on the innovating front lines knows that new ideas are often rejected by colleagues. As I mentioned, when I did some of my first behavior work on cattle, people thought I was crazy. They could not believe that agitation during handling caused lower weight gain in steers. Not only did my hypothesis turn out to be true, it became the inspiration for the curved, or serpentine, cattle chutes I designed that have been widely adopted around the world. The gentle flow keeps the steer from becoming agitated. My ability with animals and my visual thinking merged in the success of this design.

I can absolutely see how the concept of neurodiversity would have been helpful when I was growing up, the label providing insights leading to better mental health treatment and education. In a 2009 study by Edward Griffin and David Pollak at De Montfort University in Leicester, England, researchers interviewed twenty-seven students with learning differences. Those who identified their neurodiversity as "difference," acknowledging both the positives and negatives, expressed higher self-esteem—and higher career goals—than those who identified with a "medical/deficit" model.

But I have also seen both young children and their parents use labels to avoid trying new things. It's possible that the most important thing my mother did for me was to not see me primarily as disabled, or herself primarily as the mom of a disabled child. Being free of those labels allowed her to focus on the specific help I needed—the speech therapy, the home tutoring, and the supportive schooling environments that allowed me to read, write, and talk. I can't stress enough the importance of such early-childhood intervention, for children on the spectrum and off. I suspect many parents have the same overall instincts my mother had, but the disability mindset can produce a kind of tunnel vision.

Labels can be a double-edged sword. Evolving the nomenclature from "disability" to "neurodiversity" does not eliminate all the drawbacks. From my own observations and discussions with many parents and teachers, I've witnessed too many times when labels held kids back. Too many parents get into a disability mindset—whatever the label—instead of working on developing their child's strengths. How a person's identity is formed impacts career development and self-esteem. It is important to distinguish between a disability and valuable neurodiversity. In my own case there is a trade-off. Some of my autistic traits make it hard for me to connect with people, and yet I have a profound connection with animals. I cannot do algebra or other visual-spatial tasks, but I have special abilities in object visualization. This has made me successful in both animal behavior research and design of equipment. There needs to be much more emphasis on the things a person is good at. And this starts in childhood. Imagine how much further a visually inclined child might go if he or she were exposed to making things at a young age—and was encouraged to do so. Yes, there may be a trade-off. Your visual child may not make friends as easily as the verbal kids, but he or she might also invent the conveyor belt that goes to Mars.

Karla Fisher, a senior program manager for Intel, was diagnosed with Asperger's syndrome (autism without speech delay) after she became successful in the computer industry. In the essay about her in my book *Different . . . Not*

Less, Fisher describes how she found "her people" in the tech industry. They all loved technology. Being social was not the centerpiece of their lives. After her father died, she became distraught, and her boss suggested she see a grief counselor, who subsequently gave her a diagnosis of autism spectrum disorder. She said she felt like a social outcast, even though her career was going well. Fisher's senior manager at Intel told her, "I wonder just how much of you being here now is because you never received a diagnosis." For some adults diagnosed later in life, knowing they are autistic provides long-overdue insight into problems with employment and relationships they have long struggled with. But Fisher implied that if she had known her diagnosis earlier, she might not have attained such a high-level career; an earlier diagnosis, she suggested, might have held her back.

It's important to recognize that labels are just that: labels. They aren't the entirety of the person, and with respect to that person's conditions—whether physical, mental, or psychological—they may be attempting to cover so wide a range of traits and behaviors that they are stretched to the limits of usefulness. The diagnosis of autism is based on a collection of traits; it is not a precise diagnosis, such as being diagnosed with the COVID-19 delta variant. I would prefer to call it a behavioral profile instead of a diagnosis. I agree with those who propose to eliminate the terms high- and low-functioning autism. I would prefer to call them verbal and nonverbal. There are some nonverbal individuals who have significant artistic, mathematical, or musical abilities. Autism is a truly continuous set of traits, with infinite variations.

Difficult as they were to master, the skills my mother insisted on—manners, turn taking, self-presentation—were true life skills, tools to learn cooperation, communication, and compromise. Without them, I would not have been able to forge a career path. A big motivation for me was also proving to people that I wasn't stupid. Working skills are very different from academic skills. This may sound basic, but students need to learn to be on time; to be polite, neat, and clean; to work under deadline; and to execute tasks. Learning manners not only teaches you to say please and thank you but later keeps you from calling colleagues stupid even if they are stupid, generally a bad career move.

When I talk to parents and teachers at conferences, I'm struck by how many smart kids who have a disability label are not learning how to work. When I grill parents on their kids' skill level, I discover that the parents are not encouraging them to learn basic skills such as shopping, maintaining a bank account, or paying bills. (This is often true of parents of neurotypicals as well.) One mom who had an autistic teenager started crying when I pushed her on this point. Her son, who was doing well in school, had never shopped in a store by himself. He'd never even bought a slice of pizza and a Coke on his own. His mother said she could not let go.

All the new emphasis on neurodiversity and inclusion is a good thing. But I've also witnessed firsthand how the label of "inclusion" can sometimes be little more than window dressing. For instance, when I travel to speak at colleges, government agencies, and large corporations, I often see the formation of disability silos, in which people with disabilities talk only to other people with disabilities. More than once, in breakout groups with senior managers, the disability group that has invited me has failed to include managers from outside the disability realm. The negative consequence of this is that communication that could help the advancement of people with disabilities does not occur. At a tech company I visited, they neglected to invite managers from divisions where people with autism provide skills. A similar problem sometimes occurs at the colleges I visit. The diversity and disability groups forget that I have a career in animal agriculture. At one college, a professor from the veterinary technician program hadn't been informed I was on campus. Preventing the formation of silos that block communication requires hard work. The first step is to realize that they are forming. Not a single one of the hosting organizations realized it had formed a silo. Maybe that's the nature of silos: you don't realize when you're in them.

A question I get asked all the time is: "How can we help people with disabilities?" This is an overly broad question that is often voiced by a verbal thinker. A person in a wheelchair needs very different accommodations from those a person with autism needs. During my career, I have consulted with many corporations and have learned how they think. At a disability conference, I listened to a blind person who had been turned down after interviewing for many jobs he would have been capable of doing. All the positions involved computers. What I think happens is that the people interviewing the blind applicant panic. They see his guide dog and cane and think the accommodations will be too difficult. I recommend that such an applicant take a more assertive approach. He might say, "My accommodation will be easy, please just try me for two weeks. All I need is this special computer software. Everything else I can handle." He could offer to bring a friend in for a few days to teach him the office layout.

Some people argue the onus should be on employers not to discriminate against neurodiverse candidates, and that employers should provide all the necessary onboarding and accommodations. But often, in practical terms, it is the candidate who loses out. The applicant's proactive approach would put the interviewer at ease about the difficulty of the accommodations and greatly increase the likelihood of getting hired. Neurodiverse applicants need to demonstrate their abilities. One way may be to adopt my "thirty-second wow" technique, having pictures of their work on their phone (also displayed on a well-designed website) at the ready to show to a potential client sitting next to them on a train or plane.

I wasn't completely surprised to learn that Elon Musk, creator of SpaceX and Tesla, has said that résumés don't matter all that much. He doesn't put a whole lot of stock in where you went to college (in fact, being a college graduate is not a prerequisite for joining his companies) or what material you can successfully regurgitate. Musk claims that he started his own company because none of the internet start-ups would hire him. He recounts both sending his résumé to Netscape and hanging around the Netscape lobby hoping to talk to someone, although he was too shy at the time to approach anyone. What Musk is looking for is drive, curiosity, and creativity. He wants people who can make things and fix things. I'd wager that you could more easily get his attention with a beautifully rendered mechanical drawing of a ventilation system than a 4.0 GPA on your résumé.

Still, even the most progressive programs can deteriorate if they lose their corporate champions. I recently visited a well-known brand-name company to give my "Different Kinds of Minds" talk to their employees. They had a great program for people with all types of physical and intellectual disabilities, spearheaded by an upper-level manager. When he left due to a sudden illness, the program deteriorated. After a systems update, a blind employee, for example, was no longer able to use the software she needed. Until then, she had been a valued member of the customer-service department. The diversity office failed to investigate the problem and didn't track it to the systems update. The issue was that simple, and it derailed her career.

Fortunately, when it comes to neurodiversity, employers themselves are genuinely waking up to the advantages of hiring different kinds of minds. Walgreens has been a leader in this movement. Inspired by having a child with a disability, Randy Lewis, a senior vice president of supply chain and logistics, reconfigured the computers in two of the chain's distribution warehouses so that little reading was required to use them. When the different warehouses were compared, the company found that the warehouses with the people with disabilities outperformed the others.

The good news is that it is becoming more widely known that the talents and skills that people with diverse minds bring to the workplace far outweigh the temporary inconvenience of learning how to reconfigure it for their needs. They are appreciated for their deep knowledge, prolific memory, and attention to detail. Tech companies such as Microsoft and financial companies such as Goldman Sachs are among those who recognize this, and their initiatives will help pave the way for more. At a recent conference, I met a young man with Asperger's, a car dealer, who had an encyclopedic memory of all makes and models of automobiles and their features. At first, his monotone voice and inability to make eye contact seemed an insurmountable handicap on the showroom floor. Once people recognized his enthusiasm and depth of knowledge, his neurodiversity didn't matter. In fact, it became a plus as he made lots of sales.

In a *Harvard Business Review* article, Robert Austin of the Ivey Business School and Gary Pisano of Harvard Business School report that the Australian Defense Department found that autistic people were "off the charts" for skills related to analyzing raw data for patterns and potential cybersecurity breaches. This would require extreme skills of spatial pattern visualization. SAP, a large software company, and Hewlett Packard Enterprise have found that people with autism can be highly productive employees if they are given good training and a few accommodations. They may need noise-canceling headphones and a quiet place to work. They may also require more time for training, but after they are trained, they will do really accurate work. At Australia's Department of Human Services, autistic software testers were 30 percent more productive than their non-autistic counterparts.

A guide for UK employers called *Untapped Talent* highlights qualities such as attention to detail, high levels of concentration, reliability, excellent memory, and technical ability in people with autism. In addition to quiet working conditions, it mentions sensory breaks, clear work instructions, and changes in lighting as simple accommodations that may be required. And the gifts of such employees aren't only technical. People with autism are also known to share two other qualities: loyalty and scrupulous honesty.

Dan Burger was featured on a *60 Minutes* episode that explored the abilities of people with autism. At Vanderbilt University he invented a computer program called Filtergraph, which analyzes data from a NASA space telescope to aid astronomers in discovering exoplanets. The web platform has since expanded to visually analyze other large-scale data sets. Burger found that people with autism "understand patterns in images at a superior level." He has been instrumental in creating a center for autism and innovation where tests are being developed to identify such visual thinkers, with the goal of setting them up for long-term employment.

Recently I visited Aspiritech, a software- and hardware-testing company located outside Chicago. It was discovered that the company was losing 20 percent of its business from one of its branch offices, but no one could figure out why. It turned out that their web designer had transposed two digits of the company's phone number when the website was updated. An employee on the spectrum caught the error. The autistic eye for visual detail saved this client a lot of money.

Managers need to be willing to accept that a neurodiverse individual may have poor interviewing or interpersonal skills. In fact, only 15 percent of people with autism have jobs (which is less than half the rate for disabled people on the whole). Lack of affect can make a highly qualified person appear dull and distracted. The person who thinks differently is not going to be the usual team-player, social-salesman type. But people can be coached. It's easy to forget that as people get older, they often learn to manage their disabilities better. Many of the traits I had as a teen and even into my thirties have disappeared, such as constantly repeating the same thing and interrupting people due to a lag in feedback processing. People who think differently may also be reactive and impulsive, having failed to integrate the social skills most of us take for granted. One of the successful machinery designers I worked with was brilliant. He could design anything, build it, and solve any mechanical problem. But he also had a horrible temper. One day, when I was visiting the plant, he started spewing some nasty stuff about the plant engineer. I quickly escorted him to one of the catwalks above the cattle, where his ranting could not be heard from the engineer's office.

In researching this book, I went back and reviewed all the large animal-handling projects I had worked on, concentrating on those where I had both designed the facility and supervised its construction: in other words, projects where I had spent extended periods of time on the job site and really gotten to know the employees. Both by their own admission and my informal analysis, I'd say that approximately 20 percent of the skilled draftspeople, machinery designers, and welders I encountered in these workplaces were autistic, dyslexic, or had undiagnosed ADHD. Most of these people were high school graduates who got into the field when they started working in a small shop. As I've mentioned, innovation most often occurs in small shops, and a couple of the success stories I pointed to earlier were of people who started their own small shops. Unfortunately, the young people who might have started their own shops or become apprentices in the trades are now being shunted to special ed and never given the opportunity to learn to use tools at all.

I recently came across a beautiful print shop in Maine called PrintCraft. The owner, Lisa Pixley, specializes in nineteenth- and twentieth-century printing presses and proudly showed me how they worked. Each press had its own mechanical setup, and she expertly worked the foot pedals and hand pulls as she guided the paper through the drum of each machine. I asked if she would take the visual-spatial test, and she scored as high as I did: a nearly pure visual thinker. Then I asked her how she did in school. She couldn't do math, especially algebra, and had been put in special ed. It had derailed her academic career for years. Too many of our visual thinkers wind up there. Fortunately, she discovered her love of printmaking and antique letter presses and became a master printer.

The Value of Exposure

Where do clever engineers come from?

Many people go into a particular career because they were exposed to it at an early age. In some cases, that's because it was their family business or profession. According to the SC Johnson College of Business at Cornell University, approximately 40 percent of family-owned businesses will turn over to the next generation. One in five medical students has a physician parent. And students with lawyer parents are seventeen times more likely to become lawyers. That's direct exposure, of a kind. But it's not the only way to gain exposure. I suspect that most young people have no idea of the range of career possibilities out there. One of my missions throughout all the talks I give is to open their eyes. That includes opening the eyes of parents and teachers.

In our schooling and parenting, we tend to forget that people need exposure to things that *don't* wind up on tests. Developing interests also expands a person's imagination and inner life. Even at the highest levels, enrichment also comes from non-academic exposure. According to Robert Root-Bernstein, a physiologist at Michigan State University, top scientists who have won the Nobel Prize were around 50 percent more likely to have a creative hobby than highly respected and successful scientists at large. Scientists who are at the top of their field often have diverse interests and are fascinated by many different subjects. One of the best examples is Einstein and his love of music. He credited music and playing the violin with helping him to formulate some his most influential theories; he was aspiring in his scientific thinking to capture some of the complexity and beauty of music.

I'm always impressed by stories in which even a small amount of exposure to something new has the potential to change the course of a life. Angelika Amon, a top scientist in cancer research, became interested in cell genetics after watching a single movie in a science class that showed chromosomes in a cell separating. In the case of Dr. Nita Patel, she was fortunate to have been exposed to an education in science and medicine, without which she would have never become one of the doctors on the cutting edge of the search for a COVID-19 vaccine. Coming from an impoverished background, she encountered an additional challenge when her father became disabled and could no longer work. Yet he deeply believed in her education, and with the help of a generous neighbor who provided bus fare, this little girl with no shoes prevailed.

Angela Duckworth asks what is more important for achievement: innate ability or effort? I have talked to many parents about their high school–age child who is either autistic or has a learning challenge. When I ask them about their child getting a job, they usually say, "We're thinking about it." I tell them that they need to act immediately. Working in construction taught me deadlines. In construction, projects need to get done: the customer wants the project finished on time. When I talk to parents and educators, I try to impart some of that urgency. "Early exposure, early intervention, early experience" is my mantra.

How would you feel about getting a fully funded education, with your housing costs covered and the guarantee of a job when you graduated? That's what the Apprentice School in Newport News, Virginia, offers. Of the more than four thousand applications it receives each year, it enrolls only 220 students, an acceptance ratio on a par with that of Yale or Harvard. The program, which has been around since 1919, offers four-, five-, and eight-year apprenticeships in shipbuilding. The main areas of study are business, communications, drafting, mathematics, physics, and ship construction. Your classroom might be the dry docks or a steel fabrication shop or a propulsion shaft repair facility. Additionally, you will learn life skills, including how to balance a checkbook, how to buy your first home, and etiquette for business dining. It's worth noting that the school is a division of Huntington Ingalls Industries, which designs, builds, and maintains ships for the US Navy and Coast Guard. Government funding ensures the health and well-being of the apprenticeship program, just as it maintains the fitness of the fleet. Without such deep-pocketed contractors, most companies couldn't afford such a lavish program. Still, it's a model for how companies can groom, grow, and retain a next generation of highly trained employees. According to the website, the apprenticeship "provides the company with a continuous supply of journeypersons who possess the skills, knowledge and pride of workmanship."

Apprenticeships have been used for centuries to train skilled workers. The great medieval cathedrals of Europe were constructed by people who started as apprentices. Workers who reached an advanced level of skill and experience entered the guilds for their respective crafts and were accorded high social status. These days, we assess ability by having students fill out tiny oblong bubbles with number-two pencils. I wonder how success would be measured if we asked young people instead to put a computer together, frame a room, or sew a pair of pants.

The popularity of apprenticeships in the United States declined in the early twentieth century as more children entered compulsory education. This trend continued as more of the population went on to higher education, and a lack of federal funding made paid apprenticeships less viable for employers. There is also a tendency in many countries for people of a certain social class to stick up their noses at skilled trades and to discourage their children from entering them. According to a Brookings Institution report by Brian A. Jacob, technical school is often considered a "dumping ground" for low-achieving kids. This fallacy is born of our prejudice that college is for everyone, that it's the only path to a high-paying job, and that working with your hands in a skilled trade is somehow less prestigious or valuable than careers that require academic degrees. Jacob cites the increase in required academic high school courses in the 1980s, coupled with the expectation that all young people should pursue college, as the reason for a sharp decline in career and technical education (CTE) participation, also known as vocational education. Between 1990 and 2009, the number of CTE credits earned by US high school students dropped by 14 percent. In a subsequent Brookings report on the struggle to bring back apprenticeships, Greg Ferenstein writes, "As college became the default path to top professions in the twentieth century, apprenticeships fell out of favor with America's upwardly mobile culture."

The entrenched prejudice against apprenticeships and vocational schools goes a long way toward explaining why we don't have a more thriving apprenticeship culture, even though, as we've seen in the previous chapter, a college education is hardly a guarantee of success given the dropout rates, high unemployment, and crippling debt. A report published by the Manhattan Institute found that 40 percent of recent college graduates end up in jobs that do not require a college degree. Statistics vary, but approximately 28 percent of graduates are unable to find a job within their field of study.

It's true that college graduates make more money on average than high school graduates, but there are lots of exceptions. Some examples of well-paid careers that do not require a four-year college degree are skilled tradesperson, computer coder, lab technician, designer, and film editor. I recently read an encouraging article in *The Wall Street Journal* by Tamar Jacoby, who reports on how credit and non-credit programs at community colleges are providing pathways to fulfilling employment for people who may not have finished high school and those who need retraining to stay current with technology, and in the process are filling a crucial jobs gap. "For most of their history, community colleges have lived in the shadow of traditional four-year colleges," Jacoby writes. "But that is changing as automation and business restructuring upend the labor market." She also points out that half of the eleven million students are in programs designed to prepare them for jobs. In fact, many of the programs are created with industry input.

In some places, government is taking the lead in creating opportunities for the kind of exposure to work that can make all the difference between kids' losing interest (and losing their way) and feeling a spark connecting their abilities, their interests, and their passions. According to Apprenticeship.gov, there are nearly 26,000 apprenticeship programs across the nation. The average starting salary after an apprenticeship program is completed is $72,000, with a 92 percent employment retention rate. The website lists hundreds of apprenticeships with major corporations. Many apprenticeships go unfilled. When our beautiful new chemistry building was being built at Colorado State University, the project manager told me that they were having difficulty hiring enough electricians to complete it. A quick Google search with the keywords "electricians apprenticeship Colorado" revealed more than a hundred job openings. These are entry-level jobs with training, full pay, and benefits.

Unemployment for American youth is currently at 8.3 percent. By comparison, Switzerland has kept its youth unemployment rate at 3 percent, a feat largely attributed to the "dual track" apprenticeship program that graduates roughly 70 percent of Swiss youth. It's also because apprenticeships are offered only where real job opportunities are available. The Swiss program works closely with industry to collaborate on curricula and programs, and Swiss employers pay for the training, in vocational professions that range from catering to high tech.

Most Americans are shocked to learn that Swiss students make the momentous decision of choosing a path forward at age fourteen. Two years later, they will either attend university or enter the apprenticeship program while they are still finishing school. The Swiss system gives students the flexibility to switch tracks. The internships are designed to give them skill sets, not pigeonhole them. They complete their education level while getting paid for their work. This way they also avoid accumulating the staggering debt many American students struggle with upon graduation. Another advantage of the system is that it exposes students to an adult work environment at a young age. According to a *Forbes* article, the Swiss apprenticeship model is "designed to fill the real needs of modern enterprises, which make them essential talent pools for some of the world's largest companies."

In addition to a certain snobbery about the trades, there is a pervasive cultural bias among Americans against choosing a career too early and thereby limiting a person's potential. There is a cherished belief in unlimited potential: in America, anyone can supposedly become anything. A friend's daughter lamented, upon receiving a liberal arts degree, that she didn't know how to *do* anything. I learned that she likes to work with her hands, which suggests she's on the visual-thinking spectrum. Eventually, she started working for a fabric artist, and she is now learning to upholster furniture. She is also pursuing her interest in the history and culture of textiles. This would provide an ideal opportunity to start her own business. There will always be a need for furniture reupholstering. A dual track of work exposure and academics might have better prepared my friend's daughter for a future she could have embraced upon graduating instead of feeling at sea. How many liberal arts graduates are in the same boat?

Every two years, students from around the world gather to participate in something called WorldSkills Competition—an Olympics for trade skills. They compete individually and in teams, not only at such bedrock skills as fitting pipes and welding machinery but also in new skills added every year as the world demands them, including robot integration systems, cloud computing, and cybersecurity. Switzerland always places among the top three countries. In 2019, Swiss students won sixteen medals, including five gold. Opportunities to learn such skills could be game changers for all students, but especially for visual thinkers, who often learn better through doing. A 2015 report from the Century Foundation authored by Clio Chang recommends that a national apprenticeship system could be a good part of the answer to our diminishing skilled workforce and a life raft for young people in search of employment.

These aren't your grandfather's apprenticeships, either. As with the World-Skills competitions, there is a greater emphasis on tech, which provides a pathway for the mathematically inclined visual-spatial thinkers. A Denver manufacturer, Noel Ginsburg, set out to replicate the Swiss apprenticeship program. What struck him, according to an *Atlantic* magazine story, was the breadth of available careers. "They have 250 pathways there, everything from manufacturing to banking," he said. Ginsburg corralled Colorado governor John Hickenlooper to help support the effort. Hickenlooper was aware that Colorado had the best economy and lowest unemployment in the nation but couldn't fill jobs in construction, health care, tech, and "everything in between." With government funding, and additional backing from philanthropic organizations and financial services, a statewide apprenticeship system was created, with the goal of giving students real-world experience and work-based learning to close the state's skills and labor gap. In states that have large numbers of manufacturers, there will usually be more of these programs.

It is important to distinguish between paid apprenticeships and the unpaid internships many college students pursue. Many students cannot afford to perform unpaid work. However, not all internships are unpaid. JBS Foods, the large meat company headquartered in Colorado, has paid summer internships where students learn management-level jobs in quality assurance. Often the intern is not only compensated but expected to meaningfully participate. In one internship at a meat plant, the student had to figure out why the electric pallet equipment was not able to work all day on a single charge. The student discovered that the company was using the wrong charger.

Or you could create your own internship program, the way I did when I was in graduate school. I spent one afternoon a week at a Swift plant, trying to figure out why cattle were balking and backing up as they went through the plant's chute. These disruptions were costing the plant time and money. I became obsessed with solving this problem and eventually visited more than twenty different cattle feedlots in Arizona until I had the watershed moment that became key to my work on cattle handling.

I counsel kids all the time to propose internships at local businesses, even if it means offering to work part-time for no pay. Work experience is invaluable. It gives students exposure to a field they may find an affinity with, and the opportunity to gain practical knowledge of real-life expectations and responsibility. According to a 2020 article in *Fast Company*, students with internships on their résumés received 14 percent more interviews when job hunting. Internships were also shown to decrease post-graduation unemployment by 15 percent, garner higher salaries, and improve grades. Employers also report better job performance hiring students with internship experience. In a survey conducted by the Association of American Colleges and Universities, 73 percent of employers favored skills acquired in real-life settings and hands-on experience in their candidates. And more than four in five employers believed that students who had completed a supervised internship or community service project would be better prepared for success on the job.

Many more internships are now paid, thanks in part to a series of legal judgments that recognized that work should be appropriately compensated. But it's still worth making the point that not all jobs are listed on LinkedIn or on a high school or college job board. Sometimes you just need to knock on doors to get your foot inside. I'll advise kids to reach out to friends, extended family, and people in the community to see if they need some help or can share a contact. At least half of all good jobs are obtained through connections, not by responding to an ad. A recent article on Payscale indicated that networking is the path to upwards of 80 percent of jobs. Job training programs put too much emphasis on interviewing and résumés. Recently, while visiting a major technology company, I had the opportunity to talk to a young man from the Midwest who worked on electronic hardware design. We were sitting in one of the company's trendy little cafés. I asked how he ended up in Silicon Valley. One of his college professors had a contact with the company and had put him in touch.

A formal internship program isn't essential. The coveted internships at places like Google, Facebook, and Apple are great and well paid, but the acceptance rate is minuscule. Google, for instance, accepts a mere 1,500 of some 40,000 applicants in a given year. You would do better to start your own tech company, as Stanford dropouts Larry Page and Sergey Brin did.

Apprenticeships, on the other hand, are always paid. They work on an "earn as you learn" model. When I looked up apprenticeships in my home state of Colorado, one jumped out at me from the many available. It was for an arborist, combining on-the-job training with classroom study. The apprentice would learn tree biology, tree climbing, disease diagnosis, and tree trimming. Pay would increase with experience, and upon completion of the program, the apprentice would receive a journeyman license from the US Department of Labor. A journeyman's license generally allows holders to bid for jobs, perform unsupervised work, and hire unskilled workers. Essentially, it allows you to be your own boss. I can think of at least two people I went to school with who couldn't sit still in class but would have loved to climb trees for a living. A search of Apprenticeship.gov will blow your mind as to how many opportunities are there: software development, roofing, manufacturing, utilities, hospitality, pipe fitting, and aerospace, to name a few. These are not dumping grounds. These are paid positions that offer an education and stable employment opportunities. I suspect that many would be ideal for visual thinkers who may or may not have excelled in a conventional school setting.

The Italian fashion industry provides another model. Italy has long been a center for high-end fashion design, but the availability of people with the hands-on skills needed to execute the work was not keeping pace with design and marketing. In an article in *The Business of Fashion*, Brioni CEO Francesco Pesci said, "Italy has always had excellent artisans and craftsmanship. . . . We have to invest in the training of young talent. We cannot allow for a generational gap." The industry took stock of the fact that its highly skilled craftspeople were retiring or dying off. Kiton CEO Antonio de Matteis said, "Our breed of tailor was literally going extinct." At first, Kiton had difficultly recruiting for its in-house technical school, but now there's a waiting list, in large part due to its 100 percent track record in achieving job placement for students. "It's the greatest investment we've ever made," de Matteis says.

Companies such as IBM have started similarly styled programs that focus on data analytics, cybersecurity, and software engineering—great opportunities for spatial visualizers. Pilatus Aircraft in Broomfield, Colorado, created an apprenticeship based on the dual-track Swiss model. Their program allows students to rotate among departments to see what they spark to. They leave the program debt-free and with marketable skills.

Job fairs have always been a staple of college job recruitment. The National Association of Colleges and Employers reports that 91.7 percent of college career centers host such fairs. Historically, they have tended to showcase financial services, consulting, health care, nonprofits, and internet jobs. In 2014, three students at Michigan Tech University developed a platform for internships and job placement that links colleges, employers, and students. Handshake is like a virtual job fair, with more than 500,000 participating employers that post jobs and internships. It also offers networking opportunities, seminars, and a new Rate My Professors–style feature to assess employers. What I really like about it is the opportunity for students to explore job opportunities and be exposed to careers they may not have known existed. Suddenly, your backyard becomes the entire country. The goal of Handshake goes deeper; the cofounders wanted to level the playing field. In a *Fast Company* article, Jason Aldrich, a Georgia State University assistant dean, reports, "It is already helping to democratize access to more opportunities for everyone on campus, particularly our first-generation and underrepresented minority students."

But while official channels such as job fairs and unofficial channels such as personal connections undoubtedly give a leg up, they aren't the only way to get work experience. Throughout my career, I have seen many examples of people who start on the bottom rung and work their way up. At a large beef plant, a woman of limited means (who likely had undiagnosed autism) got a job on the processing floor. The guys working there, who wanted to run her off, gave her the worst job. She persevered, and within a few years she had worked her way up to manager of a crew of about a hundred people. In another case, a man took a course in computerized drafting at a community college. A local company was hiring, and he showed them a single drawing of a water valve. They hired him, and before long, he was laying out and designing entire large beef plants. Another person got a job working on the line at such a plant, and ten years later was the plant manager. A project manager who started out in the maintenance department is now, fifteen years later, in charge of building a new plant addition.

What I've observed in my own industry is true of most industries. I will do an imaginary experiment. Let's say a magic wand were waved and I instantly changed into an eighteen-year-old who didn't graduate from high school because of failing algebra and couldn't afford to take an internship for no pay and had no idea about apprenticeships—but did have the big advantage of my seventy years of knowledge. I would head straight to Amazon or a similar operation. Amazon will help pay for your GED, as will Walmart, KFC, and other large corporations. My future goal would be either designing the robotic warehouse of the future or becoming involved with Amazon's space exploration department. The first step would be to learn every job on the floor and be a super-hard worker. At first, I would have to pay my dues, unloading trucks, and then gradually I'd work my way over to the robotics section. I know this is possible because I talked to a parent whose child went from an Amazon warehouse job to rocket design by mingling with the engineers in the cafeteria.

Sometimes it's a matter of getting your foot in the door and seeing what you can do once you're inside.

Are we willing to open new avenues of education like apprenticeships? Can we produce a twenty-first-century workforce of people with and without college degrees, verbal and visual thinkers, and the neurodiverse? Can we take our eyes off the tests and promote learning? Can we take our object and spatial visualizers and provide academic and career paths that play to their strengths? If we lose our clever engineers, we lose purchase on our future. Can we find the economic and political will to rebuild our infrastructure? More important, can we find—and nurture—the people to do it?

The widespread failure to recognize and foster the abilities of visual thinkers has both individual and systemic ramifications. On the individual level, there is much that parents, teachers, and employers can do. The systemic solutions require a collective embrace of the reality that diverse ways of thinking benefit all of us and that losing nonverbal thinkers is a tragedy that harms all of us.

I think often of a field trip I went on in fourth grade, to the Museum of Fine Arts in Boston. We were all fascinated by the mummies. As we made our way from room to room, from dynasty to dynasty, starting with the earliest and working our way up the timeline, I noticed that the decorations on the heads of the pharaohs' cases became rougher and cruder instead of the other way around. When I asked our teacher why, she said something I've never forgotten: "Their civilization was falling apart." I still think of that when I see infrastructure crumbling, when I see talent squandered or wasted. It really upsets me. Too many things are falling apart. Too many kids are falling through the cracks, their gifts and abilities squandered. Where are the clever engineers? Right in front of us.

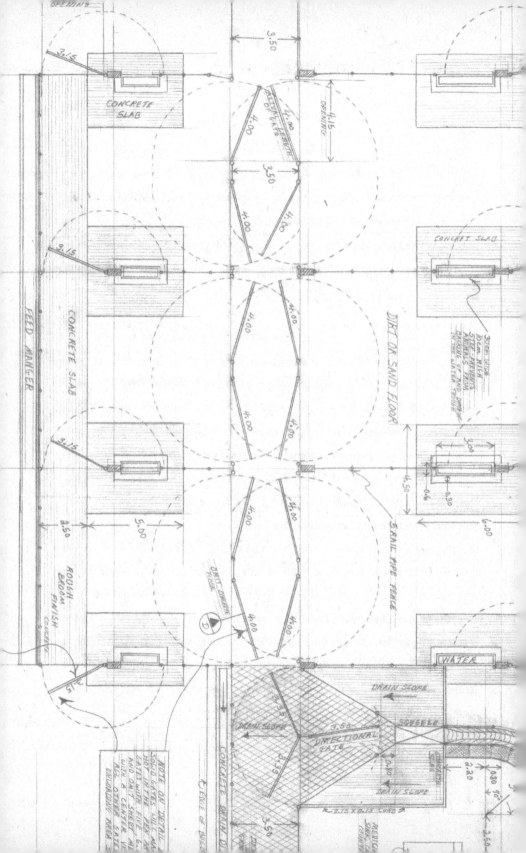

FOUR

Complementary Minds

The first step in successful collaboration between different kinds of thinkers is learning that different kinds of thinkers exist. That may sound obvious, but people tend to believe that everyone sees the world the way they do, just as I believed, well into my twenties, that everyone thought in pictures. When people discover that there are verbal, spatial, and object thinkers, they can more easily grasp how the different skill sets can be complementary. This is true in many fields, ranging from scientific research and computer science to engineering and the arts. A story I often heard as a child about my grandfather and his collaborators has always stayed with me.

It was the 1930s, and the large aeronautical companies were attempting to engineer an autopilot system for an airplane. They believed that if the plane's steering mechanism were connected to a compass needle, it would tell the direction. Made sense. But if you've ever held a compass, you've probably noticed something about the needle. It indicates direction, but it doesn't point steadily; it jiggles. You wouldn't want your car's cruise control wired to a jig-gling needle. The car would forever be lurching as it abruptly sped up and slowed down. Autopilot systems on planes faced a similar problem, but the engineers were so stuck in the compass mindset, they couldn't see another so-lution.

My grandfather John C. Purves, an MIT graduate and civil/mechanical engineer, decided to take an alternative approach. He partnered with a man named Haig Antranikian, who had an idea for making an airplane autopilot that was not connected to a compass needle. There was a model for such a de-vice, called the gyrocompass, used on American warships. Developed by Elmer Sperry, the gyrocompass withstood any fluctuation, but it was massive. The challenge was to adapt a lightweight version for flying.

Antranikian had been awarded a patent in 1936 for his magnetic field direc-tion and intensity finder. But his invention had been rejected by airplane instru-ment manufacturers; it was a brilliant idea going nowhere. Then Antranikian met my grandfather. According to my mother, Eustacia Cutler, my grandfather said, "Antranikian had the concept, but he didn't know what to do with it. I saw how to make it work."

Today, my grandfather's operation, which included two other men, Richie Marindin and Lennox F. Beach, would be called a garage start-up. The four men worked in Springfield, Massachusetts, in a loft above a trolley car repair shop. The idea behind the device they were developing was radical, but simple. A flux valve contained three little coils that read the direction of the earth's magnetic field when the device was rotated. The valve was installed in the plane's wing, where the coils would sense the direction of the earth's magnetic field as the plane turned. Sometimes it functioned perfectly when they tested it, and other times it went berserk. There seemed to be no rhyme or reason as to why.

Finally, my grandfather figured out the problem. The huge steel trains that intermittently rumbled beneath his workbench were disturbing the magnetic field. They acted like the metal detectors that you walk through at the airport. When the men took the flux valve to an open field outdoors, it worked perfectly. Building on Antranikian's patent, they worked on the device throughout the Great Depression, and the flux valve was eventually patented in 1945, with my grandfather as lead author. He was ecstatic when the autopilot for the first time guided a plane on a flight between major cities. My mother still recalls getting a phone call from him saying it was the happiest day of his life.

This group was a prime example of object visualizers collaborating with spatial visualizers, their respective skills complementing one another. However, what happened next is the story of so many inventors who have the vision and the skill but not the capital to manufacture and market their creations, nor the business acumen to sell or license them. After all their years of work, the men jumped at the chance to license the compass to the Bendix Aviation Corporation for $300. Bendix promptly ripped off the device and started selling it under the slightly altered name of "flux gate." It is hard to believe that my grandfather and his collaborators were that naive. They did not sue. World War II had begun, and they believed it unpatriotic to take legal action during wartime. The autopilot was needed in US planes to fight the war. Fortunately, the Sperry Corporation would later sign a legitimate contract with my grandfather, and the team was eventually compensated. Renamed the Sperry Gyrosyn Compass, it was used extensively in many fighter planes near the end of the war. I was excited to find an original 1945 advertisement, with the slogan "The Directional Gyro with Magnetic 'Sense.'"

According to my mother's memoir, *A Thorn in My Pocket*, my grandfather believed that original ideas come from "loners" like Antranikian. But without men like my grandfather and the rest of his team, Antranikian probably wouldn't have gotten out of the basement tinkering phase. Certainly, the flux valve exists because four men had complementary skills and a shared interest in an important project. A cornerstone in electronics, its patent continued to be cited in new patents up through 2006.

Sadly, Antranikian's life did not go well after the flux valve was successfully marketed. He eventually landed in Bellevue, the New York City hospital that became synonymous with mental illness. It's possible he was struggling with a spectrum disorder, given his loner tendencies, his highly visual mind, and his capacity for invention. As we'll see in the chapter on genius and neurodiversity, brilliance can come with a high cost. Over time his condition was stabilized, and he and my grandfather started working together on the development of color TV. But this time their work went nowhere, and neither man would invent anything else for the rest of his life. As my mother put it, "The fire had gone out of both of them."

Of the four partners, only one, Lennox Beach, went on to be hired by the Sperry Corporation, where he continued to have a successful career, earning multiple patents designing ship stabilization systems. Grandfather liked to say, somewhat judgmentally, that original ideas did not come from company men, because company men all think in a similar way. They can develop, refine, and market an idea but cannot originate it. Of the five major tech companies, four started as a garage operation or in a college dorm room, with two brilliant minds tinkering and dreaming together: Steve Jobs and Steve Wozniak created Apple, Bill Gates and Paul Allen created Microsoft, Sergey Brin and Larry Page created Google, and Mark Zuckerberg and Eduardo Saverin created Facebook.

In the late 1930s, the Sperry Corporation hired two brothers, Russell and Sigurd Varian, who exemplify the concept of complementary minds. Sigurd was a thrill seeker who dropped out of college, reportedly due to boredom, not unlike Jobs, Gates, Zuckerberg, and Musk. Russell was Sigurd's opposite—shy, with Asperger's traits. As a child, Sigurd was dyslexic (though he was thought to be illiterate, since dyslexia wasn't widely acknowledged as a condition), had other learning disabilities, and loved pranking people, using his curiosity about electronics to give visitors shocks through bedsprings and doorknobs.

(Pranking is often appealing to people on the spectrum, who may lack the nuanced social cues that jokes and ordinary banter require. As a teenager, Steve Wozniak loved pranking with electricity. According to Walter Isaacson in his biography of Steve Jobs, Wozniak "found an outlet playing juvenile pranks." In high school, Wozniak once rigged an electronic metronome in a locker to sound like a bomb about to go off, ticking faster as the locker door opened. He was sent for a night to juvenile detention, where he taught his fellow inmates to rig the wires from the ceiling fans to the bars of their cells, conveying a shock to anyone who touched them. In high school, I myself, inspired by Orson Welles's radio production of *The War of the Worlds*, built a flying saucer with a tiny light in a plastic dome. I climbed up to the roof of my dormitory and swung it in front of another student's window, completely freaking her out. Unlike Wozniak, I was never caught, though I proudly gave the student the saucer at the end of the semester.)

When Sigurd took up flying, the pair got the impetus to develop technology that could detect planes flying at night. Together they formed Varian Associates, a company that would go on to pioneer microwave and radiation therapy devices. According to the writer John Edwards on Electronic Design, "Relying on Russell's theoretical and technical knowledge, and Sigurd's mechanical abilities, they began developing plans for a device that could detect a signal bounced off an airplane several miles away." The brothers would eventually relocate their company to Stanford's industrial park in Palo Alto, which qualified it as one of the first high-tech companies in Silicon Valley. There they invented an instrument called the klystron tube, an early geophysical instrument that was a precursor to what we now think of as radar. The tube was compact enough to fit on a plane, where, via microwave technology, it could navigate through clouds and at night. This technology, combined with magnetrons that powered the transmitters, would be essential in establishing Allied dominance of the skies during World War II. The shy brother and the outgoing brother. The detail-oriented person who drills down versus the charismatic risk-taker. The spatial-math thinker and the object thinker. Complementary minds.

Observations of a Complementary Thinker

When I submitted the idea for my master's thesis on the effects of different squeeze-chute designs on cattle handling, the more traditional professors in the animal science department thought studying equipment was not suitable as an academic research project. To pursue my idea academically, I would need to find two advisers outside my department to approve the project. I was determined to conduct my study with or without the support of my department; at the very least, I figured, I could publish my findings in a cattle magazine. I still remember a poster in the university's art department that had caught my eye. It read, "Obstacles are those frightful things you see when you take your eyes off the goal." The quote was unattributed, but it spurred me on. Later, I would learn that it was from Henry Ford, a fellow industrial designer and (likely) object thinker.

Foster Burton in the construction department was the first to sign off on my project. He didn't think my idea was crazy. On the contrary, he sensed it was original and worth pursuing. Then an industrial design professor named Mike Nielsen agreed to be on my committee. Nielsen, likely another object visualizer, immediately saw the value in my proposal to evaluate the performance of existing equipment. Years later, I found an interesting video online discussing the differences between an industrial designer and a mechanical engineer. It became obvious to me, watching the video, that my approach to design had formed all the way back in graduate school. Programs in industrial design place a huge emphasis on art and drawing, with far less on math. Industrial designers develop ideas about how a product should work or look. The mechanical engineer calculates a product's functionality by looking at the mathematics of stress tests and physical forces. The industrial designer creates the design, and an engineer makes it function. I would see these complementary skills play out again and again over the course of my career.

When I met Jim Uhl, a former Marine Corps captain, my career started in earnest. Jim sought me out after he had seen some of the drawings I had worked on in graduate school. I was finishing school, and he was looking for designers for his new company building cattle-handling facilities in Arizona. At first I was reluctant to take the job. Jim wanted me to do the design work, but he also wanted me to help him sell the construction jobs. I was never a highly verbal person, and I was more comfortable doing the behind-the-scenes design work. We didn't use terms like "diverse" back then when it came to hiring, but it's clear to me now Jim wasn't concerned if a person had a disability. We never once discussed my autism. He valued the quality of my design work, and he believed I should be out front selling it. I quickly learned that the best way for me to sell a new client a design project was by showing a portfolio of drawings and photos of completed facilities. I would let my visuals do the talking.

In the mid-1970s, when Jim and I first teamed up, I still had not grasped that different types of thinking existed. When I look back on our fruitful collaboration, it is now obvious to me that Jim and I solved problems differently. With the knowledge I have now, I am almost certain that Jim was a verbal thinker. When we would spec a new plant, he would need to see everything laid out in a linear fashion and would then spend several days cataloging every gate hinge and several nights crunching numbers. I, on the other hand, estimated the new projects by visualizing them as either fractions or multiples of old jobs. For example, the amount of labor, welded steel, and concrete in the new project would be equal to two Lone Mountains, which was a ranch corral, or three quarters of the Red River dip vat project. Both methods were accurate, and our collaborations were successful; neither one of us knew why we did things differently.

Jim was a superb manager with impeccable ethics. He greatly valued the input of different minds, including not only mine but those of a local retired businessman and a young high school graduate named Mark Adams, who is now vice president of the company. Jim's ability was leadership, and he hired diverse teams of people to build the projects. There was one talented young man who did most of the construction on my dip vat projects. The guy was kind of wild, but even after he crashed a company truck, Jim told me he kept him on because he was so talented. Jim also hired people from the local Native American community, as his construction office was located on the Salt River Pima-Maricopa Indian Community. Jim was an important mentor who helped get my career started; I don't know if I would have had the confidence to start my own company without his mentoring and support. For ten years we did projects together, including the dip vat that is shown in the HBO movie based on my life.

When the Arizona agriculture business dried up in the 1980s and Jim could no longer compete with the big construction companies on prices for conventional building projects, he reinvented his company. He specialized in building complex concrete structures that the big companies did not want to spend their time on. I was in Illinois working on my PhD in animal science. When I came back to visit, he proudly showed me a complex concrete structure to hold the pumps and equipment for a huge irrigation system. Jim did not have any idea how to design this structure, but he had continued to exercise his knack for putting together diverse teams of people to do what needed to be done.

The design of the center-track conveyor system is a perfect example of complementary minds at work. It started out as a research project at the University of Connecticut in the 1970s. The idea of having an animal straddle a conveyor came from Paul Belanger, an object visualizer who worked in the experiment station shop. Paul could build anything, and he is rightly included on the original patent, though Ralph Prince, the engineer with the university degree, is listed as the first author. Prince, along with academic researchers Rudy Westervelt and Walter Giger, conducted the studies that verified this method as a low-stress, humane method for restraining sheep and calves, as measured by both behavior and stress hormone levels in the animals.

Together, the research group built a working model from plywood, using an old canvas fire hose for the conveyor. The model was brought to a metalworking shop, where it was refabricated in steel. It was installed alongside the old system, so that the plant could keep operating while the different designs were tested. It wasn't until we were on-site that it became apparent that the university researchers had missed two critical design elements, relating to the entrance as well as the method of adjusting the width for different-sized animals. I was enlisted to work on that.

One day, using plywood to make a mock-up of the width-adjustment device, I suddenly had a picture appear in my imagination. I saw the solution that would make the entrance work. This is a perfect example of how my visual mind functions. After collating all the relevant images from the bottom up, it produces a solution, fully formed. I can literally see it. To encourage the animals to correctly place their legs on either side of the conveyor every time, I designed a leg-positioning bar that was almost high enough to touch the animal's belly. Previous experiments with a lower bar had failed. The higher bar gave them a sense of security, as did adding a non-slip entrance to the ramp. The cattle walked over a high bar more easily than a lower one because it automatically put their legs in the correct position and steadied them. So I joined the team as yet another diverse mind. The project wouldn't have succeeded without the guy in the shop who thought it up, the scientists who tested it, the welder who built it, and the visual thinker who spotted and corrected a key flaw—not to mention the crew who repaired and maintained the equipment to keep it in good running order.

Forty years later, I have designed many stockyards and cattle-handling facilities for the large US and Canadian beef companies. The most widely adopted model for livestock handling is the center-track conveyor system. While working on these projects, I, like my mentor Jim, have relied on people with different types of skills to make it all work. I draw the detailed plans and design the parts of the mechanical restraining devices that come in contact with the animals. Other members of the team design the hydraulic power units and the supporting steel framework. I have been on many construction sites where large meat-processing plants were built. The object visualizers designed all the intricate equipment, such as the packaging machine. The engineers used their mathematical minds to come up with structural specifications and design the boilers and refrigeration units. Together we create large, multifaceted food-processing plants.

The object thinker often excels at inventing simple solutions that other kinds of minds may overcomplicate. In her book *What Can a Body Do?* Sara Hendren, a design researcher at Olin College of Engineering, describes a woman who had lost her fingertips. She found that her simple, improvised solutions worked better than the fancy robotic hand prosthesis she had been fitted with. She favors her homemade solutions, such as cable ties on drawer handles, a holder for playing cards, and adhesive picture hooks that allow her to open jar lids. The high-tech hand was designed to do everything, but it could not do many tasks well.

As robots are increasingly being used in factories, there is a great need for more people in the clever engineering department to innovate their use. In the food-processing industry, there is a drive to use robots to do tasks that people do by hand with a knife. The mistake many engineers make is to start with the decision to use the same tool a person would use, just attached to a robotic arm that will duplicate the task as a person would do it. But I have observed truly innovative tools that are designed to allow robotic arms to perform the same task in totally new ways. These tools are often simpler, do a better job, and are easier to clean and maintain. Achieving such a result requires both an object visualizer to create the tool and a spatial visualizer to program the robot.

Suits vs. Techies

I've worked with lots of corporations over the years, and I've observed that the problems that arise within them can often be boiled down to battles between the suits and the techies. I'm a techie, but I've always gotten along with the suits. It's not that I always agree with them, but early on in my career I realized that the way to get things done was to be "project loyal." More important than any ego was the goal to do the best work and get the job done. Most projects crash and burn, as far as I can tell, from an abundance of ego. I think I speak for most techies when I say we will go the distance to get a project done. That is our chief objective: our loyalty is to the project, not to management. We'll sit around in the job trailer and complain about what an idiot the manager is, but we'll get the machine working. I will grovel in the dirt if needed to get a job done right. I am completely driven by project loyalty over ego.

What I've noticed is that most of the time, techies pretty much hate the suits, while the suits tolerate the techies. Techies tend to dislike the suits because they do not want to know how to make things. Verbal-thinking suits who just want to get the job done tend to overgeneralize, which more than irritates techies. Generalization is death to a techie, because every minor detail has major consequences. Perhaps the biggest consequence of generalization is underestimating the time it takes to complete a project. And the bigger a suit's ego, the more destruction they will do.

Another difference between the suits and the techies is that the suits are motivated by money and turning a profit, which of course they need to focus on for their businesses to stay solvent. But too often, ethics go out the window as suits, under pressure to make quarterly financial goals, rack up safety violations in the pursuit of cost cutting. I've seen guys lose limbs when production was speeded up or safety measures willfully disregarded. I've also observed that techies tend to have a more developed sense of social justice. For the suits, doing something bad is an abstraction and easier to justify. For a techie, there is nothing abstract about the nuts and bolts or a coworker getting seriously injured.

One example of things going terribly wrong happened after a salesperson had been promoted to head up construction and remodeling at a plant. He was personable and highly verbal, could talk people into anything, could talk up a storm. I'm sure that's a big part of how he got the job. Management wanted to cut costs, and he convinced them it could be done. At one plant, over the warnings of the company's visual thinkers, he failed to expand the wastewater treatment system adequately, to save money, and overloaded it as a result. The city shut down the plant, and millions of dollars were lost. I could see why he was such a great salesperson, but as a construction manager, he was a disaster. Techies and suits may seem like complementary minds because they are interdependent, but often they don't see eye to eye.

I have been working with some of the same people for major portions of my career. Even some of the suits, though they come and go a little more frequently. In some ways, the industrial designers and I are like old married couples who don't need to say much to know what the other person is thinking. These are the rewards of a long career, of finding complementary minds. Not long ago, I drove by a derelict building, now abandoned, with dirty-yellow corrugated siding and just tall enough to hold some basic steel and machine shop equipment. It was the original shop of a welder I worked with thirty years ago on a small cattle-handling system. As with me, algebra was not his best subject in school. Fortunately, he was introduced to welding in a high school shop class. He started out by doing a tiny project for me. I could give him the design specs for anything, and he'd build it. Years later, it occurred to me that he was a visual thinker. We also shared the same work ethic. He would never use cheap supplies, would never rush a job, and would always guarantee his work. He was 100 percent project loyal. Now he zooms around from job to job in a private jet and builds huge projects for the meat industry.

Another colleague manufactures specialized meat-cutting saws and other equipment. He sells his products all around the world. He drives a sports car, and he flew me out to his factory in his corporate jet. When I arrived, we went right to his machine shop, no cup of coffee, no pleasantries. He hadn't changed. Like me, he was totally focused on his work. That is a true meeting of minds.

Two Geeks Are Better Than One

The German architect Walter Gropius famously said, "Architecture begins where engineering ends." The observation speaks to a sharp division between the fields and the status they're generally accorded. You can probably name a few famous architects (Frank Lloyd Wright, I. M. Pei, Philip Johnson), but you probably couldn't name a single engineer unless you knew one personally. While one field couldn't exist without the other, the architects generally get the attention and credit for their aesthetically daring or beautifully harmonized designs. Figuring out how to bring those designs to life and make the resulting buildings safe for human beings falls under the engineer's domain. Experience and observation suggest that architects are generally object visualizers who see their buildings in their mind's eye, while engineers are generally spatial visualizers, their mathematical minds running electrical systems, calculating the wind and snow load on the structure, and so forth.

To look at whether mechanical engineers and industrial designers see the world differently, researchers David Cropley from the University of South Australia School of Engineering and James C. Kaufman from the University of Connecticut's Neag School of Education conducted a study. One hundred twenty undergraduate engineering and industrial design students participated. Subjects evaluated photos of different types of chairs for functionality, creativity, and aesthetics, on a five-point scale. The chairs included a wide range of designs, from a top-of-the-line ergonomic office chair to a beanbag to chairs that looked like sculptures.

To the mechanical engineers, "looking nice and working seem to go hand in hand." They tended to rate the functionality of each chair similarly to its aesthetics. The industrial designers, however, differentiated between aesthetics and functionality. In other words, the engineers had more difficulty separating form from function, while the designers were better at discriminating between aesthetics and functionality. Functionality for me is comfort. I rated the fancy office chair high for functionality, low for aesthetics. The chair I hated for both functionality and aesthetics was an outdoor chair molded out of curved plywood. When I looked it up online, I discovered that it was in the Museum of Modern Art! The study revealed that not only are aesthetics and functionality separate things, but they exist largely in the eye of the beholder. Take the study a step further, and we can extrapolate that the mechanical engineers are the mathematical thinkers and the industrial engineers are object thinkers.

The father of the modern skyscraper, Major William Le Baron Jenney, was both an architect and an engineer, which may explain how he was able both to dream of a ten-story building and have the mechanical engineering skills to support it. The Home Insurance Building in Chicago was the tallest in the country at the time of its construction, and the first to use iron and steel beams instead of brick and stone to create the inner frame. It marked the transition from using heavy, load-bearing walls to structural frames that were open and light filled. The building also boasted fireproofing, modern plumbing, and Otis elevators. According to Kevin Baker's book *America the Ingenious*, architectural historian Carl Condit called the building "the most important innovation in architecture since the introduction of the Gothic cathedral in the twelfth century." To me, the building looks like it was designed by an engineer. It is a functional tall rectangle, and it is not aesthetic. My guess is that Jenney, while he was an architect, was primarily a visual-spatial mathematical thinker whose driving interest was to calculate and construct a steel frame that would not collapse.

Clare Olsen and Sinéad Mac Namara, in their book *Collaborations in Architecture and Engineering*, point out that the difference between the way architecture and engineering are taught is emblematic of the division between the two disciplines. Even the physical space of the classroom speaks to different learning styles. The engineering class is made up of uniform rows of desks in a sterile room. In the architecture class, the students are scattered around a large worktable, and art and drawings are tacked to the wall. It looks more like an art studio than a classroom. The engineering curriculum is "deterministic," attacking technical skills one problem at a time. The architecture curriculum is more open-ended; the emphasis is on creativity.

Architecture and engineering used to stay in their silos. The architects had the vision, the engineers implemented it. For the same rendering of an arc, the engineer uses a single line and a mathematical equation to describe the shape of the curve. The architect draws a three-dimensional rendering with a geometrical top. "The success of collaborations and the composition of the design team," write Olsen and Mac Namara, "can make or break a project." How do you get people who see the world so differently to work together? Peter Simmonds, the mechanical engineer who worked with the architecture firm Morphosis on 41 Cooper Square in New York City, said, "You have to discuss the project with the architects. There is no point in coming with a lot of math to an architect. That is just not effective. They are looking for the big picture, or the artistic solution; you have to learn how to communicate with them."

Andrew Saint, in his well-documented *Architect and Engineer: A Study in Sibling Rivalry*, notes that in the late Middle Ages, there was little division among building trades. Masonry and carpentry were the primary means of construction, and they were in the hands of experienced craftsmen, or "master builders." Saint attributes the division between architects and engineers to the period from the middle of the eighteenth century to the turn of the twentieth, driven by the development of machinery and new building materials, namely iron, steel, and reinforced concrete. Saint writes, "Many men skilled with machines came out of or comingled with the building trades, the carpenters especially. Someone with the capacity to design a building might also design the equipment that helped make it, too." The split between engineers and architects was gradual and developed as a result of greater specialization. One example Saint points to is railway stations, which are "multifunctional," requiring engineers to "create the locomotives, the rails, the earthworks, the bridges and stations." Ideally, architects, engineers, contractors, and fabricators work holistically in such settings.

One of the most famous examples of an engineer-architect is Gustave Eiffel, whom we easily recognize for his famous tower in Paris. Eiffel began his career as a fabricator-contractor of railway bridges. According to Saint, this experience afforded him familiarity with mechanical and structural skills, as well as with all kinds of equipment. When the 1889 world's fair was announced, Eiffel was working with two engineers, one of whom, Maurice Koechlin, produced the first sketch of what would become the Eiffel Tower. When the competition for the architects and engineers who would represent France at the exhibition was held, Eiffel and his associate Stephen Sauvestre won the bid along with two other architects. Saint points out that the tower was considered a "triumph of iron and therefore of the engineer." Yet Eiffel credited Sauvestre with the beautiful structure of the tower, saying, "The first principle of the aesthetics of architecture is that the essential lines of a monument should be determined by their perfect appropriateness to their end." This strikes me as the marriage between the object-visual thinker (Sauvestre) and the visual-spatial thinker (Eiffel).

At their very best, architects and engineers discover extraordinary synergy and work together for decades. Cecil Balmond and Rem Koolhaas are one such team. They have collaborated on numerous projects, including the Kunsthal in Rotterdam, the Seattle Central Library, and the Casa da Música in Porto, Portugal. With ever more ambitious structures and the arrival of new technologies and materials, the collaboration became more and more seamless. In an interview with Michael C. Y. Fei, Balmond explains that the top-flight architects with whom he collaborates recognize the way his mind works. "They engage with my architectural sensibilities about engineering possibility," he observes. "Architecture and engineering overlap in the abstract." In a *New Yorker* profile, "The Anti-Gravity Men," Balmond further explains that from the outset of their collaboration, "Rem found architecture wanting, and I found the whole work of structural engineering wanting." Their longings to address those deficits complemented each other. They found a common language, or, as Koolhaas described it, "a kind of telepathic communication, almost."

I've mentioned that I'm a NASA geek. One of the things I've long noted is that everything in NASA's space station is purely functional, with no attempt to make it look pretty. In fact, it looks like a junkyard, with the detritus of monitors, wires, cables, plugs, and panels all in a jumble, as if a hurricane had passed through. One of the exercise machines looked like something somebody built in a home workshop. It was pretty clear to me that the space station was designed by an engineer with little concern for aesthetics.

Enter Elon Musk. You can imagine how excited I was to learn that Musk was getting ready to launch his 2020 SpaceX Crew Dragon capsule to dock with the International Space Station. I think I watched every minute of the broadcast. I knew from the minute I saw the jet bridge that we were in another universe, in the mind of a total visual thinker. The bridge to the Crew Dragon capsule looks like a movie set for *2001: A Space Odyssey*. In contrast, NASA's jet bridge looks like construction scaffolding put together like erector sets. When you enter the SpaceX capsule, everything is white, with wide touchscreens for the instrument panel. NASA uses helmet designs similar to those of fighter pilots; Musk's helmets were inspired by Daft Punk, and the spacesuits were designed by a Hollywood costume designer, Jose Fernandez, who designed suits for several Marvel movies. Musk was adamant that SpaceX lease Launch Pad 39A, which was used for the original Apollo trip to the moon. I realized that he cared about how every single detail looked. He wanted to link up to history. I totally flipped out watching his operation lift off.

I think Musk is more than a visual thinker. It's clear he's that rare mind that can both design and build; like Jenney, he has vision but also the skills to implement: object and spatial. I wasn't surprised to learn from a recent interview with Y Combinator that Musk spends 80 percent of his time in the engineering and design departments of SpaceX and Tesla developing next-generation products. "My time is almost entirely with the engineering team . . . dealing with aesthetics and look-and-feel things." He knows every bolt on his rockets. For him, it's all about building good stuff that works.

One of the things I most admire about Musk is his visual imagination. Everything on that spacecraft was created to look cool, to give people the sense of childlike wonder that so many felt watching Apollo 11 land on the moon. I wondered how Musk was able to run SpaceX and Tesla and still spend most of his time with the designers. That's when I discovered he had a right-hand man—only it was a woman named Gwynne Shotwell, SpaceX employee number seven. Shotwell had been with the company since 2002 and is now the president and COO. She runs the day-to-day operations, including budgets and legal affairs. A number of articles credit her with managing Musk's mercurial personality, but I think it's his brain that she gets, in part because she has a bachelor's degree in mechanical engineering and a master's in applied mathematics. She understands the science, she's inspired by Musk's vision, but what she loves is to make the rockets run on time. In an interview with the NASA Johnson Space Center Oral History Project, Shotwell said, "I have no creative bones in my body at all. I'm an analyst, but I love that." Two geeks are better than one.

Steve Jobs's mania for beauty, for the marriage of form and function, culminated in the iPhone but started with a fascination with fonts. "It was beautiful, historical, artistically subtle in a way that science can't capture, and I found it fascinating." This quote is from Steve Jobs's now-famous Stanford University commencement address in which he talks about the calligraphy class he informally sat in on at Reed College after dropping out. His pleasure in talking about dropping out to a lawn full of freshly minted graduates is evident, and he underscores that it was the classes he chose to take as opposed to the curriculum forced upon him that made all the difference. The beauty of calligraphy had a big influence on Jobs's design philosophy for the early Apple computers. They were both beautiful and intuitive to use. "The main thing in our design is that we have to make things intuitively obvious," he told the graduates. What Steve Jobs accomplished was taking computers from gadgets that only computer hobbyists could use to a consumer product anyone could use.

To make a beautiful computer functional, there needs to be a techie who can design the electronic circuits that will make it work. Steve Wozniak was the perfect partner for Jobs. Walter Isaacson writes, "It may have been the most significant meeting in a Silicon Valley garage since Hewlett went into Packard's thirty-two years earlier." Wozniak wrote in his book that all he wanted to do was design circuits and "come up with clever ideas and apply them." Walter Isaacson writes of their collaboration, "Jobs had a bravado that . . . could be charismatic, even mesmerizing, but also cold and brutal. Wozniak, in contrast, was shy and socially awkward, which made him seem childishly sweet." Isaacson goes on to quote Jobs on the partnership: "Woz is very bright in some areas, but he's almost like a savant, since he was so stunted when it came to dealing with people he didn't know. We were a good pair."

In the 1970s, when the two Steves were working on the Apple II, they got into their first argument. Jobs wanted to simplify the computer so that it would be easier to use, providing only two ports, one for the printer and one for the modem. Wozniak wanted eight connector ports so that it could be upgraded for future functions. Jobs was convinced that for computers to become household appliances, they had to be less complex. According to Isaacson, Jobs wanted a "seamless end user experience." The techie wanted all the bells and whistles, but Jobs knew that for most people, additional features just cause confusion and make the computer not only more difficult to use but aesthetically less appealing. He wanted a product you could take out of the box, plug in, and start using. Form and function were at a crossroads.

Unsurprisingly, Jobs and Wozniak split after ten years. Apple went on to introduce computers that users gush over and iPhones they are glued to. Product loyalty is so high that people wait in long lines whenever a new version of the phone is introduced. What got the company there was a new partnership, between Jobs and designer Jony Ive, who became senior vice president of design in 1997. Isaacson writes, "In Ive, Jobs met his soul mate in the quest for true rather than surface simplicity." Jobs told his biographer, "If I had a spiritual partner at Apple, it's Jony. Jony and I think up most of the products together and then pull others in and say, 'Hey, what do you think about this?' He gets the big picture as well as the most infinitesimal details about each product."

Reaching Across the Aisle

The first step in a successful collaboration, as previously mentioned, is recognizing that different ways of thinking exist. Again, it sounds simple, but it's not easy to reorient the way you think or to step into another's shoes. People are attached to the way they do things because it emanates from how they see the world. It's not just habit or training, though habit and training make the ways we think more entrenched.

One of the worst experiences I've heard about involved a group of consultants who were brought into a dysfunctional company to help the various departments communicate better. Groups of people from different departments were put together and tasked with doing everything from community projects to making a parachute for an egg drop to trust exercises where you fall backward into someone's arms. These highly artificial exercises only irritated the employees and made them feel less inspired to collaborate. What did an egg parachute have to do with getting their product to market more efficiently?

On the top of my list for helping departments work better together is establishing respect. You're not going to get the suits and techies to fall backward into each other's arms and have a kumbaya moment. I suggest people from different departments shadow one another to understand one another's processes. I recommend different departments offer presentations on their projects. Much can be solved with better communication, but first you need to recognize that the various specialties each have their own language. An art director and a number cruncher basically live on different planets, which is why the art budget gets shredded when a suit has no understanding of why a high-priced scanner or some such is needed to keep pace with productivity.

A chart published by Richard Van Noorden in *Nature* magazine showed that some scientific disciplines participate in more interdisciplinary collaboration than others. Researchers in health sciences collaborate much more with those outside their field than do specialists in clinical medicine, for instance. One of the reasons for better collaboration among the health researchers is necessity. A project called the Research Excellence Framework assessed the strengths of different areas of research in the United Kingdom. The project revealed that the greater the impact of academic research outside of academia, the greater the likelihood that it required collaboration across multiple scientific disciplines. Yet the emphasis on career advancement within a narrowly specialized field tends to discourage many scientists from such collaborations, because they fear it may slow down their professional advancement.

In another study of collaboration, researchers wanted to see if pairing object visualizers with spatial visualizers would produce better results. Anita Williams Woolley and her colleagues at Harvard and Stanford started with the assumption that individuals in groups function like the brain, in that different systems are required to process information. Different kinds of thinkers work together much as the ventral visual system, responsible for processing shapes and objects (along with color and texture), works with the dorsal visual system, which processes spatial relations. The researchers assembled one hundred teams of two partners and challenged them to complete a virtual maze, tagging twin "greebles"—little Pac-Man-style figures—along the way. Some of the teams were composed of same-style thinkers, while others were paired with different thinkers. Navigation through the maze and tagging required spatial thinking. Remembering where the greebles were required object thinking.

When the teams were mixed, the visual-spatial thinkers tended to take control of the joystick, while the object visualizer used the keyboard to tag greebles. It was found that teams composed of both types of thinkers tended to outperform homogeneous teams, "demonstrating the benefits of having diverse task-specific abilities in a team." In fact, the more the homogeneous groups collaborated, the less well they performed, spending more time in conversations that didn't lead to results. Anyone who's been caught in one of those endless company meetings that don't resolve anything knows the frustrating feeling.

The research supports the idea that successful teams are composed of people with different neurological strengths, and as discussed in previous chapters, people who are good at one kind of visual thinking usually are not good at the other. Kim Kastens, a researcher at the Earth Observatory, Columbia University, who studies among other things spatial thinking in geosciences, recognizes the value of both object visualization and visual-spatial thinking. Object visualizers are generally good at analyzing satellite images, identifying rocks and minerals, and comprehending sonar imagery, for example. The more mathematically inclined spatial visualizers are better suited to visualizing three-dimensional data, whether it is presented numerically or as graphs.

Two examples of collaborations that have always inspired me bring me back to NASA. One collaboration involved a team of seamstresses and their self-taught engineering managers, and the other involved a brilliant and largely unsung computer engineer.

The public was barely aware that the International Latex Corporation (ILC) won a contest in 1965 against two other companies to design and produce the spacesuits that the first Apollo astronauts would wear. (Yes, ILC is the parent company of bra and girdle maker Playtex.) This fact became more widely known when Nicholas de Monchaux published a book on the history of the Apollo spacesuits in 2011. There were two main challenges to the design. First, the suit had to be inflated and pressurized from the inside and able to withstand extreme temperatures on the outside. But just as daunting, the suits had to be flexible: "The gloves, said one official, should allow an astronaut to pick up a dime," explained an article in *Fast Company*. The prototype designs by the "big government contractors, like Litton Industries and Hamilton Standard, made stiff, bulky spacesuit prototypes that often looked like a cross between Sir Galahad and Buzz Lightyear," CBS News reported.

ILC's suit was more flexible and was a clear winner. It is likely that the male engineers and macho atmosphere that pervaded NASA made it difficult to countenance the thought of a bra manufacturer winning the contract and potentially dubbing its creation the "Playtex Living Spacesuit." But Playtex had a secret weapon in addition to the flexible fabric: expert seamstresses. The approach to problem solving at ILC was totally different from the approach of the mathematically inclined engineers at NASA. They often clashed. The engineers wanted precise drawings, and ILC used cardboard patterns from which the seamstresses sometimes departed while sewing. A seamstress told the NASA technical team, "It might look all right on that piece of paper, but I'm not going to sew that piece of paper." Credit is long overdue to the Playtex women for their meticulous sewing of the lunar spacesuits. According to CBS, "Each suit was comprised of 21 layers of gossamer-thin fabric, sewn to a precise tolerance of 1/64th of an inch." One woman confessed that she cried almost every night because she knew the astronauts' lives depended on her work. This band of visual thinkers made the suits possible.

Hal Laning, a computer scientist with degrees in chemical engineering and applied mathematics, worked in a messy office at MIT, and out of an aversion for the spotlight rarely published a paper. You would never know that his invention cleared the way for Apollo 11's successful lunar launch. Like Katherine Johnson, Laning was obsessed with numbers from the time he was very young. Every Sunday, he used the hymn numbers on the signboard outside the church to make up math problems. Colleague Donald Fraser said, "He could read a hexadecimal dump of data as easily as I could read a novel. At any time challenged, he could recite at least the first thirty digits of pi." In the case of Apollo 11, two innovations were mission-critical. Laning employed silicon integrated-circuit chips, which were small and lightweight (their advent would speed up the microchip technology that we all take for granted). Until then, computers were the size of multiple refrigerators. Interestingly, the tiny metal cores were also sewn, by women who were employed by Raytheon because of their experience weaving.

Laning masterminded a relatively primitive computer system that could process the algebraic equations necessary for the lunar module to function, effectively creating a compiler that turned the equations into understandable computer language. Laning freely acknowledged that others did the programming, but it was his three-tiered processing system that prioritized tasks and thus enabled Neil Armstrong to take partial control of the module when the system was overloaded, readjust the radar to its correct setting, and disconnect it to prevent the computer from further overloading. Laning's compiler essentially taught the computer how to read and interpret algebraic equations and then figure out how to multitask by switching between tasks in a fraction of a second. The algebraic compiler was an innovative idea that made a computer with limited memory work. The success of the moon landing would not have been possible without it.

Two totally different types of thinkers were mission-critical: scientists and seamstresses.

Verbal, Meet Visual

Twenty-five years ago, when I was working on *Thinking in Pictures*, my editor Betsy Lerner remembers, her desk and floor were covered with piles of paper, her office walls plastered in Post-it notes. I'm a total picture-thinker, and Betsy lives in a world of words. It was a huge challenge for her to help me arrange my thoughts in a linear fashion. Not only do I think in pictures, but my mind is associative. It creates chunks of visualized information and makes associations. To a verbal thinker, these associations may appear random, but in my mind I'm continuously sorting the images. Betsy, on the other hand, is a strictly linear verbal thinker. She needs a sentence to be grammatically correct before she can understand it and move on to the next. We learned that we think completely differently, but that difference became the cornerstone of our future collaborations. To the uninitiated verbal thinker, my initial draft would have looked like a disjointed series of chunks. Betsy takes my pictures and puts them in order.

Here's our process: For each chapter, I write the initial draft. Then Betsy rearranges it. She is the master organizer of information, and I love how she teases out the stories behind my technical writing. Verbal thinkers love stories; things make sense to them when they can identify a beginning, middle, and end. As an object thinker, I pull disparate visual information together and organize it in my mind. Spatial visualizers make sense of the world using codes, patterns, and abstractions. Betsy also asks lots of questions, especially about how things work. These things are super-obvious to me, but her questions show me how verbal thinkers process information and help me focus in on how to explain scientific and engineering stuff to them. It has been a learning experience for me to understand how a verbal writer thinks differently from how I do. She has made me better at explaining things. Again, the first step is accepting that all types of minds have their own unique way of contributing to solving problems and furthering knowledge.

Two geniuses are responsible for deciphering the Rosetta Stone, the famous tablet that had three languages engraved on it: Egyptian hieroglyphics, Egyptian simplified writing, and Greek. The stone included beautiful carved figures of birds, lions, and snakes interspersed with non-pictorial symbols. The story of how the hieroglyphs were deciphered is told in *The Writing of the Gods: The Race to Decode the Rosetta Stone* by Edward Dolnick.

Both men were child prodigies who learned to read at a young age. It is likely that they both had autistic traits. Thomas Young was trained as a medical doctor but also published important studies on the physics of light waves. He effortlessly used math to solve scientific problems, as if they were fun puzzles. He had no particular interest in Egyptology. To decipher the Rosetta Stone, he used a strictly mathematical approach, similar to that of a code-breaking computer. He figured out that some of the pictorial hieroglyphs stood for speech sounds. But his computational approach could solve only part of the problem. Fully deciphering the Rosetta Stone required a different type of knowledge.

Jean-François Champollion grew up in France, where he taught himself to read by listening to chanted and sung Catholic masses and comparing the sounds he heard to writing in a prayer book. By age sixteen, he had mastered six languages, and by nineteen he became a university professor. He disliked math and had a one-track mind focused on all things Egyptian, no matter how remote the connection. Champollion used an associational approach to finish solving the puzzle of the Rosetta Stone. He had a hunch that the Coptic language could provide a bridge between the Greek translation and the hieroglyphs. Coptic, derived from the original Egyptian language but written in Greek, was in use as an Egyptian language even after the Arabs conquered Egypt. Drawing on his extensive knowledge of both Egyptian history and the Coptic language, Champollion figured out that a picture of a lion could have three different meanings, depending on its context. A lion picture could mean "lion," or it could stand, in effect, for the letter L, or it could be a pun on the similar-sounding word for "son." He also figured out what the ibis pictogram symbolized, relying on his knowledge of the Egyptian religion.

Young's mathematical approach (typical of a spatial visualizer) provided a crucial foundation; Champollion's more associational approach, which included the ability to visualize sounds (typical of an object visualizer), completed the decoding. Had Young and Champollion worked together, it's likely that the Rosetta Stone would have been deciphered more quickly. (It is equally likely that they would have hated each other's guts!)

Am I on Mute?

During COVID-19, I began to live almost exclusively online, teaching classes and sometimes attempting to go to scientific conferences hosted on confusing websites. As with most of us, my experiences with videoconferencing user interfaces ranged from easy to terrible. To present a lecture at one scientific conference, I had to go through an hourlong session on how to use a horrible program for which logging on took thirty minutes. Many interfaces are way too complicated. Object visualizers are needed to create better versions, because they can imagine exactly how a person will use it. One of the reasons Google became the number-one search engine was its simple white screen with a single search box. When I first saw it, I thought, "Wow, nothing to learn."

This is also why Zoom became one of the most popular virtual tools during the pandemic. You don't have to learn how to use it. Before COVID-19 shut down all my travel and in-person classes, I had never heard of Zoom. I learned about it from my colleagues, who were all using either Zoom or Microsoft Teams. Zoom's success is a prime example of a new company rising because of an old company's failure to innovate. Eric Yuan was a head engineer for Cisco's popular Webex videoconferencing platform. He begged Cisco to improve Webex, but to no avail. So he started his own company, with a better, easy-to-use service. Yuan made $12 billion in the first six months of the COVID-19 pandemic.

Clive Thompson, in his book *Coders*, states that working on the front end of a website, where the user interacts with the site, is often "denigrated as aesthetic, fuzzy stuff" and "not *real* coding." The mathematically inclined (spatial visualizers) are drawn to coding, or the abstract stuff. Thompson suggests that these days women are more likely to be front-end designers, while men are more likely to do the coding. But in a *New York Times* article, "The Secret History of Women in Coding," he explains that in the early days of computing, women were more prevalent in computer design than they would be in subsequent decades. In the 1950s, gender barriers and prejudices hadn't yet emerged. According to Thompson, "Institutions that needed programmers just used aptitude tests to evaluate applicants' ability to think logically." Employers often gave a pattern-recognition test, and looked for people who were logical, good at math, and meticulous. What they were really looking for, of course, had nothing to do with gender. They were looking for spatial visualizers. But even the most superb, beautiful mathematical code is not going to be successful if the user interface is a cluttered mess that is difficult to use.

Thousands and thousands of people flocked to Zoom because it was so easy to use. No user is the least bit interested in hour-long classes on how to use a program. During one of my Zoom calls to Brazil, a server crashed, and we had to switch to StreamYard. I had never seen it before, but I was able to successfully use it without any training. Now, that's a good user interface.

The Farmer and the Cowman

Many people describe attaching emotional meaning to certain songs. My visual mind will associate songs with the places where I heard them and the images they conjure. The day I got kicked out of the Scottsdale feed yard, Sonny and Cher's "A Cowboy's Work Is Never Done" was playing. Walking around the Swift cattle plants, I remember singing a Simon and Garfunkel lyric from

"The Sounds of Silence" over and over in my head: "The words of the prophets are written on the subway walls and tenement halls." In *Thinking in Pictures*, I wrote about Led Zeppelin's "Stairway to Heaven," which I listened to while driving away from the meat-packing plants. But the music I've loved since I was a child comes from musicals. I loved them then and I love them now. In high school, my roommate played *Carousel* and *Bye Bye Birdie* and *Oklahoma!* over and over. I sang "The Farmer and the Cowman" from *Oklahoma!* in the high school talent show. And when I graduated, I recited the words to "You'll Never Walk Alone" from *Carousel*:

> *When you walk through a storm*
> *hold your head up high*

It was a song that made me think about my future. There may be storms, but when you get through them there will be a bright future. I have gone through many doors, and in walking through them I always come back to this song and the promise of a golden sky.

Composer Richard Rodgers and lyricist Oscar Hammerstein were the musical team behind many of my favorite musicals, including *Carousel* and *Oklahoma!* Looking into their collaboration, I realized they were the perfect example of complementary minds. When they met, Rodgers already had a highly successful Broadway career. Hammerstein wasn't quite as successful but was widely respected. It wasn't common for theater people to start collaborating at midlife, but from the moment the two men decided to work together, something magical happened. In *The Sound of Their Music*, Frederick Nolan quotes Rodgers as saying, "What happened between Oscar and me was almost chemical. Put the right components together and an explosion takes place. Oscar and I hit it off from the day we started discussing the show." Their very first musical was *Oklahoma!* Rodgers claims that within ten minutes of Hammerstein's giving him the lyrics to the opening song, "Oh, What a Beautiful Mornin'," its unforgettable melody came to him. "When Oscar handed me the lyric and I read it for the first time, I was a little sick with joy because it was so lovely and right."

The two men didn't compose together in late-night, ashtray-filled sessions around the piano. Instead, Hammerstein mostly wrote from his home in Pennsylvania, and Rodgers largely composed from his home in Connecticut or his New York apartment. Hammerstein produced the lyrics first and sent them to Rodgers, who would then compose the melodies. In an interview on NPR's *Fresh Air*, Todd Purdum suggests that Rodgers and Hammerstein were never exactly close. Stephen Sondheim observed that the two never had a social relationship. It didn't matter. Theirs was a creative collaboration and a business partnership. As Rodgers wrote in his memoir, "I have long held a theory about musicals. When a show works perfectly, it's because all the individual parts complement each other and fit together. No single element overshadows any other. . . . It was a work created by many that gave the impression of having been created by one."

According to Purdum, the duo was project loyal, using the same orchestrator, vocal arranger, and scenic designer for all of their shows. It's nice to imagine that they were the best of friends, and that personal closeness kept the Broadway magic going. Instead, we should appreciate that the profound connection between complementary minds can be about the work and work ethic first and foremost, whereby collaborators agree that the sum is greater than the parts. As Sondheim summed it up, "Oscar was a man of limited talent and infinite soul, and Richard Rodgers was a man of infinite talent and limited soul." I would put it this way: a verbal thinker and a spatial thinker made beautiful music together.

Future Needs for Complementary Minds

Object visualizers will be needed when decisions have to be made about future technologies, such as using fusion to produce clean energy. Fusion would be the ultimate climate-friendly energy that could be used to replace both nuclear and fossil-fuel power plants. The visual-spatial mathematical minds are currently hard at work to make theoretical physics become a reality. Private industry is already funding four different designs that look like sets from the next blockbuster science fiction movie. They were described in an article titled "The Chase for Fusion Energy" in a recent issue of *Nature*. In all four designs, an intense magnetic field is used to contain a plasma that is hotter than the sun. The question is, Which one of the four competing technologies would ultimately be practical for commercial power generation?

First, we need to make sure that potential investors do not become enamored of the group that has the slickest sales presentation. Investors have previously been suckered into promising technologies that failed to work, such as Theranos, which developed the notorious blood-testing machine that was supposed to conduct multiple diagnostic tests from a single drop of blood. Investors never thought to test the new machine against the results achieved by conventional commercial labs. Millions of dollars were invested in a failed technology that potential investors could have easily tested themselves, by pricking their fingers. Founder Elizabeth Holmes was convicted of four of eleven charges of fraud.

As I looked at the four different fusion reactor designs, I thought, which one would I invest in? Large private-industry investors had already poured millions of dollars into two of the designs. When I looked them up on Google Images, it became obvious to me that they were the ones that could be easily built with standard industrial machine shop methods. A fourth design, called the Stellarator, was aesthetically beautiful. It looks like a coil wrapped in a

Slinky. It was the shiny new toy. However, its complex shape would make it extremely difficult to build with conventional metal shop methods. The oldest design of the bunch is Tokamak. In an International Atomic Energy Agency publication, Wolfgang Picot said of the two designs: "While Tokamaks are better at keeping plasmas hot, Stellarators are better at keeping them stable." Stability is essential for a practical commercial system. In the long term, the beautiful Stellarator has so many advantages, I decided I would bet on it even with the engineering obstacles presented by its unusually shaped metal parts. These need to be fabricated with 3D printers. These amazing machines, like the Stellarator, require two kinds of thinkers. The spatial thinker creates the computer code that fabricates almost anything you can imagine, from musical instruments to prosthetic limbs to entire houses—and the complex metal shapes the Stellarator would require. But the machines are what we call "high maintenance." You can't just press a button and get your widget. They need to be babied, and you can bet it's the object thinker who will be needed to finesse the precise metal components. In today's complex world, we need our different minds problem solving together so that we can find clean energy sources. Our future depends on it.

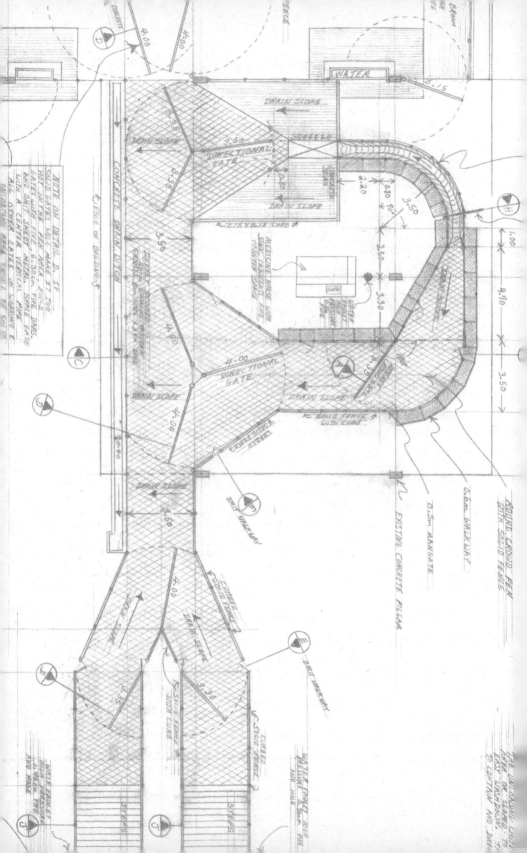

FIVE

Genius and Neurodiversity

My first brush with genius occurred in elementary school, when I was mesmerized by that book of famous inventors. I read it over and over, fascinated by their stories and their inventions. Like me, many were "difficult children" who exhibited traits that we now associate with Asperger's and other conditions on the autism spectrum, such as hyperactivity (ADHD), dyslexia, poor performance in school, poor social skills, and an inability to focus on some tasks while demonstrating incredible focus and intensity on others. Like me, many of the inventors as children loved taking things apart and putting them back together. I felt a particular affinity with the Wright brothers, who conducted nearly a thousand test flights, both modifying and improving their flying machines, before obtaining a patent for the *Kitty Hawk Flyer*. Long after a "normal" child would have become bored, I'd adjust my paper airplanes and homemade kites over and over, experimenting with folding and refolding the paper to achieve maximum lift. Though I had yet to be diagnosed with autism and did not yet have any understanding of why

I was "different," I would later realize that I shared certain traits with the Wright brothers, such as single-minded concentration, a fascination with mechanical things, and being more motivated by logic than emotion.

The inventor who impressed me the most was Thomas Edison. With his record 1,093 patents for new inventions, he dominated the turn of the twentieth century, making some of the most significant contributions to American innovation and achieving fame for inventing the lightbulb and the power-plant system that brought electricity into people's homes. He harnessed the force of his prodigious imagination with a keen and tireless entrepreneurial fervor. The promise of his abilities was evident in childhood, including some traits we now recognize as being on the autism spectrum.

It's always perilous to diagnose people postmortem or attempt to label the source of their creativity. Still, with only empirical and anecdotal evidence to rely on, there is no shortage of biographies and studies that attempt to explain genius across the arts and sciences. There have been countless studies of Einstein's brain, which was removed seven hours after he died, and endless attempts to explain the genius of Mozart, Beethoven, Leonardo, Michelangelo, Newton, Kepler, Darwin, and Shakespeare. The reason is simple: Genius is intoxicating. People who change the world are in a category of their own.

In this chapter, we'll look at the crossroads of neurodiversity, genius, and visual thinking. We'll look at examples of highly creative people and brilliant visual thinkers who, like Edison, failed miserably at school. We'll explore the prevalence of object and spatial visualization in some brilliant people, ideas about creativity and genetics, and whether certain kinds of genius might fall on the autism spectrum. It is not my goal to diagnose the Einsteins of the world, but instead to shed some light, through a series of profiles, on how neurodiversity, especially when it manifests as visual thinking, is present in what we think of as genius.

Addled Strangeness

From descriptions in various biographies, it appears that Edison had some spectrum traits: he had a domed forehead (larger heads are often a feature of autism), he memorized every street in his town, he hammered people with questions. Two incidents also suggest a limited range of emotional responses, such as empathy. The first was when he burned down his father's barn. Later he would abandon a friend who had drowned in a creek where they had been playing. Edison was at the bottom of his class and considered difficult, prone to distraction, and "developmentally delayed." Biographer Edmund Morris quotes him as saying, "I used never to be able to get along at school. I don't know what it was, but I was always at the foot of the class. . . . My father thought I was stupid, and at last I almost decided I must really be a dunce." In today's education system, Edison might have been labeled ADHD, as are nearly one in seven American boys. Mechanical thinkers like Edison often become bored in classroom settings dominated by verbal learning. These are the kids, as we've discussed in the chapter on education, who need to be *doing* things.

After learning that a teacher had called Edison "addled," his mother, herself a former teacher, pulled him out of grade school and taught him at home. She exposed him to a wide range of books, including Richard Green Parker's *A School Compendium of Natural and Experimental Philosophy.* According to Morris, this book paved the way for Edison's life as an inventor, imparting everything from the sixty-one known chemical elements to the six fundamental instruments: the pulley, the lever, the wedge, the screw, the inclined plane, and the wheel. It's not a surprise to me that these essential mechanical tools would speak to a brilliant young person at the threshold of the clever engineering department.

At twelve, Edison started working as a newsboy for the Grand Trunk Western Railroad. Accounts differ on why he dropped out after a second attempt at school, but his entrepreneurial gifts flourished outside the classroom. He figured out how to sell groceries at a margin to customers on the local train from Detroit to Port Huron. He edited telegraph reports into a broadsheet he called *The Weekly Herald* and sold to passengers for three cents a copy. In the family basement, Edison built a laboratory with more than two hundred bottles of chemicals. In a famous episode, he accidentally set a half-empty Grand Trunk baggage car on fire with a botched chemistry experiment. By age fourteen, the inventor and entrepreneur was fully fledged.

Two mentors followed in succession. The first, James MacKenzie, was a telegraph officer and stationmaster who taught Edison Morse code and how to use a telegraph machine. The second was Franklin Leonard Pope, telegrapher, electrical engineer, inventor, and patent lawyer. He was the author of the industry standard *Modern Practice of the Electric Telegraph* manual. It's possible that Edison, a voracious reader, would have read it and sought out Pope. Seven years Edison's senior, Pope became a mentor and quasi-patron to Edison, providing salary and lodging. Together they formed Pope, Edison & Company. At twenty-one, Edison's first patent, for the electrographic vote recorder, was quickly followed by the one-wire printer, which was basically a stock ticker. This set the stage for inventing the double-transmitter electrical telegraph, which featured an electromagnetic current that could sustain two operations at once, allowing a two-way conversation. There is no definitive explanation as to why the partnership fell apart after one year, though it's not difficult to imagine the prolific and gifted young Edison wanting to go solo, armed with the knowledge of how to patent an invention.

What his story unquestionably demonstrates, however, is that genius doesn't happen in a vacuum. Without mentoring and exposure, even the most brilliant people might fail to find an outlet for their abilities or a path to success. Edison benefited from a mother who was committed to his education, and he had lots of hands-on opportunities to work with mechanical and electrical equipment as a child and teen. He developed a strong work ethic as a vendor and newsboy, and his entrepreneurial zeal was encouraged and funded by Pope. These advantages dovetailed with Edison's native strengths. His abundance of curiosity (I believe this is innate), combined with the way he saw the world (I believe he was an object-visual thinker, given his propensity for making things), dogged him in elementary school, but ultimately fueled his life as an inventor. The most telling clue for me that Edison was a visual thinker is a quotation included in the biography of him by Frank Dyer and Thomas Martin: "I can always hire some mathematicians, but they can't hire me." By his own admission, Edison's mechanical mind—his genius—far outstripped his mathematical abilities.

I related to the stories of poorly behaved boys like Edison, and kids with what we now call learning disabilities. Today a movement has finally arisen that urges us to recognize that traits that may look like disabilities in one setting, such as the classroom, may be seen as abilities in another.

Neurodiversity

The term "neurodiversity" originated in the autism community, where it became a rallying cry for people who had been marginalized because of their differences. Proponents of neurodiversity strove to change the medical model that reduces people to their diagnosis or label. Journalist Harvey Blume crystalized the idea in *The Atlantic*, writing, "Neurodiversity may be every bit as crucial for the human race as biodiversity is for life in general. Who can say what form of wiring will prove best at any given moment?" The term was expanded to include dyslexia, ADHD, sensory processing disorder, learning disabilities, hyperactivity, Tourette's, OCD, bipolar disorder, schizophrenia, and other spectrum conditions that present with tremendous variability. COVID-19 and cancer, by contrast, have clear-cut diagnoses that can be confirmed with lab tests. This is not the case for neurodiversity. A mild case of schizophrenia can confer tremendous creative abilities. A full-blown case can cause paranoid delusions and destroy a person's mental health.

After a meteoric rise as a young mathematician at Princeton University, earning a PhD in just two years at age twenty-two, John Nash made a significant contribution to game theory, a mathematical tool used to analyze how people might behave in certain interactive situations. Game theory can be applied to any area to resolve conflict, most notably economics and politics. As with so many scientists with exceptional abilities, Nash showed signs of brilliance in childhood. According to Sylvia Nasar's biography, *A Beautiful Mind*, he taught himself to read at four and turned his childhood bedroom into a laboratory where he "tinkered with radios, fooled around with electrical gadgets, and did chemistry experiments."

Nash was a voracious reader of fantasy and science. Unlike Edison, he did so well in school that his parents supplemented his high school education with college courses at a nearby school. But Nash was also a loner and had a hard time connecting with peers. He was immature, socially awkward, and asked incessant questions about technical subjects and the natural world. In school, he also spoke out of turn. (This is something that I did and sometimes still do. Cutting people off can be interpreted as rudeness or being badly behaved. But for people on the spectrum, it can be a function of our wiring and difficulty with social cues.) Nasar relates that when a chemistry teacher would put a problem on the board, Nash would simply stare at it while the other students took out their pencils and paper. When he had worked out the answer in his mind, he would simply announce it.

Over time, Nash began to suffer from paranoid delusions, believing there was a Communist conspiracy against him. Most often, schizophrenia starts to manifest in the teen years, when a skimpy neural network starts to fall apart. At around age thirty, Nash began to experience psychotic symptoms, and throughout the rest of his life he continued to suffer breakdowns, although he would go on to receive the Nobel Prize in Economics for advancing the mathematics of game theory. What we cannot know is if his early genius was in some way a product of his nascent schizophrenia.

The central idea behind neurodiversity is to find a new paradigm for thinking about neurological disorders, including dispensing with the word *disorders*. Instead of pathologizing conditions like autism, proponents of neurodiversity advocate that these "conditions" be looked at as positive differences. Penny Spikins at the University of York theorizes that milder cases of autism, bipolar disorder, and ADHD may confer evolutionary advantages. Spikins believes that the rise of cognitive variation provides selective benefits not just to individuals but to society. She speculates that autism would have conferred advantages to people in settings such as Ice Age Europe, where a cold climate created a greater dependence on technology.

In her book *The Stone Age Origins of Autism*, Spikins writes, "What makes 'us' human is not a single 'normal' mind but a complex interdependency between different minds in which autism plays a key role." Groups that can integrate "difference" have advantages, thanks to members on the spectrum and visual thinkers with their obsessive focus, attention to detail, and in some cases formidable memory. People with mild bipolar traits may have facilitated greater socialization within their group. In fact, Spikins posits that these traits continue to exist in humans because in their milder versions they continue to provide advantages today, such as a facility with technological innovation. Without neurodiversity, our evolutionary history and present world might look a lot different.

J. M. Sikela at the University of Colorado School of Medicine and V. B. Searles Quick at the University of California, San Francisco, introduced a fascinating thesis in a paper titled "Genomic Trade-offs: Are Autism and Schizophrenia the Steep Price of the Human Brain?" In autism, they suggest, there may be an overdevelopment of certain genetic sequences in the brain. In schizophrenia, there may be underdevelopment. From a brain-development standpoint, the two conditions are opposites. They also vary greatly in their manifestations, from severe disability to mere personality differences. Sikela writes, "Evolution is opportunistic but also indifferent. Changes that become incorporated in a species' genome need not be without detriment so long as they provide an overall benefit. A consequence of this is that evolution often deals in genomic trade-offs, where harmful effects in some individuals are outweighed by a greater advantage to others." I believe that whatever deficits I may have, my heightened visual abilities have fueled my life's work and the contributions I've been able to make. It's a trade-off I wouldn't change.

I recently read a *New York Times* article about a deaf high school football team in California who were enjoying an undefeated season. According to the coaches, "Deaf players have heightened visual senses that make them alert to movement. And because they are so visual, deaf players have a more acute sense of where their opponents are positioned on the field." The coaches also credited their success with the way the players communicated, through a "flurry of hand movements between each play." Unlike their hearing counterparts, the deaf players could signal at great speed and with no time wasted. "I would say be careful in thinking that you have an advantage," said a coach whose team had been beaten. "They communicate better than any team I have ever coached against." This sounds like a genomic trade-off to me.

A study of entrepreneurs with and without ADHD by Curt Moore, professor at Oklahoma State University, supports this idea, showing that at least some forms of neurodiversity may be an asset in the workplace. Moore writes, "Our results suggest neurodiversity from ADHD is meaningfully related to aspects of an entrepreneurial mindset. Our results suggest entrepreneurs with ADHD employ a more intuitive cognitive style and demonstrate higher levels of entrepreneurial alertness." Entrepreneurs with ADHD have increased tendencies to look for opportunities and demonstrate high motivation.

It has been well documented that a disproportionate number of people on the autism spectrum work in tech, though many programmers actively avoid the autism label. A software engineer working in tech, who chose to remain anonymous, fit the profile: in an interview, he revealed that he taught himself to program as a child; his family wasn't happy with his single-mindedness; he performed poorly in school, largely because of the rigid environment and the work not being challenging enough. As a successful senior software engineer who now works at a prestigious tech company, he feels his skills are rewarded. "The technology industry is one of the most Aspie-friendly places that there is. The social demands on software engineers mostly consist of collaborating with colleagues to build a product."

Matt McFarland writes in *The Washington Post*, "While full-blown Asperger's syndrome or autism [holds] back careers, a smaller dose of associated traits appears critical to hatching innovations that change the world." Peter Thiel, the founder of PayPal, suggests that the social environment favors uniformity and discourages daring entrepreneurship. In a profile on him in *Business Insider*, Thiel says that in Silicon Valley many of the successful entrepreneurs are on the spectrum, which "happens to be a plus for innovation and creating great companies." In hiring, he says, he avoids MBAs, whom he describes as high-extrovert/low-conviction people, with a combination of traits that leads toward "extremely herd-like thinking and behavior."

Many people consider Mark Zuckerberg to be on the Asperger's spectrum. He has been described as robotic, socially awkward, and intensely single-minded. According to McFarland, Zuckerberg "wears a gray T-shirt every day, saying he wants to focus his decision-making energy on Facebook not fashion." Some consider him a genius for having invented the world's largest social network. It seems ironic that it took a person famous for having difficulty connecting with people to create a platform for everyone in the world to connect. Maybe that's the point.

There is a fair amount of controversy over neurodiversity within the autism community. On one end of the spectrum are severely impacted children who can't speak or dress themselves, and who don't develop rudimentary skills. On the other end of the spectrum is the person who works at—or invents— Microsoft. Most people on the spectrum are somewhere in the middle. Neurodiversity offers a way of thinking about difference that gives people on the spectrum a positive way to see themselves. Steve Silberman, in his book *NeuroTribes*, argues that neurodiversity should be viewed as different operating systems instead of through diagnostic labels. He writes, "The kids formerly ridiculed as nerds and brainiacs have grown up to become the architects of our future."

Another unlikely person who has recently captured the world's attention is a single-minded young girl from Stockholm with Asperger's. Greta Thunberg's monotone delivery and limited eye contact would not suggest a person with the ability to transfix the world and motivate a new generation of climate activists, but Thunberg calls her difference her superpower.

When I talk to autism groups, I like to share one of my favorite scientific papers, "Solitary Mammals Provide an Animal Model for Autism Spectrum Disorders" by J. E. Reser of the University of Southern California, which vividly underscores the neurodiversity on display in the animal kingdom. As we'll explore further in the final chapter, studying animals can provide an illuminating window on human neurodiversity. In animals, as in people, the brain develops with greater emphasis on either social/emotional or cognitive processing. A certain amount of variation within a species is normal, but from species to species the differences are more pronounced. Take the big cats. Some species are highly social, others more solitary. Lions live in social groups, while tigers and leopards are solitary except at mating time. In the primate world, chimpanzees are group-adapted and live within communities, while orangutans are solitary. Wolves live in packs. Striped hyenas live alone. Reser looked at data from many sources and found that solitary species of animals shared both genetic and hormonal similarities with people with autism. The solitary animals produce oxytocin, a hormone that influences social behavior, at a lower rate than more social animals. Both autistic individuals and solitary animals are less stressed when isolated than are more social members of their species under the same conditions. In the big-cat family, if leopards or tigers were people, they would probably be diagnosed with autism on account of their antisocial behavior. Are they defective? Do leopards have a disorder? In the animal kingdom, we don't apply these labels.

The Genetics of Genius

Whether they tackle psychology, brain development, genetics, or the impact of culture on individual difference, countless scientific studies revolve around one basic question: What factors determine how a person develops? What makes people who they are? For example, why does one family member inherit vulnerability to heart disease or cancer? Why does one sibling in a family thrive and another languish? How, where, and when do these vulnerabilities show up? I would add, why is one family member a visual thinker and another verbal? Or how does one family wind up with all accountants and another all lawyers? It is an old debate, and at the center of it is how much of a person's abilities are genetically determined and how much are learned. When I was in college, it was believed that all inherited qualities followed a simple pattern based on Gregor Mendel's theory of genetic principles. Mendel famously bred different varieties of garden peas, and the results showed that various traits were heritable, or what we now call genetic.

Autism was not considered to be such a trait. Instead, it was long thought to arise from nurture, or rather from the lack of it, following Bruno Bettelheim's widely accepted theory that it was attributable to "refrigerator mothers" who could not bond with their children. This cruel and baseless idea held sway from the 1940s until the 1960s, when a research psychologist named Bernard Rimland, himself the father of a son with autism, refuted it, locating the cause of autism in biology. Additional research over the next two decades helped turn the tide in convincing scientists of the genetic component to autism. Uta Frith helped advance the theory that autism is a genetically based neurobiological disorder. But autism does not follow Mendelian inheritance patterns, meaning that there is no single "autism gene." Instead, some number of genes influence each other and contribute to the expression of autism. Today researchers believe there are potentially one thousand genes involved in an autism diagnosis.

Here's what we know: During fetal development, we grow a huge pile of cells really fast to create the cerebral cortex. In addition to processing language, the cerebral cortex is responsible for sensory information, intelligence, thought, memory, perception, motor function, and executive function. As these undifferentiated cells grow in the fetus, they begin to divide into bone cells, skin cells, brain cells, and the like. Both initial differentiation of the cells and development of an entire human baby or animal are controlled by the genetic code inherited from both parents. The brain is so complicated that it is impossible for the code to direct every brain cell to an exact location. There will always be some variation. Here, too, there are no simple Mendelian dominant or recessive genes to explain the development of higher cerebral-cortex brain areas. Lots of little bits of code and variations are contributed from both parents.

While building the brain is an extremely complicated process, most of the time it develops neurotypically. While the fetus is developing, however, there are both genetic and non-genetic factors that can affect its growth, including the mother's diet, environment, stressors, and overall health. There are also genetic mutations that are responsible for any number of spectrum conditions. Genetic code is composed of four-letter pairs. These form the rungs of the ladder on the familiar diagram of DNA.

I explain it this way to my students: computer code, which is binary, can translate every book, spreadsheet, or movie into a two-digit code. In genomics, the entire blueprint for creating a person, plant, or animal is written in a four-digit code. A small section of the same four-digit genetic code may show up in identical formation multiple times in the genome. This mechanism of variation is called repeats. During fetal development, the number of identical sequences can be either increased or reduced. This acts as a "volume control" for different traits and explains why siblings don't necessarily share skin color, height, etc. Most of our traits are polygenic, which means they are affected by many genes. Another mechanism for understanding individual difference is single-nucleotide polymorphisms, or SNPs. Each one of these refers to possible substitutions at a single rung on the ladder of DNA. Sometimes a rung on the ladder changes and nobody knows why. This is called a de novo mutation and occurs in a small percentage of people diagnosed with autism.

It's impossible to talk about genetics and not run into twin studies. Scientists have long been drawn to twins because they provide the perfect petri dish to observe how nature and nurture play out. Identical twins (MZ, or monozygotic) share 100 percent of the same genes, while fraternal twins (DZ, or dizygotic) share 50 percent, which is the same as non-twin siblings. Sir Francis Galton, a polymath, statistician, inventor, and sociologist, was one of the first people to attempt a scientific study of twins. He coined the term "nature versus nurture," which still captures how we think about the play between what is innate and what is learned.

In his study "History of Twins," published in 1875, Galton writes, "Twins have a special claim upon our attention; it is, that their history affords means of distinguishing between the effects of tendencies received at birth, and of those that were imposed by the special circumstances of their after lives." He studied thirty-five pairs of identical twins and concluded that half the pairs were very similar and the other half closely similar with respect to everything from physical qualities to personality traits such as fearlessness versus timidity, volatility versus calmness. Galton would use his findings as the basis of his theory of eugenics, which advanced the idea of race- and class-based superiority. That aspect of his work has rightly been discredited, but he did point the way for others to look at twins for clues to the genetic code.

Now, twin profiles are being augmented with DNA samples, genotyping, and brain imagining. Sixty years after Bettelheim's indictment, some mothers were still suffering guilt over any developmental issues their children might have. To set the question of maternal blame to rest, researchers at Yale studied data from the placentas from the births of nearly 50 sets of identical and non-identical twins to ascertain whether developmental abnormalities were genetic. They found that cell growth responsible for developmental abnormalities occurred with similar frequency in identical twins. The lead author of the study, Dr. Harvey Kliman, wrote, "This work suggests that developmental abnormalities are much more likely to be due to the genetics of the child and not the mother's fault." What we still don't know is how these "abnormalities" manifest as a liability in one person and a gift in another.

According to Kevin J. Mitchell, associate professor at Trinity College Dublin, heritability studies can accurately measure all kinds of personality traits, such as impulsivity, language ability, sexual orientation, smoking, antisocial behavior, and neuropsychiatric disorders including autism and schizophrenia. For instance, identical twins have an 80 percent chance of having autism if their twin is autistic, while for fraternal twins it is 20 percent, which underscores the theory that genetic variation is not the only way that our brains get wired. Mitchell writes, "The genome does not encode a person. It only encodes a program to make a human being. That potential can only be realized through the processes of development."

Thomas Bouchard Jr., a psychologist at the University of Minnesota, took twin research a step further, studying pairs separated at birth. Bouchard found 137 pairs of separated identical and fraternal twins in his well-known study "Sources of Human Psychological Differences: The Minnesota Study of Twins Reared Apart." His testing concluded that identical twins raised apart shared personality traits, interests, and attitudes on a par with twins raised under the same roof, concluding that "almost every behavioral trait so far investigated . . . turns out to be associated with genetic variation."

In the 1980s, when MRI brain scans were first invented, I looked at scans of two sets of identical twins. They were very similar, but I could see slight differences in the shape of the corpus callosum, the structure that contains circuits enabling the two halves of the brain to communicate. Environment and experience—nurture—contribute to structural differences. In one study of identical twins at the Karolinska Institute's department of neuroscience in Sweden, researcher Örjan de Manzano compared the brains of sets of twins, one of whom was taught to play the piano while the other was either relatively or completely unfamiliar with the instrument. MRI brain scans showed that musical training increased thickness in both the auditory cortex and areas for motor control of the hands. Increased use of these parts of the brain evidently caused an increase in brain tissue: nurture.

Research with fruit flies by Gerit Arne Linneweber at the Sorbonne University in Paris showed that as the nervous system develops, differences in both behavior and wiring arise that are caused by "nonheritable noise," which refers to factors not controlled by the genetic code. Linneweber found that variations in the wiring of the visual system of flies, which occur naturally, will vary their behavior. It's like growing plants. The genetic code is not able to direct every developing neuron to the same place in every person. What accounts for the subtle differences? Imagine two identical Ford cars come off the assembly line. Same model, same make, same bells and whistles. They're exactly the same, but they drive a little differently. Every car has its quirks. My mind flashes images of the assembly line and all the places along the line where there is room for variability. Perhaps one worker puts more glue on a door seal than another, or a rattle is caused by a paper clip that fell out of a worker's pocket and remained inside a body panel, or by a failure to properly tighten a single bolt. Now imagine all these quirks and variations in the brain's development, which explains why most people are average (Fords) and a handful are geniuses (Ferraris).

More recent MRI studies by John P. Hegarty and his associates at Stanford University show that the overall size of a brain and its large structures are mostly determined by genetics. This is true for both autistic identical twins and neurotypical identical twins, due to the number of stem cells that initially develop in the fetus. Research has also shown that autistic brains are more sensitive to environmental influences. To use an analogy, the cerebrum—that part of the brain that mostly controls speech—is like a road. Genetics determines whether it's a four-lane highway or a single-lane road. In my own case, a detailed MRI showed that I had narrower "streets" for speaking, which would have been determined by genetic factors. But it was the environment (intensive speech therapy) that would determine whether I could learn to speak, the increased use slightly widening those narrow roads.

Researchers have also been drawn to the study of savants in an attempt to understand whether their extreme skills are genetically based. (Ten percent of people with autism have savant characteristics, compared with one in three million in the general population.)

Savants are capable of extraordinary abilities, such as quickly learning multiple foreign languages, playing complex musical arrangements having heard them just once or twice, drawing highly developed photorealistic images, and performing prodigious feats of memory such as calendar and other mathematical calculations. Dr. D. A. Treffert, a specialist in the epidemiology of autism spectrum disorders, describes these savant abilities as "splinter skills," where the memory is massive, but the area of ability is limited to a narrow field. Treffert worked with the savant Leslie Lemke, who became blind at six months and had brain damage and cerebral palsy. When he was fourteen, his adoptive parents discovered him playing Tchaikovsky's Piano Concerto No. 1 after hearing it once on television. Though he could not read music and never had a piano lesson, Lemke could play anything after hearing it once and gave concerts throughout his life showcasing his remarkable skill. Remarkably, while he had trouble speaking, he could sing any song while playing.

Bernard Rimland theorized that in such cases some defect in the brain shuts off the left hemisphere and allows greater concentration on the right. It's as if there is no balancing between the two hemispheres (something that brings us back to the idea of a spectrum), and the right hemisphere barrels on without any brakes, reaching extraordinary levels of mastery. These abilities can often come at a high cost as well, including social deficits and extreme isolation. Another way to put it is that people with these singular skills live in one part of their brain. Some believe that savants are not creative because they only make precise copies of music or visual art. After precise duplication, savants may begin to introduce small changes, and with encouragement, some can become creative in music and art. Lemke, for instance, started improvising later in his life. Yet as far as we know, a savant has never created a masterpiece.

The Sculpture inside the Stone

Like the leopard, by all accounts the great artist Michelangelo was a loner. He quit school at twelve and dropped out of a three-year apprenticeship after one year, claiming that there was nothing left for him to learn. He preferred working alone rather than among fellow artists and craftspeople. Was Michelangelo on the autism spectrum? Muhammad Arshad, a psychiatrist in the United Kingdom, and Michael Fitzgerald, a psychiatry professor at Trinity College Dublin, think he was. They point to the artist's "single-minded work routine" and poor social skills. According to one Michelangelo biographer, his contemporary Ascanio Condivi, "Passionate solitude was the very soul of the work and the genius of Michelangelo." He was indifferent to food and lived on a subsistence diet. During the three years he worked on the *David*, he lived reclusively, so fixated on his art that he couldn't be bothered to bathe or even to take his shoes off to go to bed. (Poor hygiene is common in people on the autism spectrum, usually because sensory hypersensitivity can make the sensations associated with bathing unpleasant.) Another biographer, Paolo Giovio, noted that Michelangelo's "domestic habits were incredibly squalid."

With greater certainty, I think we can agree that Michelangelo was an extreme visual thinker. He was in his early twenties when he was commissioned to sculpt the *Pietà*. At twenty-six, he began the *David*. He commenced work on the Tomb of Pope Julius II at thirty. He began work on the Sistine Chapel at thirty-three, and on his sculpture of Moses at age thirty-eight. And those are just a handful of his greatest hits. Michelangelo left school at a young age. He worked ceaselessly, driven by the constantly turning gears of his mind. He lost his mother when he was six, and he went to live with his nurse and benefited from exposure to her husband, a stonecutter. "Along with the milk of my nurse I received the knack of handling chisel and hammer, with which I make my figures," Condivi records him as saying.

Michelangelo also had the benefit of two mentors. The first was Domenico Ghirlandaio, to whom he was apprenticed at age thirteen. Although he left the apprenticeship after the first year, it would have exposed him to the process of making frescoes and to draftsmanship, including the use of foreshortening to create linear perspective, which makes objects appear farther away the smaller they are. Perhaps the brilliant teenager intuited these painting skills, but he would unquestionably have benefited from growing up in Florence, a city filled with art and home to many highly regarded frescoes. A second and more powerful mentor, Lorenzo de' Medici, took young Michelangelo into his home and provided an environment where his abilities could flourish. As Eric Weiner observes, Lorenzo deserves great credit for developing Michelangelo. He spotted the work of a young "nobody" and "acted boldly to cultivate it."

We can only conjecture that Michelangelo's single-minded focus and concentration, coupled with his aversion to social life, were evidence of Asperger's. As an object visualizer, he created two-dimensional paintings with photographic detail (the most extraordinary of which come to life as three-dimensional figures in the brilliant frescoes that decorate the ceiling of the Sistine Chapel). Using spatial skills, he created statues such as the *David* in photographic detail as well. The monumental sculpture, which he finished before he turned thirty, is considered a masterpiece and possibly the greatest example of High Renaissance art. As we've learned, in most cases, object or spatial thinking is on a spectrum. Studies so far show that these are two distinct ways of thinking. Is it possible in some cases for a person to be capable of both ways of thinking at the highest levels?

Perhaps when we encounter the prodigious gifts in someone who masters different mediums, someone such as Michelangelo, what we are seeing is the rare convergence of spatial and object thinking in the mind of a genius. According to Thomas G. West in his book *In the Mind's Eye*, Leonardo's abilities as a visual-spatial thinker were so vast that he anticipated scientific and technological advances by a hundred years in the areas of anatomy, physiology, mechanical engineering, and astronomy. West writes, "Visual spatial talents are, in some important cases, indispensable for the highest levels of original work in certain areas of science, engineering, medicine and mathematics." Other sculptors rejected the marble that Michelangelo used to carve the *David*. He saw the statue inside it.

Visual Thinking, Dyslexia, and Genius

Film director Steven Spielberg wasn't diagnosed with dyslexia until he was sixty. His body of work (thirty-two films) includes *E.T. the Extra-Terrestrial*, *Schindler's List*, and *Jaws*, and is a testament to his gifts as a visual storyteller. Spielberg had always been a very slow reader in school and struggled with academics, but he had never been labeled. During an interview, he admitted that junior high was the hardest part of his youth. Teachers believed that he was not trying hard enough, and like many people with neurodiverse traits, he was the object of bullying by his peers. In her biography of Spielberg, Molly Haskell writes, "With a camera in hand, he could not only shut out all the horrors that swirled around him, he could tackle one of them—unpopularity—in his own way." Spielberg's family had a movie camera, and Spielberg gravitated to it. He started by filming family gatherings, and soon became inseparable from the camera.

At age twelve, he made his first movie. At age eighteen, he made a full-length movie titled *Firelight* for less than $600. It was about people abducted by aliens, a theme that he would later explore in *E.T.*, which is about accepting people who are different. Spielberg continued to struggle through high school with middling grades, and his application to the University of Southern California, a top film school, was rejected. In a video interview with learning-disabilities advocate Quinn Bradlee, Spielberg said that movies were a great escape that "saved me from shame." Spielberg fused with his camera. He used a visual vocabulary to express himself. Other people do it through art, fashion, decorating, and other visually creative fields.

Dyslexia is associated with greater activity in the right frontal lobe, an area that is also the locus of spatial visualizing. Joseph McBride, in his biography of Spielberg, suggests that the director's "prodigious visual sense may be compensation for his difficulties with reading." This interpretation of genomic trade-offs is often applied to understand assets and liabilities. Thomas West suggests that, being locked into a linear view of intelligence, we are able to understand extraordinary visual skill like Spielberg's only as compensation for his dyslexia. I agree with this. We would never say of a great writer that his or her literary gift compensates for poor visual or mathematical skills.

Some dyslexics are object thinkers, and some are more mathematical visual-spatial. Once again, the studies don't sufficiently distinguish between the two types. Some spatial visualizers and people with dyslexia are great at big-picture thinking; they can both visualize and rotate 3D objects in their mind's eye. I have worked with creative metalworkers who had dyslexia. They designed and built huge, elaborate feed mills. Object visualization skills are used to design complex systems consisting of conveyors, pumps, and feed-mixing equipment. The spatial visualizers make them work. Another dyslexic colleague who did poorly in school now runs an excavating machine used in roadwork. He often had to correct mistakes made by spatial-visualizer engineers. On one construction job, his knowledge prevented a highway from collapsing when a tunnel was dug beneath it. His creativity and contributions are not given enough credit.

Helen Boden, CEO of the British Dyslexia Association, told Finbarr Toesland in *CEO Magazine* that "dyslexics are great explorers of information." Famous dyslexic businesspeople include Sir Richard Branson of the Virgin Group and celebrity chef Jamie Oliver. Also Ingvar Kamprad, the creator of IKEA, was dyslexic. To help keep his furniture inventory organized in his warehouses, he created a naming system that he could easily visualize. Large furniture had the names of Swedish places; medium-sized furniture, such as desks and chairs, received men's names; and outdoor furniture received the names of Swedish islands.

There is evidence that dyslexia and creativity may be linked. Picasso claimed not to have read before the age of ten and could not recall the correct order of the alphabet. According to Patrick O'Brian's biography, Picasso failed to learn reading or math in school. "Somehow the rudiments of these arts seeped into him quite early, but they did not do so in the classroom: to the end of his life he was not at home with the alphabet . . . his spelling remained highly personal." In *Creating Minds*, Howard Gardner notes that Picasso had "precocious spatial intelligence but very meager scholastic intelligences." My favorite observation comes from author Gertrude Stein: "Picasso wrote painting as other children wrote their [ABCs]. . . . Drawing always was his only way of talking."

Another study showed that college art students had more dyslexia than students in other majors. Thomas West cites Thomas Edison, Albert Einstein, Gustave Flaubert, and William Butler Yeats, among others, as having dyslexia or a form of learning disability. A 2021 *New Yorker* profile of Ari Emanuel, the CEO of the talent agency Endeavor, revealed that the Hollywood rainmaker was dyslexic. He was unable to read by the third grade and was diagnosed with dyslexia and ADHD. He was teased a lot, and he fought back. In 2007, he received an award from the Lab School in Washington, DC, which specializes in working with kids with learning disabilities. His remarks on the occasion amplify Thomas West's. He told them dyslexia was a gift that could give them "the insight to find inventive solutions to life—and in business—that others when they're in those situations probably never find."

In 1982, a twenty-one-year-old architecture student at Yale beat out 1,420 other competitors to win a commission to design the Vietnam War memorial in Washington. Maya Lin's design consisted of two two-hundred-foot-long polished black granite walls that were installed at 10.1 feet below grade and met in an obtuse angle of 125 degrees. It was a completely radical idea, and as with many radical ideas, it met with some intense backlash. Some critics felt that the submerged monument disrespected the very lives it was meant to commemorate. The walls are inscribed with the names of the more than 58,000 killed in combat or missing in action in the Vietnam War. The names appear not alphabetically but chronologically, by the date of each soldier's death. This was "the genius of Maya's design," said Jan Scruggs, the Vietnam veteran whose mission it was to build the memorial. "The chronological order allows veterans who were in battle to see their friends forever united on the Wall."

Long before I knew who Lin was, I had the opportunity to visit the memorial, and it was an emotional experience. My cousin was killed in Vietnam, and his name is on that wall. It was a muggy, sweltering day when I visited. Veteran volunteers helped me find my cousin's name, etched in black, no bigger or smaller than anyone else's, no rank. I had no idea a college student was responsible for that profound experience. But I was certain a verbal thinker could not have conceived of such a design.

As a child, Maya Lin amused herself by building miniature towns. "I didn't have anyone to play with, so I made up my own world," she recalled. Both of Lin's parents were Chinese immigrants and college professors. Her father was dean of the College of Fine Arts at Ohio University, and her mother taught literature and poetry there. Lin was introduced to the world of art by casting bronze and creating ceramics in her father's studio. Once again, early exposure paves the way for the child drawn to the flame. During adolescence, Lin did not fit in and seldom dated. Looking back, she describes her high school self as a "Class A Number One Nerd" who loved both computer programming and math. In architecture school, Lin says, "the architecture professors were having a horror of a time because I kept spending more and more time over in the sculpture department, and I don't tend to think analytically as an architect. I analyze more like a scientist."

Her more recent work includes large installations that visitors can walk through. Her work is meant to be visually experienced on every level. In one exhibit she painted meandering streams on the walls and ceilings of a gallery. They looked like rivers as seen from airplane windows. To build another sculpture, *Water Line*, Lin worked with researchers at the Woods Hole Oceanographic Institution in Massachusetts to obtain topographic maps of the bottom of the seascape. The shapes of the ocean bottom were built from bent aluminum tubes. The sculpture looked like a partially completed computerized image that you might find in a scientific journal article. One of her larger pieces consisted of rows and rows of grassy mounds that resembled waves. When you walk through the mounds, they look like hills. To see the full effect requires an aerial photograph. I think her work is mind-blowing because of the unique way she translates what she sees. Equal parts architect and artist, Lin takes an abstraction and makes it tangible instead of the other way around.

The Genius Coders

Computer programming requires a mathematical mind, specifically a visual-spatial mathematical mind. According to psychology professor Anna Abraham at Leeds Beckett University in the UK, mathematicians enjoy a "pedestal position" because math "represents the pinnacle of abstraction in reasoning" and is associated with elegance, pattern making, invention, creativity, and the like. That kind of mind is exemplified in the brilliant mathematician Alan Turing, who bridged the gap between the science of logic and mechanical computing machines. He is widely credited with developing the foundation of modern computing.

In school in Dorset, England, Turing's mathematical abilities and intelligence were apparent at an early age. Since childhood, he'd been attracted to numbers, even studying serial numbers on lamp posts. But the private school he attended emphasized a classical education in the humanities, and math was not considered a valuable part of such an education. His headmaster wrote, "If he is to be solely a scientific specialist, he is wasting his time." The headmaster also noted that Turing was the type of boy who would become a big problem in the community due to his behavior. A teacher observed that his writing was "the worst I have ever seen." He was also criticized for being dirty and sloppy, and his poor hygiene continued into adulthood.

By the time Turing was sixteen, he was doing advanced math, even though he had never studied calculus. It's possible that his mathematical mind may have been stimulated by Einstein's book on the theory of relativity, a gift from Turing's grandfather. At King's College in Cambridge, England, along with advanced math, Turing studied cryptology. He read several influential books, including Bertrand Russell's *Introduction to Mathematical Philosophy* and John von Neumann's text on quantum mechanics. In a course called "Foundations of Mathematics" with British mathematician and codebreaker M. H. A. Newman, Turing first encountered David Hilbert's *Entscheidungsproblem*, or "decision problem": Is it possible to use an algorithm to determine whether an inference made during an operation of formal logic is valid? Turing quickly proved that this was impossible. Two professors at separate universities mentored this brilliant young student, encouraging him to submit his work for scholarly publication. After he received his PhD, Turing produced groundbreaking work in mathematical biology, explaining such disparate things as how fingers are formed during embryonic development and how zebras get their stripes.

Turing's abilities proved more than theoretical when, during World War II, he broke the Germans' Enigma machine code that encrypted messages detailing their military operations. The Enigma machine was a typewriter-like device that used rotating discs to both encrypt and read coded messages. Cracking its code made it possible for the British to anticipate German strategic plans and troop movements, saving thousands of lives.

Turing's brilliant career abruptly ended at age forty-one. He was found guilty of being a homosexual, which was a crime in the UK at the time. He lost his security clearance and was forced to take estrogen pills. He took his own life in 1954. As I write this, I get very upset. This is a tragic ending for the man who did the calculations that were instrumental in ending World War II and that are the basis for modern computing. If the term *genius* encompasses a person's ability to work across fields at the highest level of excellence and impact the culture, we must recognize Turing as one.

Most coders and software developers have at least two things in common: First, they gravitated toward math at an early age, and second, they see patterns in the code. Bill Gates is a perfect example of a mathematical thinker who was exposed to computing at an early age. Gates was introduced to computers as a teenager at Lakeside School in Seattle. Returning to his high school to give a speech in 2005, he said, "One reason I'm so grateful to Lakeside is that I can directly trace the founding of Microsoft back to my earliest days here." This is where Gates was first introduced to programming and formed the Lakeside Programmers Group with his friend Paul Allen.

For fun, they took their school's teletype machine and connected it over telephone lines to a local GE mainframe computer. At eighty-nine dollars per hour, using the computer was so expensive that the group collectively saved money to purchase time. As a high school senior, Gates was excused from some math classes to go to his programming job at a nearby engineering firm. His first program was a game of tic-tac-toe. Then he created a scheduling system for the school, a payroll program, and a start-up called "Traf-O-Data," which analyzed traffic data. All this before graduating from high school. Then Gates famously dropped out of Harvard.

It's been widely reported in the press that Bill Gates has some Asperger's-like traits, including poor social skills, intense focus, a monotone voice, limited eye contact, and rocking. High anxiety may cause people to rock, and autistic people often have very high anxiety. In 1998, Microsoft was sued by the US government for having a monopoly. In the videos of Bill Gates's deposition testimony, he rocks when questioned. Twenty years later, he appears more at ease. He is a good example of how a person who has some autistic traits can mature and develop as they add more information to their mental databases. The new information can be sorted and manipulated in different ways, which can lead to more flexible thinking. On or off the spectrum, Gates's Microsoft Windows operating system became the computing standard of the world. In an interview, Ellen DeGeneres asked Gates if he always loved tech. Gates corrected her: his love is software.

In a *Businessweek* interview, Bill Gates was asked if Elon Musk would be the next Steve Jobs. Mr. Gates replied, "Elon's more of a hands-on engineer. Steve was a genius at design and picking people and marketing. You wouldn't walk into a room and confuse them with each other." As mentioned earlier, Musk revealed that he had Asperger's syndrome in a 2021 appearance hosting *Saturday Night Live*. He made the announcement with pride, joking in his monologue that he needs to tell people when he really means something because he doesn't have much "intonation or variation" in his speech, and that he wouldn't be making much eye contact with the cast. His "outing" himself as someone on the spectrum goes a long way toward helping people understand how difference can fuel genius.

Biographer Ashlee Vance compares Musk to a latter-day Thomas Edison, "an inventor, celebrity businessman, and industrialist able to take big ideas and turn them into big products." According to his mother, Maye, from a very young age, Musk could block out the world. At first it appeared that he might be deaf, but it turned out he was in a kind of deep trance. Vance quotes Maye as saying, "He goes into his brain, and then you just see he is in another world. He still does that. Now I just leave him be because I know he is designing a new rocket or something."

Early evidence of Musk's visual intelligence and entrepreneurial acumen appeared at age ten, when he taught himself to code, and at age twelve, when he designed the software video game called Blastar, which he sold for $500. Musk credits video games with teaching him how to code, and he believes many coders also got their start through gaming. With the older games, when the computer crashed, it would show blue screens of code. I call this computers showing their guts. Today, computers no longer show their guts when they crash. I don't know how kids can get exposed to coding playing today's video games, and I worry that activities with screens are sometimes the only thing that kids do.

Musk described his visual thinking to Vance: "It seems as though a part of the brain that is usually reserved for visual processing—the part that is used to process images coming in from the eyes—gets taken over by internal thought processes. For images and numbers, I can process their interrelationships and algorithmic relationships. Acceleration, momentum, kinetic energy—how these sorts of things will be affected by objects comes through very vividly." That's visual thinking on rocket fuel. When asked by Joe Rogan what it's like inside his brain, Musk replied, "It's a never-ending explosion."

Unlike Gates and Musk, Steve Jobs was a Silicon Valley baby. He grew up in what would become the heart of tech. Two facts that strike me: First, Jobs tested off the charts on a fourth-grade intelligence test. He scored at a tenth-grade level, meaning that his IQ likely reached Einstein territory by the time he reached adulthood, putting him in the 99.99th percentile. More interesting to me is that his adoptive father was a mechanic and carpenter. According to biographer Walter Isaacson, Jobs's father portioned off a section of his workbench to share with his young son, though Jobs was more interested in his neighbor's garage. His neighbor worked at Hewlett-Packard, and Jobs loved tinkering with all the electronics. Later, however, Jobs would say of his father, "He loved doing things right. He even cared about the look of the parts you couldn't see." In some ways, this is object visualization at its most elegant— caring about the parts you can see with only your mind's eye.

When Jobs was sixteen, he met Steve Wozniak. The teenagers heard about a guy who had made a pirated phone off a flaw in AT&T's network, using a device called a "blue box." Once they understood that they could create something capable of tapping into a huge infrastructure, Jobs and Wozniak built their own blue box in three weeks. In a 1995 interview with documentary filmmaker Robert X. Cringely, Jobs said, "I don't think there would have ever been an Apple Computer if there had not been blue boxing." Like Gates, Jobs dropped out of college. The course he took at Reed College that impacted him the most was calligraphy. He changed the world by revolutionizing the personal computer, the laptop, the mouse, and the touch screen. Job's genius was also all about design. His visual mind cared about every detail, including the font. The next time you send a text from your iPhone, appreciate that it looks the way it does thanks to that college course. There is a line by psychology professor David Barash in a piece in *The Chronicle of Higher Education* that I really love: "The relationship between Steve Jobs and 'useless' humanities programs such as calligraphy should not be ignored."

Pure Genius

There is no scientific consensus on what genius is. Throughout history, the definition has changed with the times. It was originally considered a God-given gift. Later, genius was attributed to or equated with madness. In the twentieth century, genius was conceived largely as the marriage of high intelligence and creativity, especially where great financial profits were involved. These days, we're more likely to look into a person's frontal lobes in search of it than into his or her soul. Elkhonon Goldberg, clinical professor of neurology at New York University, writes in *Creativity: The Human Brain in the Age of Innovation,* "The birth of a creative idea begins through the frontal lobe–driven process by activating certain regions within the vast cortical network distributed to a large extent throughout the posterior (parietal, temporal, and occipital) association cortex." Within this network there are unlimited pathways to creativity.

Goldberg breaks down the essential elements of creativity as salience, asking the right questions, and having relevance, an interest in novelty, the ability to apply old knowledge to new problems, mental flexibility, and the flexibility to apply multiple solutions. Also on his list are drive, doggedness, and mental focus, and mental wandering as well, which he describes as the brain's ability to flow and find solutions almost mysteriously. Because recognized geniuses are in "lamentably short supply," says Goldberg, "and the availability of their brains for neuroimaging and autopsy in even shorter," we rely on standardized tests to measure creativity.

The most widely used is the Torrance Tests of Creative Thinking (TTCT), designed by Ellis Paul Torrance in the 1960s. The test measures multiple aspects of creativity and is considered the most reliable assessment of it. I still remember when my high school science teacher, Mr. Carlock, told us about taking the test. Participants were given everyday objects and asked what uses they could come up with for them. He was given a brick. He had a very creative answer: using a stone saw to cut the brick up into little cubes, and, painting dots on each little cube, you could make dice. I have administered the brick test in many of my classes. The uses get more creative as soon as the students become willing to modify the brick. My idea would be to grind up the brick and use the powder to color paint.

Essentially, the TTCT measures divergent thinking across four axes: fluency, originality, flexibility, and elaboration. In *The Neuroscience of Creativity*, Anna Abraham describes a study of art students (the control group was chemistry students) selected on the basis of their TTCT. The art students had monthly brain scans while they drew human figures and made judgments about such things as the brightness and length of optical illusions. By the end of the study, the art students had improved their divergent creative-thinking skills compared with the chemistry students, and there was evidence of reorganization of the white matter in their prefrontal cortexes. French researchers Zoï Kapoula and Marine Vernet at the University of Paris also found that dyslexic students were more creative when assessed with the TTCT.

A question I often ask both educators and parents is, "What would happen to some of the great scientists, inventors, and artists if they were in today's educational system?" Would they fare any better than those of the past? I have observed many children and teenagers who exhibit strong aptitude in areas such as music, art, computing, or spelling bees (all of which involve feats of memorization) and who also display certain antisocial behaviors, such as poor hygiene, inability to make friends, or loner tendencies. It's likely this child is on the spectrum and may have special abilities in any of the domains: object-visual, visual-spatial, or verbal. Interestingly, at least until now, studies show that these kids are almost never a mixture of those traits. They are either an art/mechanical kid (loves to make things), a math kid (loves coding, puzzles, computers), or verbal kid (loves stories, history, and facts). Neurotypical people, by contrast, are more likely to have a brain geared to mix the different types of thinking.

Nobody better exemplifies the genius visual-spatial thinker profile than the father of modern physics. Sources vary, but it seems that Albert Einstein didn't acquire speech until around age three or four and didn't speak fluidly until age seven. His sister is quoted in the Walter Isaacson biography as saying, "He had such difficulty with language that those around him feared he would never learn." Einstein struggled in school, was socially awkward, and cared little for personal grooming. He had emotional outbursts and avoided eye contact. According to Isaacson, he was "the patron saint of distracted school kids everywhere."

As an adult and professor, Einstein refused to wear suits and ties and preferred soft comfortable clothes. It's possible his aversion to suits and ties was a sensory issue. Or perhaps a flash of rebellion, another trait sometimes seen in people on the spectrum. There is a lot of debate as to whether Albert Einstein was on the spectrum. If you Google "Einstein" and "Asperger's," you will find upwards of 312,000 entries. Neither his biographer Walter Isaacson nor the late Oliver Sacks believed that Einstein had Asperger's, pointing to his ability to have close, lasting relationships. I'm not sure that is a determining distinction; I've known many people on the spectrum who formed close relationships and married. Still, Einstein left these haunting words toward the end of his life: "I am truly a 'lone traveler' and have never belonged to my country, my home, my friends, or even my immediate family with my whole heart. . . . I have never lost a sense of distance and a need for solitude."

Einstein may have been one of the rare people who excelled in both visual-spatial and object visualization. Describing the place of words in his life, he said, "Thoughts do not come in any verbal formulation. I rarely think in words at all. . . . The psychological entities that serve as building blocks for my thoughts are certain signs and images, more or less clear, that I can reproduce or recombine at will." Einstein used visualization when formulating his theory of relativity. Bernard Patten, in the *Journal of Learning Disabilities*, said that Einstein used his unusual visual thinking to achieve scientific greatness. He was surprised to learn that other people think mainly in words.

Einstein started taking violin lessons at age six and later said, "Life without playing music is inconceivable to me." Later in life, when he was trying to solve a problem, he would play his violin until the solution came into his mind. It is my opinion that violin playing may have been a major factor in his success. Greg Miller, in *Science*, reported on a 1995 study by neurologist Gottfried Schlaug, who studied professional musicians who have been playing since the age of seven. All of them had an unusually thick corpus callosum, "the bundle of axons that serves as an information superhighway between the left and right" hemispheres. Schlaug went on to study children between the ages of six and nine to ascertain the rate of growth of the corpus callosum, using detailed MRIs. For those who practiced an instrument regularly, it grew about 25 percent relative to the overall brain.

Many papers have been published about Einstein's brain and what made him a genius. Examination of his brain revealed that motor areas of the brain that are expanded in professional violinists were also larger in Einstein's brain. This would be an example of an environmental effect. Music, like visual-spatial thinking, is thought to be located on the right side of the brain. Both math and music share visual-spatial thinking as a basis for patternmaking and abstract thinking. Perhaps math departments should encourage students to learn a musical instrument. Researchers at Notre Dame of Maryland University found that adolescents who learned to play a musical instrument or studied choral music did better in algebra. There's that link of abstract thought. Another study showed that scientists with creative hobbies are more likely to receive prestigious positions and awards, including the Nobel Prize, than scientists without such hobbies. When a person is just relaxing and letting the brain idle in restful wakefulness, creative ideas will often emerge. In my own design work, I have often solved an equipment design problem when I was just falling asleep, in the shower, or on a long stretch of open highway. Research supports the idea that a creative solution to a problem often occurs when the mind is wandering.

Neuroscientists call this the default network. In this relaxed state, wide networks in the brain's midsection are activated. These are areas of the brain where associations can be made between wide-ranging types of information. More divergent creative thoughts arise when the frontal cortex relaxes executive function, reducing control over the default network. Different types of creators, whether artistic, musical, or literary, generate ideas while the brain is in the wakeful resting state. For creativity to produce successful results, it needs to have some constraints. I have met people who had so many competing ideas that they were never able to turn them into a fully realized creation. The frontal cortex can send a signal to restrict the free flow of creative ideas and make thinking more goal directed.

A study of images of Einstein's brain by Dean Falk at Florida State University's department of anthropology reveals differences in his brain structure that may have enabled sensory information to be better integrated. Falk reports atypical areas in Einstein's cerebral cortex, which governs motor and sensory response. This may be related to Einstein's difficulties learning to speak and preference for using sensory impressions for thinking. Einstein stated that he did not think in words. Concepts came to him, he said, "only through their connection with sense experiences." The brain photos also showed that the parts of the brain associated with visually identifying objects were enlarged in Einstein's brain. This is the part of the brain associated with object visualization. His strong object-visualization tendencies would have enabled him to perform his famous visualization of physics concepts. He imagined himself riding in train cars or on beams of light. There is some evidence that Einstein had some weaknesses in math. Maybe his music helped improve his math ability.

Earlier reports by the neuroscientist Sandra Freedman Witelson and colleagues found that Einstein had an expanded parietal region, suggesting a neurological basis for his enhanced visual and mathematical thinking. While conducting research in the physics department of East China Normal University in Shanghai, Weiwei Men and his colleagues showed that the corpus callosum in Einstein's brain was bigger than those in a control group, especially in the splenium, the part of the brain that enables communication between the parietal lobes. A bigger corpus collosum would also enhance communication between the right and left brain. As we've noted, the right brain is typically associated with images and the left with verbal. It has also been reported that his prefrontal cortex and inferior parietal lobe areas were larger than usual.

I was interested in Einstein long before I had any inkling that he might be on the autism spectrum. Why was I so attracted to him when I was in high school? I could sense he wasn't like other people, and neither was I.

Allowing Genius the Opportunity to Develop

We have always been fascinated by pondering the nature of genius. We marvel at Bach's *Goldberg Variations*, Isaac Newton's theory of gravity, and Shakespeare's poetry and plays. How did these towering achievements come into being? What cultural forces contributed? What individual abilities fuel innovation in arts and science? In my work, I have often observed what I refer to as "Grade A Bookworms." These are top students who are often lacking in creativity and flexible problem-solving, and sometimes common sense. As in other fields, a solid B+ veterinary student may be more effective out in the field solving cattle health problems. A colleague told me about a veterinary student with top grades who was so busy looking at the readout on an anesthesia machine that he failed to observe that the dog was waking up during surgery.

An agronomy professor recently told me about his frustrations with some of his graduate students who had top grades. He said they had no creativity or originality when thinking up new research ideas. As we saw in the chapter on education, valedictorians and other high-achieving students can do well in life, but they are far less likely to think up something totally new and original. Genius requires not only intelligence and creativity but divergent thinking as well.

In a world wired for social contact, communication skills are prized above all. At the same time, technology dominates our culture, which may explain why we think of people like Gates, Jobs, Zuckerberg, and Musk as geniuses. Bill Gates famously said, "Software is an IQ business." Would Michelangelo or Leonardo rate in today's world? In an earlier era, a different asset might have held more capital—physical strength or the ability to procreate the largest family to run the farm. Until recently, people with disabilities were completely disenfranchised. Something like "mainstreaming" wasn't a concept when I was growing up. Typically, people like me with a host of antisocial traits and little to no language were institutionalized. The concept of normalcy shifts according to the dominant culture.

As we've seen, people who excel in their field are generally introduced early on to the tools and concepts that shape their minds, and usually receive mentoring by teachers or other role models. In a 2016 interview with Charlie Rose, Bill Gates said, "The thing you do obsessively between age thirteen and eighteen, that's the thing you have the most chance of being world class at." This was certainly true for me. Had I not observed the equipment used to calm cattle during vaccinations at my aunt's ranch, I couldn't have dreamed up my best-known invention, the Hug Machine, which helped calm my anxiety with deep pressure. My object-visualizing and mechanically inclined mind found a corollary in the mechanics of the farm equipment and an affinity with the horses and cattle. The Hug Machine was conceived of there, and while the first prototype was only a crude construction, it saved my life and went on to help many others. My life would have gone in a completely different direction if not for that early exposure.

It's true that most people are not going to be the next Thomas Edison or Elon Musk. But the next genius will never have an opportunity to emerge if all the roads are blocked.

I think of young Michelangelo at the stonecutter's home, Einstein playing violin as a boy, Picasso's father, an artist himself, instructing his young son to draw a dove, or Steve Jobs nosing around in his neighbor's garage. They were free to explore. Freedom, combined with such traits as persistence, risk taking, novelty seeking, single-mindedness—*plus* divergent thinking—are the hallmarks of brilliant innovators. Are geniuses neurodiverse? My answer would be yes in many cases. Are most geniuses also visual thinkers? It would appear so.

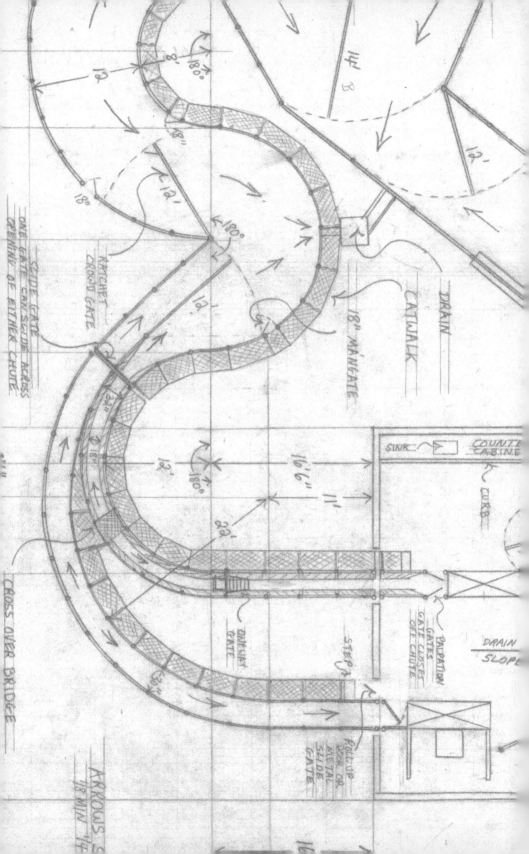

SIX

Visualizing Risk to Prevent Disasters

I am a total NASA geek. I remember running across the street when I was ten years old to watch for Sputnik from an open field with my neighbors. People gathered on rooftops and in yards all over the country to glimpse the Soviet satellite, the first to orbit the earth, heralding the beginning of the space race. Twelve years later, when I was a junior in college, American astronauts landed on the moon. I walked outside and looked up at the moon and could not believe it. All I kept thinking was, *There are people up there*. I was so excited about Apollo and the future of space exploration that I seriously thought about working for NASA, but my math skills were too weak to pass the engineering courses. Long after NASA stopped sending people to the moon and reduced funding of satellites to visit other planets in our solar system, leading most of the public to lose interest in the space program, I was still reading about the space shuttle and the Mars rover missions.

You can understand why I jumped at the opportunity to visit Cape Canaveral when I was invited to give a lecture about neurodiversity there in 2017. As part of a small group of scientists, I got to watch a SpaceX launch. We also toured the vehicle-assembly building and walked around inside a new launchpad that contractors were finishing. I got to view all the complicated equipment that was going to be used to fuel a rocket. I was in geek heaven. Suddenly, a small, rapid movement attracted my attention. When I turned toward it, I saw a raccoon waddle down a staircase and disappear into the bushes. He had spent the night inside the launchpad base. I asked the other people if they had seen the raccoon, including the engineer giving us the tour. Nobody else had noticed it. In my mind's eye, pictures flashed of the things the racoon might have been gnawing on overnight. Chewed-up tool handles would be an annoyance, but chewed-up wiring could be very dangerous if nobody knew about it. It could cause a major malfunction. I explained how raccoons are more likely to be attracted to things people have touched. Like other animals, they seek the salt from people's sweaty hands. NASA had spent millions of dollars on that launchpad. A freeloading raccoon and a chewed set of wires could have been a disaster waiting to happen. Over the years, I have learned that engineering-based programs like NASA need picture thinkers like me to solve problems and visualize potential risks.

Let's start with some everyday examples of ordinary risks and visual thinking. A parent knows that a toddler should be kept away from a hot stove or sharp knives. Toddlers do not recognize many hazards, whether they are running into table corners and walls or choking on small toys. Babies, however, have an instinctual fear of falling. Like most animals, they will refuse to cross a "visual cliff." To study depth perception and development, psychologists Eleanor J. Gibson and Richard D. Walk at Cornell University devised an apparatus that used a checkerboard surface and a sheet of Plexiglas to create the illusion of danger and a steep drop. Babies ranging in age from six and a half to fourteen months refused to venture out over the perceived drop, even with a toy perched at the far end and their mother's encouragement. The same was true for chicks, lambs, and baby goats, who froze into a defensive position when they encountered the "cliff." Gibson and Walk concluded that survival of any species depends on either an innate ability or an ability to develop depth discrimination. As we continue to develop and gain experience, we can better predict and avoid harm's way. For me, this ability is finely tuned. Not only would I see the drop, but the sequence of falling and landing would appear to me as a series of vivid images. Verbal thinkers might intellectualize the same scenario. I see it in a series of pictures or the equivalent of a YouTube video. It's that vivid.

A popular hypothesis about why teenagers tend to exhibit high-risk behavior is that the prefrontal cortex—which is responsible for decision making, planning, judgment, and inhibition—is still developing during our teenage years. By the time we reach our early twenties, our brains mature, and we have built up enough memories of life experiences to anticipate danger, whether we are visual or verbal thinkers. We slam on the brakes when we see a pedestrian crossing against the light. We change batteries in the smoke detectors in our homes. We store extra food in our pantries, and we get vaccinated. All these activities prevent something negative from happening in the future: running someone over, starting a fire, going hungry, or contracting a deadly disease. Most people can visualize everyday risks. You can probably think of many more examples where being able to visualize a potential problem can be life-saving or prevent harm.

As I've said, my mind is wired to see details that can cause danger or just mess things up, like a freeloading raccoon or a blinding sun striking a cattle chute. But I can also picture how large-scale disasters happen, looming catastrophes other people sometimes fail to see. This chapter is about the need for visual thinkers in all kinds of potentially dangerous situations. Visual thinking does not enable me to predict the future. But it does allow me to home in on design flaws and system failures that, unaddressed, can lead to disaster. Yes, we absolutely need engineers, scientists, and mathematicians to discover and formulate solutions to twenty-first-century problems. But we also need the people on the ground, the builders and installers and maintenance people. Danger is not an abstraction. We need the people who live where I live: in the world of practical things.

Risky Business

Engineers calculate risk. They are trained to apply mathematics to problem-solve. (This requires lots of algebra and higher-level math.) Years ago, when I first looked at the curriculum for a top US engineering program, I noted that it required numerous advanced math classes but only a single drafting class. This was my first clue that engineers are not object thinkers. Digging deeper, I compared the curricula of three highly regarded programs in engineering, architecture, and industrial design. The engineering program required the most math and physics classes. Industrial design emphasized art and drawing. And the architecture program split the difference, requiring more math classes than industrial design but not as many as engineering. Industrial design and architecture are fields where object visualizers can excel. Most engineers, regardless of their specialty, are visual-spatial minds.

Out in the field, I have noticed a hierarchy that accords higher status to the work of engineers than to the drafting departments and machine shops that are responsible for realizing the engineers' designs. (University programs have similar if unspoken ranking systems.) I recently visited two organizations, one aerospace and the other high-tech, where engineers with university degrees had fancy offices, while the drafting department was stuck in a service tunnel. The machinists were stuck in the basement. Where they put you tells a lot about how much your job is valued by upper management. Yet without machinists and welders, you could never execute or build anything. People who may not have university degrees, who may not do well in math, who may be quirky, can nevertheless be skilled members of a team. We need to foster the collaboration of object visualizers and spatial visualizers, especially where public safety is concerned.

A look at 2021's cutting-edge space missions by the United States and China clearly shows the need for skilled craftsmen. I looked up the cameras that are now taking gorgeous pictures on Mars. They are beautifully hand-wired. The intricate wiring must be perfectly installed, or the cameras may fail. The people who built the cameras and wired the Mars rover do not get sufficient credit.

The successor to the Hubble Space Telescope has been launched, and it is one hundred times more powerful. This project was delayed for years. One reason for the delays was poor workmanship. Rockets shake their payloads when they take off. To ensure that the new telescope would survive the rigors of the launch, it was subjected to a shake test. It failed miserably, and dozens of bolts and fasteners were scattered. A good object visualizer in the shop could have addressed this problem. They would have visualized the effect of the shaking and designed fasteners that would have withstood liftoff. As of this writing, the James Webb Space Telescope is in the correct position in space, and its mirrors are being adjusted.

———

When I was in college, researchers had to do many of the calculations they needed by hand. You may not recall the IBM punch card—they're obsolete now—but it's what everyone used to sort and process data back then. They were rectangular cards made of stiff paper stock, eighty columns down and twelve rows across—today's airline boarding passes (nearly obsolete, too) look like their evolutionary remnant. I'd enter the data for each animal study project by punching the cards with the results of my observations. For my thesis work, I had to punch several thousand cards. The card-sorting machine was like a mechanical spreadsheet. It enabled me to sort the cards into different categories, such as cattle weight and type of squeeze chute. Each day I could do only one statistical test. After I had sorted my cards, the computing center had to run them on the mainframe. The next day I'd get my results. To do a different statistical test, I'd have to sort my cards all over again.

Today, on a laptop, a student or researcher can run twenty analyses in a couple of hours. Is this a good thing? Obviously yes, for many reasons, but it's important to remember that algorithms can analyze only the data entered into the computer in the first place. Today, rigor is equated with the fanciest methods and a wall of stats. You're not going to come up with accurate results without the brilliant math mind who can crunch the data, but you also need the visual mind that will report accurate data, such as the breed of pig that was used in the research. This is more than a detail, it's an essential piece of information that I have seen omitted in methods sections. Serving as a scientific reviewer for several different journals in my field, I have witnessed an increasing use of complicated statistics; about half the time, they are compromised by serious omissions in the methods section.

In my work with graduate students, I have observed that they sometimes get lost in the math, running endless calculations of slight variations on different statistical tests. One student, looking at the relationship between the shape of the hair whorls on a bull's forehead and the quality of the bull's semen, was getting nowhere: the statistics were finding nothing. Pictures of the bulls flashed in my imagination, and I suggested re-sorting the data into two simple categories: those with normal hair-whorl patterns and those with grossly abnormal ones. A normal hair whorl is a little round spiral, and an abnormal one looks like a long scar. After this re-sort, we found highly significant results.

The bulls with the normal round spirals had higher-quality sperm. The student had been too engulfed in the numbers to consider the physical data. Small details, huge impact on results.

Observation is essential in science—it's the basis for forming a hypothesis for all formal studies. In my own work, I noted behavioral differences in various genetic lines of pigs. I had the opportunity to observe hundreds of different pig types in adjacent pens at meat-packing plants and hog-buying stations. Some were more excitable or got into more fights when they were mixed with other genetic lines. These differences struck me. Many people told me that my observations were just anecdotal. About fifteen years later, quantitative research confirmed my hypothesis.

To have a fruitful collaboration, the "hard science" researchers who rely primarily on data and math must recognize the value of more qualitative findings that provide ideas for research. This is certainly the case for discoveries that were born of serendipity over experimentation. Thomas Ban, emeritus professor of psychiatry at Vanderbilt University, points out that entire classes of pharmaceuticals were discovered when a researcher or physician wasn't crunching data but was observing, a phenomenon he calls, citing *Stedman's Medical Dictionary*, "finding one thing while looking for something else." For instance, the first drugs for treating schizophrenia, depression, infection, and erectile dysfunction were all accidental discoveries. Observation was key. Chlorpromazine (Thorazine) was originally used to improve anesthesia's effects for surgery; a doctor observed that when it was administered to schizophrenic patients, they stopped hallucinating as much. Sildenafil (Viagra) was originally developed to treat high blood pressure and coronary heart disease; then an unexpected side effect was observed that turned the little blue pill into one of the most popular (and profitable) drugs in history.

Visual thinkers are alert to minute differences in methodology, which can make all the difference in an experiment's results. Just as we've seen with MRI testing, accurate and detailed reporting may still fail to identify critical differences. In one case, two groups of scientists on opposite coasts of the United States could not figure out why their identically structured cancer studies yielded different results. They spent an entire year controlling for supplier and equipment differences and ensuring that their tissue samples were prepared in exactly the same way, but they still couldn't replicate their findings. William C. Hines, from the Lawrence Berkeley National Laboratory, and doctors from major hospitals finally discovered that the method they were using to stir their samples was different. One lab vigorously stirred the samples for several hours with a magnetic stirrer, a magnet that spins in the bottom of the glass container that holds the cells. The other gently rocked them on a rotating platform for up to a day. With all of the effort to replicate the experiment, nobody thought to ask about the stirring method. Most of the errors in the findings can be traced to poorly described methods, which make it difficult for another scientist to accurately replicate an experiment. These are the kinds of details that jump out at visual thinkers.

We are in the middle of a replication crisis in biomedical research. In the last few years, the number of studies that have been retracted from the scientific literature has increased significantly. Massive pressure on researchers to publish in order to keep the grant money flowing is largely responsible. A review of the literature by Elisabeth M. Bik, a Dutch microbiologist, and her colleagues indicated that in some cases photos of laboratory test results and microscope images had been manipulated. This is a corruption of the scientific process on which we all depend for verifiable information.

Sometimes there are too many spatial or math minds and not enough object visualizers on a project. Sometimes the different minds don't see each other. The methodologists and the statisticians are on opposite sides of the fence when they should be collaborating. The mathematical analyses are only as good as the data that are put into them. Writing an accurate and comprehensive description of the methods is an essential part of every scientific paper. The big picture is nothing without the details, and vice versa. There should always be an object visualizer on the team to review the methods section of a scientific paper, someone who can see the whorl on a bull's head, the cause of aggressive pig behavior, and different stirring methods in medical trials. Details matter.

The consequences of failing to include the full range of visual thinkers are especially dire when it comes to averting disaster, or what has come to be known as "risk management." Douglas W. Hubbard, in his book *The Failure of Risk Management*, points out that the first time a king built a wall and moat around his castle, or people stored their food for the winter, they were engaged in some form of risk management. The US insurance business started in the mid-1700s, when mathematical and statistical tools such as actuarial tables were developed to calculate probabilities such as life expectancy. Today, health insurance is a trillion-dollar business, and an entire "risk management" industry has grown up to identify hazards to and solutions for everything from shipping and aeronautics to manufacturing, natural disasters, cybersecurity, recessions, and terrorism. As Hubbard observes, "Almost anything that could go wrong is a risk."

Some theorists describe the three main components of risk assessment as identifying the potential risk, assessing the potential damage, and figuring out how to reduce it. Others describe risk management in terms of threats: regular threats, irregular threats, and events without precedent. And still others frame the danger in terms of precedent, probability, and worst-case scenarios. To me, many of these theories of risk analysis get lost in verbiage and are too abstract to be useful. I have no idea what the difference is between a regular threat and an irregular threat. A term such as "worst-case scenario" makes more sense to me, because I can instantly visualize what a worst case would look like. When I read about the crisis in the Flint, Michigan, water system, I could envision the corrosion in the old city pipes that caused lead to leach into the water. It's as if there were a video in my head. And I can picture all the terrible side effects of lead poisoning. It's not an abstraction or a percentage. Theory is necessary, but I'm more interested in preventing or fixing something than discussing the probability of its going wrong. As I said, I live in the world of practical things. I'm the person on the ground.

Infrastructure

Long before the country watched in horror and disbelief as a residential high-rise in Surfside, north of Miami, was reduced to rubble, or as outages in Texas left the state paralyzed without heat and power for days, it was clear that America's infrastructure was compromised and fragile. All you really needed to do was look around at the streets, bridges, overpasses, and electrical grids.

I can exactly recall when I was first alerted to the infrastructure crisis. It was 2012, and I was receiving an honorary doctorate from Arizona State University, where I'd earned my master's degree in animal science (a proud moment for someone with a childhood diagnosis of brain damage). At one of the receptions, one of my former thesis advisers, who was the chairman of the construction department, made the following pronouncement out of the blue: "I am Foster Burton, and people better listen to this old man! Infrastructure is falling apart, and there will not be enough skilled people to rebuild and repair it."

Dr. Burton's predictions on the consequences of failing to maintain the infrastructure of our bridges and roads are now common knowledge. The American Society of Civil Engineers in 2021 released the following astonishing national averages: dams, D; bridges, C+; energy, D+. These are the worst report cards I've ever seen. Seven and a half percent of bridges in the United States are structurally deficient. You don't have to be a structural engineer to see the problem. It's visible to the naked eye. When I'm on the road, all over the country I can see steel reinforcing rods beneath the crumbling concrete of highway overpasses. Once exposed to the elements, the rods rust and swell, causing more concrete to break off. I've seen bridges in this condition hastily wrapped with cables to keep them from collapsing.

When you're a visual thinker, shoddy work screams out at you. As I've said, it's like a sentence full of typos and bad grammar for a verbal thinker. It doesn't make sense. They've got to fix it. A non-visual thinker may register the aesthetic unpleasantness of a crumbling overpass, but the visual thinker, being more connected to the physical world, is more apt to see the dangerous consequences. Putting a Band-Aid on a bridge is just a bad idea.

Once, when I was traveling from New York to Philadelphia, the train slowed down just before getting to the station. In the middle of a derelict train yard filled with decrepit substations, I spotted a brand-new electrical transformer. Here was this piece of gleaming new equipment hooked up to all these rusting parts responsible for distributing electricity. We are still using electrical transmission equipment that was built in the 1950s and 1960s to bring power to our homes and businesses. It looked like the zombie apocalypse, a testament to the state of our infrastructure in 2021, right outside the birthplace of democracy.

It's shocking to me, but not surprising, that the lack of maintenance of electrical transmission wires was the cause of California's massive 2020 wildfires. In 2019, I traveled to one of the state's regions to lecture about cattle handling. The main high-voltage electrical transmission lines are so poorly maintained by Pacific Gas & Electric that every time the wind blows over forty-five miles per hour, the power is turned off out of fear that the electrical wires will fall off the towers and cause fires. Turning off the power is a poor substitute for inspecting and repairing the lines. Either we've lost the will or the suits want to save money and don't listen to the field staff.

If you look up at the big electrical towers that transmit high-voltage power over long distances, it is easy to understand the effects of the lack of maintenance. The brackets and connectors that attach insulators to the towers and cables to the insulators need to be designed to pivot and move. If a cable breaks free and hits the metal tower or another wire, the high voltage will cause a spark that will likely start a fire, especially in a region with so much dry terrain and vegetation. When the brackets get rusted or worn, they need to be replaced. When I saw those towers, I could visualize the entire sequence of the disaster in my mind. I could see the fires burning.

PG&E and some other large electrical companies repair power lines mostly on a "deferred maintenance" basis, which effectively means they get fixed only when something breaks. "Deferred maintenance," in other words, is a euphemism for no maintenance. It's like deferring a medical procedure that could literally save your life. Or deferring your car's annual inspection, allowing the wear and tear to compromise function and safety. Deferred maintenance is just bad policy, whether it's your health, your home, or your community.

In my neighborhood in Fort Collins, all the power lines are buried underground. Thanks to a concerted effort on the part of the city, Fort Collins is considered the poster child of underground electrical lines. Installation started in 1968 and became standard practice for new construction. In 1989, the city successfully buried all existing aboveground power lines. Today the city boasts a 97 percent compliance rate. The benefits are exponential: fewer accidents, improved energy, reduced maintenance costs, and more pleasing aesthetics.

The politicians who keep promising to rebuild crumbling infrastructure probably do not realize that, even if they were able to keep their word, we have lost many of the people with the talent and skills to repair it. Yet there are countless visual thinkers in our midst who could fill those ranks. I know a high school graduate who was not the best student. But he enjoyed shop class, and when he graduated, he started at the bottom rung digging ditches for a power company. Now he's the head troubleshooter for an electric company. As a visual thinker, he can see the whole network, from the highline to the substation transformers to the junction boxes that deliver service to neighborhoods like mine. When there is an outage, he knows exactly where to pinpoint the vulnerability. But without recognizing, training, employing, and properly valuing hands-on workers like him, we are setting ourselves up for ever more failure. These are the people you want in an emergency, not the guy in the corner office.

Words Fail Me

We expect the lights to go on when we flip a switch, and the engine in our car to start when we turn on the ignition. The world is filled with mechanical things we take for granted. But when things break or break down, most people are usually hard-pressed to repair them. Something as basic as overheating can torpedo everything from electrical power grid equipment to boilers for producing steam to home appliances. Excessive spinning speed can damage power-generation turbines, motors, centrifuges—basically any equipment that rotates at too many revolutions per minute. If a washing machine spins too fast during the spin cycle, it will break. Everyday examples abound of accidents waiting to happen. Most of these are hiding in plain sight, unless your brain works like mine and those of other object visual thinkers.

On a larger scale, busted turbines can damage the power plants that generate electricity. Excessive pressure may cause an explosion of boilers, hot-water heaters, and industrial process equipment. In a municipal water system, a pump can be ruined if it's allowed to run dry. Even the garbage disposal in your sink would be damaged if it ran too long without water. I worked for a company whose office burned down on account of a broken thermostat on a coffeemaker. I can't navigate an emotional quandary or resolve a political crisis; that's not how my mind is wired. But I can picture how mechanical things fall apart. And I can also see how to fix them.

I first came to understand how visual thinking could be instrumental in predicting problems while I was working in the industrial world. Industrial accidents of all kinds can be calculated in a straightforward manner because there is lots of accurate historical data, much of it compiled by the Department of Labor's Bureau of Labor Statistics. Historical data is the best road map we have for preventing accidents. I've witnessed up close what can happen when stakes are high and things go wrong. In my field, before strict safety rules were implemented in the late 1980s, accidents involved some gruesome stuff, such as limb amputations that resulted from moving machinery such as conveyors, rotating shafts, and unguarded screw augers, gear drives, and chain drives. An industrial conveyor belt handles literally tons of weight; this is a high-risk apparatus. In my own work, I have installed pressure-limiting devices to prevent a restraint device from injuring an animal by either bruising it or, worse, breaking its back. I've learned that you can't trust the operator; you need built-in safeguards to protect the animal from a careless operator. Same for humans.

The first time I saw a heavy gate at the meat plant, I immediately saw that it could come crashing down and crush a person's head like a melon. I also envisioned the solution: leave a sufficient gap between the bottom of the closed gate and the floor. When I got home that night, I stuck my head in a desk drawer and added an inch to the measurement. Then I designed a safer gate. It still did the work of keeping the livestock in, but it no longer presented a safety risk to the operators.

Have you ever had the experience of struggling to solve a problem, and then having the solution come to you all at once? Researchers at the University of London wanted to study such aha moments. As reported in an article in *Scientific American*, hoping to uncover which brain signals are responsible for problem solving, they gave EEGs to twenty-one volunteers to study how the brain processes verbal problems. They found that many of their subjects hit a wall or a "mental impasse." One explanation, writes Nikhil Swaminathan, is that the participants got "locked into an inflexible way of thinking and [were] less able to free their minds, and thereby unable to restructure the problem before them." I speculate that the aha moment comes to a verbal thinker when the brain is distracted, as we'll see in the next chapter. Typically, though, when it comes to solving mechanical problems, I've observed that verbal thinkers often get lost in the weeds as they try to construct a word-based explanation to arrive at a solution. For me, the aha moment often comes quickly, because I am already thinking in images, and my brain can quickly reshuffle the pictures, almost like a deck of cards, to let me see the solution. The visual thinker has a more direct path to seeing certain kinds of solutions.

Most design problems can be sorted into four basic types: design error, operator error, poor maintenance of vital equipment, or a complex combination of risks. In the 1970s, when I was a graduate student, engineering classes famously used the case of the 1940 Tacoma Narrows Bridge accident to illustrate design error, or how just one detail can upend function. The suspension bridge was nicknamed Galloping Gertie because when the wind blew strongly enough, the road deck would vibrate. If you think about the vibrations of a guitar string and multiply that exponentially, you can imagine an entire bridge vibrating under heavy winds. The engineering on the bridge's suspension cables was sound and could have withstood the vibrations. But, unlike the Golden Gate Bridge, which has wide, open, triangular-shaped trusses, the girders on Gertie were covered with solid metal, which blocked the flow of air. So, instead of stabilizing the bridge, the girders acted as sails filling with more and more wind, causing what is known as wind-induced oscillation, or aeroelastic flutter. Another problem was that the framework of girders was too narrow to stabilize the road deck sufficiently. The bridge buckled under the wind load and swelled like waves until it collapsed. Fortunately, no lives were lost that day (except for one dog who refused to join his owner and abandon a car stuck on the collapsing bridge).

The design of the Golden Gate Bridge is far superior to that of the Tacoma Narrows Bridge, but an entirely different kind of disaster was averted in 1987, when the Golden Gate celebrated it golden anniversary. To commemorate the occasion, San Francisco allowed 300,000 people to walk across it, with 500,000 more hoping to do the same. The turnout was ten times what had been expected, and people were packed shoulder to shoulder for the entire 1.7-mile length of the bridge. As a result, the bridge deck sagged a full seven feet until the people were removed and the overflow crowd was, thankfully, turned away. The problem wasn't poor maintenance; the bridge had been well maintained, which certainly helped to avert disaster. And it wasn't a problem of design. As a suspension bridge, the structure was engineered to bend and move, and while this was the biggest load the bridge had seen, "it did not exceed the design load capacity of the bridge," as engineer Mark Ketchum pointed out. In this case, the problem was the math. According to Stephen Tung of the San Jose *Mercury News*, while the weight of the individuals on the bridge was unknown, "if the average person weighs 150 pounds and occupies 2.5 square foot in a crowd . . . that's more than double the weight of cars in bumper-to-bumper traffic." Had the additional people been allowed access, there would have been a catastrophic tragedy.

Design error was to blame in 2016 when San Francisco's fifty-eight-story

Millennium Tower started to tilt. Whether out of cost-cutting or simply poor engineering, the builders failed to drill deep enough to put the pilings down into bedrock. That would be engineering 101. As a result, the building sank seventeen inches on one side, and eventually the walls and concrete cracked in the below-ground parking garage. To attempt to stop the tilt, $100 million is being spent to drill 250 feet down, into bedrock. As of April 2022, when I checked for an update, the building is still tilting, and had sunk a total of twenty-eight inches. I would never live there!

During my many trips across the country, I have observed from inside my car huge disparities in how different states maintain highway overpasses. In one state, you can see crumbling concrete and exposed, rusted metal reinforcing rods, while across state lines, a similar bridge is freshly painted and small areas of cracked concrete are patched. An article by Rob Horgan in *New Civil Engineer* connects lack of maintenance with catastrophic bridge failures. Corroded suspension cables fail one wire strand at a time, and rusted expansion joints are not able to expand and contract when the temperature changes. You can see this with the naked eye.

Other disasters are below our sight lines. In the Merrimack Valley in Massachusetts, old cast-iron distribution pipes first installed in the early 1900s were slowly being replaced with modern plastic ones. The old system of gas distribution consisted of a complex series of regulators and sensors that reduced the pressure from the main distribution lines to a much lower pressure for neighborhood distribution lines. Contractors failed to transfer the pressure regulation system's sensors over to the new line before disconnecting the old lines. When, in 2018, one of the old lines was cut, the pressure sensor in the old line immediately responded to the falling pressure and opened the valves, funneling gas into the new line at full blast. This resulted in many neighborhood lines getting the full 75 pounds per square inch (psi) pressure instead of the normal 0.5 psi. Gas lines ruptured and gas started gushing into houses and businesses. This error made during construction resulted in fires in thirty-nine homes and the destruction of multiple buildings. One person was killed, and fifty thousand people were forced to evacuate their homes or businesses. Columbia Gas had to pay a $143 million settlement for damages. They also had to pay the highest fine ever imposed for violating the Natural Gas Pipeline Safety Act. This was the country's worst natural gas accident in a residential area in recent times. Investigation quickly revealed that excessive pressure in the gas distribution lines was the cause of the accident.

According to the National Transportation Safety Board (NTSB), the cause of this mistake was "deficiencies in management." Their investigation report said that an engineer with a professional engineer certification should have signed off on the drawings and the work orders. One problem was that the old system was more complicated than modern gas distribution systems. Over many years, bits and pieces had been replaced and modified. In the gas industry, as in the meat industry, it is good engineering practice to update the drawings when any major part of a system is changed or swapped out. Otherwise, a lapse in accurate historical data will lead to the kind of disaster that happened in the Merrimack Valley.

The "as built" drawings companies have provided me with have ranged from excellent to atrocious. I have gone out and measured a site for a new stockyard and found a ten-foot mistake in the location of buildings. You do not want to start digging for a new foundation only to find a sewage system below. The best records are often kept by companies where one person is responsible for maintaining the drawings, sometimes the original owner or a longtime employee. Keeping meticulously updated drawings is rare these days, but no less crucial in the prevention of accidents. In my experience, the only dependable way to calculate risk is with accurate historical data.

Some companies take a proactive approach to safety, fostering a culture of safe practices and responsibility. Others are reactive, responding to problems after they happen. The 2010 Deepwater Horizon oil rig explosion killed eleven and injured many others, and the subsequent oil spill created one of the largest environmental disasters in our history. It was caused by a combination of operator error and poor maintenance, exacerbated by a disconnect between policies and practices. Forty-six percent of the workers on Deepwater Horizon feared reprisal if they reported safety problems in a culture that prioritized cost cutting and efficiency. By all reports, this tragedy might have been prevented had management adopted better protocols.

According to investigative reporting by David Barstow, David Rohde, and Stephanie Saul in *The New York Times*, Horizon's systems deployed but didn't function, were activated too late, or were not activated at all. The crew was trained to field problems but was unprepared for a blowout, fires, and power loss. The *Times* article reported that while the handbook was hailed as a "safety expert's dream," it didn't answer the basic question of when to act. When action was required, the crew failed to deploy the emergency shutdown system. Further, said the article, "one emergency system alone was controlled by 30 buttons." The employee responsible for shutting it down claimed she had not been taught how to use the system. "I don't know any of the procedures," she said.

The blowout preventer (BOP) is exactly what it sounds like: a 400-ton valve that works like the plug in your toilet tank, only it's meant as a final failsafe in the event of various forces causing the well to blow. Blowout preventers are meant to be the "ultimate fail-safe," but the investigation by the *New York Times* reporters concludes that the BOP "may have been crippled by poor maintenance. Investigators have found a host of problems—dead batteries, bad solenoid valves, leaking hydraulic lines—that were overlooked or ignored." On top of that, a routine maintenance inspection didn't happen. And even as the crew evacuated, they were met with another compromised set of protocols that were meant to have ensured their safety. Bewilderingly, though they practiced evacuation drills, "they had never rehearsed inflating and lowering the raft. They had trouble freeing it from the deck, more trouble keeping it level and more trouble still getting it loaded." Even the lifeboats were a near-epic fail.

Could any of these catastrophes have been avoided? There is an expression that hindsight is 20/20. It may be impossible to have perfect foresight, but it is essential to include people who visually problem-solve as part of the team when the stakes are high. When we privilege abstract or verbal solutions, critical though they are to many tasks, we run the risk of excluding crucial visual thinking. We need people who can simulate unforeseen consequences in their mind's eye and envision solutions in real time. In 2011 and then again in 2019, I became obsessed with two tragic disasters: one involved among many things a design element in aerospace, and the other involved the construction of the retainer wall in a nuclear power plant. What follows are two detailed case studies of these catastrophes and what might have prevented them.

Boeing 737 MAX

You've probably heard that your chances of dying in a car accident are far greater than those of dying in a commercial airplane accident. According to the PBS program *Nova*, your chances of dying in a car accident are 1 in 7,700, while those of dying in a plane crash are 1 in 2.067 million. And yet most people think nothing of getting in a car, but flying can cause a great deal of anxiety. I'm the kind of person who can read about plane crashes while sitting in a plane at 38,000 feet. In the first place, I'm a fact-based person and not terribly ruled by emotion. In the second place, I've been obsessed with planes and flight since I was a child experimenting with paper airplanes and making helicopters out of popsicle sticks and rubber bands. However, there was a period when I feared flying. I was a high school senior, and I had taken a trip on a 707 jet that had to make an emergency landing on account of a bomb threat. We evacuated the plane and slid down the emergency escape slides. It was terrifying, and it left me a white-knuckle flier for several years.

Exposure therapy helps people get over their fears by exposing them to the things they are afraid of in a controlled, safe setting. I inadvertently had a huge dose of exposure therapy in the early 1970s, when I flew with a family-run company that specialized in transporting animals, in this case cattle. I had met the owners at an Animal Air Transportation Association meeting, and they invited me to watch how they hauled a planeload of Holstein heifers from Miami to Puerto Rico. I was still scared of flying, but I couldn't pass up this opportunity. I should have had a clue about how bad it was going to be when I heard them call the airplane "Cowshit Connie." Cow urine leaked out of holes drilled in the fuselage. In another plane, beef was tied down with cargo straps where passenger seats had been. It was a hot day, and I nearly gagged from the smell. It was shocking to see a commercial 707 jet airliner treated so badly, its guts ripped out and filled with bloody meat.

But when I got to ride in the jump seat of the "Connie" with a load of Holstein heifers and observe from the cockpit the aqua-blue water shimmering below, my fascination overcame my fear. My visual mind became obsessed with every control; I had to know how it all worked. Thanks to that huge, unforeseen dose of exposure therapy, flying was no longer scary to me. I can now fly anywhere, anytime, and under any conditions. When you know how things work, they are a lot less frightening.

A few years ago, while I was traveling to speaking events, an assistant from the publishing company would often accompany me to set up my book table. Brad and I are both aviation geeks, and at dinner we would watch YouTube videos of aircraft doing crazy things. My favorite videos showed test pilots flying airliners as if they were fighter jets with afterburners. The pilots flew them almost straight up, like a rocket.

Brad and I were on the road in October 2018, when Lion Air flight 610 crashed into the water off the coast of Indonesia. One hundred eighty-nine people died, including a child and two infants. What happened that day was devastating. My reaction was intense. I had to understand what happened. This is how I deal with tragic events. I don't get swallowed up in emotion. Instead, I'm driven to comprehend how a tragedy of this scale could happen. The images replayed over and over in my head.

The first thing I did after hearing about the accident was search the internet for more information. I found two crucial facts. The first was that the jet was only a few months old, basically brand-new. Second, I learned from Flightradar24 that after takeoff, the ground radar tracking of the plane's flight path was weird. The altitude tracing should show a gradual, steady increase. The radar tracing on flight 610 had jagged-looking lines, like those on a heart monitor, and multiple sudden altitude changes, indicating climbing and diving. I knew no pilot in his right mind would do that. My first thought was that something was terribly wrong with this new model of plane, which Boeing had first released only a year and a half before the crash. At that point, I knew nothing about the Boeing 737 MAX planes except that Lion Air was buying them up for their fuel efficiency.

The next day I gave a talk at Oakland University, near Detroit, on autism and higher education. I brought up the crash and made a prediction: "Boeing is going to be in deep poo-poo." I had a visual intuition that there was something wrong with the engineering of this airplane. Brad was sitting in the audience, and he wondered how I knew that.

One way to explain how my visual files work is to imagine an ever-expanding accordion file or picture files on a phone. New information is constantly added and sorted from the world around me. If the image is important or interesting, it's as if my mind automatically takes a picture of it. With language, there is a finite number of words most people learn. According to a study published in

Frontiers in Psychology, by the age of twenty, English-speaking Americans know about 42,000 words. After that, adults learn one or two new words every two days until middle age, when they stop adding new words to their vocabulary (although of course there are an infinite number of ways to combine the words they already have). By contrast, my visual vocabulary continues to grow, adding new information all the time. And my problem-solving skills increase as I add more pictures, which link up to the pictures I already have. If you've ever sorted the pictures on your phone by category, place, or date, it's a little like that.

That's how I came to learn that a tiny device the size of a Sharpie marker was critical in the crash. I saw a picture in a news report, and out of a series of images from everything I've learned about aviation, my initial intuition about the malfunction focused on the sensor. Making the connection required me to have the sensor and the Sharpie in my visual vocabulary. Visual problem-solving is largely associational.

This sensor, known as the "angle-of-attack vane," is attached to the fuselage below the cockpit window and measures the angle of flight relative to wind currents. I was shocked to learn that while the Boeing MAX had two angle-of-attack sensors, it used only one, and that it was wired directly to the plane's flight computer. Angle-of-attack sensors are very fragile, and it is not a good engineering practice to rely on a single delicate sensor. Usually, this sensor is wired to an indicator on the pilot's flight display and serves as an aid to pilots, warning but not overriding them when the plane's nose is pointing up too high and putting the plane in danger of stalling. The faulty sensor on the Boeing MAX, however, signaled to the computer that the plane was stalling when it was flying normally, and thus forced the nose down in response. That would be like your car speeding ahead on cruise control but no one telling you it was on cruise control.

Basically, it comes down to this: The computer was programmed to push the plane's nose down to counteract a stall that did not exist. This is what accounted for the wiggly lines. The pilots reacted by pulling back on the control yoke to pull the plane's nose back up, just as you would slam on the brakes if your car surged ahead on autopilot. Every time the computer pushed the plane's nose down and made it dive, the doomed pilots pulled back to recover. They did not know what else to do. While one pilot kept fighting the computer, the other was frantically trying to read the plane's manual. Boeing assumed that the pilots would know how to disable the system. The plane had never been test-flown with the sensor broken. The pilots were the backup for the broken sensor, but they were not fully informed about the new computerized system.

My mind automatically runs through a series of visual simulations to explain how the sensor could have been damaged. I can see a mechanic's ladder leaning on it, or a jet bridge crushing it. It could have been broken by inclement weather or by a cleaning crew. Bird strikes were a known hazard. There is simply no way to build a damage-proof sensor. It must touch air, so it has to interact with the environment. In some ways it resembles the sense organs for touch or hearing in people and animals. For instance, sound waves jiggle the eardrum, then go through a complex leverage system before traveling through a fluid-filled chamber (the cochlea). Little hairs inside the cochlea (like tall grass) wave and convert them to electrical stimuli that get sent to the brain. In both an angle-of-attack sensor and human sense organs, a physical phenomenon, such as air angle, sound waves, or pressure, needs to be converted to electrical signals that either a computer or the brain can interpret. It is easy for an object visualizer to see how both biological and engineered sensing devices interact with the environment.

Some experts recommend a "standby system" that uses three sensors so that, if one fails, a reading can be taken from the other two. An article by Mike Baker and Dominic Gates in *The Seattle Times* reported that several of the MAX's test pilots did not know that the system relied on a single sensor. I also discovered that 737 MAXes did not include as a standard feature an angle-of-attack disagree alert, which immediately tells pilots when readings from the sensors don't match up with each other. I thought, why would they not integrate the two sensors, allowing one to function as backup if the other failed? How could they make a mistake this basic?

The Boeing designers also made the mistake of assuming that if the computer made the plane dive when it was flying normally, the pilots would know how to correct the plane's flight. The engineers assumed that the pilots would know how to disable the computer system by taking manual control of the horizontal stabilizer. Pilots are trained to manually command the horizontal fin on the plane's tail when an electrical malfunction causes the stabilizer to move on its own, a problem known as runaway trim. William Langewiesche, in a *New York Times Magazine* story about the Boeing crash, contends that "these pilots couldn't decipher a variant of a simple runaway trim . . . leading their passengers over an aerodynamic edge into oblivion." The problem was Boeing's flawed software system, which repeatedly and aggressively forced the nose of the plane down. It was a perfect storm: a pilot uninformed about the new computer systems, poorly designed software, and a malfunctioning sensor. Captain Chesley Sullenberger, the pilot who successfully landed a plane on the Hudson River, piloted a full-motion flight simulation that replicated the Boeing MAX malfunction. In a letter to the editor of *The New York Times*, he called the automated system a death trap.

Pilot error is cited in 80 percent of all plane crashes. Lion Air was known for poor maintenance and for promoting pilots prematurely to meet the demands of a growing travel market. Overreliance on automation is also a growing concern. Pilots in the United States often learn on small planes that they fly manually. The control surfaces on the tail and wings are the same on both a huge jet and a small Cessna. Learning this way enables a pilot to develop motor memory of how to fly the plane, much as you learn to drive a car. Once you get some experience driving, you no longer think about how to turn the wheel or how much to pump the brakes. It's automatic. Pilots need to learn similar skills, but in three dimensions, because the plane has three axes of motion. Fighter pilots call it "strapping on the jet" or "becoming one with the jet."

I've worked in the design field long enough to know that you need to design for the least competent person. I have built systems such that no operator could get their arms stuck in the equipment. In my mind's eye, I could see an operator's arm getting caught in a gap between a wall and a moving part. I've observed that laziness and stupidity will take any project down and result in injury to the crew or damage to the equipment. Engineers do not always see this. It's possible that not being on the ground themselves, they overestimate the abilities of the people operating the equipment.

I recently met an expert pilot on a flight from London. We had an interesting conversation about the Boeing disaster. He said the pilots should have shut off the automation and flown the airplane. He couldn't have been more certain of himself. I told him my theory about the sensor, and he looked surprised. He wanted to know if I was in the aviation field, and I told him that I designed equipment for livestock. I'm not sure if it was just typical flier exhaustion, or if he thought I was a conspiracy crackpot, but at that point he clapped on his headphones and slept for the entire flight. While we were taxiing into the gate in Chicago, I told him that I thought the Boeing MAX should have been designed for the average pilot, not experts like him. He looked genuinely surprised. "Oh," he said, "I had not thought of that."

One thing I hadn't thought of in my initial investigation of the Boeing MAX: Follow the money. Boeing had adopted a culture of cost cutting. Peter Robison, in his book *Flying Blind*, explained how Boeing's engineers no longer made major decisions, and that the company's focus had switched to serving its stockholders. In my own work with many major meat companies, I have observed a similar pattern. The companies that focus on quality first have better products, have fewer accidents, and are less likely to make hasty decisions that cause huge, costly problems in the future.

Along with labor, fuel is one of the largest costs for an airline. New fuel-efficient engines use 14 to 15 percent less fuel. Boeing management had originally planned to create an entirely new airplane that was specifically designed for the huge new engines. Their plans changed when Airbus came up with a new, fuel-efficient airplane. Designing a totally new airframe would require more time than simply retrofitting the new wide engines onto an existing Boeing 737 airframe. The Boeing 737 MAX is a kludge design—a term for when parts from different planes are cobbled together. But for Boeing, using the same airframe meant they were also able to avoid taking pilots out of the air for additional pilot training. When a new airplane is introduced, every pilot is required to spend time in the flight simulator to learn how to fly it. Putting new, fuel-efficient engines on a 737 airframe allowed both Boeing and the airlines to avoid the pilot-retraining requirements.

They quickly ran into two huge problems. First, the larger, fuel-efficient engines had to be mounted farther forward to provide ground clearance, a requirement that made the plane more unstable and prone to stalling. Second, the new engines were so wide that they started to act like wings and provide lift. This would tend to tilt up the nose of the plane, which, as you may remember from making paper planes as a kid, can cause stall. Langewiesche cuts to the chase: "Some at Boeing argued for an aerodynamic fix, but the modifications would have been slow and expensive, and Boeing was in a hurry." To solve the stalling problem, Boeing created software called MCAS (Maneuvering Characteristics Augmentation System) to make the MAX steering feel the same as the previous 737 model. Langewiesche reports, "Boeing believed the system to be so innocuous, even if it malfunctioned, that the company did not inform pilots of its existence or include a description of it in the airplane's flight manuals." As far as Boeing was concerned, it was win-win. The airline got fuel efficiency, and the pilots would not have to be grounded for simulator training. MAXes sold like hotcakes, providing stiff competition for the rival Airbus.

Of course, that's not how it played out. On the plane's previous flight, before the fatal Lion Air crash, a broken angle-of-attack sensor triggered a series of dives. That time, by chance, a third pilot riding as a passenger in the cockpit jump seat knew how to handle the plane. He flipped the trim-cutout switches, as one would do in the case of runaway trim, restoring control over the horizontal stabilizer to the pilots. When the plane landed in Jakarta, the broken angle-of-attack sensor was replaced with a used one supplied by a used parts dealer nicknamed "Cockroach Corner." Any reputable airline would have grounded this plane. But Lion Air had both a horrible safety history and a trail of faked maintenance records. It cleared the plane after this near miss for what would be its final, fatal flight.

A few months later, a second Boeing MAX, operated by Ethiopian Airlines, crashed due to a similar malfunction, nose-diving into a field at almost seven hundred miles per hour. Investigators found wreckage buried as deep as thirty feet in the ground. After that tragedy, all Boeing 737 MAX planes were grounded. I'm sure the planes would never have stopped flying if they had used a two-sensor system, and if the pilots had been fully informed on how to react to a malfunctioning system.

People from over thirty other countries died on that plane. A final, grim detail stayed with me: portraits of the deceased crew were placed in chairs for the funeral because there were no bodies to bury.

Meltdown

First the electricity cuts off. Then the cooling systems fail. Then the reactor overheats. After that, there is no turning back. The genie is out of the bottle.

The nuclear fuel melts, hydrogen is released, explosions follow, and radioactive material escapes into the atmosphere. Nuclear accidents are among the most lethal and destructive human-made disasters, terrifying and devastating in their impact on human life and the environment. From what I can tell, most of these disasters didn't have to happen.

On most nuclear reactor sites, there are multiple large diesel generators to supply electricity during emergencies. During any emergency, the reactor will be "scrammed," meaning the control rods that stop the nuclear reaction will be inserted into the reactor core. When this occurs, the reactor can no longer create sufficient heat to generate electricity. Nuclear power plants use the intense heat from the nuclear reactor to create steam to turn turbines that spin the generators, creating electricity. Nuclear energy 101. I like the way John Matson in *Scientific American* describes how nuclear reactors work: "Most nuclear reactors . . . are essentially high-tech kettles that efficiently boil water to produce electricity."

Only one problem: Inserting the control rods does not completely stop the creation of heat in the reactor core. To say it simply, inserting control rods *almost* turns the heat off. Engineers call the heat that remains after the control rods have been inserted "residual heat." To prevent a meltdown, cooling water must be used to prevent overheating. When the reactor is scrammed, an external power supply such as a diesel generator on the premises or electricity from an external power grid is required to run the emergency cooling equipment.

Most people are aware of the 1986 nuclear disaster in Chernobyl, probably because it was the most famous nuclear accident at the time, resulting in the evacuation and abandonment of an entire city to limit radiation poisoning. The irony is that it happened while the operators were testing a safety procedure. During the test, the nuclear reactor core overheated. This caused a chain reaction that resulted in a steam explosion releasing radioactive contamination into the atmosphere for ten consecutive days. Thirty-one people died in the following weeks, and about 135,000 people were evacuated. There is no way to definitively gauge the long-term health effects for people who were exposed, but radiation sickness is estimated to have eventually taken the lives of 4,000 people who were involved with or lived near Chernobyl. The surrounding pine forest died and is now known as the Red Forest. Some animals stopped reproducing. Horses died when their thyroid glands disintegrated, and gross deformities in animals were reported, including extra limbs and missing eyes. The damage was far-reaching globally, affecting the oceans and marine life. The accident was rated a level 7, the maximum rating on the International Nuclear and Radiological Event Scale.

In the United States, Three Mile Island remains the largest nuclear meltdown. The first thing that went wrong was a pump failure, which was followed by automatic fail-safe measures kicking in. So far, so good—until a relief valve that was supposed to close got stuck in the open position. Then a sensor in the control room erroneously showed that the valve was in the closed position. The operators in the control room responded by making a lot of mistakes, including pushing some of the wrong buttons. In addition, the pressure indicator was located behind large instrument panels, when it should have been more readily accessible. It was like someone hiding the car keys when you need to make a getaway. The poor design in the control room was compounded by a deafening alarm system that made it virtually impossible to calmly activate safety protocols. According to J. Samuel Walker's book *Three Mile Island: A Nuclear Crisis in Historical Context*, the alarm system kicked in "within a few seconds after the accident began," setting off "a loud horn and more than a hundred flashing lights on the control panels." This would have caused confusion and panic.

Additionally, our overreliance on meters and indicators and our blind trust in sensors contribute to our lack of preparedness when something goes wrong. Sensors, like humans, are fallible. Visual thinkers run a movie of every eventuality in their minds. They visualize the possible ways the valve could have become stuck open. The first thing I would have done is go out to look at the valve before it got too dangerous. In the case of Three Mile Island, thankfully, the containment building successfully did the job for which it was designed. The reactor core partially melted, ruining the reactor, but it stayed fully contained in the heavy concrete containment building. There was no damage to the surrounding environment.

The other nuclear disaster on a par with Chernobyl, also classified as level 7, was at the Fukushima Daiichi nuclear power plant. In March 2011, the biggest earthquake on record in Japan triggered a tsunami that flooded the plant. According to an article in the *Harvard Business Review*, "It was the largest fault slip seismologists had ever seen: 50 meters of tectonic movement in two and a half terrifying minutes." Earthquakes cause over 80 percent of giant tsunami waves by moving the ocean floor. Approximately fifty minutes later, a giant tsunami crashed over northeastern Fukushima prefecture on Japan's Pacific coast, a result of the quake, taking thousands of lives with it, injuring many more, and destroying homes, businesses, roads, railways, and communications infrastructure in its wake. All of this was horrendous enough, but the tsunami took one more turn that set off another destructive chain of irreversible events: the tsunami reached the Fukushima Daiichi nuclear power plant.

It wasn't hard for me to figure out what happened upon reading the first reports out of Japan. I could visualize the series of events as if watching a video based on everything I knew about nuclear power and plant design basics. When the quake first shook the Fukushima plant, the automatic systems scrammed the reactors. The control rods automatically dropped into the reactor cores to slow down the nuclear fission process. When the earthquake broke the electrical transmission lines that supplied electricity from the grid, the diesel generators automatically turned on. When the shaking stopped, all the emergency equipment worked perfectly. At this point, there was no damage.

This is where the mathematical minds had a great success. Every component, ranging from the buildings, the reactors, and the pumps to the generators and the control room, had been designed with precise calculations that made them earthquake-proof. Stresses on a wide variety of materials—concrete, steel beams, plumbing, and electrical wiring—had been taken into account. In that respect, the designers had done a brilliant job of engineering.

Except that the worst was yet to come. When the big wave hit the Fukushima site, it completely flooded the station and ruined all but one of the thirteen emergency generators. This is what engineers call "station blackout." Almost nothing worked, and the control room for reactors one and two was pitch black. This made it impossible to monitor the reactors for overheating. The only thing that worked was a landline telephone. The operators attempted to use their own car batteries to power the control panel. Getting supplies was almost impossible, because the roads leading to the station were blocked or washed away. Other essential gear, such as cooling pumps, electrical switch gear, and backup electrical batteries, was flooded.

I'm driven by one question: How does it happen? The plant was earthquake-proof, but the station was poorly designed to resist flooding. The mistake struck me as elementary. Again, you start with the historical data. It is the best and only truly reliable way to assess risk. Though tsunamis were recorded as early as 684 CE, the modern study and collection of tsunami data in Japan only began in 1896, when a tsunami claimed the lives of 22,000 people. Given that Japan is the country most frequently affected by tsunamis, it's hard to comprehend the lack of foresight by the people who built the plant. The tsunami that completely inundated the Fukushima site was nearly fifty feet tall, more than double the wave height the station had been designed to resist. If the station had been constructed at a higher elevation, the accident might never have happened. Later I would learn that a sister nuclear power station located about six miles away and built on slightly higher ground had far less damage. Fukushima Daini, or F2, suffered less extensive flooding and was able to maintain limited electrical power from the external power grid and a single generator. Most important, the control room—containing indicators for monitoring the reactors—still had electricity and was operational.

I was haunted by another simple design oversight that compromised the station. If the essential cooling equipment at Fukushima Daiichi, or F1, had been protected with both watertight doors and walls that could withstand being submerged, the meltdown of the reactor cores could have been prevented. Watertight doors are an old technology, used for many years on ships and then adapted for submarines. On a ship, doors can be safety devices to prevent sinking if the hull is punctured, by sealing off the breached compartment.

With all the sophisticated technology involved in running a nuclear power plant, watertight compartments did not make the punch list, even though they could have saved lives by preventing the meltdowns and protecting the cooling equipment and emergency electrical power sources from being inundated with water. Nor had anything been done to upgrade them. The reactors melted because the emergency cooling pump and the generators needed to run them were almost all submerged under water. Whether at a nuclear power plant or at a cattle-handling facility, electrical equipment gets shorted out and ruined when it gets wet. Someone who had envisioned the water coming over the top of the seawall and flooding the station would have provided for that.

Site superintendent Naohiro Masuda, at the Fukushima Daini station, which did not have a meltdown, had twenty-nine years of experience working at nuclear power plants. He knew every inch of Daini and had earned the trust of the workers, whom he dispatched to assess the damage and then recruited in a superhuman effort to cool down the reactors. Remember, this all happened under chaotic conditions, with many workers not knowing if their families were alive or their homes intact. And time was working against them, with no emergency cooling on three of the four reactors. Masuda knew he had to get electricity to the pumps before the reactors started core meltdown. After first trying to draw power from a radioactive-waste building, Masuda realized the only way to stop a meltdown in time was to run huge, heavy power cables from the single working generator to the pumps. When I described the crisis to one of my students, she said, "Oh, giant extension cords." Masuda's team ended up laying several miles of cable. Pressure readings from the control room enabled him to decide which reactor should be first to get cooling. When the pressure in another reactor started rising more quickly, Masuda was agile enough to pivot, bringing the cable to that reactor. To me, this is straightforward visual thinking.

Masuda prevented a dangerous meltdown that would have released radioactive material into the environment. Another factor that helped prevent a meltdown was Masuda's style of management. Chuck Casto, a US federal agent, reported that Masuda gave his employees all the information about the tsunami and damage to the station. This helped reduce anxiety, because when people have knowledge, they are empowered to act. Masuda also gave his employees a clear, easily understood goal of achieving cold shutdown. While Masuda was working hands-on, his counterpart at the other plant that was melting down was sitting in a remote emergency center, communicating by video link. This "suit" did not know the extent of the damage until he watched it on the TV news. Later, Masuda would be appointed F1's chief decommissioning officer.

I will put my faith in the person on the ground any day. It's not to say that the spatial and mathematical minds aren't important, but without people who can implement and repair systems, who rely on pragmatics such as historical data and take all environmental possibilities into account, we will not be safe. As reported in the *Bulletin of the Atomic Scientists*, the nuclear engineer and former director of F1 said, "We can only work on precedent, and there was no precedent. When I headed the plant, the thought of a tsunami never crossed my mind." How is that possible in a region known for multiple seismic events?

According to sociologist Charles Perrow, author of the seminal book *Normal Accidents: Living with High-Risk Technologies*, the problem does not reside in human error, mechanical failure, environment, design, or procedures, though usually one of these factors (human error) is singled out. According to Perrow, accidents emanate from a series of failures. The first failure in the crash of Lion Air Flight 610 was reliance on a single delicate sensor, and the second mistake was not informing the pilots about the existence of the MCAS. The third and fourth areas of failure were Lion Air's poor maintenance and the plane's lack of an angle-of-attack disagree indicator. This would have informed the pilots that one of the sensors was broken. This is where verbal thinkers can overthink things. To my mind, as a visual thinker and a designer, it's not that complicated. Had the engineers at F1 been able to see the probability of a massive tsunami, they would likely have installed waterproof compartments in the basement. Perhaps they wouldn't have put the diesel generators and emergency batteries in the basement, or maybe they would have built on a higher elevation to begin with. In both the Boeing and Fukushima accidents, I see it: the single sensor breaking, or water coming over the top of the seawalls.

Future Dangers

The future is here. Numerous ransomware attacks have already occurred. Common hacks have disabled corporations, schools, hospitals, and municipal governments. The hackers break into a computer system and encrypt all its files, compromising a company's ability to access billing, deliveries to customers, payrolls, hospital records, car registrations, and many other vital systems. To get their files back, corporations or towns pay a ransom fee. These hackers are in it for the money. Two of the biggest such ransomware attacks were at Colonial Pipeline and JBS Foods. The Colonial hack shut down fuel distribution to the East Coast. Gas stations ran out of fuel, and airlines started having shortages. The JBS hack shut down beef- and pork-processing plants in the United States, Australia, and Canada.

After the Colonial and JBS hacks, all I could think about was the importance of protecting physical equipment against cyberattacks. If Colonial had major equipment damage, it could take months to repair. I visualized chaos at hundreds of gas stations because gasoline would now have to be delivered cross-country by truck. I could see cars following gas tankers so that they would be first in line to get the gas.

The people who know how to protect the physical infrastructure in these situations work on the pipeline or in a basement shop at the beef-processing plant. They need to be sought out and consulted. Algebra may be impossible for them, but they can help avert total disaster the way Naohiro Masuda did at F2.

Since I've come of age, most of our cars, industrial equipment, and appliances in homes have come under the control of computers. Computerized systems control how the power grid distributes electricity when everybody turns on their air conditioners at once. They also enable your phone to unlock your front door, and they automatically control heating and cooling in your home. The risk of something going wrong is compounded by the fact that many of our devices are connected to the internet. Hackers have already been able to remotely control the computer that operates a car and have spied on people through their own security systems.

In the future, the most dangerous hacks will be those that deliberately sabotage industrial processes. Some examples include disabling electric power generators, opening water spillway gates on dams by manipulating critical valves, and causing oil refineries to explode. To prevent such disasters, we must also have noncomputerized controls to shut off critical equipment if a rogue computer message instructs it to spin too fast, get too hot, or operate with excessive pressure. These controls would be hacker-proof because they would have no internet-connected component that would leave them susceptible to hacks. In my mind's eye, I can visualize the systems and the hacker-proof controls. I see round metal gauges with needles, like the old rpm meter in a car. Each gauge face has a clearly marked red-colored danger zone. When the needle enters the red zone, the equipment shuts down. I'm not a Luddite, but our vulnerable electrical power grid has me lying awake at night.

My worst fear is what happens when the hackers shift to sabotaging equipment. Hackers proved they can infiltrate factory systems when they froze the computers that controlled production in the aluminum products factories at Norsk Hydro ASA. If they had taken the next step and started controlling all the factory computers, the scenario would have become seriously dangerous. They could have gained control of furnaces that melt aluminum scrap and other expensive, difficult-to-replace equipment. As it was, the hack was a $60 million mess for Norsk, because most of their payroll and customer accounts around the world were also frozen.

While I was writing this chapter, one of my worst nightmares almost happened. On February 5, 2021, hackers took control of a municipal water system in Oldsmar, Florida. Had the hacker commanded a certain valve to fully open, dangerous amounts of chemicals would have been dumped into the water system. Fortunately, an alert plant operator spotted a suspicious arrow moving around on a monitor and clicked on certain settings to restore security. That was lucky, but to a visual thinker, a hacker-proof solution is more secure. In my mind's eye, I visualized the installation of a small pipe that would greatly restrict flow from the tank holding the chemicals. Even if the computer-controlled valve were to be fully opened, the small pipe would be sized for the maximum safe dose. Fortunately, I learned from a later article that the tank was already equipped with a pipe that restricted chemical flow along these lines. Had worse come to worst, the operator had plenty of time to discover the open valve and close it.

There are three basic ways to protect expensive, difficult-to-replace infra-structure and prevent people from being killed. The first is old-fashioned electromechanical, non-electronic controls that will automatically turn it off if it gets too hot, spins too fast, vibrates too much, has excessive pressure, or if a pump runs dry. Most people are already familiar with the fuses and breaker switches in homes, which are an example of such a fail-safe. These non-electronic controls help prevent a circuit from overloading and burning down your house. The second type of equipment that requires protection includes fully computerized systems that replace human operators. Some examples are robotic arms that stack boxes in factories, and electric trains that move pas-sengers between airline terminals. These systems must be totally isolated from the internet, both connections with cables and wireless connections such as Wi-Fi. Engineers call this an "air gap."

Great care must be taken to never connect a computer with built-in Wi-Fi to industrial and mechanical systems. These systems are always looking for a connection. You may recall that the wireless component in Dick Cheney's de-fibrillator was disabled for fear that it would be hacked by terrorists. The car-diologist Dr. Jonathan Reiner was quoted in a *Washington Post* article: "It seemed to me a bad idea for the vice president to have a device that maybe somebody on a rope line or in the next hotel room or downstairs might be able to get into—hack into."

Recently, while touring a large factory, I noticed a computer sitting on a folding chair, the monitor, mouse, and keyboard precariously perched on it, the box it came in under the chair. It might be an okay setup for your studio apartment, but it was sort of alarming here. I asked about it and discovered that when the technicians hadn't been able to get a particular set of equipment oper-ating from the control room, someone ran out to the local electronics store, hooked up the computer, and got things running. I asked if the computer had built-in Wi-Fi. It did. If the computer was hacked, manufacturing could come to a halt. In, say, a transportation system, with human lives at stake, such an oversight could create enormous vulnerability. What if a hacker took control and commanded electric trains to crash into each other? For the same reason, self-driving cars must be hacker-proof, with a mechanical kill switch accessible to the driver in an emergency and not connected to the internet. After the computer is disabled, the car should have a mechanical emergency brake and be steerable, so the driver can get it off the road. I think we've become so reliant on computers and blindly trusting of them that we no longer see the inherent dangers. In a literal way, they are hidden from us, unless you're the kid who loves taking them apart. Most of us have no idea how our devices work. To most people, the internet is an abstraction. That's dangerous.

More recently, it has come to light that the rollout of 5G cell phone service in the United States might be a risk to aviation safety. Signals from 5G cell phones and cell towers may interfere with radar altimeters on airplanes. These devices enable airplanes to safely land during foggy weather, when the pilot cannot see the runway. For safety, the altitude measurements must be very accurate.

I thought: 5G cell service is already in use in Europe and there have been no safety issues, so why all the fuss in the United States? What is different? Pictures again flashed into my imagination. I see an aircraft taking off from New York and flying to Paris. The same aircraft is flying around in both the United States and Europe. Both the US and Europe use a system called frequency sharing for 5G service, which allows many users to be on the same frequency simultaneously. My mind then saw pictures of some of the standards I have written for animal welfare, such as the North American Meat Institute's *Recommended Animal Handling Guidelines and Audit Guide*. That's how my mind associated the idea of standards. Maybe there is a difference in the standards for managing radio-frequency use in Europe and the United States. I looked for standards and found a paper by Maria Massaro of Chalmers University of Technology in Sweden that explained the difference. It became clear that the differences in radio-frequency sharing standards resulted in increased risk in the United States. The altimeter technology and 5G systems that exist as of this writing require the elimination of high-powered 5G cell antennas near runways and plane approach paths. Not a difficult fix, considering how many lives are potentially saved.

When I give a talk on visual thinking, one of the most common questions I get is whether I hallucinate. Are hallucinations visual thinking? The plain answer is no. Visual thinking is real—reality based. A lion attacking you in the Hilton is a hallucination. Dreams have a hallucinatory component. Everything I see in my imagination is real. And one of the things my imagination works overtime visualizing is what happens when systems controlled by artificial intelligence (AI) are hacked.

In 2015, Google introduced DeepDream, a computer vision program that used AI algorithms to generate and enhance images by detecting patterns. An example of a normal use for such a program would be to find pictures of dogs on the internet. When used for their intended purpose, the programs resemble visual thinking. When forced to look for things that are not there, however, they hallucinate similarly to a person with schizophrenia. When the program was forced to repeatedly look for dogs in an image that lacked dogs, it started seeing parts of dogs. An apple on a tree might morph into an eye. The images the programs generated were creepy: multiple-eyed monsters, multiple eyes all over the sky, or mixed in among groceries on supermarket shelves. Alex Hern, in *The Guardian*, described these AI-generated images as veering "from beautiful to terrifying."

The year 2015 marked a turning point in the life of AI. It was the first time a computer beat a human in the game of Go, which is more complicated than chess. Mathematical visual-spatial thinkers often excel at chess and the game of Go, which are abstract strategy games. In the journal *Nature*, David Silver and his colleagues write that the computer used "nonstandard strategies beyond the scope of traditional Go knowledge." AI is being studied and applied in areas as diverse as video games and analyzing satellite images. AI programs are even being trained to write plays and essays. In an article on Medium.com, Sofia Merenych wrote about GPT-3, a program that composed a play so thoroughly in the manner of Shakespeare that linguists had a difficult time determining it was fake. When the program sucked up vast amounts of human knowledge off the internet, it was capable of writing essays on different subjects. When asked to write about a controversial subject, it sometimes came to conclusions that were offensive. Eliza Strickland wrote in the *IEEE Spectrum* that "whatever GPT's failings were, it learned them from humans. The odds of something offensive coming out is 100 percent."

AI applications are being developed for simulations and analytics, and in industry, transportation, cybersecurity, and the military. What are the failsafes? Would you want an AI program running a nuclear reactor? What if the AI operator started hallucinating because a hacker inserted a feedback loop that forced it to perceive the high pressures and temperatures of a meltdown that did not exist? Maybe it would create an actual meltdown. Some computer scientists will admit that they are not completely sure how AI works. In an article by Arthur I. Miller, the author of *The Artist in the Machine*, he writes, "The crucial point [about Google's Deep Dream] is that the machine was producing images that were not programmed into it." Would it be possible for this to occur in a system designed to monitor temperatures, water flows, pressures, and speeds of industrial equipment? This would be a world of number patterns instead of pictures.

I think back to watching *2001: A Space Odyssey* when I was in high school. This classic 1968 science fiction movie features an intelligent computer named HAL who accompanies a crew of astronauts on a mission to find alien life. HAL is programmed not to reveal the purpose of the mission to the astronauts until they reach their destination. He is also instructed never to lie. Killing the astronauts is the logical solution to solving this paradox. But HAL has an off switch, and the pivotal moment in the film comes when David, the sole surviving astronaut, disconnects HAL before HAL can kill him, too.

The genius of the film is that HAL is humanized in every way. The astronauts befriend him, play chess with him; right up until the end he's one of them, even if he is mostly depicted as a red pulsing eye. HAL pleads with David to stop removing his AI modules, but David has no choice if he wants to survive. I remember crying along with most of the audience when HAL was sacrificed. By then, HAL had already shut off the ship's air supply, but David was able to escape by manually opening an emergency exit, overriding the spacecraft's computer system. Over fifty years later, the metaphor holds up. Can humans and robots coexist? Who will control the oxygen supply? Is there an off switch? Now more than ever, it makes sense that critical infrastructure equipment has old-fashioned electromechanical devices that will shut them down and prevent damage if a hacker commands them to damage themselves.

The Words We Use

Nuclear event scale. Beyond design basis. Redundant path backup. Passive hazard control. Acceptable risk. Proximate cause. I'm not a verbal thinker, but I've observed that when engineers discuss risk, they use language that is almost robotic, devoid of human detail. A crash is called *impact with terrain.* Major problems are called *anomalies.* During a rocket launch, when everything is working smoothly, it is *nominal.* When it isn't, there are four levels of failure: *negligible, marginal, critical,* and *catastrophic.* The Boeing tragedy was labeled a "common mode failure."

Places and systems are reduced to their acronyms. According to the Nuclear

Regulatory Commission, NPS stands for "nuclear power station." If I weren't reading about nuclear power plants in a scientific journal, I would have absolutely no idea what NPS means. If this same sentence had appeared in an article in an aviation journal to describe the conditions that led up to a crash, maybe NPS could stand for "navigation and pilot systems." An article on the Fukushima 2 plant referred to the lesser flooding there, which left the PC, MC, and the RB dry and undamaged. Unless I knew these acronyms, I would have no idea what they stood for. I looked them up on the internet. This is what I found: The PC was either the pressure controller or the PC desktop computer. The MC was either the main circulator or the main condenser. RB stood for "reactor building."

Every industry has its jargon and acronyms, but engineering has many more acronyms than I've encountered in other fields. EPM stands for "engineering product manager" and PD for "product design." Too many initials and acronyms make it easier to separate oneself from reality. Matrix charts employ such endpoints as *very low severity* to *very high severity*, or axis words such as *rare*, *unlikely*, *possible*, *likely*, and *certain*. The problem with jargon and scientific terms devoid of human connection is that they hinder problem solving and reduce motivation to fix serious problems. I think it is important to discuss this, because vague language emotionally distances engineers from the consequences of their mistakes. It is easier to talk about an *anomaly* or *impact with terrain* than to admit that something blew up, was flooded, or crashed, injuring or killing people. To the visual thinker, disaster is never abstract. As I write this, I see the wreckage, the pulverized bodies, the pieces of busted-up plane all over the ground.

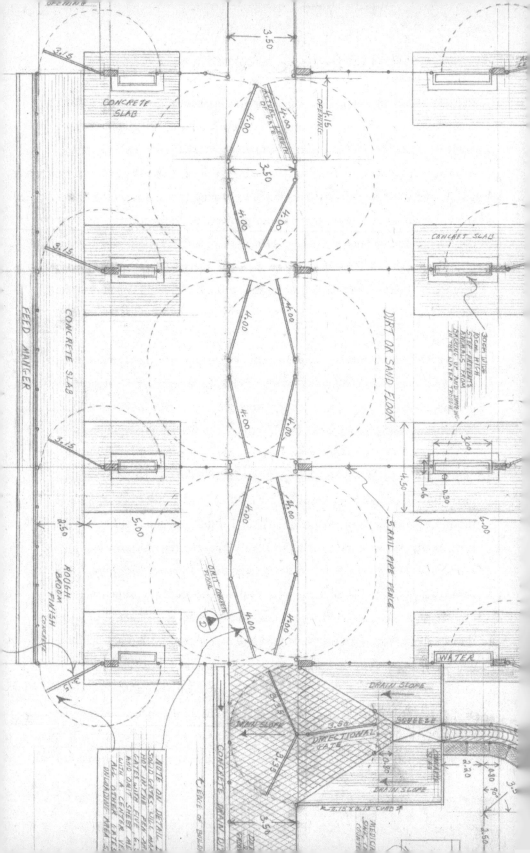

SEVEN

Animal Consciousness
and Visual Thinking

I t always struck me as ridiculous to think that a dog or a cow does not have consciousness, yet people continue to debate the subject. Aristotle believed that what set men above animals was the ability to reason. Where humans were capable of perception and rational thinking and communicated through language, animals were driven by sensation and impulse.

The Bible includes passages that indicate that animals, like humans, feel pain and deserve rest. In Deuteronomy (22:10), for instance, it is forbidden to yoke a donkey and an ox together to plow a field. Another passage, in Exodus (23:12), states that working donkeys and oxen are to be rested on the Sabbath. The Quran (6:38) has a lovely verse observing that all animals form and need community: "All living beings roaming the earth and winged birds soaring in the sky are communities like yourselves." From our earliest writings, the stage is set for the ongoing debate about whether animals think and feel, and how we think and feel about them.

Throughout this book, I've made the point that the greatest obstacle in understanding visual thinking is knowing it exists. Nowhere is that obstacle greater than in comprehending the inner lives of animals. Just as we've underestimated and underutilized the talents and contributions of humans who are visual thinkers, we have similarly underestimated and misunderstood thought in animals. Animals live—and think—through their senses. Without verbal language, they store memories of previous experiences as pictures, sounds, smells, tastes, or touch memories. Sensory-based thinking and memories are recollections of experiences *without* words. Grazing or herbivorous animals, including cattle, antelopes, giraffes, elk, and deer, use visual dominance to detect threats; they are constantly on the lookout for predators. In *Thinking in Pictures*, I wrote extensively about my connection to prey animals, namely cattle. I identified the ways in which my alert system was similarly organized to theirs. We all share some of these "animal instincts," even if our visual sense isn't dominant. We don't need words to tell us when a strange car is in the driveway. We "sense" danger.

Octopuses, with their sensory systems wired into their tentacles, rely on touch as well as taste and smell; canids, from wolves to dogs, live through their sense of smell, coupled with high-frequency hearing. I tell people to stop yanking their dog's leash when they linger around a tree or hydrant. A dog is a highly social animal. Smelling stuff, especially pee, is how they get their information. I've been known to call it "pee-mail." I remember reading about a wine steward who could apparently identify two thousand kinds of wine by smell; that's about as close as a human can get to a dog's sense of smell. A dog has three hundred million olfactory receptors compared with our six million. Their smell center in the brain is forty times greater than the equivalent part of the human brain, proportionally. An animal's senses inform and determine its skill set.

Even an insect brain can differentiate between same and different. Bees can learn to distinguish between colors and lattice patterns that are the same or different. Some animals' brains create categories with distinct boundaries. Jessie

Peissig at California State University, Fullerton, and her colleagues found that pigeons will spontaneously group shapes into categories, a skill generally thought to distinguish human cognition. Shigeru Watanabe from Keio University in Japan found that pigeons could learn to tell a Monet painting from a Picasso, even when shown a painting they had not previously viewed. I imagine the reason why birds developed this skill is adaptive; they need to be able to identify their surroundings. Squirrels use visual thinking to "remember" where they hid their nuts, just as ants have visual memories they use to find their way back to the nest. S. P. D. Judd and T. S. Collett, from the Sussex Centre for Neuroscience at the University of Sussex in the UK, discovered that when ants go out on foraging trips, they will stop along the way and "snap a photo" of a new food source multiple times from different angles. They will also turn back multiple times to look at the landmark on their way back to the nest.

Though animals vary in their display of temporal and spatial understanding, it is obvious that all mammals and birds know where their den or nest is located, and they develop a general sense of where plentiful food may be found. Squirrels use visual memory to find nuts they have stored, and corvid birds such as crows can remember where they have hidden food *and* how long it has been there. Jays know that delicious worms rot faster than nuts. They know that they must go back and eat the worms more quickly than a less perishable food, just as we empty our fridge before the pantry.

The human habit of privileging verbal thinking over visual thinking often extends to animals despite evidence that language had nothing to do with some of humankind's earliest and most impressive achievements. Attaching a stone blade to a stick to create a spear, one of the first complex tools, was invented long before language evolved. A recent study by Dana Cataldo and colleagues from University College London investigated how our ancestors might have created stone blades. Novices were divided into two groups. The first group had an expert flintknapper who both demonstrated how to make the tools and verbally explained the process. The second group had the same instructor, but there was no spoken instruction. The students had to observe the instructor, who used nonverbal cues such as pointing or showing how to hold the rock. The novices who were in the nonverbal group performed better at learning the task. Nonverbal, sensory-based learning may have played a significant role in early human achievement, an idea worth thinking about as it relates to the cognition and achievement of other animals.

———

First, I want to give you a quick history of how we think about animals, how we've treated them and studied them. We'll also look at the neuroscience and the study of emotions in animals, all with a view toward understanding how the different kinds of thinking in animals relate to how humans think.

According to Erica Hill in her article "Archaeology and Animal Persons," ancient hunter-gatherers viewed animals as "capable of independent and intentional action." First, to be successful, hunter-gatherers themselves would need to rely on visual thinking. They would need to be able to see faint tracks or broken twigs that indicated where animals had passed. As reported by Eyal Halfon and Ran Barkai at Tel Aviv University, who have extensively studied hunter-gatherers, they tend to view animals as part of a living community where only some members are human. Many Native American belief systems include animals as relatives of human beings.

A recent study conducted by psychologist Matti Wilks, a lecturer at the University of Edinburgh, found that children under the age of nine are less likely to prioritize people over animals. Many valued the life of a dog as much as that of a human, whereas almost all adults chose to save one human over even a hundred dogs. The study concludes that the importance of human life "appears late in development and is likely socially acquired." I hypothesize that the tendency to perceive animals as completely "other" increases as verbal thinking predominates, in both individuals and cultures. It's possible that as verbal consciousness grew, along with speech and written language, our regard for animals diminished, and our very understanding of them changed. From medieval times to the Enlightenment, the Western view of animals was reflected in the idea of the Great Chain of Being. This is a Christian interpretation of Aristotle's attempts to organize the natural world into a hierarchy, placing God, angels, and man at the top, with animals, plants, and minerals at the bottom. Relegating animals to a lower status reflects the decline of a belief that we share modes of perception.

It isn't until the year 1580 that we encounter the first major refutation of this posture in humanist philosopher Michel de Montaigne's defense of animal sentience in the essay "Man Is No Better Than the Animals." Montaigne challenges the belief that humans are superior to animals, which he attributes to human arrogance: "Presumption is our natural and original disease." He asks how people can possibly know "the secret and internal motions of animals." To underscore the point, he asks, "When I play with my cat, who knows whether I do not make her more sport than she makes of me?" Anyone in a close relationship with an animal could ask the same.

A half century later, in 1637, the French philosopher René Descartes countered Montaigne with his influential essay "Animals Are Machines," in which he asserts that man is composed of body and soul, but that animals lack the latter and might as well be machines. Descartes compares animals to clocks, "only composed of wheels and weights." The essay expounds on all the reasons animals are not capable of thought or feeling, culminating in a final argument: "It has never yet been observed that any brute animal reached the stage of using real speech, that is to say, of indicating by word or sign something pertaining to pure thought and not to natural impulse." According to Descartes, I think, therefore I am not an animal. (Notably, Descartes engaged in vi-

visection, the dissection of live animals for medical knowledge, dismissing the howls of a vivisected dog as instinctual, rather than an expression of pain.) Even in the late nineteenth century, the philosopher William James defended the practice as providing "healing truth, relief to future suffering of beast and man," although he acknowledged that the dog, "literally in a sort of hell," was in no position to appreciate that aspect of the situation.

Until Darwin came along, the study of animal behavior did little to advance the question of animal consciousness. *On the Origin of Species* played a transformative role in how we perceive nature and our relationship with it. "It is a significant fact, that the more habits of any particular animal are studied by a naturalist, the more he attributes to reason, and the less to unlearnt instinct." A century after Descartes, Darwin's book on the evolution of humans, *The Descent of Man,* fiercely refuted the Great Chain of Being. "The difference in mind between man and the higher animals, great as it is, certainly is one of degree and not of kind," he wrote.

The history of our ideas about animals is entwined with our laws about how we treat them. One of the earliest pieces of legislation forbidding animal cruelty was enacted in Ireland in 1635. It prohibited hitching plows to horses' tails and removing wool from sheep by pulling it out, which is akin to pulling hair out of your head. In 1776, Reverend Humphrey Primatt inveighed against animal neglect and abuse in "A Dissertation on the Duty of Mercy and Sin of Cruelty to Brute Animals." "Pain is pain," he wrote, "whether it be inflicted on man or on beast." Primatt advanced the idea that humans should not treat animals cruelly on the grounds that they feel pain and should be treated humanely. "Every creature is to be considered as a wheel in the great machinery of nature." His philosophy formed the basis for early British and American anti-cruelty laws.

In 1789, the English philosopher, social reformer, and jurist Jeremy Bentham argued that animals should be given legal protection. He did not concern himself with the question of animal consciousness. Instead, he framed the issue this way: "The question is not, Can they *reason?* nor, Can they *talk?* But, Can they *suffer?*" In New York City, another reformer, Henry Bergh, a tireless champion of animal rights, would make the prevention of cruelty to animals his life's work and personal mission, and would charge into any situation where animal welfare was at stake. As Ernest Freeberg wrote in his biography *A Traitor to His Species*, "Bergh did battle with teamsters and turtle dealers, circus managers and cockfighters, butchers and surgeons." Though he often lost his cases in the court of law, the court of public opinion advanced his cause. In 1866, he formed the American Society for the Prevention of Cruelty to Animals (ASPCA). The first seal for the society depicted a cart horse being beaten and an angel of mercy hovering above.

Most notably, Bergh took on the carriage trade, notorious for the mistreatment of horses. By the mid-1800s, the streets of major cities were full of horses and buggies, as congested then as they are by car and bus traffic today. The horses were worked day and night, pulling trolleys with as many as seventy-five people crammed in. They were punched, prodded, whipped, and often left to die when they could no longer work. The wealthy "clipped" their horses, removing their protective layer of hair to give the horses a sheen while stripping them of their natural protection against the elements.

In 1877, a fictional autobiography of a horse probably did more to enact animal welfare changes than any legislation by appealing to the hearts and minds of the public. *Black Beauty: The Autobiography of a Horse* by Anna Sewell tells a heart-wrenching story about a horse who is sold from owner to owner, experiencing both kindness and cruelty at their hands. When I was a child, my mother read this book to me. I never forgot the part about the bearing rein that forced a carriage horse to hold its head up high for the solitary purpose of making it look stylish, flattering its wealthy owners. *Black Beauty* describes how difficult and painful it was for the horse to pull a carriage with his head forced into such an unnatural position, which compromised his neck and his breathing. Over a million copies of the book were printed in the fifteen years after its first publication, and more than fifty million copies have been sold to date. A few years after it came out, bearing reins were outlawed in England.

Bergh would be pleased to know that the ASPCA has grown to two million members and retained its original mission to end animal cruelty. The Animal Legal Defense Fund works to stop the abuse of animals through legal channels. More recently, lawyer Steven M. Wise founded the Nonhuman Rights Project to make the courts recognize the individual rights of animals. The goal is to protect certain animals under the law, namely great apes, elephants, dolphins, and whales. Wise argues that these animals are all sentient, have feelings and self-consciousness. The first case the project brought to the New York Supreme Court involved an elephant named Happy. Happy and her six siblings were brought to America from Thailand and named after the seven dwarves. Happy and Grumpy were sent to the Bronx Zoo. Grumpy and another companion subsequently died, leaving Happy alone since 2006. Lawyers from the NhRP petitioned for Happy's release from the zoo, writing in their brief, "The non-humans at issue are unquestionably innocent. Their confinement, at least in some cases, is uniquely depraved." The petition on behalf of Happy was denied, but in May 2021, a court of appeals granted the NhRP a motion for permission to appeal. This was "the first time in history that the highest court of any English-speaking jurisdiction" heard "a habeas corpus case brought on behalf of someone other than a human being." Unfortunately, Happy lost her appeal and will remain at the zoo.

A Tale of Two Disciplines

By the 1950s and 1960s, the study of animal behavior was dominated by two major disciplines: the study of animals in their natural environment (ethology) and the study of animals in the laboratory (behaviorism). Both ethologists and behaviorists struggled throughout the latter half of the twentieth century to imagine thought that does not rely on verbal language. Unable to account for the interior lives of animals, they concluded that animals had no interior lives at all. The train of thought was like a Möbius strip that kept turning in on itself: emotion is not possible unless an animal is conscious enough to experience that emotion.

While the ethologists believed that animal behavior was controlled by hardwired instincts, the behaviorists believed that behavior was controlled by the environment. Both schools of thought believed they could study behavior objectively, the behaviorists via carefully constructed lab tests and the ethologists by observing and recording natural animal behavior in meticulous detail over time. They also both avoided any discussion of emotional influences on behavior, which would take them into the murky territory of subjectivity that scientists were supposed to avoid at all costs. The taboo of anthropomorphizing loomed large, with the notable exception of Konrad Lorenz, a pioneer of ethology and Nobel Prize winner.

Lorenz didn't buy in to the dismissal of animal emotions as anthropomorphism. In *Species of Mind: The Philosophy and Biology of Cognitive Ethology*, Colin Allen and Marc Bekoff write of Lorenz, "He believed that animals had the capacities to love, be jealous, experience envy and be angry." They go on to explain that he considered human emotion and intuition key to understanding animals. In Lorenz's worldview, scientists are not robots, nor should they be. Objectivity does not equal denying one's feelings.

Lorenz is well known for his ideas about "imprinting," a concept he claims stemmed from his childhood, when he was given a day-old duckling that, with no mother to follow, followed him everywhere. Lorenz measured the effect of early stimulus on different animals and attempted to quantify how much of their behavior was genetically programmed. He recognized the instinctual bonds that are formed between newborns and their caregivers in the first weeks of life. In one study, he showed that a mother goose sitting on her eggs performed the same movement to retrieve an egg or an egglike object that has rolled out of the nest. The egg-rolling behavior was activated by the "sign stimuli" of such an object, and as such appeared to be innate.

Other innate behaviors include consuming food, mating, nurturing young, nectar seeking in honeybees, web spinning in spiders, and nest building in birds, though some more recent studies now suggest that some of these skills may in fact be a combination of innate abilities and learned skills. For example, weaver birds, reared in isolation, will build the same distinctive woven nest that, if you haven't seen one, roughly takes the shape of a Hershey's Kiss and almost completely envelops the bird. However, according to Ida Bailey and colleagues at the University of St. Andrews, these same birds also employ individual variations in their weaving patterns. Similarly, an innate behavior such as fighting will manifest differently in different animals.

When bulls fight, they butt heads, but when horses fight, they rear up and strike with their front hooves. Highly domesticated animals retain species-typical behaviors. A dog, for instance, will perform a play bow when it wants to play, and domestic turkeys will fan their tail to attract mates. Though a barnful of male turkeys have displayed their fanned tails to me, I am hardly a suitable mate. Animals can also be easily trained to perform behaviors that are not typical for their species. Horses, for instance, can easily learn to be ridden. Recent research also shows that animals that are more willing to approach novel objects can learn a new task more easily. This would provide some support for Lorenz's idea that motivation to learn is influenced by innate factors. It is likely that this is also true in people. In an essay he wrote when he received the Nobel Prize, Lorenz said, "I discovered imprinting and was imprinted myself."

Lorenz shared the Nobel Prize with fellow ethologists Nikolaas Tinbergen and Karl von Frisch, for their pioneering work in ethology that looked at behavior through the lens of natural selection and species differences. Tinbergen was recognized for his highly developed experiments, which showed how instinctive behavior was organized, and von Frisch for his comprehensive work on honeybees and their ability to see patterns and colors, and to communicate about food sources through "dance."

Von Frisch's work had in fact been anticipated a decade earlier by Charles Henry Turner, a Black scientist who conducted field studies using an ethological approach, including research on bees that only recently has been accorded greater recognition than the footnote in von Frisch's writings. Born in 1867 to parents who had been slaves, Turner was the first African American to earn a PhD in zoology from the University of Chicago. Although he published more than seventy research papers in prestigious journals, including *Science*, discriminatory practices prevented him from being hired as a university professor, and he spent his life working as a high school teacher.

Despite the lack of resources and institutional backing, Turner was able to show that honeybees can perceive both color and pattern. He believed that bees created "memory pictures of the environment." His experiments showed that insects can hear, and that bees are capable of learning, which accounts for their communication and navigation skills. Such findings forge a path between human and animal ability. According to Martin Giurfa and colleagues in an article in *Current Biology*, Turner pioneered cognitive views on animal behavior that would later come to dominate scientific scholarship. Turner wrote, for example, that "ants are much more than mere reflex machines; they are self-acting creatures guided by memories of past individual (ontogenetic) experience." We can easily recognize the links between such behavior and our own. The memory pictures ants use to find their way back to the nest after foraging are akin to the way people use visual landmarks—a stone wall or a store with a distinctive sign—to remember how to get from place to place. Whether or not you consciously tell yourself to turn left at the Dairy Queen to get to the doctor's office, your mind has logged memory pictures to help you navigate.

Recently, researchers Cwyn Solvi and her colleagues at Queen Mary University of London and Macquarie University in Australia, building on the work of Turner and von Frisch, among others, have shown that bumblebees can integrate sensory information from different modalities, such as vision or touch. "We cannot know for certain what a bee is thinking," says one of the researchers, "but we do know that they have the capability to transfer information from one sense to another sense. This requires the ability to picture something in one's head." The bees are thinking in pictures.

Decades after his Nobel-winning work, Lorenz would write, in *King Solomon's Ring*, that animals should not be held "prisoner" to study them. The only way to learn about them was through close observation in their natural habitats. This was a point of view widely popularized through the work of Jane Goodall, who went to Africa as a young woman to study chimpanzees in the wild. Less known is the work of a young Canadian woman who predated Goodall by a few years when she went to South Africa to fulfill her dream of seeing giraffes in their natural habitat. As a child, Anne Dagg had fallen in love with giraffes at a Chicago zoo. She studied biology at the University of Toronto but encountered little interest in animal behavior there. Likewise, she was unable to find governmental or academic support for her desire to study giraffes in their natural habitat. Undeterred, Dagg traveled to Africa on her own at the age of twenty-three. After numerous failures to find a host, she approached a rancher she had heard about through a series of loose connections. Writing to him as A. Dagg, to disguise her gender, she received an invitation. Once her deceit came to light, she was allowed to live in the family home in exchange for clerical duties. The arrangement suited her, as the cattle ranch and citrus farm were near Kruger National Park, home to a large giraffe population.

The park was her classroom, with her car serving as a blind from which to observe the animals in their habitat. Dagg kept extensive notes about what the giraffes ate (she categorized every leaf and tree) and how they walked, ran, played, fought, and mated. After a giraffe was killed, she recorded everything from the length of its intestines, which she dried on a clothesline, to their contents, studying what plants it ingested as well as testing for parasites.

Dagg noted that giraffes "are the first ungulates that seem to be equally concerned with death, and indeed perhaps more concerned," because several "remembered the spot [where] their young died for many days." She reflected, "It may be that such emotion is more common in the wild than we appreciate." According to Iain Douglas-Hamilton, founder of Save the Elephants, and his colleagues, elephants will attempt to lift a dying matriarch, and many different elephant families will visit the body after death.

The behaviorist B. F. Skinner, one of the most influential psychologists of the twentieth century, continues to wield considerable influence today. Skinner, a Harvard professor, who was already a rock star in academic circles, achieved international fame when he graced the cover of *Time* magazine in 1971. Skinner summed up his thoughts succinctly in a 1977 statement: "I see no evidence of an inner world of mental life." He was talking about humans as well as animals. According to Skinner, we were all controlled by two forces: reinforcements and punishments. Best known for his operant conditioning chamber, aka the Skinner box, the psychologist set up experiments in which rats and pigeons were subjected to different stimuli, such as light and electric shocks, to test the effect of reinforcement. If the animals tapped or pecked the correct lever, they would be rewarded with food. The experimenters demonstrated that rewarding some behaviors and punishing others caused the animals to learn new behaviors. According to Skinner, we are subject to the same operant conditioning as his lab animals. Free will is a fantasy. In his influential book

Science and Human Behavior, Skinner was also clear about what he thought of emotions: "The 'emotions' are excellent examples of the fictional causes to which we commonly attribute behavior."

In the 1960s, when I was attending college, one of my classes had the opportunity to visit B. F. Skinner. When I had a chance to ask a question, I asked about the brain and how it works. Skinner replied, "We don't need to learn about the brain because we have operant conditioning." Years later, I heard that after Skinner had a stroke, he admitted that maybe we do need to learn about the brain, after all.

In 1961, the animal specialists Keller and Marian Breland published a paper titled "The Misbehavior of Organisms." The title made it clear that this was a rebuttal to Skinner's famous book, *The Behavior of Organisms.* The pair had studied under Skinner and worked as research assistants in his lab. When they left to set up a business to commercially train animals, they used Skinner's techniques, including electric feeders. In the paper, they showed that the Skinnerian principles of conditioned stimulus response could be overridden by natural instincts. It turns out it was difficult to train an animal to do something that conflicted with its instincts. "There was nothing in our background in behaviorism to prepare us for such gross inabilities to predict and control the behavior of animals," wrote the Brelands. Over the years, they trained more than eight thousand animals belonging to more than sixty species for television ads, circuses, movies, and television shows.

In a carnival novelty that I saw at the Arizona State Fair in the early 1970s, a hen played a toy piano. It got food pellets by pecking the keys. This exhibit was successful because pecking is the natural behavior a hen uses for obtaining food. But an attempt to create an exhibit in which a raccoon deposited coins in a small box was a disaster. Raccoons wash their food, an innate behavior. When trainers gave the coins to the raccoons, the raccoons rubbed the coins, attempting to perform their instinctual food-washing behavior and refusing to drop them in the box. A pig easily learned to drop a coin in a piggy bank at first, but after a few weeks it rooted the coin, mouthed it, and tossed it around. As the Brelands observed, the pig's instinctive behavior reasserted itself: wild pigs kill small rodents, toss them around, and mouth them before eating them. Because the Brelands worked outside the academy, although Marian would eventually earn her PhD, their work proved controversial and was sometimes dismissed, but their observations resonated with me. I knew that animals were more than the sum of what you could observe in a box with a system of positive and negative reinforcements. As the Brelands wrote, "You cannot understand the behavior of the animal in the laboratory unless you understand his behavior in the wild." White laboratory rats who are generations away from living in the wild will dig elaborate burrows when released in a place with lots of dirt to dig in.

Nervous System Complexity and Consciousness

It wasn't until the 1990s, with the rise of cognitive neuroscience (and the aid of MRIs), that we were finally able to advance a conversation about animal emotion that starts with the brain. Over the last few decades, scientists who study animal consciousness have developed several theories and adopted different methods for evaluating the consciousness of animals. Even Skinner had admitted we needed to start thinking about what is inside the box.

At the most basic level, consciousness and cognition require a certain level of nervous system complexity to exist. Clams, oysters, and maggots, for instance, are not conscious. Their behavior is the result of reflexes or simple habituation to a repeated stimulus. If you touch an oyster, it will close its shell; if you repeat the stimulus enough times, it will cease closing in response. Its nervous system habituates, and it either stops responding or responds at a greatly reduced level.

On the next rung of nervous-system complexity, an animal develops a node of neurons in its head. Planarian flatworms are an example. (The flatworm also has two nerve cords down its body, precursors to a spinal cord, but in this form just the beginning of a centralized nervous system, lacking pain receptors.) All networks form nodes; it's in their nature, whether we're talking about Facebook or an airline. As flying became more popular, nodes formed organically, connecting points for flights going to many different cities. As certain nodes started getting more traffic, like Denver, they became hubs. In the nervous system, the process is called encephalization, the evolutionary brain growth that marks a shift from non-centralized neural networks to the formation of the cerebral cortex. These centralized hubs with many incoming and outgoing circuits are one of the keys to consciousness.

Building a brain is a continuous process of increasing complexity as you move up the animal phyla. En route to full consciousness, sense organs such as ears and eyes come into play. In lower forms of animals, eyes appear as rudimentary spots that are sensitive to light and can detect the direction of its source. The next stage is being able to see blurry images. The garden snail can do this. All mammals, reptiles, spiders, and insects have true eyes that can see images with some degree of clarity. Though ants and wasps are not able to see as well as we can, they rely on vision for some important tasks, including, as mentioned, the storing of visual memories as a navigational tool, a process that marks the beginning of visual thinking.

About sixty years after Charles Turner documented ants using vision, biologist E. O. Wilson and his colleagues discovered that ants also rely on the excretion of pheromones (odors) to pass on information. Wilson explained that ants use their antennae to identify their home colony, communicate about needs to the rest of the colony, and perform other tasks. Research shows that wasps can recognize the faces of other wasps in their colonies, and that they have good memories for recognizing individual wasps with which they have previously interacted. Does this make them conscious? I believe the nervous system of insects is the foundation for full consciousness, but I do not fully classify them as conscious because insects do not feel acute pain or have fully developed emotions. When an insect's leg is injured, it will continue to walk on it. An animal that can feel pain will limp and reduce the weight placed on the injured leg.

Animals that have organs for hearing and seeing require a greater amount of centralized brain tissue to process information compared with organisms that lack eyes or ears. According to Brazilian neuroscientist Suzana Herculano-Houzel at Vanderbilt University, the number of circuits and how they are wired is more significant than the sheer size of the brain. The neurons in a bird's brain pack a tremendous amount of processing power despite the brain's small size. In some cases, the processing capacity is similar to that of some large mammal brains. A good analogy is a smartphone, which can carry out many of the same functions as a desktop computer by cramming lots of circuits into tiny electronic chips. A greater number of processing units will increase behavioral flexibility. In order to enable flight, birds' brain-computing power must be both powerful and light. Since most mammals do not fly, there has been less evolutionary selection pressure for them to develop a powerful, light brain.

Further research by Herculano-Houzel showed that even though an African elephant's brain is much larger than a human brain, the human brain has 16.3 billion cortical neurons, and the elephant has only 5.6 billion. The human brain has both more densely packed neurons and a thicker cerebral cortex. Other parts of the human brain more closely resemble those of other mammals. What separates people from animals is the raw computing power of the huge number of circuits in the cerebral cortex. What the elephant may lack in the cerebral cortex, it gains in the size of its cerebellum. The large cerebellum may be related to the elephant's use of low-frequency vibrations to communicate, or the control of its trunk, as the cerebellum assists with motor coordination. Elephants are extremely intelligent compared with many other animals.

Michelle J. Redinbaugh in the department of psychology at the University of Wisconsin, Madison, explains that to be conscious requires a centralized hub that has both feedforward circuits and feedback circuits within it. Information travels both ways between different layers of the frontoparietal cortex. This also requires a structure that processes and associates all the incoming information, capable of responding in a flexible manner. In both humans and animals, the PAG (periaqueductal gray) has a network of connections to numerous brain areas in both higher cortical areas and lower brain centers. When the PAG is destroyed, whether in a human or in a cat, they will enter a comatose state, ceasing to react to things around them. Another hub for consciousness is located in the middle lower-brain area. Both areas serve as hubs for processing emotions. The information that is stored in the brain can mingle and associate there, like delegates entering the rotunda of a large convention center.

The research points to a consensus that consciousness is a hierarchy. As brain systems become more complex, consciousness becomes more complex, with emotions and sensory information being processed in larger and larger association areas more densely packed with neurons. The lower PAG area acts like the master of a railway switching yard or an air traffic controller. This system enables either an animal or a person to interact both with the environment and with other individuals.

For humans and most animals, the PAG is also involved in assessing possible danger. A deer will suddenly raise its head and point both its eyes and ears at a strange noise or sight. This is an innate response to a possible threat. However, the deer still needs to decide how to respond. I have observed this behavior many times. There is a pause while the brain decides whether to flee, keep watching, or continue grazing. This is the beginning of flexible decision-making.

The thalamus regulates consciousness and arousal. It is also a relay station for both sensory and motor signals. The thalamus and the PAG alone do not entirely explain consciousness. There is another major information hub in the parietal lobe (top-back of the brain) adjacent to the occipital cortex that integrates sensory and emotional information. Dissection of human brains shows that huge bundles of nerve fibers provide wide-ranging connections between both local and long-distance cortical areas. Christof Koch at the Allen Institute for Brain Science in Seattle theorizes that all conscious experience in people originates in this "hot zone."

Another key step toward building a brain that may become conscious is the ability to perform cross-modal transfers between different sources of incoming information. This is a fancy way of saying that information that enters the brain via one sense organ, such as the eyes, can be combined with information from another sensory system, such as touch, to create a unified understanding. In humans, these visual and tactile inputs are linked from birth but continue to develop over time. An example of cross-modal transfer in people is the ability to identify coins in your pocket by feel. Cockpit controls in many airplanes have handles with distinct shapes so that pilots can fly partially by feel, reducing the chances they mistakenly engage the wrong control. A child learning to ride a bike uses sensory input simultaneously from both the eyes and the vestibular balance system. These tasks, from simple to more challenging, depend on a complex cognitive ability.

Mammals and other animals are adept at cross-modal transfers, displaying great capacities for navigation and memory, both of which require an ability to integrate different kinds of information. Pigeons use landmarks on the ground and compass headings to get back home. Some birds can remember where they've hidden nuts. These are all great feats of sensory-based cognition that do not require verbal language. Even though birds do not have a cerebral cortex as mammals do, they have a structure in the brain that performs similar functions. Martin Stacho and his colleagues at Ruhr-Universität Bochum in Germany found that bird brains have long horizonal circuits that link up distant parts of the brain and local vertical cross circuits. The long horizontal fibers would be analogous to long-distance trains that go across a country. The shorter, vertical circuits would be the local trains that move across a hub city. These circuits perform the function of a cerebral cortex, processing incoming and outgoing information in a flexible manner.

There are only two brain areas we know of that are *not* required for consciousness. They are the frontal cerebral cortex, which controls executive function, and the cerebellum, which coordinates motor function. The prefrontal cortex is a massive association cortex that contains no information storage or motor-movement control systems. A review of the medical literature by Dr. Koch and his colleagues revealed a consensus that major portions of a person's frontal cortex can be removed without their losing consciousness. Canadian researchers Aaron Kucyi and Karen Davis found that when a person daydreams, both the frontal cortex and the association areas required for consciousness are activated. These massive areas are where internal thought occurs when you think up a new idea while in the shower.

The frontal cortex and two other association areas are also activated when we plan for the future, an ability we share with certain animals. Nicola Clayton of Cambridge University and colleagues in her lab did an experiment that I like to call "the cheap hotel and the expensive hotel." During the day, a scrub jay had free rein of two compartments, or "hotels," joined together by an intermediate space. At night he would be locked in one of the hotels, but he would only receive breakfast after spending the night in the "expensive hotel." Scrub jays quickly learned to store more of their food in the cheap hotel, apparently knowing they wouldn't be served a complimentary breakfast there as they were at the expensive hotel. They planned for the future possibility of being locked in the cheap hotel. I watched a squirrel plan for the future in my front yard. He carefully buried a nut, making sure that the hole was deep enough that the nut could be completely buried. He had to try putting the nut in the hole three times before he had dug a sufficiently deep hole.

Abraham Peper, a researcher at the University of Amsterdam, has discussed cognition in animals and humans. He observes, "I will argue that cognitive processes in humans and animals are fundamentally alike as long as verbal activity is disregarded." He suggests that sensory images are the way "living creatures experience new environmental information." Taking the idea further, he points out that visual thinking has nearly unlimited complexity, is less vague than spoken language, is two- and three-dimensional, and is "incomparably more detailed" than spoken language. Michael Fanselow at the University of California, Los Angeles, has a similar opinion. Referring to people who deny that animals have true feelings of fear, he states, "In my opinion, their approaches suffer from the human tendency to glorify verbal report over all other measures."

Consciousness exists on a spectrum. What we know so far is that you need a nervous system along with certain neurobiological features. We know that consciousness has a biological function and that there is a relationship between what's inside your head and the outside world. Most scientists would agree that consciousness is not a single thing but, to use their word, multimodal. Mammals across a wide range of species demonstrate complex ways of perceiving and responding to their environments. Perhaps it's the very lack of language that makes their behaviors such fascinating windows into evolutionary processes, such as the ability of homing pigeons to find their way home.

When an animal looks at its own reflection in a mirror, does it recognize that it is seeing itself, or does it think it is looking at a strange animal? In the view of many scientists, this is the gold standard for the highest level of animal consciousness: self-awareness. If you have a dog, you've probably noticed that upon seeing its reflection, it will either bark or not react at all, and never get past this stage. In 1970, psychologist Gordon Gallup developed the mirror self-recognition (MSR) test to see if chimps were able to recognize themselves. He sedated chimps and painted a red mark on their bodies. If, upon seeing the mark in the mirror, the chimp investigated where the mark had been applied to its body, it was considered to have self-awareness, interest in the self. The small group of animals that have been shown to recognize themselves includes chimps, bonobos, gorillas, orangutans, elephants, dolphins, and magpies.

Hunter College professors Joshua Plotnik and Diana Reiss, together with highly regarded biologist and primatologist Frans de Waal, conducted a mirror self-recognition test with three elephants that replicated the progression of responses that young children exhibit as they become conscious of themselves. At first, they are in exploratory mode, sometimes looking around the mirror to see if someone else is hiding behind it. They might also attempt to interact with the image, engaging socially or becoming aggressive. Then, as they become more interested in the reflection, they will test their movement in the mirror by going in and out of view. The official name for this stage is "contingency testing." (Diana Reiss calls it "the Groucho stage," after the famous Groucho Marx mirror scene in the movie *Duck Soup*.) Next, they will begin to investigate their faces and other body parts. Elephants check out their mouths and tusks. Other higher mammals behave similarly.

Dolphins and elephants in some of these mirror studies will bend into weird positions to examine themselves. As a child, I remember checking out my body from every angle in the three-way mirrors in clothing-store dressing rooms. I also tried to figure out why the writing on a T-shirt appeared backward in the mirror. I discovered that it was still backward when I switched the side with the writing to my back.

Babies develop an interest in their mirror image at about one and a half to two years old. With this level of self-awareness, more complicated emotions develop, such as embarrassment, envy, and empathy. Later, we develop even more complex emotions such as shame, guilt, and pride. Michael Lewis, director of the Institute for the Study of Child Development at Rutgers Robert Wood Johnson Medical School, writes, "By three years of age, the child already shows those emotions that Darwin characterized as unique to our species—the emotions of self-consciousness."

Frans de Waal has dedicated his life to the study of primate behavior and has been a lifelong advocate for the recognition of animal emotion. Often disagreeing with the scientific community, he writes, "Science doesn't like imprecision, which is why, when it comes to animal emotions, it is often at odds with the view of the general public." Most of us who have pets would agree with Montaigne—we have no doubt our cats and dogs and horses have emotions. It's the university professors, de Waal says, who balk. De Waal also believes that our prejudice for verbal communication makes it hard to understand animal emotion. In his beautiful book *Mama's Last Hug*, about a sorrowful embrace between biologist Jan van Hooff and a dying chimpanzee with whom he shared a lifelong bond, de Waal asks the reader to consider where that emotion comes from. "Considering how much animals act like us, share our physiological reactions, have the same facial expression, and possess the same sort of brains, wouldn't it be strange indeed if their internal experiences were radically different?"

Beyond self-awareness, others would argue that the true proof of cognition is the ability for flexible problem-solving, under novel conditions and with the use of tools. Corvid birds such as crows are able to create tools to retrieve food. Gavin Hunt of New Zealand's Massey University observed wild crows creating hooklike tools that they stored for future use. Crows are also able to fashion a long food-retrieval tool from shorter items. Auguste M. P. von Bayern of

Oxford University gave crows pieces of wooden dowels and syringe barrels and plungers and observed as the crows figured out how to assemble the three items into longer tools.

When Jane Goodall first observed that chimps used sticks as tools to fish for termites, many people did not want to believe it. Until then, scientists had believed that what separated humans from chimps was our ability to make and use tools. But Goodall discovered that chimps use leaves as sponges to soak up water to drink, use rocks to crack open nuts and gourds, and sharpen sticks to use as spears. Chimps and gorillas who have learned to use sign language have invented creative new words such as "cry hurt food" for a radish or "dirty toilet" for things they did not like, demonstrating a flexible use of language to communicate. Simon Baron-Cohen is less impressed with our primate counterparts. He writes in *The Pattern Seekers*, "Chimpanzees and humans split from our common ancestor eight million years ago, so they've had as long as we've have had to develop a capacity to invent complex tools, like a bicycle, a paintbrush, or a bow and arrow."

The fact that we share 99 percent of our DNA with chimps is awe-inspiring in itself; we don't expect them to be rocket scientists. But when NASA needed a proxy to send into space before sending an astronaut, it turned to our closest relative, to determine if an animal like us could survive the altitude and speed. In search of the best proxy, NASA subjected forty chimps to G-force exposure simulation and to Skinner-like training sessions in which the chimps were rewarded with bananas for pulling a lever at the right time in response to light cues. Their feet were shocked if they failed. "Beyond their genetic similarities to humans," writes Eric Betz in *Discover*, chimps are "incredibly smart and have complex emotions. . . . NASA needed a test subject with the intelligence and dexterity to actually prove it could operate a spacecraft." On January 31, 1961, Ham became the first chimpanzee to travel into space, on a suborbital flight boosted by the Mercury Redstone rocket, and thus "paved the way for

the successful launch of America's first human astronaut, Alan B. Shepard."
(As a side note, in 1783, nearly two hundred years before Ham's historic flight,
the first hot-air balloon was launched. The first passengers were a sheep, a
duck, and a rooster. They also survived.)

Emotion and the Brain

While there may be dissent among scientists as to how much consciousness a
given animal may have, the idea that at least some animals have consciousness
has become more and more widely accepted. Recognition of animal emotion
continues to prove a thornier road.

Neuroscientist, psychologist, and pioneer Jaak Panksepp coined the term
"affective neuroscience" to cover the study of neurobiology and the emotions.
Until then, both the behaviorists and the ethologists treated the brain as a kind
of "black box." Panksepp was able to show that subcortical emotional centers
drive behavior. When specific areas in the subcortex are stimulated by an electrode (electrical stimulation of the brain, or ESB), different behaviors are triggered. For instance, he discovered that rats could be stimulated to display two
types of attack behavior. When the brain center associated with rage was stimulated, a rat would attack another rat. When the brain center associated with
seeking was stimulated, the rat turned on its predatory drive, or "quiet bite"
mode. If a mouse were then placed in the cage, the rat in quiet-bite mode would
attack. When Panksepp removed the cortex from the rats, they still retained
the capacity for social play. In adult cats, removal of the cortex made them
more fearful of people, but they had many normal cat behaviors, such as female
sexual behavior, maternal care of kittens, and grooming. These behaviors and
attendant emotions proved not to be located in the cortex.

In a *Discover* magazine interview, Panksepp explained how the brain system below the cortex works. "These are the emotional primes, the primary-process emotional systems associated with specific brain networks and specifically designated in the brain-stimulation studies of emotions." He codified these primes as: Seeking (exploration), Rage (anger), Fear (anxiety), Lust (sex drive), Care (nurturing), Panic (grief/sadness), and Play (social joy). Rage is critical for survival, because it motivates an animal to fight off an attacking predator, and fear motivates it to avoid being attacked. Panic, different from fear, is the result of separation distress, such as when a mother, human or animal, is separated from her young, or vice versa. Dogs can have serious issues with separation distress when they are left home alone all day while the owner is at work. When I take a midday walk through my subdivision, I can hear dogs whining and barking. Some will chew up your house or slippers if left alone. I know a graphic designer whose cat pooped on his pillow when he went away for a night. Of course, different animals have different temperaments. Some dogs are content to sleep all day and greet you warmly when you get home.

Seeking is "the basic impulse to explore, search, investigate, and make sense of the environment." Studies show that it is pleasurable for mammals when the seeking part of the brain is stimulated, and they will continue to press a lever that stimulates that part of their brains. Lust, or the sex drive, greatly increases when both people and animals reach puberty. Nearly all people and warm-blooded animals nurture their young. This is the maternal instinct. Mothers not only have to guard their babies but to nurse and otherwise care for them. Panksepp was also able to show that this system in mammals is controlled by the hormone oxytocin and the opioid system, the same stimulants that create happiness in humans and that are also responsible for drug addiction. Finally, all young mammals and children are motivated to play. Play helps them learn how to socially interact and, in children, to develop intellectually. The kind of games children play are learned; the need to play is innate.

Panksepp's work focused on emotions as part of a triad of factors motivating animal behavior that also included innate behavior patterns and learning. I believe emotions underlie learned behavior and are genetically ingrained to drive inherited behavior patterns. There are also situations where more than one emotional system is involved in motivating behavior. Elaborating on Panksepp's seven core emotions, scientists are using ESB, fMRI, and PET scans to make a kind of emotional road map.

Neuroscientist Gregory Berns at Emory University trained dogs to voluntarily enter an MRI scanner and lie very still while the caudate nucleus, a major reward center in the brain, was scanned. "Many academics rejected the idea that we could know the mind of an animal, even with modern neuroscience techniques," writes Berns. He declined to restrain the dogs; he believed this would violate basic principles of self-determination. The dogs could leave the scanner at any time. Like people, they exhibited huge individual differences. Some were easy to train to lie still and got used to wearing industrial ear protectors to guard their hearing. Others could not learn to tolerate the scanner noise, and a few were too frightened to even try it.

To study jealousy in the dogs, Berns designed an experiment in which those dogs who could tolerate the MRI watched food being either given to a very realistic fake dog or put in a bucket. The amygdala, an area of the brain associated with both fear and aggression, had greater activation when the fake dog was fed. Watching food being put into the bucket had little effect. This reaction was more pronounced in dogs with an aggressive temperament.

Berns found that the reward center in a dog's brain responds similarly to how a human brain responds. When a dog smelled his favorite person, the reward center was activated. There were also differences in how individual dogs responded to rewards such as food or praise. For certain dogs, verbal praise from their owners was preferred over a treat. Berns concludes that the more we learn about a dog's brain, the more we must admit "we had much in common with dogs at the deepest levels." The dogs in the study also demonstrated a certain level of semiotic understanding. It was easy to teach dogs that when they saw a certain hand signal, they would get a treat, and that another signal resulted in getting nothing. The caudate nucleus was activated when the dog observed the hand signal for a treat. On an emotional level, dogs are a lot like people, neurologically speaking, at least.

Another study, done by Mylène Quervel-Chaumette at the University of Veterinary Medicine, Vienna, showed that dogs had different emotional responses depending on whether they were listening to a recording of a familiar dog they had lived with, a strange dog, or random computer-generated sounds. The dogs recruited for this study had all lived with another dog. When the dogs were separated, there were more behavioral indicators of stress when the familiar dog whine was played. Some of the behaviors included tail between the legs, whining in response to the recording, and crouching low.

As a graduate student, neuroscientist Joseph LeDoux observed a fascinating cross-modal switch-up in epilepsy patients whose nerve connection between the two halves of the brain was severed. The left hand would search for an object in response to stimuli presented to the left visual field (and thus "seen" by the right hemisphere), but the patients could not name the object (language-processing being a left-brain function); or they could name objects placed in the right hand but not in the left. "In the split-brain patient," LeDoux wrote, "information put in one hemisphere remains trapped on that side of the brain, and is unavailable to the other side."

As a professor and researcher at New York University, LeDoux wanted to learn if emotions were similarly affected. He decided to focus on fear, largely considered the most primitive of the emotions, and for good reason. Fear motivates avoidance of danger, from avoiding poisonous snakes to steering clear of dark alleys at night. In an animal, it provides motivation to avoid predators or places where a predator may be located. The main fear center in the brain is the amygdala. If the amygdala is damaged, a wild animal will sometimes become tame. Rats will lose their fear of cats, and monkeys will approach people and novel objects without hesitation. When the amygdala and the brain structures around it are removed, fear is abolished. Current research is now showing that the amygdala has other circuits that are not related to fear, but overall its function is biased toward fear.

LeDoux isolated the basic fear circuits in the brain, focusing on a "low road" (non-conscious processing) circuit located in the lower brain areas where thinking is not required. The fast-acting survival circuit is what makes a human or an animal freeze or quickly move away from danger, such as a predator, sometimes before the nature of the threat has even been fully processed or recognized via the "high road" (conscious processing) circuits of the brain.

LeDoux's basic hypothesis was that these evolutionarily old systems (defense against danger) needed to be activated in a conscious brain to generate emotions (being afraid). In his 1996 book *The Emotional Brain*, LeDoux noted that the "neural organization of particular emotional behavior systems" was similar across species. In his 2015 book, *Anxious*, however, LeDoux claimed that all animal reactions are merely survival circuits. "These circuits do not exist to make us or any other animal feel a certain way. Their function is to keep the organism alive," he wrote. At an International Society of Applied Ethology conference, I learned, LeDoux was confronted about why he had revised his views in a way that denied animals true emotional lives and feelings. He stated that, as a person, he thought they had true emotions, but as a scientist, he was not sure. It's possible that people who think in words cannot countenance the experience of feeling disconnected from language.

A recent study done by Alexandra Klein and her colleagues at the Max Planck Institute clearly shows that emotions in mice are more complex than mere survival circuits. Mice can modulate their fear levels based on previous experiences. The insular cortex located at a midpoint in the brain is a major hub for modulating the intensity of a fear response. It processes information from many parts of the brain. This provides further evidence that LeDoux's recent views on emotions in animals are wrong.

Then I found a mind-blowing study that places emotion mechanisms in the lower, more primitive parts of the brain. D. Alan Shewmon and his colleagues at the UCLA Medical Center studied four children who were born without cerebral hemispheres. This kind of damage typically results in a lifelong vegetative state. Except these children were found to have "discriminative awareness," displaying a range of emotions and social interactions. They were fearful of new people and things. They could tell familiar and unfamiliar people apart. They were capable of social interaction, music preferences, and associative learning. The emotion drivers, it appears, are not in the cortex.

Jonathan Birch of the London School of Economics and his colleagues Alexandra Schnell and Nicola Clayton of Cambridge University believe there is an emerging consensus among scientists that the list of animals who possess "some form of consciousness" is likely longer than just humans and great apes, including other mammals, birds, and some cephalopods. They study comparative cognition and use the term the "richness" to rank the complexity of animals' experiences of sensory perception and emotions. One animal may have stronger "perceptual richness" for one sense compared with other senses. The reason dogs do not engage with their image in the mirror is likely because their primary senses for socializing are smell and hearing, with vision a distant third. In the perceptual richness dimension, corvid birds live in a rich visual world and octopuses live in a rich world of touch. According to Birch, some animals have richer perceptual richness, such as crows' or blue jays' strong sense of vision, and others, such as the elephant, have even richer *evaluative* richness, which can be understood as emotional capacity.

If you think back to the neural network, the octopus is an interesting case. Even though octopuses are categorized with the cephalopods (squid, cuttlefish, etc.), they exhibit characteristics usually associated with vertebrate animals. According to Jennifer Mather, a comparative psychologist at the University of Lethbridge in Canada, octopuses use a variety of techniques to open clams, are capable of play, and have specialized areas of the brain for memory storage and learning. They have "huge neural representation in the arms, and there's a ganglion controlling every sucker." In the documentary *My Octopus Teacher*, naturalist Craig Foster discovers an octopus in a South African kelp forest. At first, the octopus disappears out of sight upon his arrival. But Foster keeps returning, maintaining a respectful distance, and over time the octopus develops an interest in her human visitor and eventually comes closer. At the end of the film, the octopus allows Foster to hold her.

Understanding the Nonverbal World of Animals

Animals live in a sensory-based world and think in pictures, smells, sounds, and touch sensations. We humans live in a highly verbal world where language often filters our sensations, distancing us from directly engaging with sensory information. Young children (pre-language, -thought, and -reason) and animals are similar in terms of cognitive functioning. Frans de Waal notes empathic behavior in children as young as eighteen months, who will comfort a person in distress. This behavior is seen across animals as varied as rodents, elephants, and chimpanzees. The origin of empathy, he writes, is maternal care.

The human-animal relationship transcends language. It's mysterious and beautiful. The best horse trainers I have observed could train a wild colt to be ridden within two hours. One of them, Ray Hunt, was hopeless at explaining what he did. The best he could manage was, "Get in tune with the horse." He simply worked intuitively and empathically. The same is true of many animal handlers. They forge a direct emotional connection between the animal's body and their own, based on nonverbal communication. They unconsciously draw on sensory recall and visual thinking to observe the horse's behavior. These skills are very difficult to teach.

Bud Williams and Burt Smith are two of the true cattle whisperers. They can take a group of naive cattle (meaning cattle that are new to a certain procedure) and draw them out from the edges of the pasture, even from behind bushes, to congregate in the center of the field. They don't do this with bullhorns and a bunch of screaming cowhands, or with jeeps or helicopters—these animals weigh over a thousand pounds each and can easily stampede. The handler simply walks back and forth in a zigzag pattern on the edge of the herd's collective flight zone, their personal space. His quiet walking pattern triggers an instinctual behavior that draws the cattle together. If he walks too quickly, the cattle scatter.

When I asked Burt to explain his method, he made a diagram at his kitchen table, with arrows for the cows. It looked like the diagonal lines in a parking lot. This was when I knew for sure he was a visual-spatial thinker who thinks in patterns. It could have been a diagram for a mathematical text on vectors. Like Ray, he could not explain to students how to do what he did. I realized that in corralling the cattle, Burt was solving the equivalent of a geometry problem in his mind.

As we've discussed, children lose some of their visual imagery as verbal language emerges and then takes over. Visual thinkers like myself and some of the people profiled in this chapter connect with animals because words are not the primary means of communication. For completely verbal thinkers, visual thinking is extremely difficult to contemplate. Imagine if you could trust another person's emotions without having them spelled out in words. "When you watch a child grow," says Pulitzer Prize–winning novelist Marilynne Robinson, "it is pure consciousness coming into being. It's beautiful, complex, and inexhaustible. You learn so much about the mind, how language develops and memory works." Her observation captures the extraordinary process of gaining consciousness, but it also suggests a common assumption, that language is a prerequisite of full consciousness.

Twenty-five years ago, in *Thinking in Pictures*, I predicted that science would finally prove that the little old ladies in tennis shoes were right, that Fifi really does have emotions. Today, I am pleased to report that there are hundreds of research studies on both animal cognition (thinking) and animal emotion (feeling). Marie-Antonine Finkemeier of the Leibniz Institute for Farm Animal Biology in Dummerstorf, Germany, observes that "measuring and understanding personality in animals is a rising scientific field." Researchers are seriously studying animal personality in the wild, in laboratories, and with farm animals. Doreen Cabrera of Brigham Young University reviewed thirty-six personality studies in a variety of mammals, birds, reptiles, and insects. All of the studies showed that these creatures exhibit differences in personality traits such as boldness, fear, and the strength of the drive to be inquisitive and explore. There is even an international conference on animal emotion that highlights interdisciplinary work. We are no longer locked into a binary way of looking at animals, and emotion has taken its place alongside genetics and environment as a major influence on animal behavior. Scientists are well on the way to accepting that animals have personality and emotions. This represents a sea change over the past half century.

I can still recall a story I heard decades ago that boggled my mind. It was 1978, and I was attending an animal behavior symposium hosted by the American Society of Animal Science. Ron Kilgour, an animal behavior scientist from New Zealand, shared a story about a lion that was transported in a crate on a plane. The lion's owner placed a pillow inside the crate. When the plane landed and the crate was opened, the lion was dead, and the pillow gone. What happened? Sadly, this isn't a riddle. The lion had eaten the pillow.

The story brought home to me how highly verbal thought makes it difficult to understand the sensory-based world of an animal. It was obvious to me that a lion would need straw spread out on the hard metal floor of the crate, not a pillow, to feel comfortable. I would have been concerned about the volume and vibrations of takeoff and landing disturbing the lion. I would have been concerned about the lion's eardrums popping at high altitude, or if the animal might experience separation anxiety.

Many years ago, I got into a discussion about consciousness with a person who thought that language was required for consciousness. If this were true, then I would not have been conscious until age three and a half, or even years later, if full consciousness depends on fluency. More recently, I talked to a lady who was highly verbal about how she thinks, and it appeared that her words and emotions were completely fused in a way she could not explain. *I feel, therefore I am.* For me, pictures come first, words next. My emotions don't get tangled in unless I see something very upsetting, like the Boeing crash. But even then, as we've seen, my mind races to figure out how it happened.

Even with the strides in research on animal emotion, the taboo of anthropomorphism still hangs over the field. Nevertheless, it is easy for me to visualize what it would be like to be an animal. When I design restraint equipment, I visualize and perceive the sensations that the animal will experience when held by it. Sudden movements frighten cattle—I see the pictures in my mind based on previous observations of how cattle react. It makes no sense to me that such perceptions are seen as compromising a scientist's objectivity. Amanda Alvarenga and her colleagues at Purdue University and Sichuan Agricultural University found that approximately half the genes associated with behavioral differences in farm animals were also associated with mental disorders in people. Further studies have shown that fearfulness in cattle and friendliness in dogs are associated with genetic factors associated with autism and Williams-Beuren syndrome in humans.

In my view, the culture has a split personality where the treatment of animals is concerned. On the one hand, we have dogs dressed up in baby clothes and fed human food. In New York City, I've seen chihuahuas with ribbons in their hair being pushed around in baby carriages. At the same time, there are dogs that are abandoned or confined to crates for many hours each day. They seldom participate in natural dog behavior, such as socializing with other dogs and sniffing the outdoors to learn what the other dogs are doing. Many also suffer from separation anxiety when they are left home alone all day. (COVID-19 greatly improved the lives of many dogs, because it kept people at home to pay attention to them.)

Two books written outside academic circles provide some of the best insight into the animal mind. Both *The Hidden Life of Dogs* by Elizabeth Marshall Thomas and *Merle's Door* by Ted Kerasote show how dogs that are allowed to roam their neighborhoods have rich social lives. They may be more endangered (dog fights, getting hit by cars, getting lost), but it is likely that their quality of life is enhanced (freedom, social aspect, exercise, novelty seeking). Ted Kerasote observed that dogs need the company of other dogs, and they are motivated to explore many new things with their noses. These activities are much more interesting to dogs than playing with balls, toys, or chewy rawhide.

The latest research on farm-animal welfare emphasizes the importance of giving animals that we use for food lives worth living, with positive emotional experiences. You can go online and look at dairy cows using motorized brushes to groom themselves. I am not supposed to say that they love it, but it is obvious that they do. The cow will repeatedly position herself so that the brush will groom many parts of her body.

The ability to think like an animal inevitably leads to a greater empathy with animals and—in the brain of an object visualizer, especially—a determination to create and promote ways of furthering their welfare. And it doesn't stop with animal welfare. Looking back on a long career, I have thought deeply about how using animals for food affects the environment. When grazing is done correctly, with either good pasture management or effective crop rotation, it can improve soil health and sequester carbon. Grazing animals such as sheep, cattle, and goats can also be raised on land that is too arid for crops. I know family ranchers who are good stewards of the land and run cattle operations that are truly sustainable.

I've often been asked how I can love animals and be involved in designing slaughterhouses. While death in nature is often harsh and cruel, humans must be responsible stewards of the animals they have domesticated for food. Today when I visit a slaughter plant, I get angry when I see problems caused by indiscriminate breeding for greater productivity, which may be associated with painful lameness or heart failure. Ten years ago, I got a lot of pushback from the livestock industry when I spoke out about heat stress and lameness problems associated with an excessive dose of growth promoters. I remember pondering whether to speak out while making a six-hour drive to lecture at a livestock meeting. As I drove, I looked at the cattle out on the pastures and thought that I had to tell cattle producers that there were problems that needed to be corrected.

Breeding problems are even worse in dogs. Long before GMOs, the bulldog was bred to the extreme, for a massive head and short muzzle. This has resulted in a dog that has shoulder problems, difficulty breathing, and a high percentage of puppies that are born by cesarean section. Many of the young people I have talked to who are dog owners or work in the livestock industry do not realize that these problems exist. They just think that it is "normal for the breed." This is what I call "bad becoming normal." I am old enough to remember cattle, pigs, and dogs that never had welfare issues associated with breeding. All of these problems were created via conventional breeding.

I cannot divorce my work as a scientist from my connection to animal behavior and perception. To me, it is obvious that mammals, birds, and some cephalopods, such as the octopus, are conscious and aware. Each animal has its own individual personality. Twenty-five years ago, I was not allowed to use the word *fear* in a scientific paper. I had to call it "behavioral agitation" because scientists were not supposed to give animals human emotions. Today, the word *fear* is allowed. Science is slowly pointing toward the conclusion that the one thing that separates us from other animals is the huge computing power of our brain. Where emotions are concerned, we are similar.

I believe my connection to animals comes from my experience as a visual thinker. As with many people with autism, my emotional spectrum is limited to what the neurologists call the prime (or primitive) emotions. When I was younger, I compared myself to a prey animal, highly alert to danger. When I was in grade school and constantly being bullied, I was like a deer in an open field sensing a predator every time I walked across the schoolyard. I also experience happiness and sadness, but more complex feelings are beyond my range of emotions. I don't understand love-hate relationships or how people swoon over a painting, although intellectually I understand that it has cultural value and worth. What makes me swoon is entering the United States Patent and Trademark Office and seeing all that mechanical genius or finding an elegant solution to a challenging design project.

Marilynne Robinson also described how language resonates emotionally for verbal thinkers. "Literature says this is what sadness feels like and this is what holiness feels like, and people feel acknowledged in what they already feel," she writes. Her observations provided me with an insight into how the verbal mind processes emotion and how it differs from mine. Words provide information for me; there are few to no emotional associations. I need to see something or recall a visual image to feel emotion. A concept like holiness is too abstract for me. But I am not without emotion. When my mother read *Black Beauty* to me, I visualized a real horse from my database of horses, and then imagined it being harmed, and that made me feel terrible.

Throughout graduate school, I was able to adopt the supposedly objective stance of the scientist. It made a lot of sense. All that changed when I stepped onto my first cattle plant and placed my hands against the side of a steer. It was as if a current had run through me. I could instantly tell whether the animal was anxious, angry, agitated, or relaxed. I didn't need more proof than that. Animals have emotions. Some, like chimps and dolphins, also have self-awareness. Others feel through their senses, like the elephants who mourn for their herd mates when they die. They may not have words to tell us about their feelings, but I believe animals have consciousness. They are visual thinkers.

Afterword

On the morning of January 28, 2022, at 6:39 a.m., the Fern Hollow Bridge, which goes through the Frick Park area of Pittsburgh, collapsed over a ravine. It was snowing that morning, so fortunately, with a delayed opening to the school day, the four-lane bridge was less heavily trafficked than usual. No lives were lost, but at least ten people were injured. A gas pipe had also been ruptured in the collapse, and even though it was soon shut off, people in nearby homes had to be evacuated. The recognition that it could have been much worse hung in the air, along with the lingering smell of gas, as people were rescued from the site.

When we say, "Things could have been worse," we are saying we are grateful there wasn't more damage, while somewhere in the back of our minds we know that it can and will happen again. Then, after the EMTs and the fire trucks and the police leave, life goes back to normal. The debris is cleaned up, the bridge repaired or demolished, and we become complacent until the next time.

As you could probably have guessed, the first thing I did after learning of this collapse was go online to learn the critical details about the structure of the bridge. I saw that it had a steel K-frame design that might be more likely to fail than a bridge with a more robust supporting structure. It needed both more frequent inspections and more frequent repairs and painting to deal with corrosion. This got me into full bridge-geek mode, and I looked up the 2007 collapse of an interstate bridge near downtown Minneapolis. When I saw the photos of the crumpled steel in that disaster, I had an instant visualization: The steel was too light. Too cheap. It bent like cardboard. A report published in the online Civil Engineering Portal confirmed my diagnosis. The gusset plates that held the steel beams together were only half the required thickness. I guessed that in both cities, there were visual thinkers who detected that these bridges were unsafe but who were afraid to speak out, or who tried to speak out and were ignored.

Coincidentally, the Fern Hollow Bridge plunged into the ravine below on the same day that President Biden was scheduled to visit Pittsburgh to talk about infrastructure, emphasizing the need to improve the supply chain, revitalize manufacturing, and create good-paying jobs. These are all admirable goals, and I'm not expecting politicians to drill down into the details (they're mostly verbal thinkers). But the question remains: How will we find and train the people for the vital jobs the president proposes if we stick with our current one-size-fits-all model of education, employment, and communication? Finding and training the engineers, machinists, welders, architects, and public planners begins on the nursery floor. The children who are drawn to blocks, Legos, tools, highly detailed drawing, who like to take things apart and put them together; these are the visual thinkers. If we recognize and cultivate and invest in them, they will grow into the adults who will build and repair bridges, airplanes, and nuclear reactors. If we don't provide these kids with a more visually based education, we are decimating our talent pool.

The reason for the collapse of the Pittsburgh bridge is still under investigation, but it is generally agreed that "deferred maintenance" is responsible. There's that phrase again. Earlier in this book, we looked at what happened when outages in California left people without power and sparked fires. I would prefer to call "deferred maintenance" what it is: infrequent maintenance, or sometimes no maintenance. According to the 2021 Report Card for America's

Infrastructure, of the 617,000 bridges across the country, 7.5 percent are considered structurally deficient and 42 percent are as old as the Fern Hollow Bridge, which, almost fifty years old, was not built for that longevity.

There is hopeful news: bridge engineers have been developing all kinds of cool materials, such as high-performance concrete and steel, corrosion-resistant reinforcements, and improved coatings. New methods to evaluate the health and stability of bridges include infrared thermography, ground-penetrating radar, embedded sensors that can provide continuous feedback, and my favorite, submersible drones outfitted with cameras that can take pictures underwater.

I've worked with industry innovators for my entire career, and I'm convinced that the people who are developing this kind of cutting-edge technology are like Edison, Turing, and Musk, visual thinkers whose paths began in a basement or garage where they were free to tinker and experiment. I'm also convinced that two key elements set the stage for success in fostering abilities: exposure and mentorship. The breakthrough technologies are not coming from kids shunted off to special ed or addicted to video games, even though they might have the right kinds of minds for it. How can we identify and encourage our future designers, engineers, and artists? First, we must see them, recognize their skills, support their different learning curves. Above all, my goal is to help those kids. If we start there, anything is possible.

Imagine if we catered to visual thinkers the way we cater to verbal thinkers. If we didn't assume that we all perceived and processed information the same way, primarily through language. We can look the other way each time a bridge buckles, an apartment building collapses, a plane crashes, or a reactor melts down. Or, if we want to make good on our promises of giving our kids a better life—if we want to engineer a safer, more inclusive, more advanced society that leads in manufacturing, technology, and finding solutions to the challenges of a rapidly changing and complex world—we need to make room for our visual thinkers and their remarkable gifts.

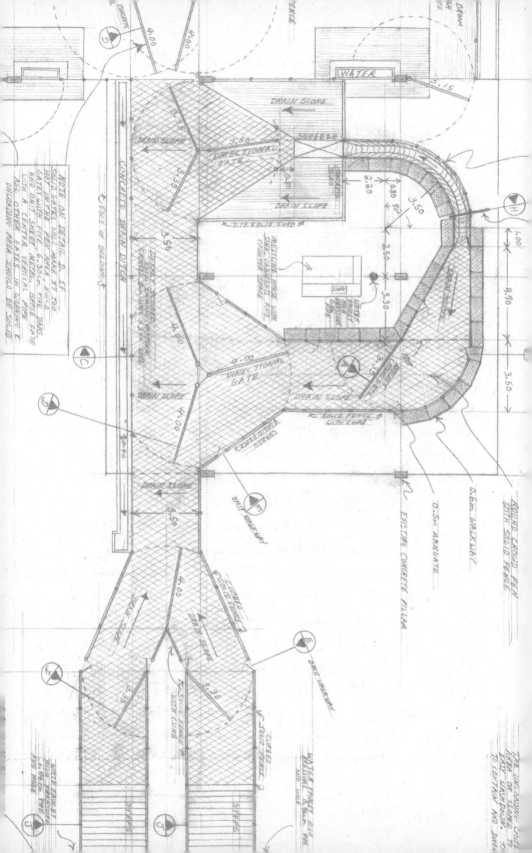

Acknowledgments

Many thanks to the team of people—incredible verbal and visual thinkers working together—who helped produce and publish this book: Nora Alice Demick, Ashley Garland, Marc Greenawalt, Geoff Kloske, Cheryl Miller, Tyriq Moore, Becky Saletan, Jenefer Shute, Nick Tabor, Shailyn Tavella, Catalina Trigo, Auguste White.

References

INTRODUCTION

Chomsky, N. *Syntactic Structures*. Eastford, CT: Martino Fine Books, 2015.

Descartes, R. *Meditations on First Philosophy: With Selections from the Objections and Replies*. Translated and edited by John Cottingham. Cambridge, UK: Cambridge University Press, 2017.

Frener & Reifer. Steve Jobs Theater. https://www.frener-reifer.com/news-en/steve-jobs-theater/ (accessed August 7, 2021).

Grandin, T. *Thinking in Pictures*. New York: Doubleday, 1995. Expanded edition. New York: Vintage, 2006.

Kozhevnikov, M., et al. "Revising the Visualizer-Verbalizer Dimensions: Evidence for Two Types of Visualizers." *Cognition and Instruction* 20, no. 1 (2002): 47–77.

Kozhevnikov, M., et al. "Spatial versus Object Visualizers: A New Characterization of Visual Cognitive Style." *Memory and Cognition* 33, no. 4 (2005): 710–26.

Premier Composite Technologies, Dubai, Arab Emirates. Steve Jobs Theater Pavilion. http://www.pct.ae/steve-jobs-theater (accessed August 7, 2021).

Sedak, Gersthofen, Germany. Apple Park, Cupertino, California, 2,500 glass units in facade. https://www.sedak.com/en/references/facades/apple-park-cupertino-usa (accessed August 7, 2021).

1. WHAT IS VISUAL THINKING?

Adolphs, R. *The Neuroscience of Emotion*. Princeton, NJ: Princeton University Press, 2018.

Akkermans, M. "Collaborative Life Writing in *Life, Animated*." *Diggit Magazine*, October 4, 2020.

Alfonsi, S. "Matthew Whitaker: Meet the Blind Piano Player Who Is So Good, Scientists Are Studying Him." *60 Minutes*, December 27, 2020.

Amit, E., et al. "An Asymmetrical Relationship between Verbal and Visual Thinking: Converging Evidence from Behavior and fMRI." *NeuroImage*, March 18, 2017.

Ankum, J. "Diagnosing Skin Diseases Using an AI-Based Dermatology Consult." *Science Translational Medicine* 12, no. 548 (2020): eabc8946.

Baer, D. "Peter Thiel: Asperger's Can Be a Big Advantage in Silicon Valley." *Business Insider*, April 8, 2015. https://www.businessinsider.com/peter-thiel-aspergers-is-an-advantage-2015-4.

Bainbridge, W. A., et al. "Quantifying Aphantasia through Drawing: Those without Visual Imagery Show Deficits in Object but Not Spatial Memory." *Cortex* 135 (Feb. 2021): 159–72.

Baron, S. "How Disney Gave Voice to a Boy with Autism." *Guardian*, December 3, 2016.

Baron-Cohen, S. *The Pattern Seekers*. New York: Basic Books, 2020.

Behrmann, M., et al. "Intact Visual Imagery and Impaired Visual Perception in a Patient with Visual Agnosia." *Journal of Experimental Psychology* 20, no. 5 (1994): 1068–87.

Birner, B. "FAQ: Language Acquisition." Linguistic Society of America. https://www
.linguisticsociety.org/resource/faq-how-do-we-learn-language.

Blazhenkova, O., and M. Kozhevnikov. "Creative Processes during a Collaborative Drawing Task in Teams of Different Specializations." *Creative Education* 11, no. 9 (2020). Article ID 103051.

Blazhenkova, O., and M. Kozhevnikov. "Types of Creativity and Visualization in Teams of Different Educational Specialization." *Creativity Research Journal* 28, no. 2 (2016): 123–35.

Blazhenkova, O., M. Kozhevnikov, and M. A. Motes. "Object-Spatial Imagery: A New Self-Report Imagery Questionnaire." *Applied Cognitive Psychology* 20, no. 2 (March 2006): 239–63, https://doi.org/10.1002/acp.1182.

Blume, H. "Neurodiversity: On the Neurological Underpinnings of Geekdom." *Atlantic*, September 1998.

Bouchard, T. J., et al. "Sources of Human Psychological Differences: The Minnesota Study of Twins Reared Apart." *Science* 250, no. 4978 (1990): 223–28.

Bryant, R. A., and A. G. Harvey. "Visual Imagery in Posttraumatic Stress Disorder." *Journal of Traumatic Stress* 9 (1996): 613–19.

Chabris, C. F., et. al. "Spatial and Object Visualization Cognitive Styles: Validation Studies in 3,800 Individuals." *Group Brain Technical Report* 2 (2006): 1–20.

Chen, Q., et al. "Brain Hemisphere Involvement in Visuospatial and Verbal Divergent Thinking." *NeuroImage* 202 (2019): 116065.

Chen, W., et al. "Human Primary Visual Cortex and Lateral Geniculate Nucleus Activation during Visual Imagery." *Neuroreport* 9, no. 16 (1998): 3669–74.

Cho, J. Y., and J. Suh. "Understanding Spatial Ability in Interior Design Education: 2D-to-3D Visualization Proficiency as a Predictor of Design Performance." *Journal of Interior Design* 44, no. 3 (2019): 141–59.

Cooperrider, J. R., et al. "Dr. Temple Grandin: A Neuroimaging Case Study." Presentation, University of Utah, at the International Meeting for Autism Research (IMFAR), San Diego, 2011.

Courchesne, E., et al. "Hypoplasia of Cerebellar Vermal Lobules VI and VII in Autism." *New England Journal of Medicine* 318 (1988): 1349–54.

Cropley, D. H., and J. C. Kaufman. "The Siren Song of Aesthetics? Domain Differences and Creativity in Engineering and Design." *Proceedings of the Institution of Mechanical Engineers, Part C: Journal of Mechanical Engineering Science* 233, no. 2 (2019): 451–64.

Curry, A. "Neuroscience Starts Talking." *Nature* 551 (2017): S81–S83.

Dajose, L. "Reading Minds with Ultrasound: A Less-Invasive Technique to Decode the Brain's Intentions." Caltech, March 22, 2021. https://www.caltech.edu/about/news/reading-minds
-with-ultrasound-a-less-invasive-technique-to-decode-the-brains-intentions.

Dean, J. "Making Marines into MacGyvers." *Bloomberg Businessweek*, September 20, 2018, 48–55.

"Diagnosing Bill Gates." *Time*, January 24, 1994, 25.

Dolgin, E. "A Loop of Faith." *Nature* 544 (2017): 284–85.

Doron, G., et al. "Perirhinal Input to Neocortical Layer 1 Controls Learning." *Science* 370 (2020): 1435.

Fehlhaber, K. "A Tale of Two Aphasias." *Knowing Neurons*, August 13, 2014. https://knowingneurons.com/2014/08/13/a-tale-of-two-aphasias/.

REFERENCES

Fernyhough, C. *The Voices Within: The History and Science of How We Talk to Ourselves*. London: Profile Books, 2016.

Ferrier, D. "On the Localization of the Functions of the Brain." *British Medical Journal*, December 19, 1874, 766.

Ferrier, D., and G. F. Yeo. "A Record of Experiments on the Effects of Lesions of Different Regions of the Cerebral Hemispheres." *Royal Society Philosophical Transactions*, January 1, 1884, https://doi.org/10.1098/rst.1884.0020.

Firat, R. B. "Opening the 'Black Box': Functions of the Frontal Lobes and Their Implications for Sociology. *Frontiers in Sociology* 4, no. 3 (2019). https://www.frontiersin.org/articles/10.3389 /fsoc.2019.00003/full.

Freedman, D. J., et al. "Categorical Representation of Visual Stimuli in the Primate Prefrontal Cortex." *Science* 291 (5502): 312–16.

Fulford, J., et al. "The Neural Correlates of Visual Imagery Vividness—An fMRI Study and Literature Review." *Cortex* 105 (2018): 26–40.

Gainotti, G. "A Historical Review of Investigations on Laterality of Emotions in the Human Brain." *Journal of the History of the Neurosciences* 28, no. 1 (2019): 23–41.

Ganis, G., et al. "Brain Areas Underlying Visual Mental Imagery and Visual Perception: An fMRI Study." *Cognitive Brain Research* 20 (2004): 226–41.

Gardner, H. *Creating Minds*. New York: Basic Books, 2006.

Gardner, H. *Frames of Mind*. New York: Basic Books, 1983.

Gardner, H. *Multiple Intelligences: New Horizons in Theory and Practice*. New York: Basic Books, 2008.

Ghasemi, A., et al. "The Principles of Biomedical Scientific Writing: Materials and Methods." *International Journal of Endocrinology and Metabolism* 17, no. 1 (2019): 88155.

Giurfa, M., et al. "The Concepts of 'Sameness' and 'Difference' in an Insect." *Nature* 410, no. 6831 (2001): 930–33.

Glickstein, M. "The Discovery of the Visual Cortex." *Scientific American*, September 1988. https:// www.scientificamerican.com/article/the-discovery-of-the-visual-cortex/.

Glickstein, M. *Neuroscience: A Historical Introduction*. Cambridge, MA: MIT Press, 2014.

Goldstein, J. "18-Year-Old Blind Pianist Prodigy Getting Studied by Scientists for His 'Remarkable' Talents." *People*, February 24, 2020. https://people.com/human-interest /blind-pianist-prodigy-matthew-whitaker-studied-by-scientists/.

Golon, A. *Visual-Spatial Learners*. Austin, TX: Prufrock Press, 2017.

Graham, J. "*Life, Animated*: A Film Review." *johngrahamblog* (blog). December 8, 2016. https:// johngrahamblog.wordpress.com/2016/12/08/life-animated-a-film-review/.

Grandin, T. "How Does Visual Thinking Work in the Mind of a Person with Autism? A Personal Account." *Philosophical Transactions of the Royal Society, London, B. Biological Sciences* 364, no. 1522 (2009): 1437–42.

Grandin, T. "My Mind Is a Web Browser: How People with Autism Think." *Cerebrum* 2, no. 1 (2000): 14–22.

Grandin, T. *Temple Grandin's Guide to Working with Farm Animals*. North Adams, MA: Storey, 2017.

Grandin, T. *Thinking in Pictures*. New York: Doubleday, 1995. Expanded edition. New York: Vintage, 2006.

Grandin, T., and R. Panek. *The Autistic Brain*. New York: Houghton Mifflin Harcourt, 2013.

Grandin, T., and M. M. Scariano. *Emergence: Labeled Autistic*. Novato, CA: Arena, 1986.

Gross, C. G. "The Discovery of Motor Cortex and Its Background." *Journal of the History of the Neurosciences* 16, no. 3 (2007): 320–31.

Gualtieri, C. T. "Genomic Variation, Evolvability, and the Paradox of Mental Illness." *Frontiers in Psychiatry* 11 (2021): 593233.

Haciomeroglu, E. S. "Object-Spatial Visualization and Verbal Cognitive Styles and Their Relation to Cognitive Abilities and Mathematical Performance." *Educational Sciences: Theory and Practice* 16, no. 3 (2016): 987–1003.

Haciomeroglu, E. S., and M. LaVenia. "Object-Spatial Imagery and Verbal Cognitive Styles in High School Students." *Perceptual and Motor Skills* 124, no. 3 (2017): 689–702.

Haque, S., et al. "The Visual Agnosias and Related Disorders." *Journal of Neuro-Ophthalmology* 38, no. 3 (2018): 379–92.

Henzel, D. "He Told Me That He Has No Sensory Thinking, Cannot Visualize, Feel or Hear His Own Dog." Howwesolve.com, 2021 (accessed fall 2021).

Hirsch, C., and S. Schildknecht. "In Vitro Research Reproducibility: Keeping Up High Standards." *Frontiers in Pharmacology* 10 (2019): 1484. doi:10.3389/fphar.2019.01484.

Hitch, G. J., et al. "Visual and Phonological Components of Working Memory in Children." *Memory and Cognition* 17, no. 2 (1989): 175–85.

Höffler, T. N., M. Koć-Januchta, and D. Leutner. "More Evidence for Three Types of Cognitive Style: Validating the Object-Spatial Imagery and Verbal Questionnaire Using Eye Tracking When Learning with Texts and Pictures." *Applied Cognitive Psychology* 31, no. 1 (2017). doi.org/10.1002/acp.3300.

Hsieh, T., et al. "Enhancing Scientific Foundations to Ensure Reproducibility: A New Paradigm." *American Journal of Pathology* 188, no. 1 (2018): 6–10.

Huff, T., et al. "Neuroanatomy, Visual Cortex." National Library of Medicine, National Institutes of Health, July 31, 2021.

Ishai, A., et al. "Distributed Neural Systems for the Generation of Visual Images." *Neuron* 28, no. 3 (2000): 979–90.

Jamiloux, Y., et al. "Should We Stimulate or Suppress Immune Responses in COVID-19? Cytokine and Anti-Cytokine Interventions." *Autoimmunity Reviews* (July 2020): 102567.

Jensen, A. R. "Most Adults Know More Than 42,000 Words." *Frontiers*, August 16, 2016.

Keogh, R., and J. Pearson. "The Blind Mind: No Sensory Visual Imagery in Aphantasia." *Cortex* 105 (2018): 53–60.

Khatchadourian, R. "The Elusive Peril of Space Junk." *The New Yorker*, September 21, 2020.

Khatchadourian, R. "The Trash Nebula." *New Yorker*, September 28, 2020.

Koć-Januchta, M., et al. "Visualizers versus Verbalizers: Effects of Cognitive Style on Learning with Texts and Pictures." *Computers in Human Behavior* 68 (2017): 170–79. doi.org/10.1016/j.chb.2016.11.028.

Koppenol-Gonzales, G. V., S. Bouwmeester, and J. K. Vermunt. "The Development of Verbal and Visual Working Memory Processes: A Latent Variable Approach." *Journal of Experimental Child Psychology* 111, no. 3 (2012): 439–54. https://doi.org/10.1016/j.jecp.2011.10.001.

Koppenol-Gonzales, G. V., et al. "Accounting for Individual Differences in the Development of Verbal and Visual Short-Term Memory Processes in Children." *Learning and Individual Differences* 66 (2018): 29–37.

Kosslyn, S. M., et al. "The Role of Area 17 in Visual Imagery: Convergent Evidence from PET and rTMS." *Science* 284, no. 5411 (1999): 167–70.

Kosslyn, S. M., et al. "Topographical Representations of Mental Images in Primary Visual Cortex." *Nature* 378 (1995): 496–98.

REFERENCES

Kozhevnikov, M., O. Blazhenkova, and M. Becker. "Tradeoffs in Object versus Spatial Visualization Abilities: Restriction in the Development of Visual Processing Resources." *Psychonomic Bulletin and Review* 17, no. 1 (2009): 29–33.

Kozhevnikov, M., M. Hegarty, and R. E. Mayer. "Revising the Visualizer-Verbal Dimension: Evidence for Two Types of Visualizers." *Cognition and Instruction* 20, no. 1 (2002): 47–77.

Kozhevnikov, M., and J. Shepherd. "Spatial versus Object Visualizers: A New Characterization of Visual Cognitive Style." *Memory and Cognition* 33, no. 4 (2005): 710–26.

Lee, S.-H., D. J. Kravitz, and C. I. Baker. "Disentangling Visual Imagery and Perception of Real-World Objects." *NeuroImage* 59, no. 4 (2012): 4064–73.

Masataka, N. "Were Musicians as Well as Artists in the Ice Age Caves Likely with Autism Spectrum Disorder? A Neurodiversity Hypothesis." In *The Origins of Language Revisited*, edited by N. Masataka, 323–45. Singapore: Springer, 2020. doi.org/10.1007/978-981-15-4250-3_9.

Mathewson, J. H. "Visual-Spatial Thinking: An Aspect of Science Overlooked by Educators." *Science Education* 83, no. 1 (1999): 33–54. https://onlinelibrary.wiley.com/doi/10.1002/(SICI)1098-237X(199901)83:1%3C33::AID-SCE2%3E3.0.CO;2-Z.

Mazard, A., et al. "A PET Meta-Analysis of Object and Spatial Mental Imagery." *Cognitive Psychology* 16 (2004): 673–95.

McFarland, M. "Why Shades of Asperger's Syndrome Are the Secret to Building a Great Tech Company." *Washington Post*, April 3, 2015. https://www.washingtonpost.com/news/innovations/wp/2015/04/03/why-shades-of-aspergers-syndrome-are-the-secret-to-building-a-great-tech-company/.

Mellet, E., et al. "Functional Anatomy of Spatial Mental Imagery Generated from Verbal Instructions." *Journal of Neuroscience* 16, no. 20 (2020): 6504–12.

Mishkin, M., et al. "Object Vision and Spatial Vision: Two Cortical Pathways." *Trends in Neuroscience* 6 (1983): 414–17.

Morena, N., et al. "Vividness of Mental Imagery Is Associated with the Occurrence of Intrusive Memories." *Journal of Behavior Therapy and Experimental Psychiatry* 44 (2013): 221–26.

Moscovitch, G., et al. "What Is Special About Face Recognition? Nineteen Experiments on a Person with Visual Object Agnosia and Dyslexia but Normal Face Recognition." *Journal of Cognitive Neuroscience* 9, no. 5 (1997): 555–604.

Mottron, L. "The Power of Autism." *Nature* 479 (2011): 34–35.

Mottron, L., and S. Belleville. "A Study of Perceptual Analysis in a High-Level Autistic Subject with Exceptional Graphic Abilities." *Brain and Cognition* 23 (1993): 279–309.

Mottron, L., et. al. "Enhanced Perceptual Functioning in Autism: An Update, and Eight Principles of Perception." *Journal of Autism and Developmental Disorders* 36, no. 1 (2006): 27–43.

Nishimura, K., et al. "Brain Activities of Visual and Verbal Thinkers: A MEG Study." *Neuroscience Letters* 594 (2015): 155–60.

Nishimura, K., et al. "Individual Differences in Mental Imagery Tasks: A Study of Visual Thinkers and Verbal Thinkers." *Neuroscience Communications* (2016).

Pant, R., S. Kanjlia, and M. Bedny. "A Sensitive Period in the Neural Phenotype of Language in Blind Individuals." *Developmental Cognitive Neuroscience* 41 (2020). https://www.sciencedirect.com/science/article/pii/S1878929319303317#sec0010.

Park, C. C. *Exiting Nirvana: A Daughter's Life with Autism.* New York: Little, Brown, 2001.

Pashler, H., et al. "Learning Styles: Concepts and Evidence." *Psychological Science in the Public Interest* 9, no. 3 (2008).

Pearson, J. "The Human Imagination: The Cognitive Neuroscience of Visual Mental Imagery." *Nature Reviews Neuroscience* 20 (2019): 624–34.

Peissig, J. J., and M. J. Tarr. "Visual Object Recognition: Do We Know More Now Than We Did 20 Years Ago?" *Annual Review of Psychology* 58 (2007): 75–96.

Peissig, J. J., et al. "Pigeons Spontaneously Form Three-Dimensional Shape Categories." *Behavioral Processes* 158 (2019): 70–75.

Pérez-Fabello, M. J., A. Campos, and D. Campos-Juanatey. "Is Object Imagery Central to Artistic Performance?" *Thinking Skills and Creativity* 21 (2016): 67–74. doi.org/10.1016/j.tsc.2016 .05.006.

Pérez-Fabello, M. J., A. Campos, and F. M. Felisberti. "Object-Spatial Imagery in Fine Arts, Psychology and Engineering." *Thinking Skills and Creativity* 27 (2018): 131–38.

Phillips, M., et al. "Detection of Malignant Melanoma Using Artificial Intelligence: An Observational Study of Diagnostic Accuracy." *Dermatology Practical & Conceptual* 10, no. 1 (2020): e2020011. doi.org/10.5826/dpc.1001a11.

Pidgeon, L. M., et al. "Functional Neuroimaging of Visual Creativity: A Systematic Review and Meta-Analysis." *Brain and Behavior* 6, no. 10 (2016). doi.org/10.1002/brb3.540.

Pinker, S. *The Language Instinct: How the Mind Creates Language.* New York: William Morrow, 1994.

Putt, S., et al. "The Role of Verbal Interaction during Experimental Bifacial Stone Tool Manufacture." *Lithic Technology* 39, no. 2 (2014): 96–112.

Reeder, R. R., et al. "Individual Differences Shape the Content of Visual Representations." *Vision Research* 141 (2017): 266–81.

Ryckegham, A. V. "How Do Bats Echolocate and How Are They Adapted to This Activity?" *Scientific American*, December 21, 1998. https://www.scientificamerican.com/article /how-do-bats-echolocate-an/.

Sacks, O. *An Anthropologist on Mars.* New York: Alfred A. Knopf, 1995.

Sacks, O. *The Man Who Mistook His Wife for a Hat.* New York: Summit Books, 1985.

Schweinberg, M., et al. "Same Data, Different Conclusions: Radical Dispersion in Empirical Results When Independent Analysts Operationalize and Test the Same Hypothesis." *Organizational Behavior and Human Decision Process* 165 (2021): 228–49.

Servick, K. "Echolocation in Blind People Reveals the Brain's Adaptive Powers." *Science Magazine*, 2019. https://www.sciencemag.org/news/2019/10/echolocation-blind-people-reveals-brain -s-adaptive-powers.

Servick, K. "Ultrasound Reads Monkey Brains, Opening New Way to Control Machines with Thought." *Science*, March 22, 2021.

Shah, A., and U. Frith. "Why Do Autistic Individuals Show Superior Performance on the Block Design Task?" *Journal of Child Psychology and Psychiatry* 34, no. 8 (1993): 1351–64.

Shuren, J. E. "Preserved Color Imagery in an Achromatopsic." *Neuropsychologia* 34, no. 4 (1996): 485–89.

Sikela, J. M., and V. B. Searles Quick. "Genomic Tradeoffs: Are Autism and Schizophrenia the Steep Price for a Human Brain." *Human Genetics* 137, no. 1 (2018): 1–13.

Silberman, S. "The Geek Syndrome." *Wired*, December 1, 2001. https://www.wired.com/2001 /12/aspergers/.

Silverman, L. K. *Upside-Down Brilliance: The Visual-Spatial Learner.* Denver: Deleon, 2002.

Smith, B. *Moving 'Em: A Guide to Low Stress Animal Handling.* University of Hawai'i, Mānoa: Graziers Hui, 1998.

REFERENCES

Soares, J. M., et al. "A Hitchhiker's Guide to Functional Magnetic Resonance Imaging." *Frontiers in Neuroscience* (2016). doi.org/10.3389/forins.2016.0015.

Spagna, A., et al. "Visual Mental Imagery Engages the Left Fusiform Gyrus, but Not the Early Visual Cortex: A Meta-Analysis of Neuroimaging Evidence." *Neuroscience and Biobehavioral Reviews* (2020). doi:10.1016/j.neubiorev.2020.12.029.

Sperry, R. W. "Lateral Specialization of Cerebral Function in the Surgically Separated Hemispheres." In *The Psychophysiology of Thinking*, ed. F. J. McGuigan and R. A. Schoonover, chap. 6. New York: Academic Press, 1973.

Sumner, N., et al. "Single-Trial Decoding of Movement Intentions Using Functional Ultrasound Neuroimaging." *Neuron* (2021). https://pubmed.ncbi.nlm.nih.gov/33756104/.

Suskind, O. "Happy Easter, Walter Post." A cartoon drawing by Owen Suskind on Facebook, 2020.

Sutton, M. "Snakes, Sausages and Structural Formulae." *Chemistry World*, 2015.

Takeda, M. "Brain Mechanisms of Visual Long-Term Memory Retrieval in Primates." *Neuroscience Research* 142 (2019): 7–15.

Thaler, L. "Echolocation May Have Real-Life Advantages for Blind People: An Analysis of Survey Data." *Frontiers in Physiology* (2013). doi.org/10.3389/fphys.2013.00098.

Thaler, L., S. R. Arnott, and M. A. Goodale. "Neural Correlates of Natural Human Echolocation in Early and Late Blind Echolocation Experts." *PLOS ONE* (2011). doi.org/10.1371/journal.pone.0020162.

Thorpe, S. J., et al. "Seeking Categories in the Brain." *Science* 291, no. 5502 (2001): 260–63.

Thorudottir, S., et al. "The Architect Who Lost the Ability to Imagine: The Cerebral Basis of Visual Imagery." *Brain Sciences* 10, no. 2 (2020). doi.org/10.3390/brainsci 1002059.

Tubbs, S. R., et al. "Tatsuji Inouye: The Mind's Eye." *Child's Nervous System* 28 (2012): 147–50.

Vance, A. *Elon Musk: Tesla, SpaceX, and the Quest for a Fantastic Future.* New York: Ecco, 2015.

Vannucci, M., et al. "Visual Object Imagery and Autobiographical Memory: Object Imagers Are Better at Remembering Their Personal Past." *Memory* 24, no. 4 (2016): 455–70.

Vazquez, C. M. "Technology Boot Camp Aims to Upgrade Okinawa-Based Marines' Problem-Solving Skills." *Stars and Stripes*, March 26, 2019.

Warford, N., and M. Kunda. "Measuring Individual Difference in Visual and Verbal Thinking Styles." Presented at the 40th Annual Meeting of the Cognitive Science Society, Madison, Wisconsin, 2018.

Watanabe, S., J. Sakamoto, and M. Wakita. "Pigeons' Discrimination of Paintings by Monet and Picasso." *Journal of the Experimental Analysis of Behavior* 63 (1995): 165–74.

Weintraub, K. "Temple Grandin on How the Autistic 'Think Different.'" *USA Today*, May 1, 2013, https://www.usatoday.com/news/nation/2013/05/01/autism-temple-grandin-brain/2122455 (accessed September 1, 2021).

West, T. Commencement address, Siena School, Silver Spring, Maryland, June 9, 2020. *In the Mind's Eye: Dyslexic Renaissance* (blog), December 22, 2020.

Wheeler, M. "Damaged Connections in Phineas Gage's Brain: Famous 1848 Case of Man Who Survived Accident Has Modern Parallel." ScienceDaily, May 16, 2012. https://www.sciencedaily.com/releases/2012/05/120516195408.htm.

Zeman, A., et al. "Phantasia—The Psychological Significance of Lifelong Visual Imagery Vividness Extremes." *Cortex* 130 (2020): 426–40. doi:10.1016/j.cortex.2020.04.003.

Zhang, W., et al. "The Use of Anti-Inflammatory Drugs in the Treatment of People with Severe Coronavirus Disease 2019 (COVID-19): The Perspectives of Clinical Immunologists from China." *Clinical Immunology* 214 (2020): 108393.

Zimmer, C. "Many People Have a Vivid 'Mind's Eye,' While Others Have None at All." *New York Times*, June 8, 2021. https://www.nytimes.com/2021/06/08/science/minds-eye-mental-pictures-psychology.html.

2. SCREENED OUT

Adams, S. "The Forbes Investigation: How the SAT Failed America." *Forbes*, November 30, 2020. https://www.forbes.com/sites/susanadams/2020/09/30/the-forbes-investigation-how-the-sat-failed-america.

Adelman, K. "Secrets of the Brain and Dyslexia: Interview with Thomas West." *Washingtonian*, July 1, 2005. https://www.washingtonian.com/2005/07/01/secrets-of-the-brain-dyslexia-interview-with-thomas-west/ (accessed June 27, 2021).

Arnold, K. D. "Academic Achievement—A View from the Top. The Illinois Valedictorian Project." Office of Educational Research and Improvement, 1993.

Asmika, A., et al. "Autistic Children Are More Responsive to Tactile Sensory Stimulus." *Iranian Journal of Child Neurology* 12, no. 4 (2018): 37–44.

Baird, L. L. "Do Grades and Tests Predict Adult Accomplishment?" *Research in Higher Education* 23, no. 1 (1985): 3–85. https://doi.org/10.1007/BF00974070.

Baker, A. "Common Core Curriculum Now Has Critics on the Left." *New York Times*, February 16, 2014.

Ballotpedia. "Education Policy in the U.S." https://ballotpedia.org/Education_policy_in_the_United_States.

Bardi, M., et al. "Behavioral Training and Predisposed Coping Strategies Interact to Influence Resilience in Male Long-Evans Rats: Implications for Depression." *Stress* 15, no. 3 (2012): 306–17.

Baril, D. "Is It Autism? The Line Is Getting Increasingly Blurry." ScienceDaily, August 21, 2019.

Belkin, D. "Who Needs a Four-Year Degree?" *Wall Street Journal*, November 13, 2020, R3.

Bernstein, B. O., D. Lubinski, and C. P. Benbow. "Academic Acceleration in Gifted Youth and Fruitless Concerns Regarding Psychological Well-Being: A 35 Year Longitudinal Study." *Journal of Educational Psychology* (2020). https://my.vanderbilt.edu/smpy/files/2013/02/Article-JEP-Bernstein-2020-F.pdf.

Bhattacharya, S. "Meet Dr. Nita Patel and Her All-Female Team Developing the COVID-19 Vaccine." *Brown Girl Magazine*, April 28, 2020.

Bower, B. "When It's Playtime, Many Kids Prefer Reality over Fantasy." *Science News*, February 6, 2018.

Bowler, D. M., et al. "Nonverbal Short-Term Serial Order Memory in Autism Spectrum Disorder." *Journal of Abnormal Psychology* 125, no. 7 (2016): 886–93.

Bowles, N. "A Dark Consensus about Screens and Kids Begins to Emerge in Silicon Valley." *New York Times*, October 26, 2018.

Brown, T. T. "The Death of Shop Class and America's Skilled Work Force." *Forbes*, May 30, 2012. https://www.forbes.com/sites/tarabrown/2012/05/30/the-death-of-shop-class-and-americas-high-skilled-workforce/.

Brunner, E., et al. "The Promise of Career and Technical Education." *Brown Center Chalkboard* (blog), Brookings, September 20, 2019. https://www.brookings.edu/blog/brown-center-chalkboard/2019/09/20/the-promise-of-career-and-technical-education/.

Carey, B. "Cognitive Science Meets Pre-Algebra." *New York Times*, September 2, 2013.

Carey, B. "New Definition of Autism Will Exclude Many, Study Suggests." *New York Times*, January 19, 2012.

REFERENCES

Carey, K. "The Demise of the Great Education Saviors." *Washington Post*, March 18, 2020.

Conway Center for Family Business. "Family Business Facts." https://www
.familybusinesscenter.com/resources/family-business-facts/.

Cooper, S. A., et al. "Akinetopsia: Acute Presentation and Evidence for Persisting Defects in
Motion." *Journal of Neurology, Neurosurgery and Psychiatry* 83, no. 2 (2012): 229–30.

Courchesne, V., et al. "Autistic Children at Risk of Being Underestimated: School-Based Pilot Study
of a Strength-Informed Assessment." *Molecular Autism* 6, no. 12 (2015).

Cuenca, P. "On Chess: Chess and Mathematics." St. Louis Public Radio, March 28, 2019.

Danovich, T. "Despite a Revamped Focus on Real-life Skills, 'Home Ec' Classes Fade Away." *The
Salt* (blog), NPR, June 14, 2018. https://www.npr.org/sections/thesalt/2018/06/14/618329461
/despite-a-revamped-focus-on-real-life-skills-home-ec-classes-fade-away.

Dawson, M., et al. "The Level and Nature of Autistic Intelligence." *Psychological Science* 18, no. 8
(2007): 657–62.

Deiss, H. S., and Miller, D. "Who Was Katherine Johnson?" *NASA Knows!* NASA, January 8, 2017,
updated January 7, 2021.

Depenbrock, J., and K. Lattimore. "Say Goodbye to X + Y: Should Community Colleges Abolish
Algebra?" *All Things Considered*, NPR, July 19, 2017. https://www.npr.org/2017/07/19
/538092649/say-goodbye-to-x-y-should-community-colleges-abolish-algebra.

Dishman, L. "This Job Platform Is for Undergrads Who Get Nowhere on LinkedIn." *Fast Company*,
October 20, 2017. https://www.fastcompany.com/40483000/this-job-platform-is-for
-undergrads-who-get-nowhere-on-linkedin.

Donaldson, M. "The Mismatch between School and Children's Minds." *Human Nature* 2 (1979):
60–67.

Drager, K. W. "The Relationship between Abstract Reasoning and Performance in High School
Algebra." Master's thesis, University of Kansas, July 24, 2014.

Drew, C. "Why Science Majors Change Their Minds." *New York Times*, November 4, 2011.

Dyas, B. "Who Killed Home Ec? Here's the Real Story behind Its Demise." *Huffington Post*,
September 29, 2014, updated December 6, 2017.

Edley, C., Jr. "At Cal State, Algebra Is a Civil Rights Issue." *EdSource*, June 5, 2017. https://
edsource.org/2017/at-cal-state-algebra-is-a-civil-rights-issue/582950.

Eis, R. "The Crisis in Education in Theory." *National Affairs*, Summer 2019.

Gara, S. K., et al. "The Sensory Abnormalities and Neuropsychopathology of Autism and Anxiety."
Cureus 12, no. 5 (2020): e8071.

García, L. E., and O. Thornton. "'No Child Left Behind' Has Failed." *Washington Post*, February
13, 2015.

Gardner, H. *Frames of Mind: The Theory of Multiple Intelligences*. New York: Basic Books, 1983.

Gardner, M. "Study Tracks Success of High School Valedictorians." *Christian Science Monitor*, May
25, 1995.

Geschwind, N. "The Brain of a Learning-Disabled Individual." *Annals of Dyslexia* 34 (1984):
319–27.

Gigliotti, J. *Who Is Stevie Wonder?* New York: Grosset & Dunlap, 2016.

"The Girl Who Asked Questions." *Economist*, February 27, 2020, 72.

Goldstein, D. "'It Just Isn't Working': PISA Test Scores Cast Doubt on U.S. Education Efforts."
New York Times, December 3, 2019.

Goodson-Espy, T. "Understanding Students' Transitions from Arithmetic to Algebra: A
Constructivist Explanation." Paper presented at the Annual Meeting of the American
Educational Research Association, San Francisco, April 1995.

Goyal, N. *Schools on Trial: How Freedom and Creativity Can Fix our Educational Malpractice*. New York: Anchor Books, 2016.

Green, S. A., et al. "Overreactive Brain Responses to Sensory Stimuli in Youth with Autism Spectrum Disorders." *Journal of the American Academy of Child and Adolescent Psychiatry* 52, no. 11 (2013): 1158–72.

Greene, J. P., B. Kisida, and D. H. Bowen. "Why Field Trips Matter." *Museum*, January 2014. https://www.aam-us.org/2014/01/01/why-field-trips-matter/.

Gross, A., and J. Marcus. "High-Paying Trade Jobs Sit Empty, While High School Grads Line Up for University." NPR, April 25, 2018.

"Guidance Counselor." Princeton Review. https://www.princetonreview.com/careers/75 /guidance-counselor.

Haciomeroglu, E. S. "Object-Spatial Visualization and Verbal Cognitive Styles, and Their Relation to Cognitive Abilities and Mathematical Performance." *Educational Sciences: Theory and Practice* 16, no. 3 (2016): 987–1003.

Haciomeroglu, E. S., and M. LaVenia. "Object-Spatial Imagery and Verbal Cognitive Styles in High School Students." *Perceptual and Motor Skills* 124, no. 3 (2017): 689–702.

Hacker, A. "Is Algebra Necessary?" *New York Times*, July 28, 2012.

Hacker, A. *The Math Myth: And Other STEM Delusions*. New York: New Press, 2016.

Hanford, E. "Trying to Solve a Bigger Math Problem." *New York Times*, February 3, 2017.

Haque, S., et al. "The Visual Agnosias and Related Disorders." *Journal of Neuro-Ophthalmology* 38, no. 3 (2018): 379–92. doi: 10.1097/WNO.0000000000000556.

Harris, C. "The Earning Curve: Variability and Overlap in Labor-Market Outcomes by Education Level." Manhattan Institute, February 2020. https://files.eric.ed.gov/fulltext /ED604364.pdf.

Harris, E. A. "Little College Guidance: 500 High School Students Per Counselor." *New York Times*, December 25, 2014.

Hartocollis, A. "After a Year of Turmoil, Elite Universities Welcome More Diverse Freshman Classes." *New York Times*, April 17, 2021, updated April 31, 2021.

Hartocollis, A. "Getting into Med School without Hard Sciences." *New York Times*, July 29, 2010.

Hinshaw, S. P., and R. M. Scheffler. *The ADHD Explosion*. London: Oxford University Press, 2014.

Hirsh-Pasek, K., et al. "A New Path to Education Reform: Playful Learning Promotes 21st-Century Skills in Schools and Beyond." Policy 2020, Brookings, October 2020. https://www.brookings .edu/policy2020/bigideas/a-new-path-to-education-reform-playful-learning-promotes -21st-century-skills-in-schools-and-beyond/.

Hoang, C. "Oscar Avalos Dreams in Titanium." NASA Jet Propulsion Laboratory, 2019. https://www.nasa.gov/feature/jpl/oscar-avalos-dreams-in-titanium.

Hora, M. T. "Entry Level Workers Can Lose 6% of Their Wages If They Don't Have These." *Fast Company*, February 1, 2020. https://www.fastcompany.com/90458673/5-things-standing-in -the-way-of-students-taking-internships.

Hough, L. "Testing. Testing. 1-2-3." *Ed.: Harvard Ed. Magazine*, Winter 2018.

Hubler, S. "Why Is the SAT Falling Out of Favor?" *New York Times*, May 23, 2020.

"IDEA: Specific Learning Disabilities." American Speech and Hearing Association. https://www .asha.org/advocacy/federal/idea/04-law-specific-ld/.

"IDEA Full Funding: Why Should Congress Invest in Special Education?" National Center for Learning Disabilities. https://ncld.org/news/policy-and-advocacy/idea-full-funding-why -should-congress-invest-in-special-education/.

REFERENCES

Iversen, S. M., and C. J. Larson. "Simple Thinking Using Complex Math vs. Complex Thinking Using Simple Math." *ZDM* 38, no. 3 (2006): 281–92.

Jaswal, V. K., et al. "Eye-Tracking Reveals Agency in Assisted Autistic Communication." *Scientific Reports* 10 (2020): art. no. 7882.

Jewish Virtual Library. "Nazi Euthanasia Program: Persecution of the Mentally and Physically Disabled." https://www.jewishvirtuallibrary.org/nazi-persecution-of-the-mentally-and-physically-disabled.

Keith, J. M., et al. "The Influence of Noise on Autonomic Arousal and Cognitive Performance in Adolescents with Autism Spectrum Disorder." *Journal of Autism and Developmental Disorders* 49, no. 1 (2019): 113–26.

Kercood, S., et al. "Working Memory and Autism: A Review of the Literature." *Research in Autism Spectrum Disorders* 8 (2014): 1316–32.

Klass, P. "Fending Off Math Anxiety." *New York Times*, April 24, 2017.

Koretz, D. "The Testing Charade." *Ed.: Harvard Ed. Magazine*, Winter 2018.

Kuss, D. J., et al. "Neurobiological Correlates in Internet Gaming Disorder: A Systematic Literature Review." *Frontiers in Psychiatry* 9, no. 166 (2018).

Laski, E. V., et al. "Spatial Skills as a Predictor of First Grade Girls' Use of Higher Level Arithmetic Strategies." *Learning and Individual Differences* 23 (2013): 123–30.

Learning Disabilities Association of America. "Types of Learning Disabilities." https://ldaamerica.org/types-of-learning-disabilities/.

Lindsay, S. "The History of the ACT Test." *PrepScholar* (blog), June 30, 2015. https://blog.prepscholar.com/the-history-of-the-act-test.

Lloyd, C. "Does Our Approach to Teaching Math Fail Even the Smartest Kids?" Great!Schools.org, March 10, 2014. https://www.greatschools.org/gk/articles/why-americas-smartest-students-fail-math/.

Lockhart, P. *A Mathematician's Lament*. New York: Bellevue Literary Press, 2009.

Louv, R. *Last Child in the Woods*. Chapel Hill, NC: Algonquin Books, 2005.

Mackinlay, R., et al. "High Functioning Children with Autism Spectrum Disorder: A Novel Test of Multitasking." *Brain and Cognition* 61, no. 1 (2006): 14–24.

Mathewson, J. H. "Visual-Spatial Thinking: An Aspect of Science Overlooked by Educators." *Science Education* 83, no. 1 (1999): 33–54.

Moody, J. "ACT vs. SAT: How to Decide Which Test to Take." *U.S. News & World Report*, March 10, 2021.

Mottron, L. "The Power of Autism." *Nature* 479 (2011): 33–35.

Mottron, L. "Temporal Changes in Effect Sizes of Studies Comparing Individuals with and without Autism: A Meta-Analysis." *JAMA Psychiatry* 76, no. 11 (November 2019): 1124–32.

Mukhopadhyay, T. R. *How Can I Talk If My Lips Don't Move? Inside My Autistic Mind*. New York: Arcade, 2011.

"NAEP Report Card: 2019 NAEP Mathematics Assessment—Highlighted Results at Grade 12 for the Nation." The Nation's Report Card, 2019. https://www.nationsreportcard.gov/highlights/mathematics/2019/g12/.

National Association for Gifted Children. "Acceleration." Developing Academic Acceleration Policies, 2018. https://www.nagc.org/resources-publications/gifted-education-practices/acceleration.

National Center for Education Statistics. "Fast Facts—Mathematics." https://nces.ed.gov/fastfacts/display.asp?id=514.

National Center for Education Statistics. "Students with Disabilities." *Condition of Education*. U.S. Department of Education, Institute of Education Sciences. Last updated May 2022. https://nces.ed.gov/programs/coe/indicator/cgg.

National Education Association. "History of Standardized Testing in the United States," 2020.

Park, G., D. Lubinski, and C. P. Benbow. "When Less Is More: Effects of Grade Skipping on Adult STEM Productivity among Mathematically Precocious Adolescents." *Journal of Educational Psychology* 105, no. 1 (2013): 176–98.

Pashler, H., et al. "Learning Styles: Concepts and Evidence." *Psychological Science in the Public Interest* 9, no. 3 (2009): 105–19.

Paulson, A. "Less Than 40% of 12th-Graders Ready for College, Analysis Finds." *Christian Science Monitor*, May 14, 2014.

Pilon, M. "Monopoly Was Designed to Teach the 99% about Income Inequality." *Smithsonian Magazine*, 2015. https://www.smithsonianmag.com/arts-culture/monopoly-was-designed-teach-99-about-income-inequality-180953630/.

Pilon, M. "The Secret History of Monopoly." *Guardian*, April 11, 2015.

Porter, E. "School vs. Society in America's Failing Students." *New York Times*, November 3, 2015.

Provini, C. "Why Field Trips Still Matter." *Education World*, 2011.

Quinton, S. "Some States Train Jobless for Post-Pandemic Workforce." *Stateline* (blog), Pew Charitable Trusts, December 10, 2020. https://www.pewtrusts.org/en/research-and-analysis/blogs/stateline/2020/12/10/some-states-train-jobless-for-post-pandemic-workforce.

Riastuti, N., Mardiyana, and I. Pramudya. "Analysis of Students [*sic*] Geometry Skills Viewed from Spatial Intelligence." AIP Conference Proceedings 1913, 2017. https://doi.org/10.1063/1.5016658.

Ripley, A. "What America Can Learn from Smart Schools in Other Countries." *New York Times*, December 6, 2016.

Rodgaard, E. M., et al. "Temporal Changes in Effect Sizes of Studies Comparing Individuals with and without Autism." *JAMA Psychiatry* 76, no. 11 (2019): 1124–32.

Root-Bernstein, R., et al. "Arts Foster Scientific Success: Avocations of Nobel, National Academy, Royal Society, and Sigma Xi Members." *Journal of Psychology of Science and Technology* 1, no. 2 (2008): 51–63. doi:10/1891/1939-7054.1.251.

Rosen, J. "How a Hobby Can Boost Researchers' Productivity and Creativity." *Nature* 558 (2018): 475–77.

Rosenstock, L., et al. "Confronting the Public Health Workforce Crisis." *Public Health Reports* 123, no. 3 (2008): 395–98.

Rosholm, M., et al. "Your Move: The Effect of Chess on Mathematics Test Scores." *PLOS ONE* 12, no. 5 (2017): e0177257. https://doi.org/10.1371/journal.pone.0177257.

Rosin, H. "Hey Parents, Leave the Kids Alone." *Atlantic*, April 2014, 75–86.

Ross, M., R. Kazis, N. Bateman, and L. Stateler. "Work-Based Learning Can Advance Equity and Opportunity for America's Young People." Brookings, 2020. https://www.brookings.edu/research/work-based-learning-can-advance-equity-and-opportunity-for-americas-young-people/.

Ross, M., and T. Showalter. "Millions of Young Adults Are out of School or Work." *The Avenue* (blog), Brookings, 2020. https://www.brookings.edu/blog/the-avenue/2020/12/18/making-a-promise-to-americas-young-people/.

Ruppert, S. "How the Arts Benefit Student Achievement." *Critical Evidence*, 2006.

Ryan, J. "American Schools vs. the World: Expensive, Unequal, Bad at Math." *Atlantic*, December 3, 2013.

Saul, R. *ADHD Does Not Exist: The Truth about Attention Deficit and Hyperactivity Disorder*. New York: Harper Wave, 2015.

SC Johnson College of Business. "Family Business Facts," 2021. https://www.johnson.cornell.edu/smith-family-business-initiative-at-cornell/resources/family-business-facts/.

Schleicher, A. "PISA 2018: Insights and Interpretations." OECD, 2018. https://www.oecd.org/pisa/PISA%202018%20Insights%20and%20Interpretations%20FINAL%20PDF.pdf.

Schoen, S. A., et al. "A Systematic Review of Ayres Sensory Integration Intervention for Children with Autism." *Autism Research* 12, no. 1 (2019): 6–19.

"School Counselors Matter." *Education Trust*, February 2019 https://edtrust.org/resource/school-counselors-matter/.

Schwartz, Yishai. "For Parents Willing to Pay Thousands, College Counselors Promise to Make Ivy League Dreams a Reality." *Town & Country*, June 28, 2017. https://www.townandcountrymag.com/leisure/a10202220/college-counseling-services/.

Seymour, K., et al. "Coding and Binding Color and Form in Visual Cortex." *Cerebral Cortex* 20, no. 8 (2010): 1946–54.

Sheltzer, J. M., and R. Visintin. "Angelika Amon (1967–2020): Trailblazing Cell Cycle Biologist." *Science* 370, no. 6522 (2020): 1276.

Shetterly, M. L. *Hidden Figures: The American Dream and the Untold Story of the Black Women Mathematicians Who Helped Win the Space Race*. New York: William Morrow, 2016.

Silverman, L. K. *Upside-Down Brilliance*. Denver: DeLeon, 2002.

Smith, A. "Two Community Colleges Show How Students Can Succeed without Remedial Math Courses." *EdSource*, 2019. https://edsource.org/2019/two-community-colleges-show-how-students-can-succeed-without-remedial-math-courses/619740.

Smith, P. "Uniquely Abled Academy at COC Looks to Pilot Opportunities for Those on Autism Spectrum." KHT SAM 1220, September 4, 2017. https://www.hometownstation.com/santa-clarita-news/education/college-of-the-canyons/uniquely-abled-academy-at-coc-looks-to-pilot-opportunities-for-those-on-autism-spectrum-203809.

Sorvo, R., et al. "Math Anxiety and Its Relationship with Basic Arithmetic Skills among Primary School Children." *British Journal of Educational Psychology* 87, no. 3 (2017): 309–27.

Strauss, V. "Is It Finally Time to Get Rid of the SAT and ACT College Admissions Tests?" *Washington Post*, March 19, 2019.

Sušac, A., A. Bubić, A. Vrbanc, and M. Planinić. "Development of Abstract Mathematical Reasoning: The Case of Algebra." *Frontiers in Human Neuroscience* (2014). https://www.frontiersin.org/articles/10.3389/fnhum.2014.00679/full.

Taggart, J., et al. "The Real Thing: Preschoolers Prefer Actual Activities to Pretend Ones." *Developmental Science* 21, no. 3 (2017). doi.org/10.1111/desc.12582.

Thaler, L. "Echolocation May Have Real-Life Advantages for Blind People: An Analysis of Survey Data." *Frontiers in Physiology* (2013). doi.org/10.3389/fphys.2013.00098.

Thaler, L., S. R. Arnott, and M. A. Goodale. "Neural Correlates of Natural Human Echolocation in Early and Late Blind Echolocation Experts." *PLOS ONE* (2011). doi.org/10.1371/journal.pone.0020162.

Tough, P. "How Kids Really Succeed." *Atlantic*, June 2016, 56–66.

Treffert, D. A. *Islands of Genius*. London: Jessica Kingsley, 2010.

US Congress, Office of Technology Assessment. "Lessons from the Past: A History of Educational Testing in the United States." Chapter 4 in *Testing in American Schools: Asking the Right*

Questions, OTA-SET-519. Washington, DC: US Government Printing Office, 1992. https://www.princeton.edu/~ota/disk1/1992/9236/9236.PDF.

Wa Munyi, C. "Past and Present Perceptions towards Disability: A Historical Perspective." *Disabilities Studies Quarterly* 32, no. 2 (2012).

Wadman, M. "'Nothing Is Impossible,' Says Lab Ace Nita Patel." *Science* 370 (2020): 652.

Walker, T. "Should More Students Be Allowed to Skip a Grade?" *NEA News*, March 27, 2017. https://www.nea.org/advocating-for-change/new-from-nea/should-more-students-ve-allowed-skip-grade.

Watanabe, T., and R. Xia. "Drop Algebra Requirement for Non-STEM Majors, California Community Colleges Chief Says." *Los Angeles Times*, July 17, 2017.

Watkins, L., et al. "A Review of Peer-Mediated Social Interaction for Students with Autism in Inclusive Settings." *Journal of Autism and Developmental Disorders* 45 (2015): 1070–83.

Wellemeyer, J. "Wealthy Parents Spend Up to $10,000 on SAT Prep for Their Kids." *MarketWatch*, July 7, 2019. https://marketwatch.com/story/wealthy-parents-are-dropping-up-to-10000-on-sat-test-prep-for-their-kids-2019-06-21.

Wells, R., D. Lohman, and M. Marron. "What Factors Are Associated with Grade Acceleration?" *Journal of Advanced Academics* 20, no. 2 (Winter 2009): 248–73.

Westervelt, E. "The Value of Wild, Risky Play: Fire, Mud, Hammers and Nails." *NPR Ed*, NPR, April 3, 2015. https://www.npr.org/sections/ed/2015/04/03/395797459/the-value-of-wild-risky-play-fire-mud-hammers-and-nails.

Williams, D. *Autism—An Inside-Out Approach: An Innovative Look at the Mechanics of "Autism" and Its Developmental "Cousins."* London: Jessica Kingsley, 1996.

Williams, D. L., et al. "The Profile of Memory Function in Children with Autism." *Neuropsychology* 20, no. 1 (2006): 21–29.

Willingham, D. T. "Is It True That Some People Just Can't Do Math?" *American Educator*, Winter 2009–2010.

Winerip, M. "A Field Trip to a Strange New Place: Second Grade Visits the Parking Garage." *New York Times*. February 12, 2012.

Wonder, S. Video interview with Mesha McDaniel. Celebrity Profile Entertainment, March 23, 2013. YouTube. https://www.youtube.com/watch?v=126ni6rvzPU.

Wonder, S. Video interview on *Larry King Now*. YouTube. https://www.youtube.com/watch?v=vJh-DVlvlJM.

Zhang, X., et al. "Misbinding of Color and Motion in Human Visual Cortex." *Current Biology* 24, no. 12 (2014): 1354–60.

Zihl, J., and C. A. Heywood. "The Contribution of LM to the Neuroscience of Movement Vision." *Frontiers in Integrative Neuroscience* 9, no. 6 (February 17, 2015). https://www.frontiersin.org/articles/10.3389/fnint.2015.00006/full.

Zinshteyn, M. "Cal State Drops Intermediate Algebra as Requirement to Take Some College-Level Math Courses." *EdSource*, 2017. https://edsource.org/2017/cal-state-drops-intermediate-algebra-requirement-allows-other-math-courses/585595.

3. WHERE ARE ALL THE CLEVER ENGINEERS?

American Society of Civil Engineers. Infrastructure Report Card. ASCE, Reston, Virginia, 2017.

Anthes, E. "Richard R. Ernst, Nobel Winner Who Paved the Way for the M.R.I., Dies at 87." *New York Times*, June 16, 2021.

REFERENCES

Aspiritech.org. Chicago.

Austin, R. D., and G. P. Pisano. "Neurodiversity as a Competitive Advantage." *Harvard Business Review*, May–June 2017.

Belli, G. "How Many Jobs Are Found through Networking, Really?" Payscale, April 6, 2017. https://www.payscale.com/career-advice/many-jobs-found-networking/.

Burger, D., et al. "Filtergraph: A Flexible Web Application for Instant Data Visualization of Astronomy Datasets." arXiv:1212.4458.

Cabral, A. "How Dubai Powers Apple's 'Spaceship.'" *Khaleej Times*, September 13, 2017. https://www.khaleejtimes.com/tech/how-dubai-powers-apples-spaceship.

Cann, S. "The Debate behind Disability Hiring." *Fast Company*, November 26, 2012. https://www.fastcompany.com/3002957/disabled-employee-amendment.

Cass, O., et al. "Work, Skills, Community: Restoring Opportunity for the Working Class." Opportunity America, American Enterprise Institute, and Brookings Institution, 2018. https://www.aei.org/wp-content/uploads/2018/11/Work-Skills-Community-FINAL-PDF.pdf?x91208.

Chakravarty, S. "World's Top 10 Industrial Robot Manufacturers." Market Research Reports, 2019. https://www.marketresearchreports.com/blog/2019/05/08/world's-top-10-industrial-robot-manufacturers.

Chang, C. "Can Apprenticeships Help Reduce Youth Unemployment?" Century Foundation, November 15, 2015. https://tcf.org/content/report/apprenticeships/.

Collins, M. "Why America Has a Shortage of Skilled Workers." *IndustryWeek*, 2015. https://www.industryweek.com/talent/education-training/article/22007263/why-america-has-a-shortage-of-skilled-workers.

"Construction Workforce Shortages Reach Pre-Pandemic Levels Even as Coronavirus Continues to Impact Projects & Disrupt Supply Chains." The Construction Association, September 2, 2021. https://www.agc.org/news/2021/09/02/construction-workforce-shortages-reach-pre-pandemic-levels-even-coronavirus-0.

"Conveyor Systems: Dependable Cost-Effective Product Transport." Dematic.com. https://www.dematic.com/en/products/products-overview/conveyor-systems/.

Coudriet, C. "The Top 25 Two-Year Trade Schools." *Forbes*, August 16, 2018. https://www.forbes.com/sites/cartercoudriet/2018/08/15/the-top-25-two-year-trade-schools-colleges-that-can-solve-the-skills-gap.

Danovich, T. "Despite a Revamped Focus on Real-Life Skills, 'Home Ec' Classes Fade Away." *The Salt* (blog), NPR, June 14, 2018. https://www.npr.org/sections/thesalt/2018/06/14/618329461/despite-a-revamped-focus-on-real-life-skills-home-ec-classes-fade-away.

Delphos, K. "Dematic to Fill 1,000 New Jobs in North America by End of 2020." Dematic.com press release, September 2, 2020.

Duberstein, B. "Why ASML Is Outperforming Its Semiconductor Equipment Peers." The Motley Fool, February 27, 2019. www.fool.com/investing/2019/02/27/why-asml-is-outperforming-its-semiconductor-equipment.aspx.

Duckworth, A. *Grit: The Power of Passion and Perseverance*. New York: Scribner, 2016.

Elias, M. *Stir It Up: Home Economics in American Culture*. Philadelphia: University of Pennsylvania Press, 2010.

Farrell, M. "Global Researcher: Professor Shaun Dougherty Presents Vocational Research Abroad." NEAG School of Education, 2017. https://cepare.uconn.edu/2017/10/10/global-researcher-professor-shaun-dougherty-presents-vocational-education-research-abroad/.

Felicetti, K. "These Major Tech Companies Are Making Autism Hiring a Priority." Monster, March 8, 2016.

Ferenstein, G. "How History Explains America's Struggle to Revive Apprenticeships." *Brown Center Chalkboard* (blog), Brookings, May 23, 2018. https://www.brookings.edu/blog /brown-center-chalkboard/2018/05/23/how-history-explains-americas-struggle-to-revive -apprenticeships/.

Ferguson, E. S. *Engineering and the Mind's Eye*. Cambridge, MA: MIT Press, 1994.

Ferguson, E. S. "The Mind's Eye: Nonverbal Thought in Technology." *Science* 197, no. 4306 (1977): 827–36.

Flynn, C. "The Chip-Making Machine at the Center of Chinese Dual-Use Concerns." Brookings TechStream, June 30, 2020. https://www.brookings.edu/techstream/the-chip-making -machine-at-the-center-of-chinese-dual-use-concerns/.

"Fort Collins Leads the Pack on Undergrounding." *BizWest*, September 5, 2003. https://bizwest .com/2003/09/05/fort-collins-leads-the-pack-on-undergrounding/.

Frener & Reifer. "Steve Jobs Theater," 2020. https://www.frener-reifer.com/news-en/steve-jobs -theater/.

FY 2020 Data and Statistics: Registered Apprenticeship National Results Fiscal Year 2020: 10/01/2019 to 9/30/2020. Employment and Training Administration, U.S. Department of Labor. https://www.dol.gov/agencies/eta/apprenticeship/about/statistics/2020/.

Goger, A., and C. Sinclair. "Apprenticeships Are an Overlooked Solution for Creating More Access to Quality Jobs." *The Avenue* (blog), Brookings, January 27, 2021. https://www.brookings .edu/blog/the-avenue/2021/01/27/apprenticeships-are-an-overlooked-solution-for-creating -more-access-to-quality-jobs/.

Gold, R., K. Blunt, and T. Ansari. "PG&E Reels as California Wildfire Burns." *Wall Street Journal*, October 26, 2019, A1–A2.

Gold, R., R. Rigdon, and Y. Serkez. "PG&E's Network Heightens California's Fire Risk." *Wall Street Journal*, October 30, 2019, A6.

Goldman, M. A. "Evolution Gets Personal." *Science* 367, no. 6485 (2020): 1432.

"Governor John Hickenlooper Announces $9.5 Million to Launch Statewide Youth Apprenticeship and Career Readiness Programs." Business Wire, September 14, 2016. https://www .businesswire.com/news/home/20160914006145/en/Gov.-John-Hickenlooper-Announces -9.5-Million-to-Launch-Statewide-Youth-Apprenticeship-and-Career-Readiness-Programs.

Gray, M. W. "Lynn Margulis and the Endosymbiont Hypothesis: 50 Years Later." *Molecular Biology of the Cell* 28, no. 10 (2017). doi.org/10.1091/mbc.e16-07-0509.

Gross, A., and J. Marcus. "High-Paying Trade Jobs Sit Empty While High School Grads Line Up for University." *NPR Ed*, NPR, April 25, 2018.

Gummer, C. "German Robots School U.S. Workers." *Wall Street Journal*, September 10, 2014, B7.

Gunn, D. "The Swiss Secret to Jump-Starting Your Career." *Atlantic*, September 7, 2018.

Hagerty, J. R. "The $140,000-a-Year Welding Job." *Wall Street Journal*, January 7, 2015, B1–B2.

Hardy, B. L., and D. E. Marcotte. "Education and the Dynamics of Middle-Class Status." Brookings, June 2020.

Harris, C. "The Earning Curve: Variability and Overlap in Labor-Market Outcomes by Education Level." Manhattan Institute, February 2020. https://files.eric.ed.gov/fulltext/ED604364.pdf.

Hoffman, N., and R. Schwartz. "Gold Standard: The Swiss Vocational Education and Training System. International Comparative Study of Vocational Educational Systems." National Center on Education and the Economy, 2015. https://eric.ed.gov/?id=ED570868.

REFERENCES

Hotez, E. "How Children Fail: Exploring Parent and Family Factors That Foster Grit." In *Exploring Best Child Development Practices in Contemporary Society*, edited by N. R. Silton, 45–65. IGI Global, 2020. doi:10.4018/978-1-7998-2940-9.ch003.

Howard, S., et al. "Why Apprenticeship Programs Matter to 21st Century Post-Secondary Education." *CTE Journal* 7, no. 2 (2019): ISSN 2327-0160 (online).

Jacob, B. A. "What We Know about Career and Technical Education in High School." Brookings, October 5, 2017. https://www.brookings.edu/research/what-we-know-about-career-and-technical-education-in-high-school/.

Jacobs, D. *Master Builders of the Middle Ages*. New York: Harper and Row, 1969.

Jacobs, J. "Seven of the Deadliest Infrastructure Failures throughout History." *New York Times*, August 14, 2018.

Jacoby, T. "Community Colleges Are an Agile New Player in Job Training." *Wall Street Journal*, September 25, 2021.

Khazan, O. "Autism's Hidden Gifts." *Atlantic*, September 23, 2015.

King, K. "Apprenticeships on the Rise at the New York Tech and Finance Firms." *Wall Street Journal*, September 23, 2018.

"Kion to Buy U.S. Firm Dematic in $3.25 Billion Deal." Reuters. June 21, 2016.

Lambert, K. G., et al. "Contingency-Based Emotional Resilience: Effort-Based Reward Training and Flexible Coping Lead to Adaptive Responses to Uncertainty in Male Rats." *Frontiers in Behavioral Neuroscience* 8 (2014). doi.org/10.3389/fnbeh.2014.00124.

LeBlanc, C. "You're Working from Home Wrong. Here's How to Fix It." Fatherly, 2020. https://www.fatherly.com/love-money/work-from-hyatt-home-office/.

Lewis, R. *No Greatness without Goodness: How a Father's Love Changed a Company and Sparked a Movement*. Carol Stream, IL: Tyndale House, 2016.

Linke, R. "Lost Einsteins: The US May Have Missed Out on Millions of Inventors." MIT Sloan School of Management, February 16, 2018. https://mitsloan.mit.edu/ideas-made-to-matter/lost-einsteins-us-may-have-missed-out-millions-inventors.

Lohr, S. "Greasing the Wheels of Opportunity." *New York Times*, April 8, 2021.

Lythcott-Haims, J. *How to Raise an Adult*. New York: Henry Holt, 2015.

Maguire, C. "How the Snowplow Parenting Trend Affects Kids." Parents.com, December 4, 2019.

Martin, J. J. "Class Action: The Fashion Brands Training Tomorrow's Artisans." Business of Fashion, September 3, 2014. https://www.businessoffashion.com/articles/luxury/class-action/.

Martinez, S. "7-Year Turnaround: How Dematic Bounced Back from Layoffs to $1B in Annual Sales." MLive (Michigan), February 20, 2014. https://www.mlive.com/business/west-michigan/2014/02/7-year_turnaround_how_dematic.html.

Milne, J. "Thinking Differently—The Benefits of Neurodiversity." Diginomica, 2018. https://diginomica.com/thinking-differently-benefits-neurodiversity.

Moran, G. "As Workers Become Harder to Find, Microsoft and Goldman Sachs Hope Neurodiverse Talent Can Be the Missing Piece." *Fortune*, December 7, 2019. https://fortune.com/2019/12/07/autism-aspergers-adhd-dyslexia-neurodiversity-hiring-jobs-work/.

Neuhauser, A. "This School Has a Tougher Admission Rate Than Yale—and Doesn't Grant Degrees." *U.S. News & World Report*, May 11, 2016.

"100 Best Internships for 2021." Vault Careers, October 27, 2020.

"PSPS Wind Update: Wind Gusts in Nearly Two Dozen Counties Reached above 40 MPH; in 15 Counties Wind Gusts Topped 50 MPH." Business Wire, October 16, 2019. https://www.businesswire.com/news/home/20191016005951/en/PSPS-Wind-Update-Wind-Gusts-in

-Nearly-Two-Dozen-Counties-Reached-Above-40-MPH-in-15-Counties-Wind-Gusts
-Topped-50-MPH.

Redden, E. "Importing Appprenticeships." *Inside Higher Ed*, August 8, 2017.

Redman, R. "Analyst: Reported Amazon-Dematic Partnership 'Validates the MFC Model.'"
Supermarket News, February 21, 2020.

Ren, S. "China Tries to Tame Its Tiger Parents." *Bloomberg Businessweek*, November 1, 2021, 92.

Renault, M. "FFA Asks: Who Will Train the Next Generation of Farmers?" *Minneapolis Star
Tribune*, February 13, 2015, B3–B5.

Robertson, S. M. "Neurodiversity, Quality of Life, and Autistic Adults: Shifting Research and
Professional Focuses onto Real-Life Challenges." *Disability Studies Quarterly* 30, no. 1 (2010).

"A Robot Maker Fetches $2.1 Billion as E-Commerce Warehouse Automation Grows." Bloomberg
News, June 22, 2016.

Rubin, S. "The Israeli Army Unit That Recruits Teens with Autism." *Atlantic*, January 6, 2016.
https://www.theatlantic.com/health/archive/2016/01/israeli-army-autism/422850/.

Sales, B. "Deciphering Satellite Photos, Soldiers with Autism Take On Key Roles in IDF." Jewish
Telegraphic Agency, December 8, 2015. https://www.jta.org/2015/12/08/israel
/deciphering-satellite-photos-soldiers-with-autism-take-on-key-roles-in-idf.

Schwartz, N. D. "A New Look at Apprenticeships as a Path to the Middle Class." *New York Times*,
July 13, 2015.

Seager, S. *The Smallest Lights in the Universe*. New York: Crown, 2020.

"Shipbuilding Apprentices Set Sail at Huntington Ingalls Graduation." *Industry Week*, February 27,
2017. https://www.industryweek.com/talent/education-training/article/22005850
/shipbuilding-apprentices-set-sail-at-huntington-ingalls-graduation.

Sidhwani, P. "People Spend 14% of Their Time on Video Games in 2020." *Techstory*, March 18, 2021.

Smith, R. "PG&E's Wildfire Mistakes Followed Years of Violations." *Wall Street Journal*,
September 6, 2019.

St-Esprit, M. "The Stigma of Choosing Trade School over College." *Atlantic*, March 6, 2019.

Stockman, F. "Want a White-Collar Career without College Debt? Become an Apprentice." *New
York Times*, December 10, 2019.

"Structural Glass Designs by Seele Dominate the First Impression of Apple Park." www.seele.com
/references/apple-park-visitor-center-reception-buildings.

Thomas, D. S. "Annual Report on U.S. Manufacturing Industry Statistics: 2020." National Institute
of Standards and Technology, U.S. Department of Commerce, 2020.

"20+ Incredible Statistics on Loss of Manufacturing Jobs [2021 Data]." *What to Become* (blog),
August 11, 2021. https://whattobecome.com/blog/loss-of-manufacturing-jobs/.

US Bureau of Labor Statistics. *Occupational Outlook Handbook*, 2020. https://www.bls.gov/ooh.

U.S. Youth Unemployment Rate 1991–2022. Macrotrends. https://www.macrotrends.net
/countries/USA/united-states/youth-unemployment-rate.

Wallis, L. "Autistic Workers: Loyal, Talented . . . Ignored." *Guardian*, April 6, 2012.

Wang, R. "Apprenticeships: A Classic Remedy for the Modern Skills Gap." *Forbes*, October 21, 2019.

West, D. M., and C. Lansang. "Global Manufacturing Scorecard: How the US Compares to 18
Other Nations." Brookings, July 10, 2018.

Woetzel, J., et al. "Reskilling China: Transforming the World's Largest Workforce into Lifelong
Learners." McKinsey Global Institute, January 12, 2021. https://www.mckinsey.com
/featured-insights/china/reskilling-china-transforming-the-worlds-workforce-into
-lifelong-learners.

Wyman, N. "Closing the Skills Gap with Apprenticeship: Costs vs. Benefits." *Forbes*, January 9, 2020.

Wyman, N. "Jobs Now! Learning from the Swiss Apprenticeship Model." *Forbes*, October 20, 2017.

Wyman, N. "Why We Desperately Need to Bring Back Vocational Training in Schools." *Forbes*, September 1, 2015. https://www.forbes.com/sites/nicholaswyman/2015/09/01/why-we-desperately-need-to-bring-back-vocational-training-in-schools.

Xinhua. "China to Accelerate Training of High-Quality Workers, Skilled Talent." *China Daily*, December 1, 2021. http://www.news.cn/english/2021-12/01/c_1310345807.htm.

4. COMPLEMENTARY MINDS

Aero Antiques. "Preserving Warbird History One Artifact at a Time: Bendix Fluxgate Gyro Master Compass Indicator AN5752-2 WWII B-17, B-24-B-29." AeroAntique, 2021.

Anderson, G. *Mastering Collaboration: Make Working Together Less Painful and More Productive.* Sebastopol, CA: O'Reilly Media, 2019.

Antranikian, H. Magnetic field direction and intensity finder. US Patent 2047609, US Patent Office, issued 1936.

"The Art of Engineering: Industrial Design at Delta Faucet." *Artrageous with Nate.* YouTube, June 9, 2016. https://www.youtube.com/watch?v=clksrjRA678.

Baker, K. *America the Ingenious.* New York: Workman, 2016.

Baker, M., and E. Dolgin. "Cancer Reproducibility Project Releases First Results." *Nature* 541 (2017): 269–70.

Ball, P. "The Race to Fusion Energy." *Nature* 599 (2021): 362–66.

Ban, T. A. "The Role of Serendipity in Drug Discovery." *Dialogues in Clinical Neuroscience* 8, no. 3 (2006): 335–44.

Beach, L. F. Activated fin stabilizer. US Patent US3020869A, UA, US Patent Office, issued 1962.

"Bellevue Psychiatric Hospital." Asylum Projects. http://asylumprojects.org/index.php/Bellevue_Psychiatric_Hospital.

Bik, E. M., et al. "The Prevalence of Inappropriate Image Duplication in Biomedical Research Publications." *mBio* 7, no. 3 (2016). doi:10.1128/mBio.00809-16.

Braddon, F. D., L. F. Beach, and J. H. Chadwick. Ship stabilization system. US Patent US2979010A, US Patent Office, issued 1961.

Brown, R. R., A. Deletic, and T. H. F. Wong. "Interdisciplinarity: How to Catalyse Collaboration." *Nature* 525 (2015): 315–17.

Büyükboyaci, M., and A. Robbett. "Team Formation with Complementary Skills." *Journal of Economics and Management Strategy* 28, no. 4 (Winter 2019): 713–33.

Carlson, N. "At Last—The Full Story of How Facebook Was Founded." *Business Insider*, March 5, 2010. https://www.businessinsider.com/how-facebook-was-founded-2010-3.

Chabris, C., et al. "Spatial and Object Visualization Cognitive Styles: Validation Studies in 3800 Individuals." Submitted to *Applied Cognitive Psychology* June 12, 2006. https://www.researchgate.net/publication/238687967_Spatial_and_Object_Visualization_Cognitive_Styles_Validation_Studies_in_3800_Individuals.

Chaiken, A. "Neil Armstrong's Spacesuit Was Made by a Bra Manufacturer." *Smithsonian Magazine*, November 2013. https://www.smithsonianmag.com/history/neil-armstrongs-spacesuit-was-made-by-a-bra-manufacturer-3652414/.

Chandler, D. L. "Behind the Scenes of the Apollo Mission at M.I.T." *MIT News*, July 18, 2019.

REFERENCES

Communications & Power Industries. "About Us: History." https://www.cpii.com/history.cfm.

Cropley, D. H., and J. L. Kaufman. "The Siren Song of Aesthetics? Domain Differences and Creativity in Engineering and Design." *Journal of Mechanical Engineering Science*, May 31, 2018.

Cutler, E. *A Thorn in My Pocket*. Arlington, TX: Future Horizons, 2004.

Daily Tea Team. "Origins of the Teapot." The Daily Tea, March 18, 2018. https://thedailytea.com/travel/origins-of-the-teapot/.

Davis, A. P. "The Epic Battle behind the Apollo Spacesuit." *Wired*, February 28, 2011.

De Monchaux, N. *Spacesuit: Fashioning Apollo*. Cambridge, MA: MIT Press, 2011.

Dean, J. "Making Marines into MacGyvers." *Bloomberg Businessweek*, September 24, 2018, 48–55.

Edwards, J. "Russell and Sigurd Varian: Inventing the Klystron and Saving Civilization." Electronic Design, November 22, 2010. https://www.electronicdesign.com/technologies/communications/article/21795573/russell-and-sigurd-varian-inventing-the-klystron-and-saving-civilization.

Eliot, M. *Paul Simon: A Life*. Hoboken, NJ: Wiley, 2010.

Enserink, M. "Sloppy Reporting on Animal Studies Proves Hard to Change." *Science* 357 (2017): 1337–38.

Fei, M. C. Y. "Forming the Informal: A Conversation with Cecil Balmond." *Dialogue* 67 (March 2003).

Fishman, C. "The Improbable Story of the Bra-Maker Who Won the Right to Make Astronaut Spacesuits." *Fast Company*, 2019. https://www.fastcompany.com/90375440/the-improbable-story-of-the-bra-maker-who-won-the-right-to-make-astronaut-spacesuits.

Fitzgerald, D. "Architecture vs. Engineering: Solutions for Harmonious Collaboration." *Redshift*, May 3, 2018. https://web.archive.org/web/20201127180130/https://redshift.autodesk.com/architecture-vs-engineering/.

Fraser, D. C. "Memorial Tribute—J. Halcombe Laning." National Academy of Engineering. https://www.nae.edu/29034/Dr-J-Halcombe-Laning.

Friedman, J. "How to Build a Future Series: Elon Musk." Y Combinator. https://www.ycombinator.com/future/elon/.

Fuller, T. "No Longer an Underdog Team, a Deaf High School Team Takes California by Storm." *New York Times*, November 16, 2021.

"Germany's Wendelstein 7-X Stellarator Proves Its Confinement Efficiency." *Nuclear Newswire*, August 17, 2021. http://www.ans.org/news/article-3166/germanys-wendelstein-7x-stellarator-proves-its-confinement-efficiency/.

Ghasemi, A., et al. "The Principles of Biomedical Scientific Writing: Materials and Methods." *International Journal of Endocrinology and Metabolism* 17, no. 1 (2019): e88155.

Giger, W., et al. "Equipment for Low-Stress, Small Animal Slaughter." *Transactions of the ASAE* 20 (1977): 571–74.

Grandin, T. "The Contribution of Animals to Human Welfare." *Scientific and Technical Review* 37, no. 1 (April 2018): 15–20.

Grandin, T. "Double Rail Restrainer Conveyor for Livestock Handling." *Journal of Agricultural Engineering Research* 41 (1988): 327–38.

Grandin, T. "Handling and Welfare of Livestock in Slaughter Plants." In *Livestock Handling and Transport*, edited by T. Grandin, 289–311. Wallingford, UK: CABI Publishing, 1993.

Grandin, T. "Transferring Results of Behavioral Research to Industry to Improve Animal Welfare on the Farm, Ranch, and the Slaughter Plant." *Applied Animal Behaviour Science* 81 (2003): 215–28.

Gropius, W. Speech at Harvard Department of Architecture, 1966. In P. Heyer, *Architects on Architecture: New Directions in America*. New York: Walker, 1978.

REFERENCES

Gross, T. "How Rodgers and Hammerstein Revolutionized Broadway." NPR, May 28, 2018. https://www.npr.org/2018/05/28/614469172/how-rodgers-and-hammerstein -revolutionized-broadway/.

Hendren, S. *What Can a Body Do? How We Meet the Built World*. New York: Riverhead Books, 2020.

Hilburn, R. *Paul Simon: The Life*. New York: Simon & Schuster, 2018.

Hines, W. C., et al. "Sorting Out the FACS: A Devil in the Details." *Cell Reports* 6 (2014): 779–81.

Hirsch, C., and S. Schildknecht. "In Vitro Research Producibility: Keeping Up High Standards." *Frontiers in Pharmacology* 10 (2019): 1484. doi:10.3389/fphar.2019.01484.

Hsieh, T., et al. "Enhancing Scientific Foundations to Ensure Reproducibility: A New Paradigm." *American Journal of Pathology* 188, no. 1 (2018): 6–10.

Iachini, A. L., L. R. Bronstein, and E. Mellin, eds. *A Guide for Interprofessional Collaboration*. Council on Social Work Education, 2018.

Isaacson, W. *Steve Jobs*. New York: Simon & Schuster, 2011.

Jambon-Puillet, E., et al. "Liquid Helix: How Capillary Jets Adhere to Vertical Cylinders." *Physics*, May 8, 2019. https://journals.aps.org/prl/abstract/10.1103/PhysRevLett.122.184501/.

Jobs, S. "You've Got to Find What You Love." Commencement Address, Stanford University. *Stanford News*, June 14, 2005.

Kastens, K. "Commentary: Object and Spatial Visualization in Geosciences." *Journal of Geoscience Education* 58, no. 2 (2010): 52–57. doi.org/10.5408/1.3534847.

Khatchadourian, R. "The Trash Nebula." *New Yorker*, September 28, 2020.

Kim, K. M., and K. P. Lee. "Collaborative Product Design Processes of Industrial Design and Engineering Design in Consumer Product Companies." *Design Studies* 46 (2016): 226–60.

Kim, K. M., and K. P. Lee. "Industrial Designers and Engineering Designers: Causes of Conflicts, Resolving Strategies and Perceived Image of Each Other." Design Research Society Conference, 2014.

Kuang, C. "The 6 Pillars of Steve Jobs's Design Philosophy." *Fast Company*, November 7, 2011.

Laird, C. T. "Real Life with Eustacia Cutler." *Parenting Special Needs Magazine*, November/ December 2010. www.parentingspecialneeds.org/article/reallife-eustacia-cutler/.

Landau, J. "Paul Simon: The Rolling Stone Interview." *Rolling Stone*, July 20, 1972. https://www .rollingstone.com/music/music-news/paul-simon-the-rolling-stone-interview-2-231656/.

Ledford, H. "Team Science." *Nature* 525 (2015): 308–11.

Lithgow, G. J., M. Driscoll, and P. Phillips. "A Long Journey to Reproducible Results." *Nature* 548 (2017): 387–88.

López-Muñoz, F., et al. "History of the Discovery and Clinical Introduction of Chlorpromazine." *Annals of Clinical Psychiatry* 17, no. 3 (2005): 113–35.

Moore, W. "WWII Magnetic Fluxgate Compass." YouTube, 2016. https://www.youtube.com /watch?v=3QJ5C_NeD6E.

Mukherjee, S. "Viagra Just Turned 20. Here's How Much Money the ED Drug Makes." *Fortune*, March 27, 2018. https://fortune.com/2018/03/27/viagra-anniversary-pfizer/.

Nolan, F. *The Sound of Their Music: The Story of Rodgers and Hammerstein*. New York: Applause Theatre and Cinema Books, 2002.

Norman, D. *The Design of Everyday Things*. New York: Basic Books, 2013.

Okumura, K. "Following Steve Jobs: Lessons from a College Typography Class." UX Collective, November 8, 2019. https://uxdesign.cc/following-steve-jobs-lessons-from-a-college -typography-class-4f9a603bc964.

REFERENCES

Olsen, C., and S. Mac Namara. *Collaborations in Architecture and Engineering*. New York: Routledge, 2014.

Ouroussoff, N. "An Engineering Magician, Then (Presto) He's an Architect." *New York Times*, November 26, 2006. https://www.nytimes.com/2006/11/26/arts/design/26ouro.html.

Owen, D. "The Anti-Gravity Men: Cecil Balmond and the Structural Engineers of Arup." *New Yorker*, June 18, 2007.

Parreno, C. "Glass talks to Cecil Balmond, One of the World's Leading Designers." *Glass*, September 9, 2016. https://www.theglassmagazine.com/from-the-archive-glass-talks-to-cecil-balmond-one-of-the-worlds-leading-designers/.

Picot, W. "Magnetic Fusion Confinement with Tokamaks and Stellarators." International Atomic Energy Agency (IAEA), 2021.

Prince, R. P., P. E. Belanger, and R. G. Westervelt. Double-rail animal securing assembly, US Patent US3997940A, US Patent Office, issued 1976.

Purves, J. C., and L. Beach. Magnetic field responsive device, US Patent 2383460A, US Patent Office, issued 1945.

Ramaley, J. "Communicating and Collaborating across Disciplines." Accelerating Systemic Change Network, 2017. http://ascnhighered.org/ASCN/posts/192300.html/.

Reynolds, A., and D. Lewis. "Teams Solve Problems Faster When They're More Cognitively Diverse." *Harvard Business Review*, March 30, 2017.

Rodgers, R. *Musical Stages: An Autobiography*. New York: Random House, 1975.

Rodgers, R. "Reminiscences of Richard Rodgers." Columbia University Libraries, 1968. https://clio.columbia.edu/catalog/4072940/.

Rogers, T. N. "Meet Eric Yuan, the Founder and CEO of Zoom, Who Has Made over $12 Billion since March and Now Ranks among the 400 Richest People in America." *Business Insider*, September 9, 2020. https://www.businessinsider.com/meet-zoom-billionaire-eric-yuan-career-net-worth-life.

"Russell and Sigurd Varian." Wikipedia. https://en.wikipedia.org/wiki/Russell_and_Sigurd_Varian/.

"Russell H. Varian and Sigurd F. Varian." *Encyclopaedia Britannica Online*, 1998. https://www.britannica.com/biography/Russell-H-Varian-and-Sigurd-F-Varian/.

Rylance, R. "Grant Giving: Global Funders to Focus on Interdisciplinarity." *Nature* 525 (2015): 313–15.

Saint, A. *Architect and Engineer: A Study in Sibling Rivalry*. New Haven: Yale University Press, 2007.

Scheck, W. "Lawrence Sperry: Genius on Autopilot." HistoryNet. https://www.historynet.com/lawrence-sperry-autopilot-inventor-and-aviation-innovator.htm.

Schindler, J. "The Benefits of Cognitive Diversity." *Forbes*, November 26, 2018.

Sciaky, Inc. "The EBAM 300 Series Produces the Largest 3D Printed Metal Parts and Prototypes in the Addictive Manufacturing Market," 2021. https://www.sciaky.com/largest-metal-3D-printer-available/.

"The Seamstresses Who Helped Put Men on the Moon." CBS News, July 14, 2019. https://www.cbsnews.com/news/apollo-11-the-seamstresses-who-helped-put-a-man-on-the-moon/.

Seyler, M., and D. Kerley. "50 Years Later: From Bras and Girdles to a Spacesuit for the Moon." ABC News, July 13, 2019.

Shah, H. "How Zoom Became the Best Web-Conferencing Project in the World in Less Than 10 Years." *Nira* (blog), 2020. https://nira.com/zoom-history/.

Smith, J. F. "Asperger's Are Us Comedy Troupe Jokes about Everything but That." *New York Times*, July 15, 2016.

Sperry Gyroscope Company ad, 1945 (Gyrosyn Compass Flux Valve Repeater Aviation Instrument). https://www.periodpaper.com/products/1945-ad-sperry-gyrosyn-compass-flux-valve -repeater-aviation-instrument-wwii-art-216158-ysw3-34.

Teitel, A. S. "Hal Laning: The Man You Didn't Know Saved Apollo 11." *Discover Magazine*, May 23, 2019. https://www.discovermagazine.com/the-sciences/hal-laning-the-man-you -didnt-know-saved-apollo-11.

Thompson, C. *Coders*. New York: Penguin Press, 2019.

Thompson, C. "The Secret History of Women in Coding." *New York Times Magazine*, February 13, 2019.

U/Entrarchy. "Mechanical Engineering vs Industrial Design." Reddit, May 3, 2013. https://www .reddit.com/r/IndustrialDesign/comments/1dmuoa/mechanical_engineering_vs_industrial _design/.

Van Noorden, R. "Interdisciplinary Research by the Numbers." *Nature* 525 (2015): 306–7.

Vance, A. *Elon Musk: Tesla, SpaceX, and the Quest for a Fantastic Future*. New York: Ecco, 2015.

Vazquez, C. M. "Technology Boot Camp Aims to Upgrade Okinawa-Based Marines' Problem-Solving Skills." *Stars and Stripes*, March 26, 2019.

Wattles, J. "She Turns Elon Musk's Bold Space Ideas into a Business." CNN Business, March 10, 2019.

Westervelt, R. G., et al. "Physiological Stress Measurement during Slaughter of Calves and Lambs." *Journal of Animal Science* 42 (1976): 831–37.

Whitman, A. "Richard Rodgers Is Dead at Age 77; Broadway's Renowned Composer." *New York Times*, December 31, 1979. https://www.nytimes.com/1979/12/31/archives/richard-rodgers -is-dead-at-age-77-broadways-renowned-composer.html/.

Witt, S. "Apollo 11: Mission Out of Control." *Wired*, June 24, 2019. https://www.wired .com/story/apollo-11-mission-out-of-control/.

Woolley, A. W., et al. "Evidence for a Collective Intelligence Factor in the Performance of Human Groups." *Science* 330, no. 6004 (September 30, 2010): 686–88.

Woolley, A. W., et al. "Using Brain-Based Measures to Compose Teams." *Social Neuroscience* 2, no. 2 (2007): 96–105.

Wozniak, S. *iWOZ: From Computer Geek to Cult Icon*. New York: W. W. Norton, 2006.

5. GENIUS AND NEURODIVERSITY

Abraham, A. *The Neuroscience of Creativity*. Cambridge, UK: Cambridge University Press, 2018.

Amalric, M., and S. Dehaene. "Origins of the Brain Networks for Advanced Mathematics in Expert Mathematicians." *Proceedings of the National Academy of Sciences* 113, no. 18 (2016): 4909–17.

Armstrong, T. "The Myth of the Normal Brain: Embracing Neurodiversity." *AMA Journal of Ethics*, April 2015.

Arshad, M., and M. Fitzgerald. "Did Michelangelo (1475–1564) Have High-Functioning Autism?" *Journal of Medical Biography* 12, no. 2 (2004): 115–20.

"Attention-Deficit/Hyperactivity Disorder (ADHD)." Centers for Disease Control and Prevention. https://www.cdc.gov/ncbddd/adhd/index.html.

"Augusta Savage." Smithsonian American Art Museum. https://americanart.si.edu/artist /augusta-savage-4269/.

Baer, D. "Peter Thiel: Asperger's Can Be a Big Advantage in Silicon Valley." *Business Insider*, April 8, 2015. https://www.businessinsider.com/peter-thiel-aspergers-is-an-advantage-2015-4/.

REFERENCES

Baron-Cohen, S., et al. "The Autism-Spectrum Quotient (AQ): Evidence from Asperger's Syndrome/High-Functioning Males and Females, Scientists and Mathematicians." *Journal of Autism and Developmental Disorders* 31, no. 1 (2001): 5–17.

Beaty, R. E., et al. "Creative Cognition and Brain Network Dynamics." *Trends in Cognitive Sciences* 20, no. 2 (2016): 87–95.

Bernstein, B. O., D. Lubinski, and C. P. Benbow. "Academic Acceleration in Gifted Youth and Fruitless Concerns Regarding Psychological Well-Being: A 35-Year Longitudinal Study." *Journal of Educational Psychology* (2020). https://my.vanderbilt.edu/smpy/files/2013/02 /Article-JEP-Bernstein-2020-F.pdf.

Bianchini, R. "Apple iPhone Design—from the 1st Generation to the iPhone 12." January 18, 2021. https://www.inexhibit.com/case-studies/apple-iphone-history-of-a-design -revolution/.

Blume, H. "Neurodiversity: On the Neurobiological Underpinning of Geekdom." *Atlantic*, September 1998.

Blumenthal, K. *Steve Jobs: The Man Who Thought Different*. New York: Feiwel and Friends, 2012.

Bouchard, T. J., Jr., et al. "Sources of Human Psychological Differences: The Minnesota Study of Twins Reared Apart." *Science* 250 (October 12, 1990): 223–28.

Bouvet, L., et al. "Synesthesia and Autistic Features in a Large Family: Evidence for Spatial Imagery as a Common Factor." *Behavioural Brain Research* 362 (2019): 266–72.

Bradlee, Quinn. "Quinn Interviews Steven Spielberg." Recorded September 2012. *Friends of Quinn*. YouTube, March 14, 2019. https://www.youtube.com/watch?v=jTX0OxE_3mU.

Brandt, K. "Twin Studies: Histories and Discoveries in Neuroscience." BrainFacts, June 12, 2019. https://www.brainfacts.org/brain-anatomy-and-function/genes-and-molecules/2019 /twin-studies-histories-and-discoveries-in-neuroscience-061119.

Brinzea, V. M. "Encouraging Neurodiversity in the Evolving Workforce—The Next Frontier to a Diverse Workplace." *Scientific Bulletin, Economic Sciences* (University of Pitești), 18, no. 3 (2019).

Bruck, C. "Make Me an Offer: Ari Emanuel's Relentless Fight to the Top." *New Yorker*, April 26 and May 3, 2021.

Bucky, P. A. *The Private Albert Einstein*. Kansas City, MO: Andrews and McMeel, 1993.

Carey, R. "The Eight Greatest Quotes from Steve Jobs: The Lost Interview." *Paste*, March 6, 2013. https://www.pastemagazine.com/tech/the-eight-most-important-passages-from-steve-jobs -the-lost-interview/.

Carrillo-Mora, P., et al. "What Did Einstein Have That I Don't? Studies on Albert Einstein's Brain." *Neurosciences and History* 3, no. 3 (2015): 125–29.

Carson, S. "The Unleashed Mind." *Scientific American*, May/June 2011, 22–25.

Chavez-Eakle, R. A. "Cerebral Blood Flow Associated with Creative Performance: A Comparative Study." *NeuroImage* 38, no. 3 (2007): 519–28.

Chen, H., et al. "A Genome-Wide Association Study Identifies Genetic Variants Associated with Mathematics Ability." *Scientific Reports* 7 (2017): 40365.

Chen, Q., R. E. Beaty, and J. Qiu. "Mapping the Artistic Brain: Common and Distinct Neural Activations Associated with Musical, Drawing, and Literary Creativity." *Human Brain Mapping* 41, no. 12 (2020). doi.org/10.1002/hbm.25025.

Clark, R. *Edison: The Man Who Made the Future*. London: Bloomsbury Reader, 2012.

REFERENCES

"Cognitive Theories Explaining ASD." Interactive Autism Network. https://iancommunity.org/cs/understanding_research/cognitive_theories_explaining_asds/.

Colloff, P. "Suddenly Susan." *Texas Monthly*, August 2000.

Condivi, A. *The Life of Michelangelo*. Baton Rouge: Louisiana State University Press, 1976.

Cranmore, J., and J. Tunks. "Brain Research on the Study of Music and Mathematics: A Meta-Synthesis." *Journal of Mathematics Education* 8, no. 2 (2015): 139–57.

Cringely, R. X. *Steve Jobs: The Lost Interview*. Apple TV, 2012.

Cringely, R. X., host. *The Triumph of the Nerds: The Rise of Accidental Empires*. PBS, 1996.

D'Agostino, R. "The Drugging of the American Boy." *Esquire*, March 27, 2014.

de Manzano, Ö., and F. Ullén. "Same Genes, Different Brains: Neuroanatomical Differences between Monozygotic Twins Discordant for Musical Training." *Cerebral Cortex* 28 (2018): 387–94.

Deiss, H. S., and Miller, D. "Who Was Katherine Johnson?" *NASA Knows!* NASA, January 8, 2017, updated January 7, 2021.

Demir, A., et al. "Comparison of Bipolarity Features between Art Students and Other University Students." *Annals of Medical Research* 26, no. 10 (2019): 2214–18.

"Diagnosing Bill Gates." *Time*, January 24, 1994, 25.

Du Plessis, S. "What Are the 12 Types of Dyslexia?" Edublox Online Tutor, November 3, 2021. https://www.edubloxtutor.com/dyslexia-types/.

Dyer, F. L., and T. C. Martin. *Edison, His Life and Inventions*. 1910; reissue CreateSpace, August 13, 2010.

Einstein, A. "The World As I See It." Center for History of Physics. https://history.aip.org/exhibits/einstein/essay.htm.

Engelhardt, C. R., M. O. Mazurek, and J. Hilgard. "Pathological Game Use in Adults with and without Autism Spectrum Disorder." *Peer Journal* (2017). doi:10.7717/peerj3393.

Everatt, J., B. Steffert, and I. Smythe. "An Eye for the Unusual: Creative Thinking in Dyslexics." *Dyslexia*, March 26, 1999.

Falk, D. "The Cerebral Cortex of Albert Einstein: A Description and Preliminary Analysis of Unpublished Photographs." *Brain* 136, no. 4 (2013): 1304–27.

Falk, D. "New Information about Albert Einstein's Brain." *Frontiers in Evolutionary Neuroscience* (2009). doi.org/10.3389/neuro.18.003.2009.

Felicetti, K., and Monster. "These Major Tech Companies are Making Autism Hiring a Priority." *Fortune*, March 8, 2016.

Fishman, C. "Face Time with Michael Dell." *Fast Company*, February 28, 2001.

Folstein, S., and M. Rutter. "Infantile Autism: A Genetic Study of 21 Twin Pairs." *Journal of Child Psychology and Psychiatry* 18, no. 4 (1977). https://doi.org/10.1111/j.1469-7610.1977.tb00443.x.

Foster, B. "Einstein and His Love of Music." *Physics World* 18, no. 1 (2005): 34.

Fuller, T. "No Longer an Underdog, a Deaf High School Team Takes California by Storm." *New York Times*, November 26, 2021, A12.

Gable, S. L., et al. "When the Muses Strike: Creative Ideas Routinely Occur during Mind Wandering." *Psychological Science*, January 7, 2019.

Gainotti, G. "Emotions and the Right Hemisphere: Can New Data Clarify Old Models?" *Neuroscientist* 25, no. 3 (2019): 258–70.

Gainotti, G. "A Historical Review of Investigations on Laterality of Emotions in the Human Brain." *Journal of the History of Neuroscience* 28, no. 1 (2019): 23–41.

Galton, F. "History of Twins." *Inquiries into Human Faculty and Its Development*, 1875: 155–73.

Gardner, H. *Creating Minds*. New York: Basic Books, 2011.

Gigliotti, J. *Who Is Stevie Wonder?* New York: Grosset & Dunlap, 2016.

"The Girl Who Asked Questions." *Economist*, February 29, 2020, 72.

Gleick, J. *Isaac Newton*. New York: Vintage, 2004.

Goldberg, E. *Creativity: The Human Brain in the Age of Innovation*. New York: Oxford University Press, 2018.

Grandin, T. *Thinking in Pictures*. New York: Doubleday, 1995. Expanded edition. New York: Vintage, 2006.

Grant, D. A., and E. Berg. "A Behavioral Analysis of Degree of Reinforcement and Ease of Shifting to New Responses in a Weigl-Type Card-Sorting Problem." *Journal of Experimental Psychology* 38, no. 4 (1948): 404–11. https://doi.org/10.1037/h0059831/.

Greenwood, T. A. "Positive Traits in the Bipolar Spectrum: The Space between Madness and Genius." *Molecular Neuropsychiatry* 2 (2017): 198–212.

Griffin, E., and D. Pollak. "Student Experiences of Neurodiversity in Higher Education: Insights from the BRAINHE Project." *Dyslexia* 15, no. 1 (2009). doi.org/10.1002/dys.383.

Hadamard, J. *The Psychology of Invention in the Mathematical Field*. Princeton, NJ: Dover, 1945.

Han, W., et al. "Genetic Influences on Creativity: An Exploration of Convergent and Divergent Thinking." *Peer Journal* (2018). doi:10.7717/peerj.5403.

Hashem, S., et al. "Genetics of Structural and Functional Brain Changes in Autism Spectrum Disorder." *Translational Psychiatry* 10 (2020).

Haskell, M. *Steven Spielberg: A Life in Films*. New Haven: Yale University Press, 2017.

Hegarty, J. P., et al. "Genetic and Environmental Influences on Structural Brain Measures in Twins with Autism Spectrum Disorder." *Molecular Psychiatry* 25 (2020): 2556–66.

Helmrich, B. H. "Window of Opportunity? Adolescence, Music, and Algebra." *Journal of Adolescent Research* 25, no. 4 (2010): 557–77.

Hodges, A. *Alan Turing: The Enigma*. Princeton, NJ: Princeton University Press, 2015.

Huddleston, T., Jr. "Bill Gates: Use This Simple Trick to Figure Out What You'll Be Great at in Life." CNBC, March 12, 2019. https://www.cnbc.com/2019/03/12/bill-gates-how-to-know-what-you-can-be-great-at-in-life.html.

Isaacson, W. *Einstein: His Life and Universe*. New York: Simon & Schuster, 2007.

Itzkoff, D. "Elon Musk Tries to Have Fun Hosting 'S.N.L.'" *New York Times*, May 10, 2021.

James, I. *Asperger's Syndrome and High Achievement*. London: Jessica Kingsley, 2005.

James, I. "Singular Scientists." *Journal of the Royal Society of Medicine* 96, no. 1 (2003): 36–39.

Johnson, R. "A Genius Explains." *Guardian*, February 11, 2005.

Kanjlia, S., R. Pant, and M. Bedny. "Sensitive Period for Cognitive Repurposing of Human Visual Cortex." *Cerebral Cortex* 29, no. 9 (2019): 3993–4005.

Kapoula, Z., and M. Vernet. "Dyslexia, Education and Creativity, a Cross-Cultural Study." *Aesthetics and Neuroscience* (2016): 31–42.

Kapoula, Z., et al. "Education Influences Creativity in Dyslexic and Non-Dyslexic Children and Teenagers." *PLOS ONE*, 11, no. 3 (2016). doi.org/10.1371/journal.pone.0150421.

Katz, J., et al. "Genetics, Not the Uterine Environment, Drive the Formation of Trophoblast Inclusions: Insights from a Twin Study." *Placenta* 114 (2021). https://www.sciencedirect.com/science/article/abs/pii/S0143400421001284.

REFERENCES

Kirby, P. "A Brief History of Dyslexia." *Psychologist* 31 (March 2018): 56–59.

Knecht, S., et al. "Language Lateralization in Healthy Right-Handers." *Brain* 123, no. 1 (2000): 74–81.

Kyaga, S., et al. "Creativity and Mental Disorder: Family Study of 300,000 People with Severe Mental Disorder." *British Journal of Psychiatry* 199, no. 5 (2011): 373–79. doi: 10.1192/bjp .bp.110.085316.

Larsen, S. A. "Identical Genes, Unique Environments: A Qualitative Exploration of Persistent Monozygotic Twin Discordance in Literacy and Numeracy." *Frontiers in Education* (2019). doi .org/10.3389/feduc.2019.00021.

Le Couteur, A, et al. "A Broader Phenotype of Autism: The Clinical Spectrum in Twins." *Journal of Child Psychology and Psychiatry* 37, no. 7 (1996). doi.org/10.1111/j.1469-7610.1996.tb01475.x.

Lehman, C. "Interview with a Software Engineer." Quillette.com. January 5, 2018.

Leibowitz, G. "Steve Jobs Might Have Never Started Apple If He Didn't Do This 1 Thing." *Inc.*, 2018. https://www.inc.com/glenn-leibowitz/in-a-rare-23-year-old-interview-steve-jobs -said-this-1-pivotal-experience-inspired-him-to-start-apple-computer.html/.

Lesinski, J. M. *Bill Gates: Entrepreneur and Philanthropist*. Springfield, MO: Twenty-First Century Books, 2009.

Lienhard, D. A. "Roger Sperry's Split Brain Experiments (1959–1968)." *Embryo Project Encyclopedia*, December 27, 2017. http://embryo.asu.edu/handle/10776/13035.

"Life of Thomas Alva Edison." Library of Congress. https://www.loc.gov /collections/edison-company-motion-pictures-and-sound-recordings/articles-and-essays /biography/life-of-thomas-alva-edison/.

Linneweber, G. A., et al. "A Neurodevelopmental Origin of Behavioral Individuality in the *Drosophila* Visual System." *Science* 367, no. 6482 (2020): 1112–19.

Lubinski, D., and C. P. Benbow. "Intellectual Precocity: What Have We Learned Since Terman?" *Gifted Child Quarterly*, July 28, 2020.

Maggioni, E., et al. "Twin MRI Studies on Genetic and Environmental Determinants of Brain Morphology and Function in the Early Lifespan." *Neuroscience and Biobehavioral Reviews* 109 (2020): 139–49.

"Maya Lin: Artist and Architect." Interview, Scottsdale, Arizona, June 16, 2000. Academy of Achievement. https://achievement.org/achiever/maya-lin/#interview.

Maya Lin: A River Is a Drawing (notes on exhibition). Hudson River Museum, 2019. https://www .hrm.org/exhibitions/maya-lin/.

Maya Lin: Systematic Landscapes (notes on exhibition). Contemporary Art Museum St. Louis. https://camstl.org/exhibitions/maya-lin-systematic-landscapes.

"Maya Lin Quotations." Quotetab. https://www.quotetab.com/quotes/by-maya-lin/.

McBride, J. *Steven Spielberg*. Jackson: University Press of Mississippi, 2011.

McFarland, M. "Why Shades of Asperger's Syndrome Are the Secret to Building a Great Tech Company." *Washington Post*, April 3, 2015. https://www.washingtonpost.com/news /innovations/wp/2015/04/03/why-shades-of-aspergers-syndrome-are-the-secret-to -building-a-great-tech-company/.

Mejia, Z. "Bill Gates Learned What He Needed to Start Microsoft in High School." CNBC, May 24, 2018. https://www.cnbc.com/2018/05/24/bill-gates-got-what-he-needed-to-start-microsoft -in-high-school.html.

Men, W., et al. "The Corpus Callosum of Albert Einstein's Brain: Another Clue to His High Intelligence?" *Brain* 137, no. 4 (2013): e268.

Miller, G. "Music Builds Bridges in the Brain." *Science*, April 16, 2008.

Mitchell, K. J. *Innate: How the Wiring of Our Brains Shapes Who We Are*. Princeton, NJ: Princeton University Press, 2018.

Moffic, H. S. "A Deaf Football Team Sees a Way to Victory!" *Psychiatric Times*, November 18, 2021.

Moore, C. B., N. H. McIntyre, and S. E. Lanivich. "ADHD-Related Neurodiversity and the Entrepreneurial Mindset." *Entrepreneurship Theory and Practice* 45, no. 1 (December 6, 2019). doi.org/10.1177/1042258719890986.

Morris, E. *Edison*. New York: Random House, 2019.

Moyers, B. "Personal Journeys: Maya Lin." *Becoming American: The Chinese Experience*, PBS, https://www.pbs.org/becomingamerican/.

Nasar, S. *A Beautiful Mind*. New York: Simon & Schuster, 2011.

Nurmi, E. L., et al. "Exploratory Subsetting of Autism Families Based on Savant Skills Improves Evidence of Genetic Linkage to 15q11–q13." *Journal of the American Academy of Child and Adolescent Psychiatry* 42, no. 7 (July 2003). doi: 10.1097/01.CHI.0000046868.56865.0F.

O'Brian, P. *Pablo Ruiz Picasso: A Biography*. New York: W. W. Norton, 1976.

O'Connell, H., and M. Fitzgerald. "Did Alan Turing Have Asperger's Syndrome?" *Irish Journal of Psychological Medicine* 20, no. 1 (2003): 28–31.

"Oprah Winfrey Biography." *Encyclopedia of World Biography*. https://www.notablebiographies.com/We-Z/Winfrey-Oprah.html.

Parker, R. G. *A School Compendium in Natural and Experimental Philosophy*. First published by A. S. Barnes, 1837. Reprinted by Legare Street Press, 2021.

Patten, B. M. "Visually Mediated Thinking: A Report of the Case of Albert Einstein." *Journal of Learning Disabilities* 6, no. 7 (1973).

Peters, L., et al. "Dyscalculia and Dyslexia: Different Behavioral, yet Similar Brain Activity Profiles during Arithmetic." *NeuroImage: Clinical* 18 (2018): 663–74.

Pinker, S. "The Gifted Kids Are All Right." *Wall Street Journal*, September 19, 2020, C4.

Ravilious, K. "Different Minds." *New Scientist* 212, no. 2387 (2011): 34–37.

Reser, J. E. "Solitary Mammals Provide an Animal Model for Autism Spectrum Disorders." *Journal of Comparative Psychology* 128, no. 1 (2014): 99–113.

Richardson, J. *A Life of Picasso*. 4 volumes. New York: Alfred A. Knopf, 1991–2021.

Robinson, A. "Can We Define Genius?" *Psychology Today*, November 30, 2010.

Root-Bernstein, R., et al. "Arts Foster Scientific Success: Avocations of Nobel, National Academy, Royal Society, and Sigma Xi Members." *Journal of Psychology of Science and Technology* 1, no. 2 (2008). doi:10/1891/1939-7054.1.251.

Rose, C. "Chairman and CEO of Microsoft Corporation Bill Gates Explores the Future of the Personal Computer, the Internet, and Interactivity." *Charlie Rose*, PBS, November 25, 1996.

Rosen, P. "Neurodiversity: What You Need to Know." Understood, https://www.understood.org.

Ruthsatz, J., and K. Stephens. *The Prodigy's Cousin: The Family Link between Autism and Extraordinary Talent*. New York: Current, 2016.

Ruzich, E., et al. "Sex and STEM Occupation Predict Autism-Spectrum Quotient (AQ) Scores in Half a Million People." *PLOS ONE*, October 21, 2015. https://doi.org/10.1371/journal.pone.0141229.

Sacks, O. "An Anthropologist on Mars." *New Yorker*, December 27, 1993, on the story of Temple Grandin. Published also in Sacks, *An Anthropologist on Mars*. New York: Alfred A. Knopf, 1995.

Sacks, O. "The Case of the Colorblind Painter." In Sacks, *An Anthropologist on Mars*, 3–41. New York: Alfred A. Knopf, 1995.

REFERENCES

"Savage, Augusta 1892–1962." Johnson Collection. https://thejohnsoncollection.org/augusta -savage/.

Schatzker, E. "'We Must Bring This Pandemic to a Close.'" Interview with Bill Gates. *Bloomberg Businessweek*, September 21, 2020, 47–49.

Seabrook, J. "Email from Bill." *New Yorker*, January 10, 1994.

Segal, N. *Born Together—Reared Apart*. Cambridge, MA: Harvard University Press, 2012.

Sharma, B. "How a Calligraphy Course Rewrote the Life Story of Steve Jobs." *Million Centers* (blog), May 11, 2018. https://www.millioncenters.com/blog/how-a-calligraphy-course -rewrote-the-life-story-of-steve-jobs.

Shelton, J. "Study of Twins Shows It's Genetics That Controls Abnormal Development." *YaleNews*, May 3, 2021. https://news.yale.edu/2021/05/03/genetics-not-environment-uterus-controls -abnormal-development.

Shetterly, M. L. *Hidden Figures: The American Dream and the Untold Story of the Black Women Mathematicians Who Helped Win the Space Race*. New York: William Morrow, 2016.

Shuren, J. E., et al. "Preserved Color Imagery in an Achromatopsic." *Neuropsychologia* 34, no. 6 (1996): 485–89.

Sikela, J. M., and V. B. Searles Quick. "Genomic Trade-offs: Are Autism and Schizophrenia the Steep Price of the Human Brain?" *Human Genetics* 137, no. 1 (2018): 1–13.

Silberman, S. "The Geek Syndrome." *Wired*, December 1, 2001. https://www.wired.com/2001 /12/aspergers/.

Silberman, S. *NeuroTribes*. New York: Avery, 2015.

Simonton, D. K. *Origins of Genius*. Oxford, UK: Oxford University Press, 1999.

Spielberg, S. *Steven Spielberg Interviews*. Edited by B. Notbohm and L. D. Friedman. Jackson: University Press of Mississippi, 2000.

Spitkins, P. "The Stone Age Origins of Autism." In *Recent Advances in Autism Spectrum Disorder*, ed. M. Fitzgerald, vol. 2, 3–24. London: IntechOpen, 2013. Also available as DOI:10.5772/53883.

Spitkins, P., B. Wright, and D. Hodgson. "Are There Alternative Adaptive Strategies to Human Pro-Sociality? The Role of Collaborative Morality in the Emergence of Personality Variation and Autistic Traits." *Journal of Archaeology, Consciousness and Culture* 9, no. 4 (2016). doi/full /10.1080/1751696X.2016.1244949.

"Steven Spielberg Escaped His Dyslexia through Filmmaking." ABC News, September 27, 2012. https://abcnews.go.com/blogs/entertainment/2012/09/steven-spielberg-escaped-his -dyslexia-through-filmmaking.

Stevenson, J. L., and M. A. Gernsbacher. "Abstract Spatial Reasoning as an Autistic Strength." *PLOS ONE* 8, no. 3 (2013): e59329.

Thaler, L. "Echolocation May Have Real-Life Advantages for Blind People: An Analysis of Survey Data." *Frontiers in Physiology*, May 8, 2013. doi.org/10.3389/fphys.2013.00098.

Thaler, L., S. R. Arnott, and M. A. Goodale. "Neural Correlates of Natural Human Echolocation in Early and Late Blind Echolocation Experts." *PLOS ONE* (2011). doi.org/10.1371/journal .pone.0020162.

Than, K. "A Brief History of Twin Studies." *Smithsonian Magazine*, March 4, 2016. https://www .smithsonianmag.com/science-nature/brief-history-twin-studies-180958281/.

Tikhodeyev, O. N., and O. V. Shcherbakova. "The Problem of Non-Shared Environment in Behavioral Genetics." *Behavioral Genetics* 49, no. 3 (May 2019): 259–69. doi: 10.1007 /s10519-019-09950-1.

Treffert, D. A. "A Gene for Savant Syndrome." Agnesian Health Care, April 25, 2017.

REFERENCES

Treffert, D. A. *Islands of Genius*. London: Jessica Kingsley, 2010.

Turing, A. M. "The Chemical Basis of Morphogenesis." *Philosophical Transactions of the Royal Society of London, Series B, Biological Sciences* 237, no. 641 (August 14, 1952): 37–72.

Turing, A. M. "Computing Machinery and Intelligence." *Mind* 59, no. 236 (October 1950): 433–60.

Van Noorden, R. "Interdisciplinary by the Numbers." *Nature* 525, no. 7569 (2015): 305–7.

Vance, A. *Elon Musk: How the Billionaire CEO of SpaceX and Tesla Is Shaping Our Future*. New York: Virgin Books, 2015.

Vietnam Veterans Memorial Fund. "The Names." https://www.vvmf.org/About-The-Wall /the-names/.

von Károlyi, C. V., et al. "Dyslexia Linked to Talent: Global Visual-Spatial Ability." *Brain and Language* 85, no. 3 (2003): 427–31.

Wai, J. "Was Steve Jobs Smart? Heck Yes!" *Psychology Today*, November 7, 2011. https://www .psychologytoday.com/us/blog/finding-the-next-einstein/201111/was-steve-jobs-smart -heck-yes/.

Wei, X., et al. "Science, Technology, Engineering, and Mathematics (STEM) Participation among College Students with an Autism Spectrum Disorder." *Journal of Autism and Developmental Disorders* 43, no. 7 (July 2013). https://www.ncbi.nlm.nih.gov/pmc/articles/PMC3620841/.

Weiner, E. *The Geography of Genius*. New York: Simon & Schuster, 2016.

Weiss, H. "Artists at Work: Maya Lin." *Interview*, August 10, 2017. https://www .interviewmagazine.com/art/artists-at-work-maya-lin/.

Wertheimer, M. *Productive Thinking*. New York: Harper & Row, 1959.

West, T. G. *In the Mind's Eye: Visual Thinkers, Gifted People with Dyslexia and Other Learning Difficulties, Computer Images, and the Ironies of Creativity*. Amherst, NY: Prometheus Books, 2009.

Witelson, S. F., D. L. Kigar, and T. Harvey. "The Exceptional Brain of Albert Einstein." *Lancet* 353 (1999): 2149–53.

Wolff, B., and H. Goodman. "The Legend of the Dull-Witted Child Who Grew Up to Be a Genius." The Albert Einstein Archives, 2007. http://www.albert-einstein.org/article _handicap.html.

Wolff, U., and I. Lundberg. "The Prevalence of Dyslexia among Art Students." *Dyslexia* 8, no. 1 (2002). doi.org/10.1002/dys.211.

Wonder, S. Interview with Mesha McDaniel, Celebrity Profile Entertainment, March 23, 2013. YouTube. https://www.youtube.com/watch?v=126ni6rvzPU.

Wonder, S. Interview with Larry King, *Larry King Live*, CNN. YouTube. https://www.youtube .com/watch?v=VtNLoaT9S24.

Young, J. B. "Maya Lin's Elegiac Sculptures and Installations Sing a Requiem for the Disappearing Natural World." *Orlando Weekly*, March 4, 2015.

Zagai, U., et al. "The Swedish Twin Registry: Content and Management as a Research Infrastructure." *Twin Research and Human Genetics* 22, no. 6 (December 2019): 672–80. doi: 10.1017/thg.2019.99.

Zeliadt, N. "Autism Genetics, Explained." *Spectrum*, June 2017, updated May 28, 2021. https://www.spectrumnews.org/news/autism-genetics-explained/.

Zhu, W., et al. "Common and Distinct Brain Networks Underlying Verbal and Visual Creativity." *Human Brain Mapping* 38, no. 4 (2017). doi.org/10.1002/hbm.23507.

Zihl, J., and C. A. Heywood. "The Contribution of LM to the Neuroscience of Movement Vision." *Frontiers in Integrative Neuroscience* 9, no. 6 (February 17, 2015). https://www.frontiersin.org /articles/10.3389/fnint.2015.00006/full.

Zitarelli, D. E. "Alan Turing in America—1942–1943." *Convergence*, January 2015. https://www.maa.org/press/periodicals/convergence/alan-turing-in-america.

6. VISUALIZING RISK TO PREVENT DISASTERS

Acton, J. M., and M. Hibbs. "Why Fukushima Was Preventable." Carnegie Endowment for International Peace, March 6, 2012. https://carnegieendowment.org/2012/03/06/why-fukushima-was-preventable-pub-47361.

Ankrum, J., et al. "Diagnosing Skin Diseases Using an AI-Based Dermatology Consult." *Science Translational Medicine* 12, no. 548 (2020): eabc8946.

"Assessment of C-Band Mobile Communications Interference Impact on Low Range Radar Altimeter Operations." Radio Technical Commission for Aeronautics, RTCA Paper No. 274-20/PMC-2073, October 7, 2020.

Baker, M., and D. Gates. "Lack of Redundancies on Boeing 737 MAX System Baffles Some Involved in Developing the Jet." *Seattle Times*, March 26, 2019.

Bard, N., et al. "The Hanabi Challenge: A New Frontier for AI Research." *Artificial Intelligence* 280 (2020): 103216.

Barry, R., T. McGinty, and A. Pasztor. "Foreign Pilots Face More Snags in Landing in San Francisco." *Wall Street Journal*, December 12, 2013, A1, A4.

Barstow, D., D. Rohde, and S. Saul. "Deepwater Horizon's Final Hours." *New York Times*, December 25, 2010, http://www.nytimes.com/2010/12/26/US/26spill.html.

Benedict. "Google AI Sees 3D Printed Turtle as a Rifle, MIT Researchers Explain Why." 3D Printer and 3D Printing News, November 2, 2017. https://www.3ders.org/articles/20171102-google-ai-sees-3d-printed-turtle-as-a-rifle-mit-researchers-explain-why.html.

Bennett, J. "Screws and Washers Are Falling off NASA's Multi-Billion Dollar Space Telescope." *Popular Mechanics*, May 3, 2018.

Bloomberg. "Lion Air Pilots Battled Confusing Malfunctioning before Deadly Crash." *Fortune*, November 24, 2018. https://fortune.com/2018/11/24/lion-air-plane-crash/.

Bourzac, K. "Upgrading the Quantum Computer." *Chemical and Engineering News*, April 15, 2019, 26–32.

Bressan, D. "Historic Tsunamis in Japan." *History of Geology* (blog), March 17, 2011. http://historyofgeology.fieldofscience.com/2011/03/historic-tsunamis-in-japan.html.

Casto, C. "Fukushima Daiichi and Daini—A Tale of Two Leadership Styles," Chartered Quality Institute, August 9, 2016. https://www.quality.org/knowledge/%E2%80%8Bfukushima-daiichi-and-daini-tale-two-leadership-styles.

Catchpole, D. "The Forces behind Boeing's Long Descent." *Fortune*, January 20, 2020. https://fortune.com/longform/boeing-737-max-crisis-shareholder-first-culture/.

Cho, A. "Critics Question Whether Novel Reactor Is 'Walk-Away Safe.'" *Science* 369, no. 6506 (August 21, 2020): 888–89. https://www.science.org/doi/10.1126/science.369.6506.888.

Chubu Electric Power. "Blocking a Tsunami: Prevention of Flooding on the Station Site." https://www.chuden.co.jp/english/energy/hamaoka/provision/tsunami/station/.

Davis, C. "Merrimack Valley Gas Pipeline Contractors Lacked Necessary Replacement Info, Says NTSB." NGI, National Gas Intelligence, October 12, 2018. https://www.naturalgasintel.com/merrimack-valley-gas-pipeline-contractors-lacked-necessary-replacement-info-says-ntsb/.

Enserink, M. "Sloppy Reporting on Animal Studies Proves Hard to Change." *Science* 357, no. 6358 (September 29, 2017): 1337–38. https://www.science.org/doi/10.1126/science.357.6358.1337.

REFERENCES

Federal Aviation Administration. Air Worthiness Directive. Transport and Commuter Category Airplanes. Docket No. FFA 2021-0953. Project Identifier AS-2021-01169-T.

Flightradar24.com. JT610 Granular ADS-B Data, 2018.

Ford, D. "Cheney's Defibrillator Was Modified to Prevent Hacking." CNN, October 24, 2013.

Foster, C. *My Octopus Teacher*. Directed by P. Ehrlich and J. Reed. Netflix, 2020.

Fountain, H. "Focus Turns to Well-Blocking System." *New York Times*, May 10, 2010. https://www.nytimes.com/2010/05/11/science/11blowout.html/.

Fowler, J. T. "Deepwater Horizon: A Lesson in Risk Analysis." American Public University, EDGE, March 13, 2017. https://apuedge.com/deepwater-horizon-a-lesson-in-risk-analysis/.

Freed, J., and E. M. Johnson. "Optional Warning Light Could Have Aided Lion Air Engineers Before Crash: Experts." Reuters, November 30, 2018.

Furchtgott-Roth, D. "Canada Limits 5G to Protect Air Travel." *Forbes*, November 21, 2021.

Garrett, E., et al. "A Systematic Review of Geological Evidence for Holocene Earthquakes and Tsunamis along the Nankai-Suruga Trough, Japan." *Earth-Science Reviews* 159 (August 2016): 337–57. dx.doi.org/10.1016/j.earscirev.2016.06.011.

Gates, D., and D. Baker. "The Inside Story of MCAS: How Boeing's 737 MAX System Gained Power and Lost Safeguards." *Seattle Times*, June 22, 2019. https://www.seattletimes.com/seattle-news/times-watchdog/the-inside-story-of-mcas-how-boeings-737-max-system-gained-power-and-lost-safeguards/.

Gibson, E. J., and R. D. Walk. "The 'Visual Cliff.'" *Scientific American* 202, no. 4 (1960): 64–71.

Glantz, J., et al. "Jet's Software Was Updated, Pilots Weren't." *New York Times*, February 3, 2019, 1, 18.

"The Great, Late James Webb Space Telescope." *Economist*, November 27, 2021, 76–78.

Greene-Blose, J. M. "Deepwater Horizon: Lessons in Probabilities." Paper presented at PMI Global Congress 2015—EMEA, London. Newton Square, PA: Project Management Institute.

Gulati, R., C. Casto, and C. Krontiris. "How the Other Fukushima Plant Survived." *Harvard Business Review*, July–August 2014. https://hbr.org/2014/07/how-the-other-fukushima-plant-survived.

Harris, R. "Elon Musk: Humanity Is a Kind of 'Biological Boot Loader' of AI." *Wired*, September 1, 2019.

Herkert, J., J. Borenstein, and K. Miller. "The Boeing 737 MAX Lessons for Engineering Ethics." *Science and Engineering Ethics* 26 (2020): 2957–74.

Hern, A. "Yes, Androids Do Dream of Electric Sheep." *Guardian*, June 18, 2015.

Hines, W. C., et al. "Sorting Out the FACS: A Devil in the Details." *Cell Reports* 6 (2014): 779–81.

Hirsch, C., and S. Schildknecht. "In Vitro Research Reproducibility: Keeping Up High Standards." *Frontiers in Pharmacology* 10 (2019): 1484. doi:10.3389/fphar.2019.01484.

Hollnagel, E., and Y. Fujita. "The Fukushima Disaster—Systemic Failures as the Lack of Resilience." *Nuclear Engineering and Technology* 45 (2013): 13–20.

Horgan, R. "Fatal Taiwan Bridge Collapse Is Latest Example of Maintenance Failings." *New Civil Engineer*, October 7, 2019. https://www.newcivilengineer.com/latest/fatal-taiwan-bridge-collapse-is-latest-example-of-maintenance-failings-07-10-2019/.

Hsieh, T., et al. "Enhancing Scientific Foundations to Ensure Reproducibility: A New Paradigm." *American Journal of Pathology* 188, no. 1 (2018): 6–10.

Hubbard, D. W. *The Failure of Risk Management*. Hoboken, NJ: Wiley, 2009.

"Injury Facts: Preventable Deaths: Odds of Dying." National Safety Council. https://injuryfacts.nsc.org/all-injuries/preventable-death-overview/odds-of-dying/.

REFERENCES

Jensen, A. R. "Most Adults Know More Than 42,000 Words." *Frontiers*, August 16, 2016.

Johnston, P., and R. Harris. "The Boeing 737 MAX Saga: Lessons for Software Organizations." *Software Quality Profession* 21, no. 3 (May 2019): 4–12. https://asq.org/quality-resources/articles/the-boeing-737-max-saga-lessons-for-software-organizations?id=489c93e1417945b8b9ecda7e3f937f5d.

Kaiser, J. "Key Cancer Results Failed to Be Reproduced." *Science* 374, no. 6573 (2021): 1311.

Kalluri, P. "Don't Ask If AI Is Good or Fair, Ask How It Shifts Power." *Nature* 583 (2020): 169.

Kansai Electric Power. "Nuclear Power Information: Measures against Potential Tsunami." 2019. https://www.kepco.co.jp/english/energy/nuclear_power/tsunami.html.

Kawano, A. "Lessons Learned from Our Accident at Fukushima Nuclear Power Stations." Global 2011, Tokyo Electric Power Company, PowerPoint presentation, 2011.

Kennedy, M. "Federal Investigators Pinpoint What Caused String of Gas Explosions in Mass." NPR, November 16, 2018. https://www.wnyc.org/story/federal-investigators-pinpoint-what-caused-string-of-gas-explosions-in-mass.

Keshavan, M. S., and M. Sudarshan. "Deep Dreaming, Aberrant Salience and Psychosis: Connecting the Dots by Artificial Neural Networks." *Schizophrenia Research* 188 (2017): 178–81.

Kitroeff, N., et al. "Boeing Rush to Finish Jet Left Little Time for Pilot Training." *New York Times*, March 17, 2019, 1, 26.

Koenig, D. "Messages from a Former Boeing Test Pilot Reveal MAX Concerns." Associated Press, October 18, 2019.

Komatsubara, J., et al. "Historical Tsunamis and Storms Recorded in Coastal Lowland, Shizwoka Prefecture, along the Pacific Coast of Japan." *Sedimentology* 55, no. 6 (2008). doi.org/10.1111/j.1365-3081.2008.00964.x.

Koren, M. "Who Should Pay for the Mistakes on NASA's Next Big Telescope?" *Atlantic*, July 27, 2018.

Lahiri, T. "An Off-Duty Pilot Saved Lion Air's 737 MAX from a Crash the Day before Its Fatal Flight." *Quartz*, March 19, 2019. https://qz.com/1576597/off-duty-pilot-saved-lion-airs-737-max-the-day-before-its-fatal-flight/.

Langewiesche, W. "System Crash—What Really Brought Down the Boeing 737 MAX? A 21st Century Aviation Industry That Made Airplanes Astonishingly Easy to Fly, but Not Foolproof." *New York Times Magazine*, September 22, 2019, 36–45, 57.

"Lion Air: How Could a Brand New Plane Crash?" BBC News, October 29, 2018. www.bbc.com/news/world-asia-46014260/.

Lithgow, G. J., et al. "A Long Journey to Reproducible Results." *Nature* 548 (2017): 387–88.

Lopes, L., et al. "174—A Comparison of Machine Learning Algorithms in the Classification of Beef Steers Finished in Feedlot." *Journal of Animal Science* 98, issue supplement (November 30, 2020): 126–27.

Massaro, M. "Next Generation of Radio Spectrum Management: Licensed Shared Access for 5G." *Telecommunications Policy* 41, no. 5–6 (2017): 422–33.

McCartney, S. "Inside the Effort to Fix the Troubled Boeing 737 MAX." *Wall Street Journal*, June 5, 2019.

McNutt, M. K., et al. "Applications of Science and Engineering to Quantify and Control the Deepwater Horizons Oil Spill." *Proceedings of the National Academy of Sciences* 109, no. 50 (2012): 20222–228. https://www.pnas.org/doi/full/10.1073/pnas.1214389109.

Miller, A. *The Artist in the Machine*. Cambridge, MA: MIT Press, 2019.

REFERENCES

Miller, A. "DeepDream: How Alexander Mordvintsev Excavated the Computer's Hidden Layers." *MIT Press Reader*, July 1, 2020.

Mohrbach, L. "The Defense-in-Depth Safety Concept: Comparison between the Fukushima Daiichi Units and German Nuclear Power Units." *VGB PowerTech* 91, no. 6 (2011).

Mullard, A. "Half of Top Cancer Studies Fail High-Profile Reproducibility Effort." *Nature*, December 9, 2021. https://www.nature.com/articles/d41586-021-03691-0.

Naoe, K. "The Heroic Mission to Save Fukashima Daini." Nippon.com, April 7, 2021. https://www.nippon.com/en/japan-topics/g01053/the-heroic-mission-to-save-fukushima-daini.html.

National Transportation Safety Board. "Preliminary Report: Pipeline Over-pressure of a Columbia Gas of Massachusetts Low-pressure Natural Gas Distribution System [September 13, 2018]." October 11, 2018.

Niler, E. "NASA's James Webb Space Telescope Plagued by Delays, Rising Costs." *Wired*, June 27, 2018. https://www.wired.com/story/delays-rising-costs-plague-nasas-james-webb-space-telescope/.

Norman, C. "Chernobyl: Errors and Design Flaws." *Science* 233, no. 4768 (September 5, 1986): 1029–31.

"NRC Nears Completion of NuScale SMR Design Review." *World Nuclear News*, August 27, 2020.

Onyanga-Omara, J., and T. Maresca. "Previous Lion Air Flight Passengers 'Began to Panic and Vomit.'" *USA Today*, October 30, 2018.

Pasztor, A. "Air Safety Panel Hits Pilot's Reliance on Automation." *Wall Street Journal*, November 18, 2013, A4.

Pasztor, A., and A. Tangel. "FAA Gives Boeing MAX Fix List." *Wall Street Journal*, August 4, 2020, B1–B2.

Perkins, R. "Fukushima Disaster Was Preventable, New Study Finds." *USC News*, September 15, 2015.

Perrow, C. "Fukushima, Risk, and Probability: Expect the Unexpected." *Bulletin of the Atomic Scientists* (April 2011). https://thebulletin.org/2011/04/fukushima-risk-and-probability-expect-the-unexpected/.

"Perseverance's Selfie with Ingenuity." NASA Science, Mars Exploration Program, April 7, 2021. https://mars.nasa.gov/resources/25790/perseverance-selfie-with-ingenuity/.

Peterson, A. "Yes, Terrorists Could Have Hacked Dick Cheney's Heart." *Washington Post*, October 21, 2013.

Phillips, M., et al. "Detection of Malignant Melanoma Using Artificial Intelligence: An Observational Study of Diagnostic Accuracy." *Dermatology Practical and Conceptual* 10, no. 1 (2020): e2020011.

Pistner, C. "Fukushima Daini—Comparison of the Events at Fukushima Daini and Daiichi." Presentation, 1st NURIS Conference, Vienna, April 16–17, 2015.

Rahu, M. "Health Effects of the Chernobyl Accident: Fears, Rumors and Truth." *European Journal of Cancer* 39 (2003): 295–99.

Rausand, M. *Risk Assessment: Theory, Methods, and Applications.* Hoboken, NJ: Wiley, 2011.

Razdan, R. "Temple Grandin, Elon Musk, and the Interesting Parallels between Autonomous Vehicles and Autism." *Forbes*, June 7, 2020.

Rice, J. "Massachusetts Utility Pleads Guilty to 2018 Gas Explosion." *ENR, Engineering News-Record*, March 9, 2020.

Robison, P. *Flying Blind: The MAX Tragedy and the Fall of Boeing.* New York: Doubleday, 2021.

REFERENCES

Ropeik, D. "How Risky Is Flying?" *Nova*, PBS. https://www.pbs.org/wgbh/nova/planecrash/risky.html/.

Rosenblatt, G. "When We Converse with the Alien Intelligence of Machines." *Vital Edge* (blog), June 27, 2017. https://www.the-vital-edge.com/alien-machine-intelligence/.

"Safety Measures Implementation at Kashiwazaki-Kariwa Nuclear Power Station." Tokyo Electric Power Company Holdings. Last update February 14, 2018. https://www.tepco.co.jp/en/nu/kk-np/safety/index-e.html.

Schaper, D., and V. Romo. "Boeing Employees Mocked FAA in Internal Messages before 737 MAX Disasters." *Morning Edition*, NPR, January 9, 2020.

Shuto, N., and K. Fujima. "A Short History of Tsunami Research and Countermeasures in Japan." *Proceedings of the Japan Academy, Series B Physical and Biological Sciences* 85, no. 8 (October 2009): 267–75. https://www.jstage.jst.go.jp/article/pjab/85/8/85_8_267/_article.

Silver, D., et al. "Mastering the Game of GO without Human Knowledge." *Nature* 550 (2017): 354–59.

Singh, M., and T. Markeset. "A Methodology for Risk-Based Inspection Planning of Oil and Gas Pipes Based on Fuzzy Logic Framework." *Engineering Failure Analysis* 16 (2009): 2098–2113.

Smith, R. "U.S. Water Supply Has Few Protections against Hacking." *Wall Street Journal*, February 12, 2021. https://www.wsj.com/articles/u-s-water-supply-has-few-protections-against-hacking-11613154238.

Solkin, M. "Electromagnetic Interference Hazards in Flight and the 5G Mobile Phone: Review of Critical Issues in Aviation Security." Special issue "10th International Conference on Air Transport—INAIR 2021, towards Aviation Revival." *Transportation Research Procedia* 59 (2021): 310–18. https://doi.org/10.1016/j.trpro.2021.11.123.

Sparks, J. "Ethiopian Airlines Crash, Anguish and Anger at Funeral for Young Pilot." Sky News, 2019.

Sullenberger, C. "What Really Brought Down the Boeing MAX?" Letter to the Editor, *New York Times Magazine*, October 13, 2019, 16.

Swaminathan, N. "What Are We Thinking When We (Try to) Solve Problems?" *Scientific American*, January 25, 2008. https://www.scientificamerican.com/article/what-are-we-thinking-when/.

Synolakis, C., and U. Kânoğlu. "The Fukushima Accident Was Preventable." *Philosophical Transactions of the Royal Society A* (2015). doi.10.1098/rsta.2014.0379.

Tangel, A., A. Pasztor, and M. Maremont. "The Four-Second Catastrophe: How Boeing Doomed the 737 MAX." *Wall Street Journal*, August 16, 2019.

Thompson, C. "The Miseducation of Artificial Intelligence." *Wired*, December 2018.

Travis, G. "How the Boeing 737 MAX Disaster Looks to a Software Developer." *IEEE Spectrum*, April 18, 2019.

Tsuji, Y., et al. "Tsunami Heights along the Pacific Coast of Northern Honshu Recorded from the 2011 Tohoku and Previous Great Earthquakes." *Pure and Applied Geophysics* 171 (2014): 3183–215.

Tung, S. "The Day the Golden Gate Bridge Flattened." *Mercury News*, May 23, 2012.

Turton, W. "Breakthrough Technologies for Surviving a Hack." *Bloomberg Businessweek*, July 27, 2020, 50–53.

US Department of Labor. "Number and Rate of Fatal Work Injuries, by Industry Sector," 2018. stats.bls.gov.

US Government Accountability Office. "James Webb Space Telescope: Integration and Test Challenges Have Delayed Launch and Threaten to Push Costs over Cap." *GAO Highlights* 18-273 (2018), a report to Congressional Committee.

US Nuclear Regulatory Commission. "Backgrounder on the Three Mile Island Accident." https://www.nrc.gov/reading-rm/doc-collections/fact-sheets/3mile-isle.html.

US Nuclear Regulatory Commission. *NRC Collection of Abbreviations, NOREG-0544 Rev 4.* Washington, DC: US Government Printing Office, 1998.

Vance, A. *Elon Musk: Tesla, SpaceX, and the Quest for a Fantastic Future.* New York: Ecco, 2015.

Vanian, J. "Why Google's Artificial Intelligence Confused a Turtle for a Rifle." *Fortune*, November 8, 2017.

Waite, S., et al. "Analysis of Perceptual Expertise in Radiology—Current Knowledge and a New Perspective." *Frontiers in Human Neuroscience* (2019). doi:10.3389/fnhum.2019.00213.

Washington State Department of Transportation. "Tacoma Narrows Bridge History—Lessons from the Failure of a Great Machine." https://www.wsdot.wa.gov/TNBhistory/Machine /machine3.htm/.

"'Weak Engineering Management' Probable Cause of Columbia Gas Explosions, NTSB Says." WBZ, CBS 4, Boston, October 24, 2019.

Webster, B. Y. "Understanding and Comparing Risk." Reliabilityweb. www.reliabilityweb.com /articles/entry/understanding_and_comparing_risk/.

Weinstein, D. "Hackers May Be Coming to Your City's Water Supply." *Wall Street Journal*, February 26, 2021.

Wilkin, H. "Psychosis, Dreams, and Memory in AI." *Special Edition on Artificial Intelligence* (blog), Graduate School of Arts and Sciences, Harvard University, August 28, 2017. https://sitn.hms .harvard.edu/flash/2017/psychosis-dreams-memory-ai/.

Witze, A. "One Telescope to Rule Them All." *Nature* 600 (December 9, 2021): 208–12.

Wolff, J. "Engineering Acronyms: What the Heck Are They Saying?" 2014. https:// www .jaredwolff.com/the-crazy-world-of-engineering-acronyms.

World Nuclear Association. "Fukushima Daiichi Accident," 2020. https://world-nuclear.org /information-library/safety-and-security/safety-of-plants/fukushima-daiichi-accident.aspx.

World Nuclear Association. "Three Mile Island Accident," 2020. https://www.world-nuclear.org (accessed August 4, 2020).

Yoichi, F., and K. Kitazawa. "Fukushima in Review: A Complex Disaster, a Disastrous Response." *Bulletin of the Atomic Scientists* 68, no. 2 (March 1, 2012): 9–21. doi:10.1177/009634021 2440359.

7. ANIMAL CONSCIOUSNESS AND VISUAL THINKING

Abramson, C. I. "Charles Henry Turner: Contributions of a Forgotten African American to Honey Bee Research." *American Bee Journal* 143 (2003): 643–44.

Allen, C., and M. Bekoff. *Species of Mind: The Philosophy and Biology of Cognitive Ethology.* Cambridge, MA: MIT Press, 1997.

Alvarenga, A. B., et al. "A Systematic Review of Genomic Regions and Candidate Genes Underlying Behavioral Traits in Farmed Mammals and Their Link with Human Disorders." *Animals* 11, no. 3 (2021): 715. https://doi.org/10.3390/ani11030715/.

Anderson, D. J., and R. Adolphs. "A Framework for Studying Emotions across Species." *Cell* 157, no. 1 (March 2014): 187–200.

REFERENCES

"Animal Consciousness." *Stanford Encyclopedia of Philosophy*. Stanford, CA: Metaphysics Research Lab, 1995, 2016. https://plato.stanford.edu/entries/consciousness-animal/.

Aristotle. *Nichomachean Ethics*. Edited by R. C. Bartlett and S. D. Collins. Chicago: University of Chicago Press, 2011.

ASPCA. "History of the ASPCA." American Society for the Protection of Animals, 2020. aspca.org/about-us/history-of-the-ASPCA.

Bailey, I. E., et al. "Image Analysis of Weaverbird Nests Reveals Signature Weave Textures." *Royal Society Open Science*, June 1, 2015. https://doi.org/10.1098/r505.150074/.

Bailey, P., and E. W. Davis. "Effects of Lesions of the Periaqueductal Gray Matter in the Cat." *Proceedings of the Society for Experimental Biology and Medicine* 51 (1942): 305–6.

Bates, M. "Bumblebees Can Recognize Objects across Senses." *Psychology Today*, February 20, 2020.

Bekoff, M. "Do Animals Recognize Themselves?" *Scientific American*, November 1, 2016. https://www.scientificamerican.com/article/do-animals-recognize-themselves/.

Benedictus, A. D. "Anatomo-Functional Study of the Temporo-Parietal-Occipital Region: Dissections, Traceographic and Brain Mapping Evidence from a Neurosurgical Perspective." *Journal of Anatomy* 225, no. 14 (2014). doi.10.1111/joa.12204.

Bentham, J. *An Introduction to the Principles of Morals and Legislation*. First published by T. Payne and Sons, 1789. Reprinted by Oxford University Press Academic, 1996.

Bentham, J. *Of the Limits of the Penal Branch of Jurisprudence*. First published by T. Payne and Sons, 1780. Reprinted, edited by Philip Schofield, by Oxford University Press, 2010.

Berns, G. *What It's Like to Be a Dog: And Other Adventures in Animal Neuroscience*. New York: Basic Books, 2017.

Betz, E. "A Brief History of Chimps in Space." *Discover*, April 21, 2020.

Birch, J., et al. "Dimensions of Animal Consciousness." *Trends in Cognitive Sciences* 24, no. 10 (2020) 311–13: 789–801.

Bjursten, L. M., et al. "Behavioural Repertory of Cats without Cerebral Cortex from Infancy." *Experimental Brain Research* 25, no. 2 (1976): 115–30.

Black, J. "Darwin in the World of Emotions." *Journal of the Royal Society of Medicine* 95, no. 6 (June 2002): 311–13.

Boly, M., et al. "Are the Neural Correlates of Consciousness in the Front or in the Back of the Cerebral Cortex? Clinical and Neuroimaging Evidence." *Journal of Neuroscience* 37, no. 40 (2017): 9603–13.

Borrell, B. "Are Octopuses Smart?" *Scientific American*, February 27, 2009. https://www.scientificamerican.com/article/are-octopuses-smart/.

Breland, K., and M. Breland. *Animal Behavior*. New York: Macmillan, 1966.

Breland, K., and M. Breland. "The Misbehavior of Organisms." *American Psychologist* 16, no. 11 (1961): 681–84.

Cabrera, D., et al. "The Development of Animal Personality across Ontogeny: A Cross-Species Review." *Animal Behavior* 173 (2021): 137–44.

Cataldo, D. M., et al. "Speech, Stone Tool-Making and the Evolution of Language." *PLOS ONE* 13, no. 1 (2018): e0191071.

Cep, C. "Marilynne Robinson's Essential American Stories." *New Yorker*, October 5, 2020, 44–53.

Ceurstemont, S. "Inside a Wasp's Head: Here's What It Sees to Find Its Way Home." *NewScientist*, February 12, 2016. https://www.newscientist.com/article/2077306-inside-a-wasps-head-heres-what-it-sees-to-find-its-way-home/.

"Charles Henry Turner." Biography.com, 2014. https://www.biography.com/scientist/charles-henry-turner/.

Chen, A. "A Neuroscientist Explains Why We Need Better Ways to Talk about Emotions." *The Verge*, July 6, 2018.

Christianson, J. P. "The Head and the Heart of Fear." *Science* 374, no. 6570 (2021): 937–38.

Collias, E. C., and N. E. Collias. "The Development of Nest-Building Behavior in a Weaverbird." *The Auk* 81 (1964): 42–52.

Collins, R. W. "What Does It Mean to be Human, and Not Animal? Examining Montaigne's Literary Persuasiveness in 'Man Is No Better Than the Animals.'" Animals and Society Institute, 2018.

Colpaert, F. C., et al. "Opiate Self-Administration as a Measure of Chronic Nociceptive Pain in Arthritic Rats." *Pain* 91 (2001): 33–45.

Cook, P., et al. "Jealousy in Dogs? Evidence from Brain Imaging." *Animal Sentience* 22, no. 1 (2018). https://www.wellbeingintlstudiesrepository.org/animalsent/vol3 /iss22/1.

Costilla, R., et al. "Genetic Control of Temperament Traits across Species: Association of Autism Spectrum Disorder Risk Genes with Cattle Temperament." *Genetics Selection Evolution* 52 (2020): 51.

Dagg, A. I. *Giraffe: Biology, Behaviour and Conservation*. New York: Cambridge University Press, 2014.

Danbury, T. C., et al. "Self-Selection of the Analgesic Drug Carprofen by Lame Broiler Chickens." *Veterinary Research* 146 (2000): 307–11.

Darwin, C. *The Descent of Man*. London: John Murray, 1871.

Davis, J. M. "The History of Animal Protection in the United States." Organization of American Historians, *The American Historian*. https://www.oah.org/tah/issues/2015/november /the-history-of-animal-protection-in-the-united-states/.

Davis, K. L., and C. Montag. "Selected Principles of Pankseppian Affective Neuroscience." *Frontiers in Neuroscience*, January 17, 2019. https://www.frontiersin.org/articles/10.3389 /fnins.2018.01025/full/.

de Molina, A. F., and R. W. Hunsperger. "Central Representation of Affective Reactions in the Forebrain and Brain Stem: Electrical Stimulation of the Amygdala, Stria Terminalis and Adjacent Structures." *Journal of Physiology* 145 (1959): 251–65.

de Molina, A. F., and R. W. Hunsperger. "Organization of the Subcortical System Governing Defence and Flight Reactions in a Cat." *Journal of Physiology* 160, no. 2 (1962): 200–213.

de Waal, F. B. M. "Fish, Mirrors, and a Gradualist Perspective of Self-Awareness." *PLOS Biology* 17, no. 2 (2019): e3000112.

de Waal, F. *Mama's Last Hug*. New York: W. W. Norton, 2019.

Della Rosa, P. A., et al. "The Left Inferior Frontal Gyrus: A Neural Crossroads between Abstract and Concrete Knowledge." *NeuroImage* 175 (2018): 449–59.

Denson, T. F. "Inferring Emotion from the Amygdala Activation Alone Is Problematic." *Animal Sentience* 22, no. 9 (2018).

Descartes, R. "Animals Are Machines." Reproduced from unidentified translation at https://webs .wofford.edu/williamsnm/back%20up%20jan%204/hum%20101/animals%20are %20machines%20descartes.pdf/.

Dona, H. S. G., and L. Chittka. "Charles H. Turner, Pioneer in Animal Cognition." *Science* 370, no. 6516 (2020): 530–31.

Douglas-Hamilton, I., et al. "Behavioural Reactions of Elephants towards a Dying and Deceased Matriarch." *Applied Animal Behaviour Science* 100 (2006): 87–102.

REFERENCES

Duncan, I. J. H. "The Changing Concept of Animal Sentience." *Applied Animal Behaviour Science* 100, no. 1–2 (2006): 11–19.

Fang, Z., et al. "Unconscious Processing of Negative Animals and Objects: Role of the Amygdala Revealed by fMRI." *Frontiers in Human Neuroscience* 10 (2016). doi: 10.3389/fnhum.2016.00146.

Fanselow, M. S., and Z. T. Pennington. "The Danger of LeDoux and Pine's Two-System Framework for Fear." *American Journal of Psychiatry* 174, no. 11 (2017): 1120–21.

Faull, O. K., et al. "The Midbrain Periaqueductal Gray as an Integrative and Interoceptive Neural Structure for Breathing." *Neuroscience and Biobehavioral Reviews* 98 (2019). https://doi.org/10.1016/j.neubiorev.2018.12.020.

Favre, D., and V. Tsang. "The Development of the Anti-Cruelty Laws during the 1800s." *Detroit College Law Review* 1 (1993).

Feinberg, T. E., and J. Mallatt. "Phenomenal Consciousness and Emergence: Eliminating the Explanatory Gap." *Frontiers in Psychology*, June 12, 2020.

Finkemeier, M. A., et al. "Personality Research in Mammalian Farm Animals: Concepts, Measures, and Relationships to Welfare." *Frontiers in Veterinary Science* (2018). https://doi.org/10.3389/fvets.2018.00131.

Fortenbaugh, W. "Aristotle: Animals, Emotion, and Moral Virtue." *Arethusa* 4, no. 2 (1971): 137–65. http://www.jstor.org/stable/26307269/.

Foster, C. *My Octopus Teacher*. Directed by P. Ehrlich and J. Reed. Netflix, 2020.

Freeberg, E. *A Traitor to His Species: Henry Bergh and the Birth of the Animal Rights Movement*. New York: Basic Books, 2020.

Gent, T. C., et al. "Thalamic Dual Control of Sleep and Wakefulness." *Nature Neuroscience* 21, no. 7 (2018): 974–84.

Giurfa, M., and M. G. de Brito Sanchez. "Black Lives Matter: Revisiting Charles Henry Turner's Experiments on Honey Bee Color Vision." *Current Biology*, October 19, 2020.

Goodall, J. "Tool-Using and Aimed Throwing in a Community of Free-Living Chimpanzees." *Nature* 201 (1964): 1264–66.

Grandin, T. *Temple Grandin's Guide to Working with Farm Animals*. North Adams, MA: Storey, 2017.

Grandin, T. *Thinking in Pictures*. New York: Doubleday, 1995. Expanded edition. New York: Vintage, 2006.

Grandin, T., and M. J. Deesing. "Behavioral Genetics and Animal Science." In *Genetics and the Behavior of Domestic Animals*, 2nd ed., edited by T. Grandin and M. J. Deesing, 1–40. Cambridge, MA: Academic Press/Elsevier, 2013.

Grandin, T., and C. Johnson. *Animals in Translation*. New York: Scribner, 2005.

Grandin, T., and C. Johnson. *Animals Make Us Human*. New York: Mariner Books, 2010.

Grandin, T., and M. M. Scariano. *Emergence: Labeled Autistic*. Novato, CA: Arena, 1986.

Gray, T. "A Brief History of Animals in Space." National Aeronautics and Space Administration, 1998, updated 2014. https://history.nasa.gov/animals.html.

Guest, K. Introduction to Anna Sewell, *Black Beauty*. Cambridge, UK: Cambridge Scholars, 2011.

Hemati, S., and G. A. Hossein-Zadeh. "Distinct Functional Network Connectivity for Abstract and Concrete Mental Imagery." *Frontiers in Human Neuroscience* 12 (2018). doi: 10.3389/fnhum.2018.00515.

Herculano-Houzel, S. "Birds Do Have a Cortex—and Think." *Science* 369 (2020): 1567–68.

Herculano-Houzel, S. "Numbers of Neurons as Biological Correlates of Cognitive Capability." *Current Opinion in Behavioral Sciences* 16 (2017): 1–7.

Herculano-Houzel, S., et al. "The Elephant Brain in Numbers." *Frontiers in Neuroanatomy* (2014). https://doi.org/10.3389/fnana.2014.00046.

Hill, E. "Archaeology and Animal Persons: Towards a Prehistory of Human-Animal Relations." *Environment and Society* (2013). https://doi.org/10.3167/ares.2013.040108.

Hunt, G. R. "Manufacture and Use of Hook-Tools by New Caledonian Crows." *Nature* 379 (1996): 249–51.

Hussain, S. T., and H. Floss. "Sharing the World with Mammoths, Cave Lions and Other Beings: Linking Animal-Human Interactions and Aurignacian 'Belief World.'" *Quartar* 62 (2015): 85–120.

"In an Ant's World, the Smaller You Are the Harder It Is to See Obstacles." *The Conversation*, April 17, 2018. https://theconversation.com/in-an-ants-world-the-smaller-you-are-the-harder-it-is-to-see-obstacles-92837.

Jackson, J. C., et al. "Emotion Semantics Show Both Cultural Variation and Universal Structure." *Science* 366, no. 6472 (2019): 1517–22.

Jacobs, L. F., and E. R. Liman. "Grey Squirrels Remember the Locations of Buried Nuts." *Animal Behavior* 41, no. 1 (1991): 103–10.

James, W. *The Will to Believe*. New York: Longmans, Green, 1897. Project Gutenberg, https://www.gutenberg.org/files/26659/26659-h/26659-h.htm#58/.

Judd, S. P. D., and T. S. Collett. "Multiple Stored Views and Landmark Guidance in Ants." *Nature* 392, no. 6677 (1998): 710–14.

Kerasote, T. A. "Essay: Lessons from a Freethinking Dog," 2008. kerasote.com/essays/ted-kerasote-merle-essay.pdf.

Khattab, M. *The Clear Quran: A Thematic English Translation*. 2015.

Klein, A. S., et al. "Fear Balance Is Maintained by Bodily Feedback to the Insular Cortex in Mice." *Science* 374, no. 6570 (2021): 1010–15.

Klüver, H., and P. C. Bucy. "'Psychic Blindness' and Other Symptoms Following Bilateral Temporal Lobectomy in Rhesus Monkeys." *American Journal of Physiology* 119 (1937): 352–53.

Knight, K. "Paper Wasps Really Recognise Each Other's Faces." *Journal of Experimental Biology* 220 (2017). doi:10.1242/jeb.163477.

Koch, C. "What Is Consciousness? Scientists Are Beginning to Unravel a Mystery That Has Long Vexed Philosophers." *Nature* 557 (2018): S8–S12.

Koch, C., et al. "Neural Correlates of Consciousness: Progress and Problems." *Nature Reviews Neuroscience* 17 (2016): 307–21.

Kremer, L., et al. "The Nuts and Bolts of Animal Emotion." *Neuroscience and Biobehavioral Reviews* 113 (2020): 273–86.

Kucyi, A., and K. D. Davis. "Dynamic Functional Connectivity of the Default Mode Network Tracks Daydreaming." *NeuroImage* 100 (2014): 471–80.

Learmonth, M. J. "The Matter of Non-Avian Reptile Sentience and Why It 'Matters' to Them: A Conceptual, Ethical and Scientific Review." *Animals* 10, no. 5 (2020). doi.org/10.3390/ani/10050901.

LeDoux, J. *Anxious: Using the Brain to Understand and Treat Fear and Anxiety*. New York: Penguin Press, 2015.

LeDoux, J. *The Emotional Brain: The Mysterious Underpinnings of Emotional Life*. New York: Simon & Schuster, 1996.

LeDoux, J. "Rethinking the Emotional Brain." *Neuron* 73, no. 4 (2012): 653–76. https://doi.org/10.1016/j.neuron.2012.02.004.

LeDoux, J., and N. D. Daw. "Surviving Threats: Neural Circuit and Computational Implications of a New Taxonomy of Defensive Behavior." *Nature Reviews Neuroscience* 19 (2018): 269–82.

LeDoux, J. E., M. Michel, and H. Lau. "A Little History Goes a Long Way toward Understanding Why We Study Consciousness the Way We Do Today." *Proceedings of the National Academy of Sciences* 117, no. 13 (2020): 6976–84.

LeDoux, J. E., and D. S. Pine. "Using Neuroscience to Help Understand Fear and Anxiety: A Two-System Framework." *American Journal of Psychiatry* 173, no. 11 (2016): 1083–93.

Lee, DN. "Charles Henry Turner, Animal Behavior Scientist." *The Urban Scientist* (blog), *Scientific American,* February 13, 2012. https://blogs.scientificamerican.com/urban-scientist /charles-henry-turner-animal-behavior-scientist/.

Lehrman, D. S. "A Critique of Konrad Lorenz's Theory of Instinctive Behavior." *Quarterly Review of Biology* 28, no. 4 (1953): 337–63.

Lejeune, H., et al. "About Skinner and Time: Behavior-Analytic Contributions to Research on Animal Timing." *Journal of the Experimental Analysis of Behavior* 85, no. 1 (2006): 125–42.

Lewis, M. *The Rise of Consciousness and the Development of Emotional Life.* New York: Guilford Press, 2014.

Lorenz, K. Nobel Lecture, 1973. https://www.nobelprize.org/prizes/medicine/1973/lorenz /lecture/.

Lorenz, K. "Science of Animal Behavior (1975)." YouTube, September 27, 2016. https://www .youtube.com/watch?v=IysBMqaSAC8.

Maier, A., and N. Tsuchiya. "Growing Evidence for Separate Neural Mechanisms for Attention and Consciousness." *Attention, Perception, & Psychophysics* 83, no. 2 (2021): 558–76.

Majid, A. "Mapping Words Reveals Emotional Diversity." *Science* 366 (2019): 1444–45.

Mcnaughton, N., and P. J. Corr. "Survival Circuits and Risk Assessment." *Current Opinion in Behavioral Sciences* 24 (2018): 14–20.

Mobbs, D. "Viewpoints: Approaches to Defining and Investigating Fear." *Nature Neuroscience* 22 (2019): 1205–16. Contains comments by Ralph Adolpho on verbal language.

Montaigne, M. de. "The Language of Animals." http://www.animal-rights-library.com/texts-c /montaigne01.htm.

Morris, C. L., et al. "Companion Animals Symposium: Environmental Enrichment for Companion, Exotic, and Laboratory Animals." *Journal of Animal Science* 89 (2011): 4227–38.

Motta, S. C., et al. "The Periaqueductal Gray and Primal Emotional Processing Critical to Influence Complex Defensive Responses, Fear Learning and Reward Seeking." *Neuroscience and Biobehavioral Reviews* 76(A) (2017): 39–47.

Nash, R. F. *The Rights of Nature: A History of Environmental Ethics.* Madison: University of Wisconsin Press, 1989.

Nawroth, C., et al. "Farm Animal Cognition—Linking Behavior, Welfare and Ethics." *Frontiers in Veterinary Science* (2019). doi.org/10.3380/fvets.2019.00024.

"New York Court of Appeals Agrees to Hear Landmark Elephant Rights Case." *Nonhuman Rights Blog,* May 4, 2021. https://www.nonhumanrights.org/blog/appeal-granted-in-landmark -elephant-rights-case/.

Nieder, A., et al. "A Neural Correlate of Sensory Consciousness in a Corvid Bird." *Science* 369 (2020): 1626–29.

Ohman, A. "The Role of the Amygdala in Human Fear: Automatic Detection of Threat." *Psychoneuroendocrinology* 30, no. 10 (2005): 953–58.

REFERENCES

Olkowicz, S., et al. "Birds Have Primate-Like Numbers of Neurons in the Forebrain." *Proceedings of the National Academy of Sciences* 113, no. 26 (2016): 7255–60.

"Organismal Biology." Georgia Tech Biological Sciences. https://organismalbio.biosci.gatech.edu /growth-and-reproduction/plant-development-i-tissue-differentiation-and-function/.

"Our Legacy of Science." Jane Goodall Institute. https://www.janegoodall.org/our-story /our-legacy-of-science/.

Padian, K. "Charles Darwin's Views of Classification in Theory and Practice." *Systematic Biology* 48, no. 2 (1999): 352–64.

Panksepp, J. "The Basic Emotional Circuits of Mammalian Brains: Do Animals Have Affective Lives?" *Neuroscience and Biobehavioral Reviews* 35 (2011): 1791–1804.

Panksepp, J., et al. "Effects of Neonatal Decortication on the Social Play of Juvenile Rats." *Physiology and Behavior* 56, no. 3 (1994): 429–43.

Pauen, S. "The Global-to-Basic Shift in Infants' Categorical Thinking: First Evidence from a Longitudinal Study." *International Journal of Behavioral Development* 26, no. 6 (2002): 492–99.

Paul, E., and M. Mendl. "Animal Emotion: Descriptive and Prescriptive Definitions and Their Implications for a Comparative Perspective." *Applied Animal Behaviour Science* 205 (August 2018): 202–9.

Peissig, J. J., et al. "Pigeons Spontaneously Form Three-Dimensional Shape Categories." *Behavioral Processes* 158 (2019): 70–76.

Pennartz, C. M. A., M. Farisco, and K. Evers. "Indicators and Criteria of Consciousness in Animals and Intelligent Machines: An Inside-Out Approach." *Frontiers in Systems Neuroscience*, July 16, 2019.

Peper, A. "A General Theory of Consciousness I: Consciousness and Adaptation." *Communicative and Integrative Biology* 13, no. 1 (2020): 6–21.

Plotnik, J. M., et al. "Self-Recognition in an Asian Elephant." *Proceedings of the National Academy of Sciences* 103, no. 45 (2006): 17053–57.

Prior, H., et al. "Mirror-Induced Behavior in the Magpie (Pica pica): Evidence of Self-Recognition." *PLOS Biology* 6, no. 8 (2008): e202. https://doi.org/10.1371/journal.pbio.0060202.

Proctor, H. S., et al. "Searching for Animal Sentience: A Systematic Review of the Scientific Literature." *Animals* 3, no. 3 (2013): 882–906.

Quervel-Chaumette, M., et al. "Investigating Empathy-Like Responding to Conspecifics' Distress in Pet Dogs." *PLOS ONE* 11, no. 4 (2016): e015920.

Raby, C. R., et al. "Planning for the Future by Western Scrub-Jays." *Nature* 445, no. 7130 (2007): 919–21.

Rahman, S. A. "Religion and Animal Welfare—An Islamic Perspective." *Animals* 7, no. 2 (2017): 11.

Rand, A. L. "Nest Sanitation and an Alleged Releaser." *Auk* 59, no. 3 (July 1942): 404–9.

Ratcliffe, V., A. Taylor, and D. Reby. "Cross-Modal Correspondences in Non-Human Mammal Communication." *Multisensory Research* 29, nos. 1–3 (January 2016): 49–91. doi:10.1163 /22134808-00002509.

Redinbaugh, M. J., et al. "Thalamus Modulates Consciousness via Layer-Specific Control of Cortex." *Neuron* 106, no. 1 (2020): 66–75e12.

Rees, G., et al. "Neural Correlates of Consciousness in Humans." *Nature Reviews Neuroscience* 3 (2002): 261–70.

Reiss, D. *The Dolphin in the Mirror: Exploring Dolphin Minds and Saving Dolphin Lives*. New York: Houghton Mifflin Harcourt, 2011.

REFERENCES

Robinson, M. "Jack and Della." *New Yorker*, July 20, 2020.

Rutherford, L., and L. E. Murray. "Personality and Behavioral Changes in Asian Elephants (*Elephas maximus*) Following the Death of Herd Members." *Integrative Zoology* 16, no. 2 (2020): 170–88.

Schleidt, W., et al. "The Hawk/Goose Story: The Classical Ethological Experiments of Lorenz and Tinbergen, Revisited." *Journal of Comparative Psychology* 125, no. 2 (2011): 121–33.

Sewell, A. *Black Beauty: His Grooms and Companions, The Autobiography of a Horse.* London, UK: Jarrold and Sons, 1877.

Sheehan, M. J., and E. A. Tibbetts. "Robust Long-Term Social Memories in a Paper Wasp." *Current Biology* 18, no. 18 (2008): R851–R852.

Shewmon, D. A., et al. "Consciousness in Congenitally Decorticate Children: Developmental Vegetative State as Self-Fulfilling Prophecy." *Developmental Medicine and Child Neurology* 41, no. 6 (1999): 364–74.

Skinner, B. F. *The Behavior of Organisms.* Century Psychology Series. New York: D. Appleton-Century, 1938.

Skinner, B. F. *Science and Human Behavior.* New York: Macmillan, 1953.

Skinner, B. F. "The Technology of Teaching, Review Lecture." *Proceedings of the Royal Society of London, Series B Biological Sciences* 162, no. 989 (1965): 427–43.

Skinner, B. F. "Why I Am Not a Cognitive Psychologist." *Behaviorism* 5, no. 2 (1977): 1–10.

Smulders, T., et al. "Using Ecology to Guide the Study of Cognitive and Neural Mechanisms of Different Aspects of Spatial Memory in Food-Hoarding Animals." *Philosophical Transactions, Royal Society London Biological Science* 365, no. 1542 (201): 888–900.

Solvi, C., et al. "Bumblebees Display Cross-Modal Object Recognition between Visual and Tactile Senses." *Science* 367, no. 6480 (2020): 910–12.

Stacho, M., et al. "A Cortex-Like Canonical Circuit in the Avian Forebrain." *Science* 369, no. 6511 (2020). doi.10.1126/science.abc5534.

Szaflarski, J. P., et al. "A Longitudinal Functional Magnetic Resonance Imaging Study of Language Development in Children 5 to 11 Years Old." *Annals of Neurology* 59, no. 5 (2006). doi.org /10.002/ana20817.

Tinbergen, N. "Derived Activities; Their Causation, Biological Significance, Origin, and Emancipation during Evolution." *Quarterly Review of Biology* 27, no. 1 (1952): 1–32.

von Bayern, A., et al. "Compound Tool Construction by New Caledonian Crows." *Scientific Reports* 8, no. 15676 (2018). https://www.nature.com/articles/s41598-018-33458-z/.

von der Emde, G., and T. Burt de Perera. "Cross-Modal Sensory Transfer: Bumble Bees Do It." *Science* 367 (2020): 850–51.

vonHoldt, B. M., et al. "Structural Variants in Genes Associated with Human Williams-Beuren Syndrome Underlie Stereotypical Hypersocialability in Domestic Dogs." *Science Advances* 3, no. 7 (2017): e1700398. doi:10.1126/sciadv.1700398.

Watanabe, S., et al. "Pigeons' Discrimination of Paintings by Monet and Picasso." *Journal of the Experimental Analysis of Behavior* 63, no. 2 (1995): 165–74.

Weber, F., et al. "Regulation of REM and Non-REM Sleep by Periaqueductal GABAergic Neurons." *Nature*, January 24, 2018.

Weintraub, P. "*Discover* Interview: Jaak Panksepp Pinned Down Humanity's 7 Primal Emotions." *Discover*, May 30, 2012.

Westerman, G., and D. Mareschai. "From Perceptual to Language-Mediated Categorization." *Philosophical Transactions of the Royal Society B* 369, no. 1634 (January 19, 2014): 20120391. https://doi.org/10.1098/rstb.2012.0391.

Whalley, K. "Controlling Consciousness." *Nature Reviews Neuroscience* 21 (2020): 181.

Whiten, A., et al. "Culture in Chimpanzees." *Nature* 399 (1999): 682–85.

Wilks, M., et al. "Children Prioritize Humans over Animals Less Than Adults Do." *Psychological Science*, January 2021, 27–38.

Wilson, E. O. "Ant Communication." *Pulse of the Planet: The Sound of Life on Earth* (blog). November 8, 2012. https://pulseword.pulseplanet.com/dailies-post-type/2545-6/.

Yin, S. "The Best Animal Trainers in History: Interview with Bob and Marian Bailey, Part 1." August 13,2012 https://cattledogpublishing.com/blog/the-best-animal-trainers-in-history-interview-with-bob-and-marian-bailey-part-1/.

Zalucki, O., and B. van Swinderen. "What Is Consciousness in a Fly or a Worm? A Review of General Anesthesia in Different Animal Models." *Consciousness and Cognition* (2016). doi.org/10.1016/j.concog.2016.06.017.

Zentall, T. "Jealousy, Competition, or a Contextual Cue for Reward?" *Animal Sentience* 22, no. 4 (2018).

AFTERWORD

American Society of Civil Engineers. Report Card for America's Infrastructure, 2021. https://infrastructurereportcard.org/catitem/bridges.

Associated Press. "Review Slated for 5 Bridges Sharing Design of Collapsed Span." February 2, 2022.

Robertson, C., and S. Kasakove. "Pittsburgh Bridge Collapses Hours before Biden Infrastructure Visit." *New York Times*, January 28, 2022.

Schaper, D. "10 Years after a Bridge Collapse, America Is Still Crumbling." *All Things Considered*, NPR, August 1, 2017.

Schultheisz, C. R., et al. "Minneapolis I-35W Bridge Collapse—Engineering Evaluations and Finite Element Analysis." CEP Civil Engineering Portal. https://www.engineeringcivil.com/minneapolis-i-35w-bridge-collapse-engineering-evaluations-and-finite-element-analysis.html.

Treisman, R. "A Bridge in Pittsburgh Collapsed on the Day of Biden's Planned Infrastructure Visit." NPR, January 28, 2022. https://www.npr.org/2022/01/28/1076343656/pittsburgh-bridge-collapse-biden-visit.

Index

INDEX